AN HISTORICAL ACCOUNT

OF THE ENGLISH

TRANSLATIONS.

"SURE I AM, THAT THERE COMMETH MORE KNOWLEGE AND VNDERSTONDINGE OF THE SCRIPTURE BY THEYR SONDRIE TRANSLACYONS, THEN BY ALL THE GLOSES OF OURE SOPHISTICALL DOCTOURS. FOR THAT ONE INTERPRETETH SOMTHYNGE OBSCURELY IN ONE PLACE, THE SAME TRANSLATETH ANOTHER (OR ELS HE HIM SELFE) MORE MANIFESTLY BY A MORE PLAYNE VOCABLE OF THE SAME MEANYNG IN ANOTHER PLACE." MYLES COUERDALE—'A PROLOGE VNTO THE CHRISTEN READER'—BIBLE, M.D.XXXV.

LONDON:

Samuel Bagster and Sons, Paternoster Row:

AT THE WAREHOUSE FOR BIBLES, NEW TESTAMENTS, CONCORDANCES, PRAYER-BOOKS, AND PSALTERS, IN ANCIENT AND MODERN LANGUAGES.

ΠΟΛΛΑΙ μεν θνητοις ΓΛΩΤΤΑΙ, μια δ'αθανατοισιν.

M.DCCC.XLI.

Lazarus Ministry Press

An Historical Account of the English Translations: 1841

Vintage Archives
2020 Builders Place
Columbus, OH 43204

ISBN 1-58329-009-5

CONTENTS.

PART I.

PERIOD PRIOR TO THE REIGN OF HENRY VIII.

PART II.

THE FORMER PART OF THE REIGN OF HENRY VIII.

PART III.

THE LATTER PORTION OF THE REIGN OF HENRY VIII.

AN HISTORICAL ACCOUNT

OF THE

ENGLISH VERSIONS OF THE SCRIPTURES,

IN CONNECTION WITH THE PROGRESS OF THE REFORMATION

WITH BIOGRAPHICAL NOTICES OF VARIOUS TRANSLATORS.

PART I.

PERIOD PRIOR TO THE REIGN OF HENRY VIII.

I.

THE ANGLO-SAXON AND ENGLISH VERSIONS, PRIOR TO THE MIDDLE OF THE FOURTEENTH CENTURY.

In this account it is particularly intended to trace the workings of the hand of God, in introducing the circulation of the Scriptures, and thus bringing about the Reformation in this country. In England, it has to be specially noticed, that the great instrument of the Reformation was the reading of the word of God, just as, in Germany, the attention excited by Luther's personal testimony is seen bringing the truth before all men, and as in Switzerland, we see the labours of many evangelists who preached Christ in many places.

The Anglo-Saxon and early English versions have first to be noticed, tracing out what appears to have been done prior to the days of Wiclif:—then the version of Wiclif, its causes and consequences:—a century and a half later, the labours of Tyndale and Coverdale have to be especially rested on,—and, subsequently, the various versions executed up to the year 1611, when the translation which we have in daily use, was published.

Scripture addressed to the consciences of all.

The outline of the history of the translation and diffusion of the Scriptures in English, is one from which we may learn how much cause we have for thankfulness, that we are permitted the unhindered use of the Word of God in our own tongue. The Scripture, as being the record of the Holy Ghost, concerning the love which God has shown in the gift of his Son, that his blood should be shed for sinners, was not given forth for a few merely; but it is that which is set before the eyes of all, not for them to exercise respecting it any supposed right or ability of forming a judgment of their own, but for them to acknowledge the authority of God to speak, and their responsibility to hear.

Saxon invasion of Britain and its consequences. A. D. 450.

Conversion of the Saxons. A.D. 596.

Scriptures among them in Latin.

The Saxon invasions of Britain from the middle of the fifth century and onward, issued in the peopling of almost the whole of the southern part of the island with idolators; Christianity, such as it was, could only be found in the western edges of South Britain. The conversion of the Saxons to a profession of Christianity was effected by three means.—the mission of Augustine, the labours of Scottish Christians, and the efforts in some places of the conquered Britons. After the profession of the Christian religion became general on the part of the Saxons, the Scriptures were among them only in Latin, as found either in some of the versions anterior to Jerome's revision, yet extant in that day, or else in the Vulgate as more ordinarily used.

The people little acquainted

There appears to have been no objection made to vernacular translations of the Scriptures; but still no particular desire seems to have been felt for any such version; this implies at least that the Scriptures

with the revelation of God.

were in the hands of the hierarchy, and that the people in general received what they knew of the revelation of God from their instructions. It is impossible to say when, or by whom, the first Anglo-Saxon version of any portion of Scripture was executed: what is known respecting any of these versions has been carefully collected by Mr. Baber, from whom the facts relative to these early versions are principally derived.*

Seventh century, Cædmon's paraphrase in verse.

The first attempt, of which we have certain knowledge, at any thing like a paraphrase of Scripture in the Anglo-Saxon tongue to which a date can be assigned, is the poem of Cædmon in the seventh century. He is thus mentioned by the Venerable Bede; "Cædmonus divinâ gratiâ specialiter insignis carmina religioni et pietati apta facere solebat ...... Canebat autem de creatione mundi et origine humani generis *et totâ Genesis historiâ*, de egressu Israel ex Ægypto et ingressu in terram repromissionis, ac de aliis plurimis sacræ Scripturæ historiis." This poem, although containing Scripture histories, seems to be as little of a translation, or even paraphrase, of the Scriptures as any modern poem on Scripture subjects. but still it was a commencement; it gave some narrations of the Scripture in the vernacular tongue, and thus it may have been the precursor of real *translations*. The poem of Cædmon was published by Junius, at Amsterdam, in 1665. Its subject is pretty well described in the brief notice given by Bede. It opens with the fall of the angels, the creation, the deluge, the history of the children of Israel in their departure from Egypt and entering into the promised land. Nebuchadnezzar and Daniel, with portions of their histories, are also introduced.

Cædmon's poem, published in 1665. Its contents.

Literal translations in the eighth century.

This portion of Scripture history in verse was succeeded, in the following century, by literal translations of the Scripture lessons read in the daily services of the church. The early part of this century (the eighth) is the date to which two Anglo-Saxon versions of the Psalter are attributed; the translators are reputed to have been ALDHELM, Bishop of Sherborn, and GUTHLAC the first Saxon anchorite. It is, however, doubtful, whether either of these versions be yet in existence; one of them may, however, be possibly contained in a very ancient Psalter in which an interlinear Anglo-Saxon version has been added to the Latin text; this Psalter is said to have been one which was sent by Pope Gregory to Augustine, the monk, after his mission to this country (A.D. 596); whether the book really belongs to so very early a period can hardly be questioned with any reason;† whatever the history of this copy may be, the Latin text is very ancient, and the more modern version, which has been added between the lines, belongs likewise to a very remote period.

Two versions of the Psalter. Aldhelm and Guthlac.

Latin Psalter with interlined version. Cotton MSS. Vesp. A. 1.

Bede in the eighth century translates the Gospel of St. John. Baber, p. lix. Cuthberti vita Ven. Bedæ.

There can be no doubt that the Venerable BEDE did in this century translate into the Anglo-Saxon tongue, the Gospel of St. John; this appears to be the first portion of the New Testament of which we have any account as being translated into the vernacular language of this country.

A manuscript of the four Gospels of Jerome's Latin version was copied by Eadfrid, afterwards Bishop of Lindisfarne, in the year 680; this manuscript was greatly adorned by Ethelwold, his successor in his see, (with the assistance of Bilfrid, an anchorite), with golden bosses and precious stones as well as very curious illuminations. To this manuscript, an interlined Anglo-Saxon version was, at some subsequent period, added by a priest named ALDRED the date of this version is much questioned, but the reign of Alfred appears to be regarded as about the most probable period. This manuscript is known by the name of THE DURHAM BOOK.

Durham Book, A.D. 680. Cott. MSS. Nero, D. iv.

The Rushworth Gloss a version of the gospels, by Farmen and Owen.

There is another Anglo-Saxon version of the four gospels, probably of the same antiquity as the one just mentioned. This version, like the former, is interlined, the Anglo-Saxon word being placed over the corresponding Latin. The version, or *gloss*, as it is termed, appears to have been the work of two individuals FARMEN and OWEN; the former having made the translation of St. Matthew's Gospel, the latter the rest of the work; this is indicated by the subscriptions at the end of the respective portions; to St. Matthew's Gospel there is subjoined "Farmen presbyter thas boc thus gleosode;" (*Farmen the presbyter this book thus glossed* [i. e. interpreted]). At the end of the book there is subjoined; "The min bruche gebidde fore Owun the thas boc gloesede Færmen, thæm preoste æt Harawada; (*He that of mine profiteth bede* [pray] *he for Owen that this book glossed* [and] *Farmen the priest at Harewood.*) After this, the transcriber of the manuscript has added his own subscription in Saxon characters, "Macregol depincxit hoc euangelium,

* Baber's "Historical Account of the Saxon and English Versions of the Scriptures previous to the opening of the Fifteenth Century" is prefixed to his edition of Wiclif's New Testament. It consists of but a few pages altogether, but the labour and research are such as to stamp upon them a very peculiar value.

† Baber says (p. lviii.) "It has well-grounded pretensions to be one of the books which Pope Gregory the Great sent to Augustin, first archbishop of Canterbury, soon after his arrival in England. The Latin text is written in that thin light [rather *firm clear*] hand, which characterizes manuscripts penned in Italy." From a collation of part of this manuscript, I find that it contains the text of the *Roman* Psalter, which was introduced at Canterbury, whereas the *Gallican* obtained a footing in other parts of England, this confirms the reputed history of the book. The interlinear Anglo-Saxon version is written in a very neat minute hand, each word standing over the corresponding Latin.

quicumque legerit et intellegerit istam narrationem orat pro Macreguil scriptori." From this subscription of Macgregol, or Macreguil, we may learn two things; first, that vernacular versions were not at that time at all prohibited; and, secondly, that the transcriber deemed that in multiplying copies, he was doing a deed which might claim on his behalf the prayers of those who read or understood the book. This valuable and interesting Manuscript is in the Bodleian Library; it is called from the name of a former owner the RUSHWORTH GLOSS.

Bibl. Bodl. D 24. No. 3964.

ALFRED, commonly called the Great, translated the Ten Commandments, together with passages from the twenty-first, twenty-second, and twenty-third chapters of Exodus; these were prefixed to the body of laws which he promulgated. Other translations of parts of Scripture have been ascribed to him; but nothing else appears certain as having been done by him: he undertook a version of the Psalter, but did not live to execute it.

Alfred translates the Ten Commandments, &c.

In the tenth century there was a partial gloss of the book of Proverbs executed, the version being inserted between the lines of a Latin copy, through a considerable portion of the book. No part of this is a finished translation; sometimes but one Latin word in a whole line has any thing in Anglo-Saxon above it; so that it would be too much if we were to suppose that it gives any evidence that a translation of the Proverbs once existed.

10th Century. A partial gloss on the Proverbs. Cott. MSS. Vespas. D. vi.

In the latter part of the same century were executed the versions and paraphrases of ÆLFRIC of the historical books of the Old Testament. He appears to have done this work with the express intention of enabling his countrymen to read the Scripture history for themselves, and to this end his work is most decidedly *popular* in its character: thus, some parts are literal and exact versions of select parts, while again others are loosely paraphrastic abridgments or condensations of the sacred narrative. He wrote, also, a summary account of the Old and New Testaments, from which we learn what the portions of Scripture were which he turned into Anglo-Saxon. The following appears the result of his labours;—the Pentateuch, Joshua, Judges, part of the history of the Kings as found in the six books, Samuel, Kings, and Chronicles; Esther, Job (perhaps), Judith, and the two books of Maccabees.

Ælfric's versions, &c.

Some parts literal.

His own account of his labours.

Of these books, the Pentateuch, Joshua, Judges, Job, (if indeed it be his) and part of Judith, have been published in print; that is, in fact, the whole of his versions of which we have any account, excepting the summary of the history of the Kings, the Maccabees, Esther, and the rest of Judith. It is most probable that these books are not now extant.

Part of the version of Ælfric printed in 1698.

There exists a third Anglo-Saxon version of the four Evangelists; which appears to have been made at a later period than the other two, one of the existing manuscripts was written, probably, but a little before the time of the Norman Conquest, and the version itself, may belong to a period not much more remote. The translator is unknown, but he appears, in several places at least, to have translated from the Latin version which was in use before the time of Jerome, if, indeed, he has not wholly followed such a copy. This version has been several times printed, first of all in 1571, with a preface by the learned and laborious John Fox, author of "The Acts and Monuments of the Martyrs." This edition was not very accurate, but other editors have bestowed care in amending the text; for this purpose Junius collated four manuscripts of this version, as well as the two earlier translations which have been mentioned as contained in the Durham Book and the Rushworth Gloss; these two last, however, though very valuable as separate translations, could be but of little assistance in correcting the text of *another* version.

A third later version of the Gospels.

The Ante-hieronymian text used.

This version printed 1571, &c.

Besides this translation of the Gospels, a few manuscripts containing the Psalter are mentioned as having been written shortly before the time of the conquest. A little later than this there appears to have been an Anglo-Norman version of the Gospels, or at least a transcript of the Gospels into the dialect which was now displacing the genuine Anglo-Saxon: there are three such manuscripts known to be in existence, one of which is attributed to the time of William the Conqueror, the other two to about the time of Henry the Second. The first mentioned of these must be, I should think, *ante-dated*, for it does not seem to me likely that the effects of Norman intercourse could have so soon shown themselves in producing a marked dialect. These three manuscripts all exhibit the same translation, although with variations made by copyists; it is probable that each one sought to frame the language of the version according to what was most intelligible to himself.

Anglo-Saxon MSS. of the Psalter.

Anglo-Norman version of the Gospels.

Three such MSS.

One, of the days of Will. I

Two, of the time of Henry II.

With these gospels ends the series of Anglo-Saxon translations of parts of Scripture; it will be plainly seen that no attempt was made to form a complete version of the Bible, or even of the New Testament; the histories of the Old Testament, the Psalms, so much used in the public services of the church, and the narratives of the four evangelists seem to have been the only parts completed. It may be, that other portions of Scripture were translated which have not come down to us.

The last of the series of Anglo-Saxon versions.

Summary of the versions and paraphrases.

The following is a Summary of the Anglo-Saxon Translations and Paraphrases:—

PENTATEUCH, JOSHUA, JUDGES, and ESTHER, paraphrased by ÆLFRIC, in the latter part of the tenth century.

Some of the HISTORY of the KINGS, and perhaps JOB, by the same.

THE TEN COMMANDMENTS in Exodus xx., and parts of the three following chapters, by KING ALFRED, in the latter part of the ninth century.

THE BOOK OF PSALMS; two versions in the beginning of the eighth century by ALDHELM and GUTHLAC.

The same book, as found in manuscripts of the eleventh century.

PART OF THE PROVERBS, translated probably in the close of the ninth century.

[THE APOCRYPHAL BOOKS OF JUDITH and the MACCABEES, by ÆLFRIC in the latter part of the ninth century.]

THE GOSPEL OF JOHN, by the VENERABLE BEDE in the eighth century.

THE FOUR GOSPELS by ALDRED, probably in the end of the ninth century.

THE GOSPEL OF MATTHEW by FARMEN, probably in the tenth century.

THE GOSPELS OF MARK, LUKE, and JOHN, by OWEN, about the same period.

THE FOUR GOSPELS somewhat later. [The published translation.]

And, again, the FOUR GOSPELS in the ANGLO-NORMAN DIALECT.

To what degree the books in the above list were circulated, cannot of course be in any way ascertained. They were probably not all of them intended for the use of the priests, who ought to have known the Bible in Latin; but still it is likely that few comparatively of the people could read their own tongue: this may have been one reason why no complete version of the Scriptures was made in those days; the unlearned could not use it, the learned would prefer to read the Scriptures in Latin; it is not improbable that some of the interlined versions were made for the instruction of the priests themselves, that they might really understand what they were reading to the people. However this may be, no restraint appears to have been imposed upon the translating or the reading of the Scriptures in the vernacular tongue; and in the possession of a large portion of the word of God thus translated, the inhabitants of this country were much better off than they were at a later period, when the Anglo-Saxon dialect was become obsolete. It is not too much to conclude, that two centuries after the Norman conquest, there was far less knowledge of the Scriptures in England than had been the case in Saxon days.

Less knowledge of the Scriptures two centuries after the Conquest than in Saxon days.

After the English tongue, such as it then was, had supplanted the Anglo-Saxon, the history of Scripture translations recommences just in the same way as it did before; for as Cædmon had by his paraphrase, or compendium in verse, led the way to actual translations, so at this later period all the earliest attempts of which we know any thing to give any portion of Scripture truth in English are found in paraphrases in *verse*. The first of these was executed by one ORME, or Ormin, and hence his work is known by the name of "Ormulum;" it is a paraphrase on the Gospels and the Acts of the Apostles, in the style of Saxon poetry without rhyme; exhibiting the English language in its early state. No date appears to be assigned to this work, of which, in fact, comparatively little seems to be known; the language *may*, perhaps, indicate it to belong to some part of the twelfth century.

Gospels, &c. paraphrased. Orme's work, "Ormulum." Bibl. Bodl. Junius 1.

Sowlehele MSS. Bodl. 779.

The next attempt at Scripture paraphrase in English is likewise in metre; it is contained in a very large volume in the Bodleian Library bearing this title; "Here begynnen the tytles of the book that is cald in Latyn tonge Salus Animæ, and in Englysh tonge Sowlehele." Its contents are very various, although almost entirely consisting of religious poetry; amongst the rest is a metrical paraphrase of the Old and New Testaments; this work is supposed to have been executed before the thirteenth century; but like the Paraphrase of Orme, it is very difficult to assign a date to it.

A similar version of Genesis and Exodus. C.C.C.C.

In Corpus Christi College, Cambridge, there is a somewhat similar version of the history contained in the books of Genesis and Exodus; the date is supposed to be about the same as that of "Sowlehele;" the dialect differs, this being (according to Baber) evidently northern.

The Psalms in metre in English. Cir. 1300.

In the same college there is also an English metrical version of the book of Psalms, supposed to belong to about the year 1300. In other manuscripts (in the Bodleian Library and in the British Museum,) a version is also found partly similar, but with amendments and revisions, probably the partial adaptation of the same version to a more modern diction and orthography. These Psalters are almost the first thing that can be called an attempt at a *translation* into English. They follow the Latin Psalter which was ordinarily used in the church services, namely the *Gallican;* that is, the version of the Psalter corrected

The same version improved.

Taken from the Gallican Latin text.

by Jerome in accordance with the Greek text of Origen's Hexapla; this version was adopted in the end of the sixth century in Gaul, and afterwards in Britain. This Psalter is followed as closely by this English version as the verse will permit.

The hundredth Psalm is thus given in the two forms of the English version, the original and the revised:— The hundredth Psalm of both these versions.

ORIGINAL. C.C.C. CANT. MS. 278.	LATER VERSION. COTTON MS. VESP. D. VII.
Mirthes to god al erthe that es	Mirthes to lauerd al erthe that es,
Serves to louerd in faines.	Serues to lauerd in faienes.
In go yhe ai in his siht,	Ingas of him in the sight
In gladnes that is so briht	In gladeschip bi dai and night.
Whites that louerd god is he thus,	Wite ye that lauerd he god is thus,
He us made and our self noht us,	And he us made and ourself noght us;
His folke and shep of his fode ·	His folk and schepe of his fode:
In gos his yhates that are gode ·	In gas his yhates that er gode:
In schrift his worches belive,	In schrift his porches that be,
In ympnes to him yhe schrive.	In ympnes to him schriue yhe.
Heryhes his name for louerde is hende,	Heryes oft him name swa fre,
In all his merci do in strende and strende.	For that lauerd soft es he.
	In euermore his merci esse
	And in strende and strende his sothnesse.

With these metrical versions of the Book of Psalms ends the history of known attempts to embody the Scriptures in English prior to the fourteenth century. It will thus be seen that there was far less executed than there had been in Saxon days; so that three hundred years previously an inhabitant of England would have found much more of Scripture in his vernacular tongue than would one who lived at this time. These the only English versions known, prior to the 14th century.

I say *known* attempts, because assertions have been not unfrequently made of the existence of very early English translations of the whole of the Scriptures, and of course the *possibility* of such having existed is not to be denied, while, at the same time, the execution of any such version has never been *proved.* I think that it is not impossible, that any persons (such as Sir Thomas More when writing against Tyndale) who have alluded to a translation of the Scriptures into English prior to the fourteenth century, have been misled by supposing a metrical paraphrase (such as that contained in "Sowlehele") was a version of the Scriptures. Metrical paraphrases probably mistaken for versions.

Before giving any account of the English versions of the fourteenth century, it will be well to consider the statements of Sir Thomas More respecting translations of the Scriptures made *long previous* to the days of Wiclif. It is clear, that any version made in the fourteenth century could not have been accurately spoken of by More as made long before the days of Wiclif. Sir T. More's statements considered.

In the year 1408, when the opinions which Wiclif taught, and his translation of the Scriptures, had excited very general attention, a convention was held by Archbishop Arundel, at which several constitutions were decreed, of which the seventh runs thus:—"It is a dangerous undertaking, as St. Jerome assures us, to translate the Holy Scriptures; it being very difficult in a version to keep close to the sense of the inspired writers: for, by the confession of the same father, he had mistaken the meaning of several texts. We therefore decree and ordain, that from henceforward no unauthorized person shall translate any part of the holy Scripture into English, or any other language, under any form of book or treatise. *neither shall any such book, treatise, or version, made either in Wiclif's time, or since,* be read, either in whole or in part, publicly or privately, under the penalty of the greater excommunication, till the said translation shall be approved, either by the bishop of the diocese, or a provincial council, as occasion shall require." The proceeding of Abp. Arundell, 1408. Collier's Ecc. Hist. iii. 280. Danger of translating Scripture asserted. Prohibition to translate the Scriptures.

On this constitution and its intent, Sir Thomas More thus remarks:—"Ye shal understande that the great arch heretike Wickliffe wheras *yͤ hole byble was long before his dayes* by vertuous & wel lerned men *translated into yͤ englysh tong*, & by good & godly people wͪ deuotion & sobreness wel and reuerently red, toke vpon hym of a malicious purpose to translate it of new. In which translacion he purposely corrupted yͤ holye text, maliciously planting therin such wordes as might in yͤ reders eres serue to yͤ profe of such heresies as he went about to sowe, which he not only set furth with his own translacion of the Bible, but also wͭ certain prologes and glosis whiche he made therupon........ After that it was perceiued what harme yͤ peple toke by yͤ translacion prologes and gloses of Wickliffe, & also of some other that after him holpe to set Sir Thomas More's assertion, that the whole had been translated long before Wiclif's. Dialogues, b. iii. c. 14.

furth his secte, than for that cause, and for as much as it is daungerous to translate the text of scripture out of one tong into another, as holy S. Hyerome testifieth, for as much as in translacion it is hard alway to kepe the same sentence whole: it was I say for these causes at a counsayle holden at Oxenford prouided, upon great payn, y^{t} no man should from thencefurth translate into the englishe tongue or any other language, of his own authoritie, by way of boke, lybel or tretice, nor no man openly or secretly anye such boke lybel or tretice reade newly made in ye time of the said John Wicliffe or since, or that should be made any time after, till the same translacion wer by the dyocesane, or, if need shoulde require, by a provinciall counsayl approued. . . . It neither forbiddeth the translacions to be read that wer *already wel done of old before Wicliffes dayes,* nor damneth his because it was new, but because it was nought, nor prohibited new to be made, but prouydeth that they shall not be read if they be miss made til they be by good examinacion amended, excepte they bee such translacions as Wicliffe made and Tyndall, that the malicious minde of the translator had in such wise handled it as it were labor lost to go about to mende them." In another dialogue More's interlocutor objects that the clergy burned the English Bible, without respect to the translation be it good or bad; to this More answers: "Myself haue seen and can shew you Bybles fayr and old written in English which haue been knowen & sene by the byshop of the dyoces, and left in leymens handes & womens to such as he knew for good and catholike folk that used it with deuocion and sobrenes. But of truth al such as are founden in the handes of heretikes they use to take away; but they doe cause none to be burned, as farre as euer I coulde wit, but onely such as be founden faultie. Wherof many be sette forth with euill prologes or glosses maliciouslye made by Wickliffe and other heretikes. For no good man would (I wene) be so mad to burn up the Byble wherin they found no fault, nor any lawe that letted it to be looked on and read."

The constitution of Abp. Arundell referred to.

More's charges against Wiclif's and Tyndale's versions.

More's statement, that he himself had seen such previous versions. Dialogues, b. iii. c. 15.

All versions to be taken out of the hands of heretics.

More's object to defend Bp. Tonstall.

This statement of Sir Thomas More's was occasioned by the point which he wished to establish, namely, that Bishop Tonstall had performed a defensible, or even praiseworthy act, in burning Tyndale's New Testament; and here it is first of all to be observed, that he says, that all translations found in the hands of heretics, were taken away; this is part of the truth, but not the whole. He does not say, that within seven years before this dialogue was written, as well as at different times for more than a century previously, many persons were condemned as heretics, merely because they possessed, or had read, or had learned some portion of the Scripture in English. No question seems to have been made as to *who* was the translator of the portions in question; the Scripture, in English, was in itself made sufficient to brand men with the charge of heresy. Farther, there exists no proof, nor indeed has it been alleged, that the Scriptures of any translation at all were circulated, or commonly used by any of the laity in England; so that all that More says about translations, prior to that of Wiclif, being still *permitted,* is but an empty sound.

A man who had the Scriptures judged to be a heretic.

A question of chronology.

As to the distinct assertion, that the whole Bible was translated into English *long before* Wiclif's days, and that he himself had seen such copies, all that can be said is, that it is a mere question of chronology. He may, indeed, have meant the old metrical paraphrases; but I think it more probable that he looked on the constitution of 1408, which prohibits versions made in the days of Wiclif or since, as implying that there were previous translations in existence; he seems farther to have supposed, that Wiclif's translation was characterized by prologues *and explanatory glosses;* and thus a copy in which these were found, he would attribute to Wiclif, while one in which they were absent, he would regard as being what he termed the far older version. But, indeed, I believe that in all this, More knew very little about what he was speaking of, as little as he did of Tyndale's Testament; and thus he praised a translation which really was Wiclif's, while he condemned, most sweepingly, another, with glosses, which was made a little afterward.

More's mistakes with regard to Wiclif's version.

Dialogues, b. iii. c. 16.

Sir Thomas More again speaks to the same import, with regard to the Scriptures being kept by the clergy from the people. "I haue shewed you, y^{t} they kepe none from them, that can no more but theyr mother tong," "but such translacion as be either not yet approued for good; or such as be alredy reproued for naught as Wickliffes was and Tyndals. For as for other olde ones y^{t} were before Wickliffes daies, remain lawful, and be in some folkes hands." This was very little in accordance with known facts; and More himself lets us know that he was *not very certain* about the date of those Bibles which he attributed to periods anterior to that of Wiclif: he seems to wonder that no translation had been made, and formally approved by the clergy or some one bishop, so that it might be printed without fear of penalty, like other books; he had before asserted the free use of translations, made before the days of Wiclif, to be permitted, but adds, "Yet I thinke ther will no printer lightly be so hote to put anye Byble in prynte at hys own charge, wherof ye losse shoulde lie hole on his own necke, & *than hang upon* A DOUBTFUL TRYAL *whether ye first copy of his translacion was made before Wickliffes days or since*; for if it were made synce it must be approued before the prynting."

Opposed to facts.

More's wonder that no approved English translation had been printed.

Thus, after all, More lets us know that it would hang upon *a doubtful trial* whether any of the English copies of the Scriptures, then in existence, were translated before the days of Wiclif or not; observe, More had stated such a translation to have been made *long before* Wiclif's, this could not then have been in the fourteenth century; likewise he had said, that *the whole Bible* had been so translated, so that no versions of particular parts would help him out of his difficulty. I think that I need say no more to make it plain that Sir Thomas More's statements afford NO PROOF of the execution of a version of the whole Bible, anterior to that of Wiclif. Those who have affirmed this, seem to have commonly copied either from Sir Thomas More, or from one another.

More thoroughly contradicts himself.

There does not thus appear any thing like evidence of the existence of an English version of the Scriptures, either of the Old Testament or of the New, prior to the fourteenth century; and further it may be said, that to the same century may be ascribed the first translation, of which there is authentic information, of any portion at all of the word of God into *English prose.* The first of the translators of this period was RICHARD ROLLE, hermit of HAMPOLE, who has been most commonly known by the latter name, being designated agreeably to the custom of the age, Richard Hampole, or simply Hampole; the place from which he took this appellation, is near Doncaster. This hermit lived in the early half of the fourteenth century, and his object in making translations of parts of the Scripture appears especially to have been occupation and amusement. The portion of Scripture, the translation of which may be with certainty ascribed to Hampole, is the book of Psalms; which he turned together with the Hymns of the Church into English, subjoining a comment to each verse. Hampole thus speaks in the prologue to the Psalms: "In this worke y seke no straunge Englishe, bot esieste and communeste, and siche that is moost lyche to the Latyne: so that thei that knoweth not the Latyne by the Englishe may come to many Latyne wordis. In the translacione y folewe the lettre as much as I may, and there y fynde no proper Englice I folewe the wit of the wordis so that thei that shal reede it, thar not drede erryng. In expownyng I folewe hooly Doctors, and resoun: reprouyng synne... Ffor this boke may comen into summe envyous manns honde... and suche wolle seye that I wiste not what I seyde, and so do harme to hymsilf and to othur."

No evidence of an English version of the Old or New Testament prior to the fourteenth century. Richard Rolle of Hampole. Fourteenth century. The Psalms with a comment. Hampole's prologue, Bib. Reg. Mus. Brit. 18. D. I. His manner of translating, and of expounding.

The following may be taken as specimen of Hampole's version: the Latin Psalter which he follows is the Gallican. Psalm xxiii (Lat. xxii).

"Our lord gouerneth me and nothyng to me shal wante stede of pasture that he me sette.
"In the water of hetyng forth he me brougte: my soule he turnyde.
"He ladde me on in the stretis of rygtwisnesse: for his name.
"For win gif I hadde goo in myddil of the shadewe of deeth · I shal not dreede yueles, for thou art with me.
"Thi geerde and thi staf · thei haue coumfortid me. Thou hast greythid in my sygt a bord. agens hem that angryn me.
"Thou fattide myn heued in oyle: and my chalys drunkenyng what is cleer.
"And thi mercy shal folewe me: in alle the dayes of my lyf.
"And that I wone in the hous of oure lord in the lengthe of dayes."

Psalm xxiii. A specimen of Hampole's version. The first in English prose. Bib. Reg. Mus. Brit. 18. D. I. Psalm 1—79.

But although Hampole commenced thus the translation of Scripture into English prose, he seems to have preferred greatly to follow in the path which had been trodden before him; he made a translation in verse of the seven penitential psalms; a paraphrase in verse of certain portions of Job; and also a profuse paraphrase on the Lord's prayer.

Hampole's translation in verse.

Besides this translation of the Psalter by Hampole, there are two other versions of the same book extant, the date of which appears to be about the same as his; one of these resembles Hampole's version, the other is widely different.

Two other versions of the Psalter.

Besides these three versions of the Psalter, there is likewise mentioned by Lewis a manuscript in the library of Benet College, Cambridge, containing a gloss on the following books of the New Testament:— the gospels of St. Mark and St. Luke, the epistles to the Romans, Corinthians, Galatians, Ephesians, Philippians, Colossians, [the apocryphal epistle to the Laodiceans,] Thessalonians, Timothy, Titus, Philemon, and Hebrews. From the existence of a gloss comprehending so very large a portion of the New Testament, I think it very probable that the whole of this division of the Scriptures was about that period thus rendered into English; this manuscript may in fact be a portion of such a work.

A gloss on part of the New Test. (Lewis Hist. Trans. p. 16) MS. Benet Coll. Camb. P vi.

The following is a sample of this gloss, as communicated to Mr. Lewis by Dr. Waterland:

Mark i. 1. "And he prechyde sayande, a stalworther thane I schal come efter me of whom I am not worthi downfallande, or knelande, to louse the thwonge of his chawcers."

A specimen of this gloss.

Mark vi. 22. "When the doughtyr of that Herodias was in comyn and had tombylde and pleside to Harowde, and also to the sittande at mete, the king says to the wench."

Mark xii. 1. "A man made a vynere, and he made aboute a hegge, and grofe a lake & byggede a tower."

Mark xii. 38. "Be se ware of the scrybes whylke wille go in stolis and be haylsede in the market and for to sit in synagogis in the fyrste chayers."

Luke ii. 7. "... and layde hym in a cratche: for to hym was no place in the dyversory."

The comment like that of Hampole.

Lewis states the accompanying comment to be much like that of Hampole upon the Psalter; whether this version be the production of Hampole or not, it is at least the most important step in biblical translation which had as yet been made in English. I know of no data upon which to ascribe this work to Hampole, except that which may be supposed to be deduced from similarity of style, and this is very far from a sure criterion. In this, however, we have the labour of some one who in a remote age diligently toiled in the then unwonted field of Scripture translation; and who did far more than had ever been accomplished since Anglo-Saxon days. This work was probably executed for private edification rather than for public circulation, by some priest seeking (as Mr. Baber conjectures,) to instruct those over whom he was set.

A partial translation of the gospels. MSS. Harl. 5035, called in the catalogue "Mirror of Sermons for the whole Year." A specimen. John i. 19—28.

A partial translation of the Evangelists in the northern dialect is found in a manuscript in the British Museum, which contains the Gospels for the Sundays throughout the year, translated into English, together with an exposition. The following is a specimen of this version:—

John i. 19—28. "And this is the testimoninge of Ion whan the Iues of ierulm sent prestes & dekenes vnto Ion baptist forto aske him what ertow. And he graunted what he was, & aȝensaide noȝt. And he graunted & said, for y nam nouȝt crist. And hii asked him, what ertow than, ertow ely? And he answered, I nam nouȝt eli. And hii saiden, Ertow a p̄phete? And he answered and said, nai. And hii said to him, what ertow, that we may ȝif answer to hem that sent us, what sais tow of the seluen? I am a uoice of the criand in desert that dresceth our lordes wai as Isaie saith. And hii that were sent thei were of phariseus. And hii asked him and said to him wharto baptizes too, ȝif thou ne be noȝt crist, ne heli, ne prophete? Ion answered to hem and saide. I ȝow baptize in water: fforsothe he stode in middes of ȝou that ȝe ne wot nouȝt, he schal com efter me that is made tofore me of whom inam nouȝt worthi to undo the thwonge of his schoes. Thes thinges ben don in bethaine beyond iordan ther Ion baptized."

The object of the translation.

The object which the translator of these portions proposed to himself was probably that of making those events of our Saviour's life which are narrated in the Sunday Gospels intelligible to those who were ignorant of Latin. As yet there does not appear to have been in England, either a desire on the part of the people to possess the whole of the Scripture in their own language, or an attempt on the part of the ecclesiastical authorities to forbid this. The close connexion of the translations hitherto noticed with the services of the church is to be borne in mind these versions have been mostly Psalters and Church Hymns, or else portions of the New Testament which were frequently read in the Latin services, which were clothed in an English dress, apparently by those who belonged to the Roman priesthood, and who carefully guarded the text so translated by their own commentary.

These early versions closely connected with the services of the church.

These partial translations probably instruments of blessing. Although but little circulated.

I do not question that these partial translations were instruments of blessing to some of those into whose hands they came. There is a power in the word of God, even if it be but partially known, and the Holy Ghost may apply to the conscience of a sinner even a small portion of His own revelation concerning Christ. But it does not appear even likely that these versions were at all widely circulated; indeed this would be contrary to all probability, when the state of literature in England at that time is considered. Thus something was yet to be waited for, which should give a sufficient impulse to cause laborious pains to be taken to transcribe and circulate the English Scriptures. It was not enough that they should be translated. If they were to be known by the people, they must be forced upon their attention by some new and unwonted means. This was not long delayed.

These versions belonging to the earlier half of the fourteenth century. No evidence to warrant Sir T. More's assertions.

It is probable that these versions already mentioned, which appear to belong to the fourteenth century, were executed in either the earlier half or not much beyond the middle of it; what others were made at that time (if any) I cannot find. I have noticed all of those to which any allusion is made by Mr. Lewis or Mr. Baber, together with making what farther inquiry was within my power. It will be seen, that nothing which has been mentioned has at all borne out the assertion of Sir Thomas More, as to the Scripture, both of the Old and the New Testaments, having been translated into English before the days of Wiclif. More's assertion is utterly unsupported so far as evidence goes, even though the length of time, "*long before* Wiclif's days," were not rested upon as a material point. The fallacy of the assertion, if strictly taken, I have already shewn.

There was thus an open field left in biblical labours in England with regard to two points; first, the making of an English version of the whole of the Old and New Testaments; and secondly, the circulation of such a translation after it had been made. We have no account of any attempt to attain either of these objects.

It may be well to re-state what the translations and paraphrases of Scripture in English were which had been made previous to the latter part of the fourteenth century. Summary of the English versions or paraphrases prior to the middle of the fourteenth century.

THE PARAPHRASE IN METRE, WITHOUT RHYME, OF THE GOSPELS, AND THE ACTS OF THE APOSTLES, executed by ORMIN.

THE METRICAL PARAPHRASE OF THE OLD AND NEW TESTAMENTS contained in the collection entitled "SOWLEHELE," supposed to be prior to the year 1300. The metrical versions, &c.

THE NORTHERN PARAPHRASE OF GENESIS AND EXODUS (of about the same date), in Corpus Christi College, Cambridge.

THE METRICAL PSALTER, of about the same date.

THE REVISED VERSION OF THE PSALMS, somewhat more modern than the preceding.

THE PROSE VERSION OF THE PSALTER, by RICHARD ROLLE of HAMPOLE, before the middle of the fourteenth century. The prose translations.

THE METRICAL VERSION OF THE PENITENTIAL PSALMS, part of JOB, and THE LORD'S PRAYER, by the same.

Two other PROSE VERSIONS of the PSALMS.

THE GOSPELS OF MARK AND LUKE, and the EPISTLES OF ST. PAUL.

THE NORTHERN TRANSLATION OF THE DOMINICAL GOSPELS.

II.

SOME ACCOUNT OF WICLIF TO THE TIME OF HIS TRANSLATION OF THE SCRIPTURES.

THE earliest version of the Scriptures into English, which either excited much attention, or was the instrument of any known important results, is most certainly that of JOHN WICLIF. I say this without hesitation, although I neither forget the Anglo-Saxon translations of various portions of the word of God, nor do I overlook the objections which have been from time to time raised against the claim of Wiclif as being the first English translator of the whole of the Scriptures. Wiclif's version the first which excited much attention, or produced important results in England.

The Anglo-Saxon versions have been already spoken of, but I again advert to them in connection with the translation of Wiclif: I do it for this simple reason, that those versions do not in any way stand in competition with his. They may have been very important in the days in which they were made; they may have afforded the means of learning the revealed will of God to many whose eyes had been otherwise blinded; God may thus have made them instruments of blessing to those who needed the light of his truth; but still, it must always be remembered, that in Wiclif's day they were utterly obsolete. They occupy, it is true, an important place in the history of the vernacular versions of this country, but it would be as unreasonable to call the Vulgate *Italian*, as the Anglo-Saxon Gospels *English;* there is as little parity, as to language, between the translation of Ælfric and that of Wiclif, as there is between those of Jerome and Diodati. No one would put the Latin versions of the Scripture amongst the Italian translations, and just so the Anglo-Saxon versions belong to a wholly different category from that of Wiclif. The Anglo-Saxon versions in no sense competitors of Wiclif's. Obsolete in the fourteenth century.

But we have this question to examine, "Was WICLIF's the first *English* translation?" This is, of course, a point of considerable interest; and it becomes especially so, when we have that translation, together with the effects which it produced, as the objects under examination. Even if I should not be able to give an answer wholly explicit or satisfactory to this inquiry, I shall, I believe, be at least able to bring forward certain collateral points which throw some light upon the claim of Wiclif to originality, even if they do not establish it. Some remarks on this point have already been made. Was Wiclif's the first *English* translation?

The point which I wish first to bring forward and prove is, that Wiclif's was the first *published* English version of the Scriptures. I use the word *published* in the sense in which it was continually used, prior to the invention of printing; *now* we have affixed a certain conventional sense to the term, which never *could* have been used before the present mode of multiplying books was introduced; and thus, in speaking of the publication of Wiclif's version, I speak according to the use of the word in the fourteenth century, and not according to that which was introduced in the latter half of the fifteenth. Wiclif's the first *published* English version.

Publication of works prior to printing.

What then would have been formerly regarded as the publication of a work? This was commonly done, either by the author employing copyists, and thus multiplying transcripts for sale, or else by his depositing his work in any place (a convent or college library, or the like), to which learned men might both have access, and have the opportunity of making copies; or else the author used some means for letting the contents of his work be publicly known, and then preparing transcripts for any who might be sufficiently interested to have such copies made. It was in this last mentioned manner that Giraldus Cambrensis published some of his works. He lived in the reign of Henry II., and was one of the companions of Baldwin, archbishop of Canterbury, during his journey through Wales, in preaching the Crusades. Giraldus, wishing to publish some of his works, had a pulpit erected in an open thoroughfare at Brecon (of which place he was archdeacon), and there he read his works aloud, so that those who passed might listen, and any who wished for copies, had the opportunity of having them transcribed. This may serve to illustrate the means which, in former days, were taken to publish any works which had been written or translated.

Giraldus Cambrensis publishes some of his works by reading them in an open place.

To return, then, to Wiclif. I do not believe that it has been objected by any, that an English translation previous to his had ever been published; and even if this objection were raised, I do not think any *proof* could be brought forward in support of such an opinion. Observe, it is not enough that a translation be *made*, for this is not in itself publication; but means must be taken to diffuse such a translation amongst those who would read it. This attempt to diffuse constitutes the very essence of publication; and I do not think that this can be even alleged of any version prior to Wiclif's. Let individuals have made versions to any number for their own private use, let copies of these have been preserved among the secluded treasures of many libraries, still nothing whatever would have been done, which could at all render the labour of Wiclif an uncalled-for work.

Multiplication of copies of Wiclif's version.

It is most evident that Wiclif must have used no small diligence in his publication of the English Scriptures: this is proved; first, by the numerous copies which have come down to our day in spite of the prohibition issued in the year 1408;—and, secondly, by the notice which was taken of the fact of this version being so much diffused. The testimony of the enemies of Wiclif sufficiently proves this point;—thus Knyghton* says, "The gospel, which Christ delivered to the clergy and doctors of the church, that they might, themselves, sweetly administer to the laity and to weaker persons with the hunger of their mind according to the exigency of the times and the need of persons, did this Master John Wyclif translate out of Latin into English .... whence through him it became vulgar and more open to the laity, and women who could read, than it used to be to the most learned of the clergy, even to those of them who had the best understanding." Knyghton then goes on to speak of the contempt which, he says, was thus cast upon the Scripture. Unless we suppose that this Romish writer was led by his zeal to exaggerate greatly the effect which Wiclif's version produced, we cannot help concluding that the diffusion of copies almost as soon as the translation was made, must have been very wide: but let every allowance be made for Knyghton's zeal that may be thought needful, it is impossible to doubt that much of what he says, must rest upon the simple facts of the case. Knyghton thus continues his lament over the diffusion of God's word; "And in this way the gospel pearl is cast abroad, and trodden under foot of swine, and that which used to be precious to both clergy and laity, is rendered, as it were, the common jest of both. The jewel of the clergy is turned into the sport of the laity, and what was hitherto the principal talent of the clergy and doctors of the Church, is made for ever common to the laity." I do not wonder at these remarks; they are just what might have been expected concerning the reading of the word of God from the mind of one who knew not its value as being the revelation of God. Strange, indeed, that the book which testifies of Christ and His precious blood, should be deemed unfit for the eyes of sinners who need the knowledge of that truth of God; but yet this is not stranger than the fact, which continually occurs, of this book being owned and upheld as coming from God, and yet of its testimony being utterly disregarded.

Knyghton de Eventibus Angliæ, col. 2644.

The publication of the Scriptures made a ground of accusation against Wiclif.

Knyghton's heavy complaints.

I rest upon the unsuspected testimony of Knyghton as a proof of the publication of Wiclif's translation;—he proves this in two ways, first, in direct statement of this diffusion; and secondly, in mentioning the resulting consequences: with his sentiments in connection with the subject, of course I can have no sympathy, but this in no way renders his testimony suspicious.

The peculiar interest attaching to Wiclif's version.

There is thus a peculiar interest attaching to the version of Wiclif; it came forth in a day when Christ's Gospel was scarcely preached, and when human observances of every kind were substituted for that faith through which man, in himself a lost sinner, is justified before God: but although the darkness around were such, yet there was thus a ray of light introduced, a ray which served to show how foul was the

* Henry Knyghton was a cotemporary of Wiclif, and a canon of Leicester.

atmosphere in which it was shining. Surely it is impossible not to see the overruling hand of God in this: surely we have to ascribe this precious testimony to His truth and Gospel, as having been brought about by His grace. The fact of such a version having been made and diffused at such a period, does, I think, manifest this working of God: but it will make this still more evident, if the causes which led Wiclif to this work be duly considered. In order to ascertain these causes of his undertaking, it will be needful briefly to glance at his previous history and circumstances.*

Birth of John Wiclif, 1324. 1340. Is at Queen's College, Oxford. Removes to Merton College. He writes "The Last Age of the Chirche," 1356. MS. Trin. Col. Dub. class c. tab. 3. No. 12.

John Wiclif is supposed to have been born in the year 1324, at a village in Yorkshire, from the name of which he, like other ecclesiastics of that period, took his surname, if indeed it were not his family name also, which is not impossible. In the year 1340, he was one of the original students at Queen's College, Oxford, but he removed shortly after to Merton College, which was then the most distinguished in Oxford. In 1356 his first treatise was written, bearing this title: "The Last Age of the Chirche." It was occasioned by the manner in which England and other countries had been visited with a devastating pestilence, a little while previous to the writing of the tract in question. Its contents exhibit a conscience deeply exercised by the evil and corruption which on every side prevailed in that which was called the Church of God, and the calamities which were to be expected in consequence of these abominations. He looked upon two periods of especial suffering to the Church previous to the coming of the Lord Jesus in the clouds of heaven. Two such periods had already elapsed since Christ had set up His church upon earth; the one, the persecution of the Church by Pagan rulers; the second, the entrance of heresy: "That is put of bi wisdom of seyntis, as the firste was cast out bi stedfastnesse of martiris." With regard to the two periods of peculiar evil to the Church which were yet to be expected, the first would be (as he judged), calamity arising from "the pryui heresie of symonyans;" the last would be the time of the dominion of *Antichrist* (whom he clearly regarded, in common with almost all early writers, as an individual person), the period of whose "comynge oonly to God is knowen."†

p. xxv. Two periods of peculiar evil expected. Simony. Antichrist.

I rest particularly upon this first publication of Wiclif's, because (although the greater part of it is filled with fanciful calculations out of the Abbot Joachim) I think that in it is to be traced the germ which was developed in his after life and writings, his version of the Scripture itself not excepted. He saw corruption in every class of those who bore the name of Christians; and this was the more manifest in those who were especially standing in eminence of station in the Church. Every thing being thus out of course, there was but one thing for which he looked, and that speedily—the righteous vengeance of God. While all around him were glorying in the name of *Church*, he testified that this boast was but adding to the condemnation of those that made it. In fact, *the apostasy of the Church* is plainly pointed out, and the resulting consequences are dwelt on. He supposes that secular power would rise on the ruins of ecclesiastical. However peculiar the sentiments and opinions, and wildly fanciful as are both his citations from the real or pretended writings of the Abbot Joachim and others, and also his own comments as contained in this tract, may now seem to some, yet, in parts, there appear points of valuable truth, setting forth principles which are often overlooked in this day, as they were in his.

The apostasy of the Church marked out.

But in this tract, Wiclif does not only speak of judgment as being the inevitable consequence of the apostasy of the body (according to Romans xi. 22.), but he likewise points out that security which God giveth to those who believe in the name of the Lord Jesus Christ. He thus concludes his tract:—"Whanne we weren synful & children of wraththe, Goddis sone cam out of heuene, & preyying his fadir for his enemyes, & he deyed for vs thanne myche rathere we ben maad riȝtful bi his blood schule be saued. Poul writith to the romayns, v. c°. He schal praye for vs. Ihūs wente into heuene to apere to the semlant of God for vs. Poul to the hebrees: The whiche semlant he graunte vs to see that lyueth & regneth without eende, Amen."

The inevitable consequence of apostasy marked out, as well as the security of any and every believer. p. xxxvi. Rom. v. 9. Heb. ix. 24.

* In these notices, I have mostly followed Baber and Vaughan; the work of the latter is valuable for the light which it throws upon the periods at which the various works of Wiclif were written. in this way his conduct becomes much more intelligible, and the insinuations of Milner and others are shewn to be undeserved. If the researches of Vaughan have not all the importance which he claims for them, they are at least as far, or farther, from the insignificance which some have chosen to ascribe to them. His researches as to the events of Wiclif's life, and the dates of his writings, have, I should think, much more precision than his account and estimate of his opinions. Indeed this latter field was much the more difficult.

† While these pages were in the press, I received a little book entitled, "The Last Age of the Church, by John Wyclyffe, now first printed from a Manuscript in the University Library, Dublin. Edited, with Notes, by James Henthorn Todd, D. D., &c." This little volume contains 103 small pages, of which fourteen only comprise Wiclif's tract. The preface and notes of the Editor form the rest of the volume: had these been omitted, there are but few to whom the tract would have been intelligible. The opportunity which I have thus had of comparing Vaughan's account with the book itself, makes me much regret that I am obliged, in several instances, to take my citations from him. A modernizer of an ancient writing ought to take care that he does not make his author say something which he never intended. I thank Vaughan for what he has done, but I should have been still more obliged, if he had given his citations *verbatim et literatim*.

The general corruption of the Church marked by covetousness.

The true key to the understanding of the motive of this tract is to be found in the corruption which existed in the Church of Rome at this time; a corruption which is only equalled by its boldness and freedom from all attempts at concealment. *Money* seemed to be the one object sought by all classes in the Church, while every portion of Christian doctrine was of course frittered away. It is impossible to say by what means God had wrought upon the soul of Wiclif, we simply have the fact as proved by the results; his conscience was evidently deeply aroused. We shall find that his mind gradually opened to more and more truth, but many of the principles which were afterwards farther developed had been contained in this tract. So far as I know, his later writings were not replete with fanciful speculations.

1360. Wiclif opposes the mendicant friars.

It was in 1360, four years after the time when the tract just mentioned was written, that Wiclif was known at Oxford as the opponent of the mendicant friars, a body of men whose conduct and character had undoubtedly led to many of his previous reflections on the condition of the Church. We shall find that from that time and onward, these friars were continually harassing and opposing the reformer. The mendicant friars had by their encroachments excited much opposition on the part of those who hated fraud and duplicity. Richard Fitzralph (commonly called Armachanus), who was chancellor of the University of Oxford in 1333, was their determined opponent, both at that time as well as subsequently, when he became (in 1347) archbishop of Armagh. He died in 1360, the year in which Wiclif succeeded to his place in this contention. With regard to these new orders, Wiclif considered that if God had indeed conferred them on the Church, it was done just in the same manner as that in which the Israelites received a king, namely, in chastisement. The controversy with the friars appears to have led Wiclif to the close study of God's word, a circumstance of considerable subsequent importance.

The mendicant friars opposed by Armachanus, Abp. of Armagh, 1347.

Wiclif's opinion with regard to the origin of the friars.

1361. Rector of Fillingham, and warden of Baliol College.

The following year (1361) Wiclif was presented to the rectory of Fillingham, and chosen Warden of Baliol College, in the University of Oxford. In December 1365, however, he accepted the office of warden of Canterbury Hall, being so appointed by Simon Islip, then archbishop of Canterbury. This situation involved him in no small trouble; and circumstances connected therewith first brought him into direct collision with the Papacy. Archbishop Islip was himself the founder of Canterbury Hall, which was to consist of a warden and three scholars (all chosen from amongst the monks of Christ Church, Canterbury), and eight secular clergy. This arrangement he afterwards saw fit to alter, by removing the warden and the other three monks, and placing in their stead secular scholars. The first warden who had been appointed was a monk named Woodhall, a doctor of divinity, a man apparently of ability, but of a most ungoverned temper. This he shewed in his management of Canterbury Hall, where the disputes between the regular and the secular clergy (*i. e.* those who belonged to monastic orders and those who did not) ran high: in fact, it could hardly be otherwise, when such incongruous materials were attempted to be blended together. In consequence of the dissensions, Archbishop Islip availed himself of a right which he had intended to have reserved to himself in his deed of foundation, for the subsequent regulation of the Hall.

1365. Warden of Canterbury Hall.

The constitution of the house.

Woodhall the first warden.

Dissensions.

The constitution of the house changed.

Woodhall appeals to Abp. Langham, and is restored, March, 1367.

As soon as Archbishop Islip was dead, the rejected warden, Woodhall, appealed to the new archbishop, Peter Langham, in hopes of obtaining the wardenship from which he had been deprived by the preceding archbishop. In March, 1367, Woodhall was restored, although it was done in direct contravention of the intention of the founder of the Hall; and in consequence, Wiclif appealed from the archbishop to the Pope. The decision at length, after some years, was given in favour of the monks, and against Wiclif; and not only was the secular warden thus excluded, but it was declared that none except monks were to have any claim to admission to that Hall. This contest is so far of importance, as having been the first direct contact into which Wiclif was brought with the Papacy, as well as because the whole of the opposition which was made to him by the monks resulted from their enmity having been excited by his testimony against their corruptions. It is of course evident, that at the time of Wiclif's appeal to the Pope, he did not question the authority of the Papacy in ecclesiastical matters, while at the same time he was actually engaged in opposing the temporal authority of the Roman bishop.

Wiclif appeals to the Pope, who decides against him.

Urban V. claims sovereignty over England, 1365.

In 1365, not long before the appeal respecting Canterbury Hall had been brought before the Pope, the claim of temporal authority over England was revived by Urban V. and the annual tribute of a thousand marks, and the whole of the arrears for thirty-three years was now demanded. This demand having been made to Edward III. in 1365, he submitted the question to the decision of Parliament in the following year. They went so far as to threaten the Pope with war in case he should attempt to enforce his claim. A monk, one probably of those who had felt the lash of Wiclif's testimony on the corruption of the Church, published a book upholding the papal claim, asserting the realm of England to be forfeited to the Pope, and calling upon Wiclif to disprove the assertion. To this Wiclif replied, stating what was involved in the question. He refers to the proceedings of the English Parliament relative to the

The demand laid before Parliament.

A monk challenges Wiclif.

His reply.

claim, adopting, it is clear, a considerable portion of the sentiments which are introduced. It comes, in fact, to a question of *simony*. If the Pope had a pecuniary claim on England, it must be for some advantage to be bestowed by him: the Pope could only dispense spiritual blessings; thus the admission of the papal claim would be a direct sanction of the sale of spiritual advantages, and thus it would be the admission of sanctioned simony. Thus this was no mere political question, there were far higher principles involved; it was one which displayed the utter rottenness of the whole system of things called spiritual then existing in Europe.* It is no marvel that the Pope should have given his judgment against such a free-spoken appellant.

The question simply one of simony.

The principle involved.

In 1368, while the appeal was yet pending, Wiclif exchanged the rectory of Fillingham for that of Ludgershall, also in the diocese of Lincoln.

Fillingham exchanged for Ludgershall, 1368.

In 1370, the Pope gave his definite sentence in favour of Woodhall: and, two years after, a confirmation was procured from the king, a bribe of two hundred marks (equal to a very large sum of the present day) having been employed to obtain it.

The Pope decides against Wiclif, 1370.

The king confirms the decision.

In 1372, John Wiclif took his degree of doctor in divinity, and became theological lecturer at Oxford—a position of no small importance, when occupied by such a man,—in which he both had, and used, the opportunity of expounding scripture to his auditors; which not only produced important results in many of them, but which likewise appears to have imbued the mind of Wiclif himself more and more with the truth of God, set forth by the Holy Ghost in the Word. In fact, Wiclif, who had before been known as the steady opponent of the friars, the bearer of a righteous testimony against simony, even though it were found in the Pope himself, the deplorer of the apostasy of the Church, now stood as the setter forth of the truth of God, before those by whom the theological lectures were attended; he had not merely to combat error, but likewise to teach *truth*.

Wiclif takes his degree of D.D. and becomes theological lecturer at Oxford.

In the documents which have come down to us, as portions of the theological lectures of Wiclif, it is interesting to see how earnestly the person and the work of the Lord Jesus Christ are pressed upon the attention of the auditors; no introduction of any thing whatsoever save the blood of Christ between the soul of a sinner and God. This becomes a point of exceeding importance, when the testimony of Wiclif, in a corrupt age, is considered; he was not merely one who saw how simony and corruption abounded on every side in the nominal church of God;—this might have been noticed by any observer through dint of mere intellect;—but he saw the enormity of these things in their true light, from regarding them as set in contrast to the revelation of God. Services, of one kind or another, were introduced and recognized as having something to do with the acceptance of the sinner; and, after all, the degree of nearness wholly depended upon certain things to be done by certain priests; these matters were, in that day, *fully relied on;* men had confidence in them, instead of depending only on that blood which has been shed for many for the remission of sins. I give one extract, which shows how firmly Wiclif opposed even the most dearly cherished superstitions of his age:—"Many think that if they give a penny to a pardoner, they shall be forgiven the breaking of all the commandments of God, and therefore they take no heed how they keep them. But I say thee for certain, though thou have priests and friars to sing for thee, and though thou each day hear many masses, and found chauntries and colleges, and go on pilgrimages all thy life, and give all thy goods to pardoners; all this shall not bring thy soul to heaven. While if the commandments of God are revered to the end, though neither penny nor halfpenny be possessed, there shall be everlasting pardon, and the bliss of heaven!" On this extract I would remark, that the contrast which Wiclif draws, is between the commandments which *men* had framed, and the commandments which had been given by *God;* if this distinction be not borne in mind, it may lead to the strange mistake of supposing that the doctrine of Wiclif savoured of a righteousness of our own, wrought out by our own obedience, instead of the righteousness of Christ, which is made ours by faith. This is hardly the place to enter upon specific proof that the doctrinal sentiments of Wiclif were utterly opposed to every thing of self-righteousness, and that they fully recognized the teaching of Scripture as to human depravity and inability. *Man's* commandments he speaks of with condemnation, while he upholds *God's* commandments as being the way of salvation:—"And this is *His* commandment, that we should believe on the name of His Son Jesus Christ, and love one another, as He gave us commandment."

The person and the work of the Lord Jesus pressed in the theological writings of Wiclif.

Contrast of this to the then current doctrines.

Extract from Wiclif on the Decalogue, Vaughan i., p. 329.

Commandments of men contrasted with the commandments of God.

Wiclif no advocate for self-righteousness.

1 John iii. 23.

Such, then, was the manner in which Wiclif gave his instructions as divinity lecturer at Oxford; standing, be it remembered, in the midst of Papal abuse, and not merely displaying the deformity of error, but

Wiclif's lectures stand in striking contrast to the errors of his day.

* It is probable that the monkish controvertist made his appeal to Wiclif on account of the situation which the latter held. it appears from his reply, that he was at that time chaplain to the king.

opening, likewise, the word of God, and giving forth its blessed testimony of revealed truth; a work which not only fitted him for the labour of translating the word of God, but which likewise appears to have led him onward to the undertaking of the arduous task.

July 26, 1374. Wiclif sent to Bruges by Edward III., on a mission to the Pope. Delegates arrive at Bruges August, 1374, where they remain till July, 1376. Wiclif made prebend of Aust, and rector of Lutterworth, by the king.

Two years after Wiclif became the professor of Divinity at Oxford, he was sent as such by Edward III., together with the bishop of Bangor, and others, on a mission to Pope Gregory XI., respecting certain encroachments with regard to reservations of benefices, &c. which he had attempted to make in England. The place at which the negotiation was to be carried on was Bruges; where the commissioners appear to have arrived in or about the month of August, 1374. The proceedings were lengthened out for a considerable time, so that Wiclif does not appear to have left Bruges till July, 1376; having thus been for nearly two years in contact with the utter corruption of the Papal emissaries. The principal English commissioner was subsequently richly rewarded by the Pope, being immediately translated to the see of Hereford, and thence, in 1389, to St. David's, both of these translations having taken place by virtue of papal "provisions." Wiclif, during his absence (November, 1375,) was presented by the king with the prebend of Aust in the collegiate church of Westbury, and subsequently with the rectory of Lutterworth. These facts show pretty plainly how these men had respectively conducted themselves in their mission.

The sufficiency of the revelation of God urged by Him. He opposes the whole papal authority.

The protracted stay of Wiclif, at Bruges, was probably not a wasted period of his life. We have seen how his heart had learned to mourn over the corruption of the church visible,—how he traced back these evils to that sin which first brought corruption into the early church in the case of Ananias—the sin of covetousness;—how afterwards he traced this simony up even to the visible and ostensible earthly head of Christendom, the Pope himself;—and how in his public teaching he had pointed away from the many things which had been introduced "after the commandments and doctrines of men," to the sufficiency of the revelation of God in His word, as setting forth the atonement of Christ:—but now we see him in a new position, he is brought into immediate personal contact with the venality of the Roman bishop, a position in which he not only had his previous impressions strengthened, but, likewise, he was led to act even with more decision than before, in opposition to that which was so contrary to God and his truth. From the time of Wiclif's return from Bruges to the time of his death, we find that his mind was rapidly opened to see one truth after another as standing in opposition to papal delusion; and, also, that his testimony was so marked as to call forth all the vindictive feelings of those who sought to uphold the existing circumstances and condition of the Church.

John of Gaunt at Bruges at the same time as Wiclif.

The stay of Wiclif at Bruges appears to have brought him into contact with the duke of Lancaster—John of Gaunt—one who had but little liking for either the conduct or the principles of prelates, priests, or monks; but this prince appears to have regarded them rather in a *political* than in any other light; and his subsequent protection of Wiclif appears to have proceeded from this political feeling, and not from any true apprehension of the principle of obedience to the truth of God by which Wiclif himself was guided. The patronage of John of Gaunt was an exceeding hindrance to the testimony of Wiclif, instead of being a help as many have vainly thought.

Wiclif summoned before the convocation, Feb. 19th, 1377. John of Gaunt befriends him; this leads to a disturbance.

Seven months after the return of Wiclif from Bruges, his unwelcome doctrines had obtained such a degree of notoriety, that he was summoned to appear before the convocation; this assembly met on the third of February, 1377; and the day, on which he was to meet the charges made against him, was the 19th of the same month. It does not precisely appear what the exact charges were which were brought against Wiclif, but it is probable that they resembled those which were, a little while afterwards, made the ground of accusation against him by the Pope himself. In appearing before the convocation, Wiclif, doubtless, encountered no inconsiderable danger. At this juncture, John of Gaunt saw fit to befriend him with his patronage, which, however kindly meant, produced only disastrous consequences: for, instead of Wiclif having an opportunity of defending himself, and testifying for the truth, the convocation at St. Paul's became a scene of disgraceful contention between the duke of Lancaster and Courtney the bishop of London, in which, however, the decency of the conduct of the latter put that of the duke to shame.

When Wiclif appeared at St. Paul's according to the citation, he went thither accompanied by John of Gaunt, and Henry, Lord Percy, Lord Marshal of England; the former of these was, at this time, the king's eldest surviving son, and, in fact, was the most important person then alive belonging to the royal family of England. St. Paul's was crowded with persons, so that it was with difficulty that Wiclif, and those with him could make their way to the place where the bishops were assembled. This occasioned some tumult, of which William Courtney, bishop of London, took notice, and his indignation was increased when he saw the companions who were with Wiclif. As Lord Percy was making way for Wiclif through the crowd, the bishop regarding him as taking too much upon him, said to him,—"Lord Percy, if I had known beforehand what *maisteries* you would have kept in the church, I would have stopt you out from coming hither."

The contention between the duke and Bp. Courtney. Fuller's Chur. Hist. p. 135.

The duke of Lancaster.—" He shall keep such maisteries here, though you say nay."

Lord Percy.—" Wiclif, sit down, for you have many things to answer to, and you need to repose yourself on a soft seat."

Bishop Courtney.—" It is unreasonable that one cited before his ordinary, should sit down during his answer. He must and shall stand."

The duke of Lancaster.—" The Lord Percy his motion for Wiclif is but reasonable. And as for you, my Lord Bishop, who are grown so proud and arrogant, I will bring down the pride not of you only, but of all the prelacy of England."

Bishop Courtney.—" Do your worst, Sir."

The duke of Lancaster.—" Thou bearest thyself so brag upon thy parents, which shall not be able to help thee, they shall have enough to do to help themselves."

Bishop Courtney.—" My confidence is not in my parents, nor in any man else, but only in God, in whom I trust, by whose assistance I will be bold to speak the truth."

The duke of Lancaster [in a low tone].—" Rather than I will take these words at his hands, I would pluck the bishop by the hair out of the church." These intemperate words of the duke in addition to what had before passed, occasioned a furious tumult, owing to which all proceedings against Wiclif were for the present dropped.

Wiclif in no way implicated in the disturbance.

It is but an act of justice to state most fully, that there appears no ground whatever for charging Wiclif with being in any way accessory to this disgraceful disturbance.

The position in which Wiclif was now placed.

Thus ended the citation to St. Paul's, leaving Wiclif, in one respect, in a new position; not merely that of a witness for the truth of God against its enemies, but also that of one whose testimony drew forth the enmity not merely of his old antagonists the friars, but likewise of his ecclesiastical superiors. Not having the particulars of the life of Wiclif, from the time of his return from Bruges, up to the meeting of the convocation, we are, of course, uncertain as to the grounds of accusation which the assembled prelates had against him. These grounds must have been either something found in his writings, or else what he had advanced in his public lectures at Oxford, or else in his parochial instructions at Lutterworth. The only question for Wiclif now was, whether he should succumb to the weight of human authority, or go on in obedience to God at all hazards.

The Pope's bulls against him. 11 Cal. an. 1377.

Some months passed away before any incident occurred in the life of Wiclif of which we have received any account: this period was probably spent partly at Lutterworth and partly at Oxford. Meanwhile his adversaries were not idle. This is evinced by the fact of the papal thunders having been called down upon the devoted head of the reformer. Four bulls were sent forth by Pope Gregory XI., bearing date May 22, 1377.* Three of them were addressed to the archbishop of Canterbury (Simon Sudbury), and the bishop of London (Courtney), authorising and requiring them to cite, restrain, and imprison John Wiclif on certain charges; they were to ascertain his opinions, and transmit them to Avignon for judgment. The fourth was addressed to the University of Oxford, in the fear lest Wiclif and his doctrines found succour and support there. These four bulls were accompanied by a letter to Edward III., reciting the powers with which the archbishop and bishop were invested by the accompanying bulls, and requiring his countenance and support in carrying them into effect. The charges were such as shewed how sensibly the Pope felt any thing like a questioning of his authority. They appear to me to be probably the same in substance as the charges before the convocation, and they may have been thus transmitted from the Pope in consequence of intelligence of the termination of the citation of Wiclif to St. Paul's. This is made the more probable, from the fear which the bulls express, lest the king and princess of Wales, and others of the royal family, should be tainted with the doctrines of Wiclif, a fear, for which the previous conduct of

The charges against Wiclif.

* Vaughan, in common with others, gives the date June 11, (vol. i. p. 370), but this clearly is a mere oversight. He likewise speaks of the prelates being "instructed to employ their vigilance that the king, the *prince* of Aquitain and Wales, and others of the nobility, and the counsellors of the sovereign, may not be defiled with the errors adverted to" (vol. i. p. 371). It should be "princess of Aquitain and Wales;"—Johannam *principissam* Aquitaniæ et Walliæ. The Prince of Wales, Richard of Bordeaux, was then a child, while his mother was a person (as was shortly after shewn) of no small power or influence. I mention these things, because accuracy is very desirable, especially when controverted subjects are to be treated of; I can generally rely upon the *facts* stated by Vaughan, but in these minutiæ his work needs correction. Vaughan's appendix contains the documents which supply the data required for the detection of these errors. It may also be well to state, that the princess of Wales is styled shortly after by Vaughan "the queen-mother," when, in fact, she was really but princess dowager of Wales and Aquitain, and mother of the king (Richard II.)

John of Gaunt gave some grounds, and which was likewise borne out by the subsequent conduct of the princess.

The "conclusions" with which Wiclif was charged.

A few words may be needful to explain the charges themselves:—They were the "*conclusions*" deduced in part from the writings of Wiclif, and in part, apparently, from some of his instructions which had been reported by those who took offence at them. These "conclusions," let it be observed, were not expressed in Wiclif's words, nor did they contain in any sense an epitome of his doctrines: they were simply certain conclusions attributed to him, expressed in the terms of his accusers; the subjects of them being those which were supposed more or less to affect the power of the Pope. I say, *were supposed*, because really it quite betrayed the weakness of all papal claim, for the very first of these conclusions to be objected to. I will give

The first of the "conclusions." "Totum genus humanum concurrentium citra Christum non habet potestatem simplicem ordinandi, ut Petrus et omne genus suum dominetur in perpetuum politicè supra mundum."

this *first* "conclusion," in order that the over-sensitiveness of Gregory XI. may be fully seen:—"The whole race of men agreeing, has no power, apart from Christ, of simply ordaining that Peter and all his race should rule politically for ever over the world." Truly he who styled himself the successor of St. Peter must have had strange thoughts, if he imagined that this absurdly phrased "conclusion" was one of such magnitude. All thought of authority derived from Christ himself seems to have left the pontiff's mind. The oft-quoted "Tu es Petrus," was for a while forgotten, and the Pope wished something to be asserted which would ascribe to *man* little short of omnipotence. I notice this "conclusion" thus particularly, because we learn in this manner how little the Pope had really to lay to the charge of the reformer, and on what absurd grounds he framed these charges against him.

Edward III. dies June 21, 1377. The first Parliament of Richard II.

There are other things to be noticed, before we arrive at the citation of Wiclif in consequence of these charges, and the answers which he made to them. One month after the date of the Bulls and the letter to Edward III., that king died (June 21, 1377), and this doubtless occasioned some delay in acting upon these formidable powers. When the first Parliament of Richard II. met, questions came before them connected with the right of the Pope to demand the treasure of the kingdom. This was, in fact, the question regarding simony, which had been before taken up by Wiclif. He again used the opportunity to bear his testimony against the principle of pecuniary demands being made upon nations, for what were

The question of the temporal power of the pope answered by Wiclif out of Bernard.

termed spiritual objects. The question of the political power of the Pope, which was put before him by the House of Commons for his opinion, he meets by an apposite citation from Bernard, who himself had argued against this from the words of the Apostle Peter, and of Christ himself. This testimony of Wiclif, at such a juncture, with the torrent of papal wrath ready to break forth upon him, is valuable, as shewing how calmly he could look at the existing state of things irrespective of the circumstances in which he, as

October, 1377.

an individual, stood. It was in October 1377, that Wiclif gave this memorable testimony against the simony of the nominal church.

The first public notice taken of the papal bulls. Causes of delay.

No public notice appears to have been taken in England of the papal Bulls, until about a month after this time. It is probable that the death of Edward III., and the subsequent events, occasioned this delay. Perhaps there was no one who saw fit to act according to the request which the Pope in his letter had made to Edward III., seeing that this might have drawn forth the enmity of John of Gaunt, whose power had

The university of Oxford receive with great reluctance the bull addressed to them.

rather increased in consequence of his father's death. However this may be, the papal Bull was at length presented to the University of Oxford; but it was very reluctantly received, and the authorities there do not appear to have been inclined in any way to act upon it. Archbishop Sudbury wrote to the chancellor of the University, requiring him to cite Wiclif to appear at St. Paul's, in answer to the mandate of the Pope, within thirty days from the 18th of December, 1377. Wiclif's actual appearance was at Lambeth,

Abp. Sudbury requires the chancellor to cite Wiclif within thirty days, Dec. 18, 1377.

Wiclif appears at Lambeth; nothing decided against him.

Sir L. Clifford forbids them to condemn him.

and not at St. Paul's; it may be that the prelates did not wish to renew the tumultuous scenes of the preceding year. However, nothing was decided against Wiclif. Many persons, avowing their attachment to his doctrines, entered the chapel where the assembly was held, and this appears to have intimidated the prelates; and after this Sir Lewis Clifford coming, it is said, as a messenger from the widow of the Black Prince, the mother of the reigning monarch, forbade the prelates to injure Wiclif, or to proceed to any definite condemnation of him or his doctrines. It is to be remembered, that the Pope had reserved for himself the right of passing sentence upon Wiclif; what the prelates had to do as the delegates of the Pope, was to imprison Wiclif, examine him on the articles of accusation, and transmit the results to Rome. With the injunction of Sir Lewis Clifford the bishops complied. thus the Lambeth citation produced no results which could harm the intended victim. The conduct both of the people and of the princess dowager of Wales, proves how widely the doctrine of Wiclif was known and respected.

A document presented to the Prelates by Wiclif; he remarks on the "conclusions."

But although the proceedings against him were thus cut short, yet there exists a document which he appears to have presented to the bishops on this occasion. He makes his observations upon the "conclusions" transmitted by the Pope, refuting the charges based on them, and on some points stating his own doctrines

—those doctrines to which he judged his mind had been opened by the Spirit of God out of the Word. In order to understand this document aright, it is needful to recollect what he was commenting upon. he had the Pope's "conclusions" about his doctrine; and for that which had been absurdly stated by the Pope, of course Wiclif cannot be deemed responsible; and yet, strangely enough, Wiclif has been condemned for meeting the objections against some of the "conclusions" in the way in which such strange propositions deserved. The first of the "conclusions" has already been given; he now remarks upon it, that as all power and dominion will be put down by Christ, according to 1 Cor. xv., so it is impossible for men to give any perpetual government to Peter and his successors. This has been called an evasion, if it be so, I am unable to perceive it: to me it only appears to be a truth, the statement of which was elicited by the foolish charges contained in the "conclusion." His opposition to the *whole* character and claim of the papacy was not yet that which it afterwards became.

Wiclif's "Sort of Answer to the Bull."

Wiclif's exhortation to the Pope.

The reading of the Scriptures not to be prohibited.

After the Lambeth citation, Wiclif published some remarks upon the articles of accusation. In these remarks, he speaks freely of the conduct of the papacy; one sentence has an especial importance when the subsequent labours of Wiclif are borne in mind.—"Let him [the Pope] not be ashamed to perform the ministry of the church, since he is, or at least ought to be, the servant of the servants of God. But A PROHIBITION OF READING THE SACRED SCRIPTURES, and a vanity of secular dominion, would seem to partake too much of a disposition towards the blasphemous advancement of Antichrist, especially while the TRUTHS OF A SCRIPTURAL FAITH are reputed tares,* and said to be opposed to Christian truth by certain leaders, who arrogate that we must abide by their decision respecting every article of faith, notwithstanding they themselves are plainly ignorant of the faith of the Scriptures. But by such means, there follows a crowding to the court [of Rome] TO PURCHASE A CONDEMNATION OF THE SACRED SCRIPTURES AS HERETICAL, and thence come dispensations contrary to the articles of the Christian Faith." From this extract from Wiclif's "Sort of Answer to the Bull," we learn, I think, that the conduct of the Pope had resulted from influence backed by pecuniary considerations; and also, that in the opposition to the doctrines which he held, he looked on it as being directed against the Scriptures, and not against himself. We see how he had learned the authority and sufficiency of the Scriptures as the means which God had provided for the communication of truth; and this may, I judge, be regarded as one of the indications that his mind was tending towards that labour for which his name is to be held in most grateful remembrance—the translating and publishing of the Scriptures in English. These expressions may, however, have been occasioned by his having already commenced his work of translating; and this being known, may have led to further attempts to crush him. I merely suggest this as being *possible*, while the title which Wiclif gave to the document in question, seems to intimate that it referred to the previous bulls, and in them no mention is made of any thing so obnoxious as a vernacular translation of the word of God.

The Romish court bribed.

Wiclif regards the attack as being against the Scriptures.

Wiclif's mind turned towards the translation of the Scriptures.

"Mixtus Theologus" attacks Wiclif.

He regards the popedom as being essentially evil.

The assertions of "Mixtus Theologus."

Wiclif's appeal to Scripture.

Its authority above all popes.

An anonymous adversary, whom Wiclif calls "Mixtus Theologus," appears at once to have attacked him on the point of the infallibility and jurisdiction of the Pope. To this attack Wiclif replied, and there appears little doubt but that the positions assumed by "Mixtus Theologus" led the mind of Wiclif into more distrust of the authority of the papacy than he had before felt. He had looked on it as having become corrupt, he now began to regard it as essentially evil. It is of great consequence in judging of the conduct and principles of Wiclif, to observe that this change was wrought *subsequent* to the Lambeth citation. The assertion of papal infallibility, brought forward by "Mixtus Theologus," had amounted to this:—that it was not possible that the Pope could commit mortal sin, and that every thing which he ordained must be just. Wiclif's reply is remarkable; his mind instantly recurs to *Scripture;* and it is the authority of the Scripture which in itself destroys this claim on behalf of the papacy. He says, that if "Mixtus Theologus" were right in the doctrine which he had advanced, the Pope might exclude any book of the Scripture from the canon, that he might introduce any novelty in its place, that he might thus alter the whole Bible, make the very Scripture heresy, and establish that which is contrary to truth for catholic doctrine. In this reply, reference is made to the papal decision, which was yet pending, respecting the doctrines advanced in connection with the "conclusions;" but Wiclif's mind was becoming, at this very time, more emancipated than it had been from subjection of any kind to the see of Rome.

Wiclif meanwhile was at liberty: the prelates were hindered from using the papal authority with which

* In the Bull of Pope Gregory XI., addressed to the University of Oxford, he speaks of a tare having sprung up amongst the pure wheat,—lolium inter purum triticum—of their university. To this Wiclif alludes, understanding apparently the doctrine which he had taught to be compared to the tare. The Bull goes on to lament that the University took no pains for the extirpation of this tare—circa extirpationem hujus lolii. What can this be called but "handling the word of God deceitfully?" The framer of this Bull gathered his phrases from the words of our Lord in Matt. xiii., and yet he uses them in direct contravention of the words, "*Let both grow together until the harvest.*"

they were commissioned to touch his person, and they were restricted by the papal Bulls themselves from pronouncing judgment with regard to his doctrine. Thus, until the decision of the court of Rome could be transmitted to England, the prelates could not restrain Wiclif from propagating his doctrines; thus strangely had the resolve of the Pope to be himself the judge, defeated the purpose which it was intended to answer, namely, the effectual repression of the obnoxious tenets.

The unrestrained freedom of Wiclif, both as to person and testimony, would probably have not continued long, had not very peculiar circumstances occurred relative to the papacy in this very year. Gregory XI. died on the twenty-seventh of March, probably without having received from Archbishop Sudbury, and Bishop Courtney, any account of the examination of Wiclif, as to his doctrines, or of the ineffectual attempts to imprison him. On the death of Gregory, there was a warm contention for the papal chair, between Urban VI. and Clement VII.; this schism of the papacy was undoubtedly one of the causes of Wiclif's tranquillity. Nor was this time unemployed by the Reformer, for he used it not only to write on the refutation which the schism gave to the claim of infallibility, and on "The Truth and Meaning of the Scripture," but also to execute HIS ENGLISH TRANSLATION OF THE SCRIPTURES. Few things were ever more marked by the guiding hand of Providence than was this; how was Wiclif, whom popes and prelates sought to crush, to find leisure for this mighty labour? Was he to give up defending those doctrines of truth, to which his mind had been gradually opened by the Holy Ghost, in order to accomplish the work of Scripture translating? or was he to leave his countrymen just as he found them, ignorant of the word of God, and devoid of it in their own tongue? The good providence of God rendered neither of these alternatives needful, and thus ample time was afforded to Wiclif to carry on and complete his version.

Death of Pope Gregory XI. March 27, 1378.

The papal schism a cause of Wiclif's continued tranquillity.

He writes "The Papal Schism."

"The Truth and Meaning of Scripture."

His English version of the Bible.

The marked providence of God respecting this translation

It is not difficult to trace the motives which influenced him in engaging in this work; he had spoken boldly of the state of the church, he had questioned the authority of the Pope; first, as to things temporal, and, at length, as to things spiritual; and the only ground on which he found that he could rest, was *the Word of God;* he had felt, step by step, his individual responsibility to God; this responsibility he had, both in preaching and in writing, enforced upon others; his testimony was not given merely to the learned at Oxford, but likewise to his parishioners at Lutterworth, and in his writings, to his countrymen at large. How, then, were those, on whose consciences he was thus pressing individual responsibility, to know *what* is, and what is not, the truth of God? It became necessary to translate the Scriptures, or else to give up all the ground on which he was contending. Even if it were granted that other versions of the whole Bible then existed, at least they were not in common circulation; and thus that work was done by Wiclif, by which the memory of the doctrine which he taught, and the appeal which he made to the word of God, was kept alive.

The motives which influenced Wiclif to translate the Scriptures.

A version of the Scriptures needful, if he would not give up the ground on which he contended.

The period during which Wiclif appears to have been unmolested in the continuance of his labour of translating the Scriptures, and defending, by various writings, the doctrines which he had learned from them, continued from the Lambeth citation, in 1378, to the spring of 1381. The works which he put forth during this interval, prove how unwearied was his assiduity in upholding the truth of God against all opponents; marvellous, indeed, does the retrospect appear of the position which Wiclif occupied during these three important years.

Wiclif's period of repose, 1378—1381.

Many works written at this time.

But, although he was unmolested by either ecclesiastical or secular authority, he had other hindrances. In the early part of the year 1379, he was severely ill with palsy at Oxford. It was during this illness, that some of his old antagonists, the mendicant friars, came to him, and exhorted him to repentance of his testimony against them; he was then supposed to be almost at the point of death; but being raised in his bed, he addressed the reproaching friars, "I shall not die, but live, and again declare the evil deeds of the friars!" And so, indeed, he did; not merely in his tract, entitled, "Objections to Freres," but far more in the publishing of the Scriptures in English,—the testimony of God Himself against all and every form of false doctrine, or of corrupt practice.

Wiclif's illness at Oxford, 1379.

The friars visit him.

It is probable that some of the friends of Wiclif were his coadjutors in the making of his translation: this is confirmed by a notice which is found written in one MS. of this version, at the end of a portion of the apocryphal book of Baruch, "Explicit translacionem Nicolay de Herford;" from this it appears that Nicholas Hereford, who was one who had received many of Wiclif's doctrines, had translated a particular portion, concluding with part of this book.* But be Wiclif's fellow-workers who they may, this is certain, that to him was the work attributed, in his own day, by his adversaries: he was the individual through whose energy it had been carried on and executed.

Wiclif's coadjutors in his work of translation.

Nicholas Hereford. Baber, p. lxix.

Notice in Mr. Douce's MS.

* "This remarkable notice is subscribed by a different hand, and with a less durable ink, than that used by the transcriber of the MS., and, if not written by Hereford himself, was probably done by one who had good authority for what he thus asserted by his pen."—*Baber*, p. lxix.

The version, when made, was widely diffused; even if the transcribers were the only persons in England who were imbued with the doctrines which Wiclif taught, then the number of those who had received them must have been far from inconsiderable. It is remarkable how *sensitively* the name of Wiclif was connected in the minds of those who upheld the Papal doctrine and dominion, with the translation of the Scriptures; in fact, his name, his testimony against Rome, and that great work, seemed as though they were inseparably conjoined, and that they must thus stand or fall together. The opposition of the ecclesiastical authorities was soon manifested against Wiclif's translation, so that it became a dangerous matter for any part of it to be transcribed or possessed; this opposition became, in 1408, an absolute prohibition, and thus it is almost certain, that the copies of this version which have come down to us, were mostly made previous to that year; it is even probable that many, or the greater part of them, were copied immediately on the translation having been executed. I shall have occasion shortly to notice the prohibition of 1408 more particularly

Wide diffusion of the version.

Opposition raised against Wiclif's version in 1408.

Such, then, were the circumstances which led to the first publication of the Scriptures in English. A priest, whose heart God had opened to receive successively many portions of truth; who was so thrown into contact with the papal intrigues, as to see the full working of the evil of the system; and who had before his eyes the deeds of the friars, so that he found the corruption to pervade the whole of the nominal church, from the highest to the lowest; stood forth as a witness for the Truth in the midst of the corruption, and pressed home upon the consciences of men their responsibility of individual allegiance to God. his voice was heard far and wide; many were induced to question the papal authority, and ceased to rely upon what was then given forth as truth; while he, who had taken the bold stand in testimony, puts into their hands the Word of God, the written record which declares both what are the *grounds* of our allegiance, and *what* the obedience which we, as true to our allegiance. are called upon to render.

Circumstances which led to the circulation of the Bible in English.

Wiclif's testimony leads to his version of the Scripture.

III.

SOME ACCOUNT OF WICLIF'S VERSION.

THE importance of this version is such, that some account of its execution, and other circumstances connected with it, seem almost to be required; at least, without them, the notice of the labours of Wiclif would be very defective.

Notice of the version itself.

This translation of the New Testament was made (as has been already said) from the Latin Vulgate, and not from the original Greek. This was rendered necessary for two reasons; first, it is exceedingly improbable that the knowledge of Greek possessed by Wiclif was at all sufficient to enable him to translate from that language. He introduces Greek words in some of his writings, but this by no means implies that he was more learned in this respect than his cotemporaries in the west of Europe; and, also, it is not likely, even if Wiclif had been competent to translate from the Greek, that he could have found a Greek copy of the New Testament to have used for the purpose; since it was not until after the taking of Constantinople by the Turks in 1453, that copies of the Scriptures and other manuscripts in Greek became dispersed by the fugitive Greeks throughout the western parts of Europe. These two reasons shew completely, that if the New Testament were to be translated into English at all, it must be from the Latin. Until Dr. Linacre introduced Greek literature into England, there was scarcely any thing known in this country either of that language or of works therein.

The version made from the Vulgate, and why.

Greek scarcely known in the West of Europe at that time.

Greek MSS. not then to be obtained.

Greek literature introduced into England by Linacre.

The Old Testament was translated from the Latin for reasons similar in their kind to those which rendered the translation of the New from that language a matter of necessity: it belonged to a later and more critical age to use the originals in forming vernacular versions of the Scriptures. However desirable it may be constantly to recur to the fountain, in order that the water may be drawn in all its purity, it is the part of wisdom for those who are prevented from having access to the well-spring, to take from the stream lower down.

The original text not used for translation till a later period.

The Latin Vulgate having then been the medium from which Wiclif translated, the inquiry arises, how far is the *Version of a version* to be trusted as conveying the revealed truth of God? I have already spoken of the wisdom of using and circulating a translation made from another version, when it is impracticable for one to be framed from the original. Now in considering the merit of a version when formed from another, there are these two things to be considered; first, the character of the primary version from which the other is made; secondly, the accuracy with which that primary version is represented by the second translator. In the case before us then, we have to look at the Latin Vulgate, and to inquire what are its merits

The value of a *Version of a version.*

What are the

merits of the Vulgate as a version.

Some account of the early Latin versions.

The Old Test. translated from the Septuagint.

The labours of Jerome.

He translates the Old Test. from Hebrew into Latin.

His correction of the Latin versions of the New Test.

as a version. This must be contemplated apart from all considerations as to its elegance of language or the contrary. How far does it accurately represent the original Greek? To this question but one reply would I believe, be *now* given by any who have critically examined that version, viz. that it is, on the whole, an accurate version, one which at the time when it was made did very tolerably represent in Latin the Greek original. Very soon after the diffusion of Christianity in the western provinces of the Roman empire, especially in those of Africa around Carthage, versions of the Greek Scriptures were executed for the use of those Christians to whom the Latin was the vernacular language. The books of the Old Testament were translated out of the Septuagint Greek version, in consequence of the inability of the translators to make use of the Hebrew original. These versions (of the New Testament especially) were exceedingly numerous; and from various causes, partly from the mistakes of transcribers, and partly from the want of any one established version, these translations became very inaccurate, many interpolations creeping into the text through the insertion of glosses and other scholia. In the latter part of the fourth century Jerome undertook the task of translating the books of the Old Testament out of the original Hebrew, so that there might be in Latin an *immediate* version; and thus the translations formed mediately from the Septuagint were no longer the channel through which the Old Testament was known. With regard to the New Testament, Jerome did not undertake any labour so onerous as he had with regard to the Old; he simply corrected some of the copies then in use, so as to form a version which should not be very discrepant from the original.

Jerome's corrected version gradually supersedes those which had preceded it: the Psalms an exception.

The Latin Vulgate never strictly identical with the version of Jerome.

A mixed text formed.

Various readings in course of transmission.

Inaccuracy of the common copies of the 14th century.

The testimony of the author of "Elucidarium Bibliorum."

Latin copies compared to form a text; this probably done previous to the execution of Wiclif's version.

This corrected version of Jerome gradually superseded those inaccurate translations which had previously been used in the West; the Psalms, however, were retained in all the services of the Church according to the old or ante-hieronymian version with but little alteration, because from their being so frequently used, it was thought to be too great a change to substitute a version altogether new. With regard to other portions of the Scripture, the version and recension of Jerome were in the main adopted, yet not without some portions of the older translations being retained; this appears to be especially the case in the New Testament; so that even in its early days the Latin Vulgate was never strictly identical with the version of Jerome; while at the same time it was chiefly the text of his recension. The manner in which the Latin Vulgate text was thus formed, may, I believe, be traced to two causes, 1st. The difficulty that was felt in entirely giving up the versions which were in common use, led to the retention of not a few terms, expressions, and glosses, which had been extruded by the critical labours of Jerome; and, 2nd. The practice of *altering* copies in which the text of some of the older versions was found, so as to make them in some sort conformed to Jerome's recension. The consequence of this was the formation of a mixed text, in which the influence of the earlier versions is plainly to be traced.* Thus, if the Vulgate had simply been the version or recension of Jerome, it would have more accurately represented the original; but still even when every allowance is made it must be acknowledged that the Vulgate was a tolerably fair version for accuracy. Of course, in its transmission, various readings have crept in just as in other ancient writings which have come down to us; so that no one Manuscript copy is to be relied on as truly and precisely giving the original text of that combination of the version of Jerome with the preceding translations which was at first the Vulgate; and thus we cannot judge from the commonly printed copies what in all respects this version once was. In the fourteenth century, it is certain that the commonly circulated copies were generally *less* accurate than those which are printed, although in some respects there have been alterations made for the worse. Such then was the state of the version from which Wiclif undertook his translation. How then did he form or select a text from which to frame his version? The author of the prologue,† entitled "Elucidarium Bibliorum," at the end of the year 1395, says, "The commune latyne bybles haue more nede to be correctyd ..... than hath the englyshe bible late translated." This implies that there was some particular reason which rendered the copy which Wiclif used peculiarly accurate; and when we find in the same prologue an interesting account of the collation of various Latin copies so as to form a standard text, previous to translating, it seems most probable that something of the kind had been done previous to the execution of the version of Wiclif. It is true that the collation mentioned in the prologue is spoken of as being introductory to the making of the *second* version (1395), but this does not at all preclude a similar process having been carried on as a preparation for the former version. I rest upon

* Amongst the Harleian Manuscripts in the British Museum there is a curious example of this systematic method of correction. This Manuscript (1772) contains some of the Epistles and the Revelation written by a very ancient hand, and corrected in the manner above described by a more recent but still an ancient corrector.

† This prologue belongs to a version of the Bible into English which was made a very little time after that of Wiclif; the prologue and the version itself will be noticed in their proper place.

these two things, 1st. the author of the prologue knew the inaccuracy of the common Latin Bibles, and yet asserts the comparative correctness of the English version which had then been for some little while executed; 2nd. he also mentions the process by which he and others obtained a more correct copy for the basis of their version; thus it becomes more than probable that some similar means had been taken by Wiclif and his coadjutors. Indeed it may be that John Purnay himself, who appears to have been the author of this prologue, and was much associated with Wiclif, was one of those assisting in a previous work of collating Latin Bibles, and this collation was the commencement of a more extended labour previous to the making of the later version. These will not be regarded as mere conjectures, when the direct testimony to the comparative accuracy of Wiclif's text, is duly weighed.

Ed. 1550. Chap. xv.

The author of this prologue probably an assistant of Wiclif.

Having thus briefly considered the first of the two questions which arise in connection with a *Version of a version*, namely, the character of the primary version from which the other is made,—I have now to examine the second, i. e. the *accuracy* with which that primary version is represented by the second translator. We have seen that Wiclif had a very tolerable ground-work for his version in the Latin Vulgate, and that in some manner there was an accuracy more than was then common in the text from which his version was made: how far did Wiclif acquit himself as a competent translator from the Latin? In discussing this, it is well again to refer to Purnay's prologue, in order that we may see how this version was appreciated in the time in which it was made. The passage already quoted from this prologue, in which the version is spoken of as needing correction less than the common Latin Bibles, proves not only the general accuracy of the *text* employed, but likewise that the *translation* was well executed; because if *this* had been incorrectly done the commendation would have been wholly misplaced. This testimony is not to be regarded as that of merely a blind admirer, it comes from one whose critical labours must have been in that non-critical age very extraordinary; and what is more, although the writer thus commends the earlier version, yet he himself takes in hand another, thus shewing that in his judgment it might be amended in some respects. Now what was the objection which the author of the prologue had against the version of Wiclif? Why, after having commended it, did he think it an advisable work to put forth another? Now I think that if the *intended character* of the version to which the prologue belongs be considered, it will be seen that he looked on the translation of Wiclif as being *too literal*, and too close in following the Latin idiom. He says that in making the new translation, they resolved that it should *not be literal*, but that it should be according to the *sense* and meaning of the text. Thus we find from Purnay's prologue, a cotemporary testimony to the exactitude and fidelity with which Wiclif had made his version.

How far does the version of Wiclif accurately represent the Latin text.

The testimony of the author of the prologue.

This testimony not that of a mere blind admirer.

Wiclif's version very literal.

This judgment, so soon expressed after the death of Wiclif, is fully supported by the closest examination which can be given to the version. It is impossible to compare it with the Vulgate without seeing how attentively the translator has sought, without being *too* servile, to express all that the Latin expresses, and if possible in the same manner. It is not improbable, that Wiclif was the more particular in thus adhering, when he could, to the *form* of the Latin phrase, in order that his version might be used as a help to those who wished to learn to read the Scriptures in Latin: we know that this influenced Hampole in causing him to use the Latin idiom when he could, and even words of Latin origin in preference to those which are more purely Saxon.

This testimony fully borne out by examination.

In speaking of the comparative purity of the Latin text used by Wiclif, it is not of course affirmed that he possessed any peculiar power of detecting and eliminating mistakes and intrusive glosses; I merely take the testimony of Purnay's prologue, and what I should understand would be this, that Wiclif's text was that which appeared the most correct from a comparison of old copies; whatever had crept into the text in them was of course retained in Wiclif's version. The following may be taken as instances:—1 Pet. iii. 22. *Vulg.* "Qui est in dexterâ Dei, *mortem deglutiens ut vitæ æternæ hæredes efficeremur;* profectus in cœlum subjectis sibi angelis, et potestatibus, et virtutibus." *Wiclif*—"That is in the riȝthalf of god. [And swolowith deeth: that we schulden be made eiris of euerlastynge liif,] he ȝede in to heuene: and aungels ⁊ poweris and vertues ben made sugetis to hym."

What is to be understood by the comparative purity of Wiclif's Latin text.

Glosses in the Latin retained. 1 Pet. iii. 22.

2 Pet. i. 10. *Vulg.* "Quapropter, fratres, magis satagite, ut *per bona opera* certam vestram vocationem et electionem faciatis." *Wiclif*—"wherfor britheren be ȝe more bisie, that [bi good werkis] ȝe make ȝoure clepyng ⁊ chesynge certeyn."

2 Pet. i. 10.

These are manifest instances of glosses which have obtained insertion in the Latin text, so early as to appear like an integral portion of it. In fact there were many such interpolations in the old ante-hieronymian versions, and several have been transferred from thence into the Vulgate. Were any object to be answered by so doing, a list of such passages retained by Wiclif might be swelled to a considerable amount.

Numerous glosses in the Ante-hieronymian versions.

Wiclif's variations from the Clementine Vulgate.

The following are instances of variation in the text of Wiclif from the Clementine, or *now* commonly received text of the Latin Vulgate.

1 Cor. x. 17.

1 Cor. x. 17: "for we many ben o breed and o bodi, alle we that takun part of o breed and of o cuppe." These last four words are found in some manuscripts, and in the *Sixtine* edition of the Vulgate, although now rejected.

1 Cor. x. 27.

1. Cor. x. 27: "if ony of hethen men clepith ȝou to soper and ȝe wolen go." "To soper" is a phrase circumstanced precisely like that which has last been mentioned.

Introduced words originally part of the Vulgate.

It is probable that in both of these passages the words which stood in Wiclif's Latin text were a part of the Vulgate originally, I mean a part of the *mingled* version formed from Jerome's and those which preceded, and that their extrusion, although perfectly right in conformity with the Greek and critical exactness, is but a departure from what the *composite* version called the Vulgate truly was when the blending was first made. It was in the insertion of such adventitious scholia that the version of Jerome was conformed in some measure to those previously in use, and thus the Vulgate was produced. The existence of such interpolations does not, therefore at all destroy the character of the Latin text used by Wiclif, as far as concerns antiquity and accuracy, however much it may shew that the pure gold of God's word was in parts impaired by a slight admixture of alloy. Wiclif could not aid himself in getting his text free from these adscititious glosses.

Scholia in the Latin text of Wiclif do not make against its antiquity.

A passage shewing Wiclif's Latin text to have been old.

There is one passage which shews that Wiclif has kept to a more ancient reading of the Latin in preference to one which afterwards was set forth with great authority by the Church of Rome.

1 John v. 7, 8. Words omitted in some Latin copies, on the authority of Thomas Aquinas. Joachim's dispute on the unity of persons. His supposed proof.

1 John v. 7, 8. "for thre ben that ȝeuen witnessynge in heuene, the fadir the sone the holi goost: and thes thre ben oon, and thre ben that ȝeuen witnessynge in erthe, the spirit watir and blood, and thes thre ben oon." The last clause is excluded from some of the printed Latin copies, and also from the more modern Latin manuscripts. Why is this done? It appears simply to rest upon the *ipse dixit* of Thomas Aquinas. The circumstances are these: the Abbot Joachim in the thirteenth century disputed concerning the unity of persons in the Godhead, alleging that it was an unity of love and consent, and not an unity of essence. In support of this confused and false doctrine, he adduced the words "et hi tres unum sunt," as standing in the Latin copies after the mention of the testimony of the earthly witnesses—the Spirit, the Water, and the Blood, as well as after that of the heavenly witnesses—the Father, the Word, and the Holy Ghost. His argument rested on this: that the unity, whatever it be, must be *identical* as regards the respective witnesses in heaven and on earth; and thus, if in the one case the expression were supposed to denote unity of essence, then it must also in the other; but as unity of essence cannot be predicated of the Spirit, the Water, and the Blood, no more (he alleged) can they in this passage be predicated of the Father, the Word, and the Holy Ghost. The reply of Thomas Aquinas was, that in the eighth verse the "et hi tres unum sunt" was an interpolation of Arian heretics in order to counter-argue the orthodox creed of the Church. The consequence of this was, that the clause, from that time and onward, was very commonly omitted in Latin Bibles, the authority of Thomas Aquinas being deemed quite sufficient to warrant the change. Hence it is to be inferred, that the Latin text used by Wiclif was one of an older date than the occurrences which led to this passage being thus altered.

The reply of Thomas Aquinas. The clause in consequence omitted. Wiclif's Latin text of an older date.

The manner in which this passage stands in the older Latin copies. All mention of the heavenly witnesses omitted in the older copies.

In *very early* Latin Bibles, however, the seventh verse, in which the heavenly witnesses are mentioned, is subjoined to the eighth, while in others which are still older, it stands merely in the *margin* as a scholion, while in more than forty of the very oldest it is, according to the Greek manuscripts and all other versions, entirely omitted. Wiclif's oldest manuscript must then have been more modern than any of these, that is to say, more modern than the eighth century. It may not be amiss to state, that the concluding clause of ver. 8 is restored in the Clementine edition of the Vulgate, in spite of the authority of Thomas Aquinas.

Wiclif's MS. substitutes "filius" for "verbum." This indicates an early date.

Another circumstance to be observed is, that Wiclif has "the sone" instead of "the word," plainly shewing that what he regarded as his authoritative manuscript had "filius" and not "verbum;" now this indicates an early date, as that which must be ascribed to his copy, because in the course of a couple of centuries or less, after these two verses had become fixed in their order in the Latin copies, the phraseology and the individual words of the verse became settled likewise; whereas previously they had abounded in variations. This makes it probable that Wiclif mistrusting the faulty Latin copies which were then common, used the best that he could obtain at Oxford,* or elsewhere, or else collated (as has been

* Perhaps at Oxford, Latin bibles were at this period scarce enough. About twenty years before this time, Armachanus sent two persons from Ireland to Oxford to study divinity; after two years they returned, not being able to comply with his wishes, from their inability to purchase for themselves a Bible at Oxford.

suggested), more than one of such old copies;—the date of which may probably be about four hundred years before his own time. This may sufficiently account for any slight variations which exist between the text of Wiclif and that of the printed Vulgate,—although these discrepancies will be found to be of small magnitude.

Wiclif probably used a copy 400 years old

Many of the peculiarities of the version of Wiclif are to be attributed to the phraseology of the time in which he lived; and it is remarkable that, in his version of the Scriptures, he writes far more intelligible English than is found in his original works; the dignity of the book which he translated seems to have imparted an excellence of expression to the version itself. It is indeed wonderful that the language of four hundred and sixty years ago should be so intelligible to us as is the version of John Wiclif. Surely we may ascribe it to the good providence of God, not merely that an English version of the Scriptures was made in such a day as that of Wiclif, but likewise that the version itself is such a one as it is.

Peculiarities in Wiclif's version as to language.

The providence of God with regard to the version

IV.

THE LATTER PART OF WICLIF'S LIFE.—HIS TESTIMONY.

It will be well to *glance* briefly at the three concluding years of the life of Wiclif. His period of freedom from molestation continued, as we have seen, until the spring of 1381: it was then that Wiclif took a yet more decided stand at Oxford against the *doctrines* of Popery than he had previously done. Before this we find him controverting the power of the Pope, denying the authority which men in ecclesiastical stations could have, apart from the truth of God and the authority of Christ; we find him opposing the then almost universal doctrine which put the merits of saints as an object of reliance for sinners, and setting forth the one oblation of Christ as that alone through which God forgives sins gratuitously: we find him condemning all the means then used of procuring spiritual benefits through the observances of priests; and shewing how all these things more or less had sprung from the deeply-rooted simony of the church—" the love of money is the root of all evil;" but there was one thing regarded by both clergy and laity as the most sacred and profound of mysteries, against which he had yet to testify, and to shew that the commonly received doctrine concerning it was not only in itself contrary to Scripture and to truth, but that it also led to very numerous errors, and upheld in fact almost every one of the doctrines which he had previously opposed.

A glance at the three concluding years of Wiclif's life. 1381—1384

His stand against the *doctrines* of Popery at Oxford

His previous testimony

1 Tim, vi 10

This doctrine, against which Wiclif now directed his testimony, was that of *transubstantiation;* a doctrine which, if true, did absolutely contradict all that he had taught respecting the one sacrifice of Jesus Christ, and which in itself upheld the power and authority of the Romish priesthood. It may be asked why did not Wiclif raise his voice against this dogma of Rome before? Why did he wait until after there was an open rupture between him and the Pope before he took his position on such obnoxious ground? This may, I believe, be answered quite satisfactorily; his own mind opened *gradually* to the truths revealed in the Scriptures; and it was as his mind became more and more fully imbued with the truth of Scripture, that he received more light, and thus saw how utterly all that he taught was nullified by the popular doctrines respecting the Lord's Supper. In thus having his mind gradually opened to a clearer and fuller perception of truth, Wiclif was not peculiar; the same has been the case with many others; it is thus that we find Apollos commencing to preach boldly " knowing only the baptism of John;" his imperfect testimony was not therefore rejected, for when Aquila and Priscilla heard him they took him, " and expounded unto him the way of God more perfectly." Our blessed Lord does not then refuse to own a feeble or imperfect testimony, but He leads on into a more full apprehension of truth those who really are acting in the desire of doing the will of God, " If any man will do [desire to do] His will he shall know of the doctrine, whether it be of God."

He at length opposes transubstantiation

Why did Wiclif delay his testimony against it till this time?

The gradual opening of his mind

The case of Apollos, Acts xix

The grace of the Lord in owning even imperfect service

John vii 17

The consequences of the dogma of transubstantiation are such, that I must briefly allude to them in their connection with the testimony of Wiclif:—I. If Christ's very body, which suffered on the cross, be actually present, it was argued, that *worship* is to be paid thereto; especially so, according to the decrees of councils, which define that the substance of the bread is changed into, and actually becomes, the body, blood, human soul, and Godhead of Christ*:—II. also, if the Lord's death be shewn forth in this celebration,

Four conclusions resulting from the real presence and "concomitancy."

I Worship

* The doctrine of transubstantiation, in Wiclif's days, had not gone so far; this was reserved for the council of Trent. The definition of the fourth Lateran council, 1215, was this:—" There is one catholic church of the faithful, out of which no one whatever can be saved In which Christ Jesus Himself is the priest and the sacrifice, whose body and blood are truly contained in the sacrament of the altar; the bread being *transubstantiated* into the body, and the wine into the blood, by the divine power "

The council of Trent carried the matter so far, as to con-

II "Sacrifice" of the mass

III Propitiation.

IV Priestly power to make the Creator of all things.

These four conclusions fully held by the church of Rome.

and He be bodily and substantially present therein, as bodily and as substantially as when he suffered on the cross, it follows, that every celebration of the Lord's supper is an *actual sacrifice:*—III. farther, as the offering of Christ upon the cross was a *propitiation* for the sins of men, so must the repetition of it in the Lord's supper also be:—IV. also, if every one in priest's orders possessed the power of consecrating the bread, then it must follow, that every priest possessed full power to cause Christ to be substantially present; or, in other words, to *make Him*, by whom all things were made. These four conclusions are fully held and adopted by the church of Rome; in fact, the necessary consequences of transubstantiation are not attempted to be disguised.

Wiclif commences his opposition to transubstantiation

1381 His Twelve Conclusions published at Oxford

William de Berton, then chancellor, and twelve other doctors, uphold the Romish doctrine

Their definition of transubstantiation.

See Vaugh. ii App No III.

It was not with the spirit of an impatient dogmatist, but with that of a Christian, earnest for the truth of God, that Wiclif commenced his opposition to the doctrine of transubstantiation. It is interesting to observe his steadiness of purpose, and his singleness of aim, in beginning an attack which would, he was conscious, bring upon him no small danger and difficulty. He had probably preached on the subject before to his parishioners at Lutterworth, but in the spring of 1381 he drew public attention to the subject by twelve *conclusions*, which he published at Oxford. William de Berton, who had been one of Wiclif's colleagues in his mission to Bruges, was at that time the chancellor of the university. As soon as Wiclif's conclusions were published, he convened twelve doctors, and with them drew up a contradiction of the doctrines of Wiclif: in this, after reciting the statements which he had made, they adjudge them to be contrary to the determinations of Holy Church; these they declare to be, "That through the sacramental words duly uttered by a priest, the bread and wine upon the altar are transubstantiated, or substantially converted, into the very body and blood of Christ; so that after the consecration, there do not remain in that venerable sacrament material bread and wine (which were previously under their own substances or natures), but only the appearance [species] of the same things; under which appearances [speciebus] the true body and blood of Christ are really contained, not only figuratively, or tropically, but essentially, substantially, and bodily; so that Christ is truly there in his proper bodily presence: this is to be believed; this is to be taught; this is manfully to be defended against all who contradict." They likewise determined that the penalty of the greater excommunication, suspension from all scholastic exercises, and imprisonment, should be put in force against any member of the university who should inculcate these doctrines of Wiclif. All who *listened* to them were likewise to be similarly punished.

A message from the chancellor brings tidings of the condemnation of his doctrines

Wiclif appeals to the civil power.

He is prevented from lecturing on the subject at Oxford

Wiclif was, at the very time when this convention was held, lecturing in the school of the Augustinians, in virtue of his professorship, on this identical doctrine, when a messenger entered the hall, and in the name of the chancellor, and the doctors who had united with him, published their sentence respecting the "sacrament of the altar," and all who should uphold the doctrines taught by Wiclif concerning it. Wiclif was taken by surprise; his personal liberty was in question; he wished to have an opportunity of meeting his opponents, and discussing the condemned doctrines; and at length he appealed to the civil power, thus denying the summary authority of the chancellor to imprison him: this appeal seems to have had this consequence, that he continued at liberty, although prohibited from teaching the obnoxious doctrines *at Oxford*. His appeal was one which could really only come before the ensuing parliament; and thus, until that should meet, the chancellor and the divinity professor could not have their respective liberties and jurisdictions accurately determined.

Wiclif writes his "Ostiolum"

Meanwhile, Wiclif was not idle; he wrote his "Ostiolum," or "Wicket," a tract on the debated subject. This work is interesting on another account, besides that which was the occasion of its being written; he alludes to the opposition which the Scriptures in English excited. He says, that his opponents denounced it as "heresy to speak of the holy Scripture in English, and so they would condemn the Holy Ghost;" this gives the first certain mention, in which the date is evident, of the notice which his translation had excited. The tract continues to speak of the Lord's supper, and the wondrous mistakes which were made relative to it.

Wat Tyler's insurrection, 1381

The disturbances in England which prevailed in the summer of 1381, were probably a means of postponing any farther proceedings against Wiclif. In June of that year, the mob, under the command of Wat Tyler, took possession of London; on the 14th of that month Simon Sudbury, archbishop of

tradict what had been previously determined and held. It decreed (in accordance with the Romish views at the time) that "the entire Christ," i e flesh, blood, human soul, and divinity, exist equally in the bread and in the wine; and that this entire Christ exists in each particle of each

The *accidents* (properties or qualities) of bread and wine, were allowed still to remain, although it was said that *subject* (the actual substance) had disappeared: mention is frequently made with regard to this question, of "an accident without a subject;" this the Romanists affirmed to exist in the Lord's supper.

Canterbury was beheaded by them; and this vacancy of the primacy was again, it is probable, the reason why no immediate notice was taken of the alarming doctrines. Sudbury was succeeded in his archbishoprick by Courtney, bishop of London; but it was not until May 1382, that he received the *pall* from Rome which was necessary "for the completion of his *character*." This prelate shewed himself far more prompt in action than his predecessor, whose want of firmness at the Lambeth citation of Wiclif has been much blamed by Romish writers.

Abp. Sudbury beheaded by the mob, June 14.

Courtney, bp. of London, succeeds him.

On the 17th of May, he convened an assembly, consisting of eight bishops and fourteen doctors together with others, at the Grey Friars in London, for the purpose of formally condemning the doctrines held by Wiclif. Twenty-four "conclusions" were read as having been generally preached throughout England; and after three days' deliberation, this convention condemned ten of the "conclusions" as being heretical, and the other fourteen as being erroneous. At the meeting of this synod, a shock of an earthquake alarmed some of those who were present; but the archbishop turned the circumstance to good account, applying it as an intimation of the need which there was of preserving the purity of the church. The decisions of this convention were speedily published, in order that they might be carried into effect; the archbishop transmitted the decree not only to the bishop of Lincoln, Wiclif's diocesan, but even to the clergy of the parishes around Lutterworth: it was likewise sent to the bishop of London, in whose diocese many who held the opinions of Wiclif might be supposed to reside.

An assembly convened at the Grey Friars' May 17, 1382.

The storm was, however, kept for a while from breaking upon the head of Wiclif. A Carmelite, Dr. Peter Stokys, a zealous opponent of Wiclif, was sent to Oxford to publish the mandates there, where the teaching of the Reformer had gained much ground. But Robert Rigge, who had succeeded William de Berton as chancellor, was one of the admirers of Wiclif, one who, if he did not himself hold his doctrines, was little inclined to hear them condemned.* He called on Dr. Nicholas Hereford to preach before the University: this was one of Wiclif's adherents, as also was Philip Rappyngton, who was also thus employed during the visit of Stokys. The latter of these defended Wiclif and his doctrines at some length. "Amongst other things, he told the audience, that those who did not mention the secular magistrate before either the bishop or the Pope, broke the order prescribed in holy Scripture." This conduct of Dr. Robert Rigge rendered him the immediate object of the resentment of the archbishop, and he was authoritatively commanded both to abstain from opposing Stokys, and to support him in his mission at Oxford.

Peter Stokys sent to Oxford to publish the mandates. Collier, iii p. 166; Fox, i. 504 [Ed 1684]

Robert Rigge, the chancellor, an adherent of Wiclif.

Hereford and Rappyngton preach at Oxford

Collier, iii. 167.

Archbishop Courtney strengthened the authority of the convention, which had condemned the twenty-four "conclusions," by procuring an ordinance from the king against all itinerant preachers who should uphold the condemned doctrines: the sheriffs and others were commanded, at the requirement of the prelates, to arrest all such persons. This ordinance rested of course upon the royal authority only, and yet it assumed the form of an act of parliament. The pretended enacting part ran thus:—"It is ordained and assented in this present Parliament, That the King's Commissions be made and directed to the Sheriffs and other ministers of our Sovereign Lord the King, or other sufficient persons learned, and, according to the certifications of the prelates thereof, to be made in the Chancery from time to time to arrest all such preachers, and also their fautors, maintainers, and abettors, and to hold them in arrest and strong prison, till they will justify themselves according to law and reason of holy Church. And the King willeth and commandeth, that the Chancellor make such commissions at all times that he, by the Prelates or any of them, shall be certified and thereof required, as is aforesaid."

Courtney obtains the king's aid Fox i 503

The enactments of the fictitious statute.

It is to be observed, that this ordinance possessed not a particle of legal validity: it was in fact a mere forgery, and, as such, complaint was made against it in the ensuing Parliament; the Commons alleging that they had never passed any bill authorizing commissions for the imprisoning of suspected or itinerant preachers, for they would not (they said) be more bound to the prelates than their ancestors had been. In consequence of this, the fictitious statute was declared to be repealed; and yet the ecclesiastical influence was so great, that the invalid ordinance remained amongst the acts of parliament, and has been *printed* as such, while the act of repeal was altogether suppressed. Commissions continued to be issued under the forged act as though it had been a real one.

Its invalidity

Its repeal; yet continues to be acted upon.

On the 13th of June, the king issued his writ to the chancellor and proctors of the University of Oxford, ordering strict search to be made for those who should be suspected of heresy or error, especially with regard to the points which had lately been condemned by Archbishop Courtney and his coadjutors; any

Fox i. 504 The king's mandate to the university of Oxford, June 13, 1382.

* It is, however, not a little remarkable that he was one of the twelve doctors associated in the preceding year with William de Berton, the then chancellor, in the condemnation of Wiclif's "conclusions;" he must either have been a dissentient from the determinations of that assembly, or else new light must in the interval have dawned upon his mind.

persons, likewise, who entertained John Wiclif, Nicholas Hereford, Philip Rappyngton, and others of the same sentiments were to be expelled the University, and not to be received again until such time as they should be cleared of the charge of heresy before the archbishop of Canterbury; the writings of Wiclif and Hereford were likewise to be sought for and transmitted to the archbishop.

Proceedings against the chancellor and others at Oxford.

Many difficulties were thrown by the chancellor of the university in the way of these orders being fully complied with: at length, however, the contumacious parties were brought before the archbishop. Various proceedings connected with them took place in June and July 1382. Wiclif meanwhile was at Lutterworth, and in some of the sermons which he preached while these prosecutions were pending, he expresses his opinion that the secret ground in the archbishop's mind was the publication of the Scriptures in English.

Wiclif at Lutterworth; he refers in his sermons to the proceedings.

Lewis's Hist. p 22

He calls Courtney "on gret byschop of englelond," who "as men sayen is yuel payed that Goddes lawe is written in englysche to lewede [lay] men; and he pursueth a prest, for he wryteth to men this englysche and sompneth him and traveleth him, that hyt is hard to hym to route. And thus he pursueth another prest by the helpe of the pharyses, for he precheth cristes gospel frely withouten fables. O men that ben of cristes halfe, helpe ye nowe ageyns Antecrist. For the perelouse tyme is comen that crist and poule tolden byfore."

It is probable that the priest, who was thus spoken of as being pursued by the bishop for writing Scripture in English, was not Wiclif himself but Hereford, whom we have already seen to have been, in some measure, a coadjutor of Wiclif in his work. The other, who was persecuted for preaching, seems to me to have been Ashton, an itinerant labourer of much note. Others may, perhaps, judge that Rappyngton was intended. Archbishop Courtney continued his opposition with unwearied zeal, Hereford and Rappyngton being the two most obnoxious to him. Submissions, on the part of the accused—some more entire than others—some indeed very partial, were the consequence of the archbishop's proceedings against the Oxford divines.

The submission of the suspected heretics.

Wiclif still untouched

His statement presented to the king and Parliament at Oxford, Nov. 1382.

Wiclif was still untouched. It is possible that a man whose death from palsy was expected, was deemed unfit to be summoned; but so far was he from succumbing to the menaces of Archbishop Courtney, that in the following November he presented a statement of his doctrine to the king and the Parliament which assembled at Oxford. With regard to the Lord's supper, he prays that the doctrine concerning it, set forth by Christ and his apostles in the Gospels and Epistles, may be openly taught in the churches. The authority and sufficiency of the New Testament, as the Christian's directory, is put very pointedly in opposition to the multiform additions which had been appended to it. The effect of this appeal was remarkable; it led the Commons to petition the king to withdraw the illegal ordinance by which he had empowered the prelates to imprison those who held the twenty-four condemned "conclusions." The result of this petition has been already stated.

The convocation at Oxford

Wiclif summoned before it, Nov. 1382

But the archbishop was not idle: the convocation which met at Oxford at the same time as the Parliament summoned Wiclif to appear before them. This summons was duly obeyed; and here we see Wiclif meeting the combined spiritual authority of the hierarchy *alone*—for his Oxford adherents were silenced:—and *unsupported*,—for John of Gaunt, who once upheld him, now avowedly abandoned him, and recommended him not to maintain the doctrines which he had taught.

He presents two confessions of his doctrines against transubstantiation.

Wiclif deprived of his professorship, and banished from Oxford

When he appeared before the archbishop and other prelates, he presented to them two confessions on the subject of the Lord's supper, the one in English, and the other in Latin, each re-asserting that transubstantiation did not really take place. In his Latin confession, he enters into questions as to how, or in what sense, "the bread which we break is the communion of the body of Christ," but he concludes where he began, that there is no change of substance. The consequence of the Oxford citation was, his being deprived, by the authority of the king, of the office which he held as professor of divinity, and likewise banished from the University.

He now left Oxford, the place in which he had for many years taught the truth as his own mind was gradually opened to apprehend it; and where, during the last six years, his testimony had been the means of bringing a flood of light amongst his cotemporaries. One of the most remarkable facts in the history of Wiclif is, the comparative shortness of the period in which his testimony was directly pointed against the spiritual pretensions of Rome, from which results so apparently incommensurate took place. The Lord had prepared the ground, even as He sent forth Wiclif to sow the truth.

Cited by Urban VI. to appear at Rome.

It would seem as though the prelates contemplated farther proceedings against Wiclif: at all events, Urban VI. was apprised of his opinions, and he was in consequence cited to appear at Rome. It is not probable that this citation had any connection with the former proceedings, in which Gregory XI. had reserved to himself the place of authoritatively giving sentence concerning Wiclif's explanation of the Pope's "conclusions," as to what he had taught; and yet it is possible that the English prelates were still restrained by the authority of the Bull of 1377, from touching Wiclif's person, unless they received authority from Rome. The citation to appear at Rome reached Lutterworth at a time when Wiclif was so suffering from paralysis, as to render his obedience, even if he had been disposed, impossible; however, he wrote to the Pope very freely, speaking of the authority and obligation of Holy Scripture, and its superiority to even an Apostle, if he were present; this is urged on the simple ground, that apostles both could and did err, whereas the Scripture is certain and of absolute authority; he then applies this to the conscience of the Pope, speaking the truth to him both boldly and faithfully, thus showing that even though he were disabled in body, he was still vigorous in mind for the cause of God.

Wiclif writes to the Pope

Wiclif's retirement at Lutterworth must have been diligently employed in setting forth his opinions in writing. It is probable, that in this he was assisted by the pens of others; but, in spite of his paralysis, his vigour of mind, and affiance of soul upon God and his truth, were in no way weakened. The remaining months of his life do not seem to have been molested; although, in some of his writings, he appears to have expected more trouble from his opponents. But his days were near their close: he was seized with a fatal attack of paralysis, on the 29th of December, 1384, and on the 31st of the same month, aged sixty years, he "departed to be with Christ, which is far better."

Wiclif writes diligently

His death, Dec. 31, 1384.

I have thus briefly looked at the life and labours of this remarkable man, whose efforts will not, in their result, be fully known till the day when the secrets of all hearts shall be revealed. The whole course of his testimony stands more or less in connection with his publication of the Scriptures in English, either as leading onward to it, or as resulting from it. The events of his life are, it is true, seen through an obscure medium, and he rises, as it were, an object, dim, but vast, in the horizon; but though the lapse of years, and the bitter persecutions of those who were taught by him, cause many of the exact features of his character, and the incidents of his life, to be little known, yet this we do know, that his testimony in his life and writings was faithful; and that, after his death, the effects of truth received through him, continued to draw forth the opposition of its foes. Wiclif stands, indeed, in such prominence, that others who held his doctrines after him, seem to be almost forgotten, until, after a century and a half, the light of God's truth again shone forth.

But there continued, through all this dark interval, not a few who prized the truth of God more dearly than their own lives; we know of such as William Sautrè (the proto-martyr of England's papal persecution), Lord Cobham, William White, Richard Hoveden, John Goose, Tylsworth of Amersham, and of many more who yielded their bodies to be burned at various times during this period; and of many others likewise, who were *confessors*, if they were not called to suffer death. One of these, who deserves particular attention, is William Thorp, who, by his writings, formed a connecting link between John Wiclif and William Tyndale. The decrees of the convention at the Grey Friars, under Archbishop Courtney, were, as I have already mentioned, directed against any itinerant preachers who should teach the doctrines of Wiclif. Of these there appear to have been no inconsiderable number then in England. Itinerant preaching, on the part of the mendicant friars, was nothing strange; but it gave no small offence for Wiclif's "poor priests" to act in the same manner. But they were acting in obedience to the word of God, and they accounted it to be their duty to preach to the people, even though the prelates gave them no licenses. They were, in fact, acting upon the same principle as those of whom we read, who were dispersed in consequence of the persecution at Jerusalem, "They that were scattered abroad, went every where, preaching the word."

Many continued to hold the doctrines which Wiclif had taught

Many martyrs and confessors

W Thorp is, as it were, a link between Wiclif and Tyndale Fox, i 600, et seqq.

Itinerant preaching in England.

Wiclif's "poor priests"

Acts viii. 4

V.

THE ENGLISH VERSION EXECUTED BY WICLIF'S FOLLOWERS.

Before giving an account of the proceedings which were instituted soon after the death of Wiclif, for the suppression of the English Scriptures, it is needful to notice the other versions, real or supposed, which were executed about the same time or a little after.

One other version at least cotemporary with that of Wiclif.

It is a certain fact that another translation beside that of Wiclif was made about the same time; some Manuscripts of a version exist, which when compared with that of Wiclif appear in many parts to have been formed very much on the model of his translation; the terms employed and the collocation of words often seem to shew, that the translator of the one had the other version before him, and that he used it in the composition of that which he executed.

Elucidarium Bibliorum

A previous version referred to

The book entitled "Elucidarium Bibliorum" has been already referred to; this prologue to the Bible contains an intimation that a version existed which had been made a little before that which was executed by the author of that tract and certain coadjutors. The question naturally occurs, When was this prologue written? Is there any evidence to determine the author? Can the version be ascertained to which this prologue properly belongs? To these questions answers can, I believe, be returned more or less satisfactory, principally from the statements of the prologue itself.

Date of the prologue, 1395.

Events of previous years are alluded to.

1st. The date;—this is intimated by certain references made to the proceedings of the "*last Parliament*," at which some of the grievous vices of the clergy had been brought into notice. This can refer to nothing but the sad and disgusting exposure which took place in the Parliament in the year 1395, so that we may assign this prologue to that year or the beginning of the next; the translation was apparently completed just before the prologue was written. Reference is made to the contentions of the scholars at Oxford and the consequent bloodshed; these events took place in the years 1388 and 1389. A statute of the university of Oxford (enacted in 1251) was revived in 1387, which the author of this prologue thus recites:—"That no man schal lerne dyuynite neither hooly writ, no but he that hath doon his fourme in art, that is that hath comensid in art and hath been regent tweyne yeer aftir, this wolde be ix year either x before that he lerne hooly writ." The first reference gives a date to this work, which the other particulars stated, amply confirm.* A further proof that this prologue was written after the time of Wiclif, is to be found in the reference made to the writings of John Gerson, the celebrated chancellor of the University of Paris; he is cited by the name of "Parisience," which is given more explicitly in the printed edition, "Johan Gerson Parisiensis." He was not known as an author till after Wiclif's death.

John Purnay almost certainly the author of this prologue.

Wiclif's curate at Lutterworth.

2nd. The next point to be inquired into is, Who was the author of this prologue, and consequently of the version to which it belonged? It is very evident that the writer was one whose views and doctrines were similar to those of Wiclif himself; and this makes it *primâ facie* probable that the translator was one whose "Lollardism" would be so notorious, that his name would be transmitted to us amongst the learned followers of Wiclif. Of these, one of the most remarkable was John Purvy, or Purnay, who, during the life of Wiclif, appears to have lived with him, and is supposed to have acted as his curate at Lutterworth. Copies of a version of the Bible into English have the name of this person written in them, and also the prologue annexed; and hence the supposition has been very reasonably entertained that he was the translator of the version which varies from that of Wiclif. This answers also the third of the questions which have been put. This version and prologue have thus been ascribed to Purnay; and as it seems as if there could have been no reason to ascribe it to him if he had not been the author, it may be regarded as his work.†

Purnay's competency as a translator

Purnay appears, from what has been said of him by various writers, to have been very competent to the task of the translation. Walden calls him "The Library of the Lollards, and Wiclif's glosser, an eloquent divine, and famous for his skill in the Law." The manner in which the version was executed is very

* The circumstances just mentioned prove that this was not the work of Wiclif, as was formerly supposed The edition printed in 1550, under the title of "A Pathway to Perfect Knowledge," is stated on the title-page as being apparently by him If it had been, it would be clear that a previous version to his existed, for the writer expressly speaks of *the English translation lately made;* but the date which is above assigned (after Lewis and Baber) proves that this prologue presents no impediment to the full reception of the testimony of Knyghton; according to which it is clear that no English translation of the Scripture was known and circulated at large prior to that of Wiclif.

† If it be objected that the evidence is not absolutely conclusive as to Purnay having been the author of this prologue and translation, let it be observed that this does not in the slightest degree affect the account of the version itself: other things remain the same, even though we look on it as anonymous.

interesting. The following account is given at the end of the prologue of the process pursued by Purnay and his assistants in preparing for, and producing their version.*

"Fyrste thys symple creature had mych trauaile wyth diuers felowis & helpars to gather mani eld bibles and other doctouris & comune glosis, & to make oo latine bible some dell trwe, and than to studie it of the newe, the text with the glose, & other doctours as he might get, and specially Lire on the elde testamente, that helpyd full miche in hys werke. The thyrde tyme to counsell wyth elde gramariens and elde diuinis, of harde wordis and harde sentensis, how they myght beste be vnderstanden & translated. The fourth tyme, to translate as cleerly as he could to y[e] sentence, and to haue many good fellowis and kunnyng, at the correctinge of the translation. First it is to know that y[e] beste translatyng out of Latyne into Englysh is to translate after the sentence, and not only after the wordis.

The translator's account of the version. Old Latin Bibles collated

Nicolaus Lyranus

"So that the sentence be as opyn (either opener) in Englyshe as in latyne, and go not farre fro the letter. And if the letter may not be suid in y[e] translatynge, let the sentence euer be whole and open. For the wordis owen to serue to y[e] entente and sentence: and elles the wordis bene superfluouse either false. In translatyng into English, many resolusions moune make the sentence open, as an ablatyfe case absolute maye be resolued into these three words w[t] couenable verb the while, for, if, as gramarians seine. As thus, The master reding, I stode, maye be resolued thus, while y[e] master readith, I stonde. Either if the master read, ether for the master, &c. And somtime it wold accord well w[t] the sentence to be resolued into whan, either into afterward, thus, whan the master red, I stode. Either after the master read I stode. And sometime it may well be resolued into a verbe of the same tyme, as other ben in the same reason, and this worde et, that is, and, in English, as thus. *Arescentibus hominibus pre timore*, that is, And men shulen were drie for dread. Als a participle of a presente tens, either preter tens of actyfe voicis, either passife: may be resolued into a verb of the same tens, and a coniunction copulatyfe, as thus. *Dicens.* that is seynge may be resolued thus, and seythe, eyther that seythe . . . .

The version not literal

"Also whan ryghtful constructions is lettyd by relation I resolue openly thus. Where this reason, *Dum formidabunt aduersarii, eius* shuld be englyshid thus bi the letter. The lorde hys adversaries sholden dred: I english it thus by resolucyon, the aduersaries of the lorde shulen dread hym. And so of other reasons that bene like. At the byginnynge I purposyde wyth Goddys helpe: to make the sentence as true and open in englyshe as it is in latine, either more trwe and moore open than it is in latyne. And I praye for charitie and commune profyte of chrysten soulys, that if any wyse man fynd any default of the trueth of translation, let hym set in the true sentence and open the holy wryte. But loke y[t] he examyne trulye hys latyn byble: for no doubt he shall fynde many byblis in latyne ful false, if he loke mani. And namely newe, and the commune latyne bybles haue more nede to be correctyd (as many as I haue sene in my life) than hath the english bible late translated. And where the Hebru, by witnes of Jerom of Lire and other expositours dyscordith fro our Latyne biblis: I haue set in y[e] margent bi manner of a glose what y[e] Hebreu hath and howe it is vnderstonden in some place. And I did this most in the psalter, y[t] of al our bokis discordith most fro Hebru. For the chirch readeth not the psalter by the laste translation out of Hebru into Latine: but an other translacion of other men y[t] hadden mich lasse kunninge, and holiness than Jerome had."

A previous English translation referred to.

This prologue shews that the translation to which it belongs must vary considerably in its plan from that of Wiclif; this latter keeping especially close to the literal sense of the Latin, while Purnay sought to preserve the English idiom; how far this object was *attained* in the execution of the version, and what are its comparative merits as compared with Wiclif's, are questions which may admit of varying judgments; the more closely a version adheres to literal renderings of the text, the more, in my judgment, would it accurately represent the meaning: of course I do not mean that a departure from the vernacular idiom should be resorted to for the sake of precision; but that a literal adherence to the text is commonly the best mode of expressing the sense.

The plan of the version differs from that of Wiclif.

It is not perhaps easy to give an exact account of the Manuscripts, now extant, containing the version of Purnay. Lewis says, that his name is written on a copy of a translation of the New Testament, differing from Wiclif's, in Trinity College, Dublin; and, farther on, he gives a quotation from the Manuscript itself. He says, "the Prologue before-mentioned is bound up with it at the end of the Apocalypse, and written in the same hand as the New Testament."

The MSS of Purnay's version

His name in a MS at Dublin; Lewis, p 34

Lewis gives, as an extract from this Manuscript, the first verses of St. Matthew's Gospel; I give them from him, together with the same portions of Wiclif's translation.

The more literal a version the better

* The extract given from the prologue is taken from the printed edition of 1550; the British Museum copy of the Manuscript being defective at the end.

Extracts from Wiclif and Purnay, Matt i

Wiclif 1380.	Purnay 1395. (MS. Trin. Col. Dubl. 237. 97.)
The book of the generacioun of ihesus crist: the sone of dauith, the sone of abraham. abraham bigat Isaac, Isaac bigat Iacob, Iacob bigat Iudas and hise britheren.	The booke of generacioun of jesus crist the sone of davith, the sone of abraham. abraham generide or bigaat ysaac, ysaac forsothe bigate jacob, jacob forsothe bigate judas and his brethern.

Bishop Butler's MS. *now* (Feb 1841) *penes* Messrs Payne & Foss, Pall Mall.

This version, attributed to Purnay, and belonging evidently to the author of the prologue, agrees *verbatim* with a manuscript in the possession of the late Bishop Butler, of Lichfield and Coventry; this last-mentioned Manuscript differs *in the Gospels* in many respects from Wiclif's translation, and is clearly another version. I therefore give a few more specimens of it, comparing them with Wiclif.

LUKE I.

Luke i 1—5

Wiclif.	Purnay (Bp. Butler's MS.)
[The four first verses of this gospel do not appear to belong to Wiclif's translation as actually executed; if found in any manuscript apparently of Wiclif's translation, they are probably taken from that which was executed afterwards.]	Forsothe for manye men enforceden to ordeyne the tellyng of thingis whiche ben filled in vs as thei that seyn atte the bigynnyng & weren ministris of the word bitaken: it is seen also to me hauynge fro the bigynnyng alle thingis diligentli bi ordre to write to thee thou beest theofile that thou knowe the truthe of tho wordis of whiche thou art lerned.
In the daies of eroude kyng of iudee, there was a preest zacarie bi name of the sorte of abia, and his wiif was of the douȝtris of aaron: and hir name was elizabeth.	There was sum preest zacharie by name in the daies of heroude Kyng of Judee of the sort of Abia and his wyf of the douȝtris of aaron: & hir name Elizabeth

The following passage will serve to shew how far this later translation coincides with that of Wiclif in the use of terms and phrases.

LUKE X. 23—30.

Luke x. 23—30.

Wiclif.	Purnay (Bp. Butler's MS.)
blessid ben the iȝen: that seen tho thingis that ȝe seen, for I seie to ȝou that many profetis and kyngis wolden haue seen tho thingis that ȝe seen: and thei saien not, and heren tho thingis that ȝe heren: and thei herden not, and lo a wise man of the lawe roos up, temptynge hym and seiynge, maistir what thing schal I do to haue euerlastynge liif, and he seide to hym, what is writun in the lawe? hou redist thou, he answerid and seid, thou schalt loue thi lord god of al thin herte: and of all thi soule, and of al thi stryngthis and of al thi mynde and thi neiȝbore as thi silf, ¢ ihesus seide to hym, thou hast answerid riȝtli, do this thing, and thou schalt lyue but he willynge to iustifie hym silf: seid to ihesus, and who is my neiȝbore? and ihesus bi helde and seide, A man cam doun from ierusalem in to ierico, and filde among theues, and thei robbeden hym, and woundiden hym, and wenten aweie: and leften the man half alyue.	blessid ben the iȝen: whiche seen tho thingis that ȝe seen, sotheli I seie to ȝou for many pfetes & kyngis wolden see tho thingis whiche ȝe seen & sawen not and heere tho thingis that ȝe heeren & thei herden not, and lo a wise man of law roos temptynge him & seyinge; maystir what thing doynge schal I welde eulastynge lyf; and he seyde to him; what is writen in the lawe? how redist thow? he answerynge seide, thou schalt loue the lorde thi god of al thin herte & of al thi soule *eithr lyf* & of al thi myȝtes & of al thi mynde; and thi neyȝbor as thi silf. and iesu seyde to him thou has answeride riȝtly do thou this thing & thou schalt lyue. forsothe he willynge for to iustifie himself seyd to iesu, and who is my neiȝbore? sothely iesu biholdynge seyde, sum man cam doune fro ierlm in to iericho. & felde among theeues whiche also robbiden him and woundes putte inne wenten awaye the man lefte halfe quyke.

If it be thought that in anything this version seems less clear and modern in phraseology than that of Wiclif, it must be borne in mind that many of the explanatory terms with which Manuscripts are sometimes glossed, are now less intelligible than the word which they are given to explain.

This version appears to be identical with one which has been *alleged* to be more ancient than Wiclif's. Bishop Butler's Manuscript appears to coincide with that at Dublin, which has Purnay's name, and also with a specimen lately published as part of an older version.

It is, however, also to be observed, that Bishop Butler's Manuscript appears to agree in the Epistles with Wiclif's version; hence it may be supposed to have been transcribed from two different copies and versions.

A Manuscript in the British Museum (Bibl. Reg. 1 B. VI.) contains throughout a version varying from

Wiclif's; this appears in the Gospels to be identical with the version contained in Bishop Butler's Manuscript, and in the Epistles to be the rest of the same translation.

The first four verses of St. Luke's Gospel are, however, omitted in this copy, as well as in those of Wiclif's version. In the passage already cited from Bishop Butler's Manuscript from Luke x, there are only a few slight variations.

The following are specimens as compared with Wiclif:—

1 COR. VIII.

WICLIF.

But of these thingis that ben sacrified to idolis we witen for alle we han kunnynge, but kunnynge blowith, charite edifieth, but if ony man gessith that he kan ony thing, he hath not ȝit knowe hou it bihoueth hym to kunne.

MS. BRIT. MUS. BIB. REG. 1 B. VI.

Forsothe of thes thingis that ben offrid to ydolis *that ben symulacris maid to manns lyknesses.* we witen for alle we han kunnyng. sotheli science *or kunnyng* in bloweth with pride. charite edifyeth forsothe if ony man gesse *or deme* him forto wite ony thing he hath not ȝit knowun hou it bihoueth him for to kunne. 1 Cor viii 1, 2

HEB. IV.

WICLIF.

Therfor drede we leest parauenture, while the biheest of entrynge in to his reste is lefte, that if ony of us be gessid to be awei, for it is toold also to us: as to hem, and the word that was herd, profitid not to hem, not meynde to feith, of tho thingis that thei herden, for we that han bileued, schulen entre in to reste, as he seide, as I swoor in my wraththe: thei schuln not entre in to my reste.

MS. BIB. REG. 1 B. VI.

Drede we thrfore brithren leste paruenre the biheest of entring into "reste" his [*sic*] left or forsaken *or* deniyd forto be ony of us be gessid aweye. forsothe it is tolde to us as & to hem and the worde herde pfited not to hem not mengid to feith of thes thingis that thei herden forsothe we that han bileued schulen entre in to reste as he seide as I swoor in my wrath if thei schulen entre into my reste. Heb. iv. 1—3

Another Manuscript, in the British Museum, (Arundel 254), contains an English harmony of the Gospels, on the plan of that drawn up by Clement, of Lanthony, together with the Catholic Epistles, all of which are of the translation differing from Wiclif's.

Bishop Butler's Manuscript contains some peculiarities; for instance, in Matt. ii. "Kinges" is the word in the text for "wise men", and "astronomers" is placed in the margin. The word "kinges" is of course derived from the Romish legend of Gaspar, Melchior, and Balthasar. This could not have proceeded from the translator, it must have been the alteration of a copyist.

Mr. Baber gives Luke ix. 1, &c., and 1 Cor. viii. 1, &c. as specimens of a version contained in a Manuscript then in the possession of Mr. Douce: from these citations, the Manuscript in question appears to contain the version here attributed to Purnay.* Mr. Douce's MS cited by Baber.

There is a MS. in the Bodleian Library, which has this notice written at the end, "ye eer of ye lord m cccc c viii. yis book wa endid." The fourth c in the date has been erased, so as to make the book appear older; but there can hardly be a question that the date really is 1408, the very year when Archbishop Arundel's Oxford Constitutions were enacted. This MS. is worthy of notice, because, from the alteration of date, it has been supposed to be far earlier than the days of Wiclif, and also because it has been stated by Lewis to be of a different version. MS. in the Bodleian, Fairfax, 2 Date

Bishop Bonner mentioned, in 1555, an old Bible which he possessed, written about eight score years previous, from which he gives some extracts; the following is a comparison of these passages (as found in Lewis), with Wiclif's version. Bp. Bonner's MS. Lewis, p 25, 27

EXOD. XX.

WICLIF.

And the lord spak alle these wordis. I am the lord God that ladde thee out of the lond of egypt fro the hous of seruage thou schalt not haue alien goddis bifore me. thou schalt not make to thee a grauin ymage, nethir ony licnesse *of thing* which is in heuene aboue, and which is in erthe binethe, neythir of the thingis that ben in watris undir erthe, thou shalt not herie tho nether thou schalt worshippe.

BONNER'S MS.

And the lord speek alle thes wordes I am the lord thi god that hath lad the out of the londe of Egypte from the house of thraldome: thou schalt not have alyen goddys before me, thou schalt not make to the graven thing, ne eny lycknesse that is in heven abown and that is in erthe benethe, ne of hem that ben in waters under erthe, thou schalt not anoure hem ne herye hem. Exod xx 1—5

* The same version appears to be contained in a Manuscript in the Advocates' Library, Edinburgh; of which various specimens have been kindly furnished for comparison, by J. Thomson, Esq. This Manuscript does not contain the introductory verses to the Gospel of St Luke

LEVIT. XXVI.

Lev. xxvi

Ye shulen not make to you an ydol and a grauen ymage, nether ye schulen reyse tytlis, nether ȝe schulen sette a noble stoon in your lond that ȝe worschipe it.	Ghe schuln not make to ghou a mawmett and graven thing, ne tytles ghe schuln rere, ne huge stone ghe schuln putten in ghor erthe that ghe honour it.

Glosses introduced

In this passage, some Manuscripts of Wiclif's translation add, after the word "tytlis," "*yt is auteris for ydolatrie*," underscored, so as to distinguish it from the text itself. This may serve as a specimen of the kind of glosses which were early added to Wiclif's translation; they were probably appended, in many copies, almost as soon as the version itself was executed; and, indeed, it is not improbable that the copy of the New Testament in English, with glosses, which was used by Anne of Bohemia, queen consort of Richard II., was one of this description.

DEUT. V.

Deut. v. 7—9.

Wiclif.	Bonner's MS.
Thou schalt not have alien goddis in my sight, Thou schalt not make to thee a grauen ymage neyer a licnesse of all thingis that been in heuene above & that ben in erthe binethe & that ben in watris under erthe, thou schalt not herie tho & thou schalt not worshippe tho	Thou schalte not haue alyen goddys in my syght, thou schalt not make to thee graven thinge, ne lyckenesse of alle thinges that in hevene ben above and in erthe benethe, and that dwellen in waters under erthe, thou schalt not honoure hem ne herye hem

Bodleian MS, Fairfax 2, is Wiclif's.

Lewis says, that the Manuscript cited by Bonner, appears to be the same that is now in the Bodleian, marked Fairfax, No. 2; which is the Manuscript of which the date has been falsified, to make it appear a century older. In this he is clearly mistaken, for a comparison of these very passages with that MS., proves that it contains the version of Wiclif; the same is true of a passage which has been copied from the New Testament of that MS. Another Bodleian Manuscript, which Lewis speaks of as containing the same version, is also simply one of Wiclif's.* It yet remains to be shown, what Manuscripts contain the version which Bishop Bonner cites.

Purnay's version never widely spread

Thus much, then, appears certain, that in the latter part of the fourteenth century, *two* English versions of the Scriptures were made, both of which are extant; the one, John Wiclif's, a translation made very literally from the Latin; the other, executed by Purnay and others, in which an attempt was made to express the *sense* in English more than the exact words. This latter version appears never to have been so much circulated as the former, which may be attributed to three causes. 1st. That Wiclif's was so diligently copied at once, that it had acquired a sort of standing in the affections of readers; 2nd. That the troubles of Purnay commenced so very soon after the completion of his work, that *he* was not able himself to superintend the multiplication of copies; and, 3rd. That the prohibitory constitution of Archbishop Arundel was enacted only *thirteen* years subsequent to the completion of the version, whereas it was twenty-eight years posterior to the translation of Wiclif.

Glosses found in various MSS

Lewis, p 29.

Glosses of various kinds to explain passages, or, more commonly, single words, are of frequent occurrence in some Manuscripts of Wiclif's and the other early version; but especially in those of the latter: the following are a few specimens of verbal glosses:—" Incorruptible, *that may not dye ne ben peyred;*"—" Creatore, *that is, maker of noughte.*"—" Yvel fame, *or, schendeschepe.*"—" Maales, *or men.*"—" Acorden not, *or bysemen not.*"—" Bakbyters, *or soweres of discorde.*"—" Detractours, *or open bakbyteres.*"—" Proude, *high ouer measure.*"—" Affeccion, *or love.*"—" Benignite, *or good-will.*"—" Acception of persones, *that is put oon bifore another that is withouten deserte.*"—" Sacrilegie, *that is theft of holy thenges.*"—" Prepucie, *or custom of heathen men.*"—" Iustified, *or founden trew.*"—" Prevarication, *or trespassing.*"—" Allegorie, *or gospels undirstonding.*"—" A libel, *that is a little book.*"—" A bylibre of wheat, *that is, a weighte of tweye pound.*"—" With wonder and extasi, *that is, lesyng of mynde and resoun and lettyng of tonge.*"—" Oolde botellis, *or wyne vessells.*"

The object of the greater part of these glosses is very evident; in some of them, however, the explanatory term is *now* become less simple than the word to be explained. Some of the elucidations are not a little singular, while others appear to be inserted for the purpose of giving a synonyme of Saxon origin as an equivalent for some term derived from the Latin. This one thing is very clear that all the

* I am much indebted to the kindness of Dr. Bandinell, the Keeper of the Bodleian Library, for extracts from various MSS; and also to Mr Henry Gough, for information relative to these and others

labour bestowed upon the making of versions, and upon elucidating them when made, was directed to the diffusion of the knowledge of the word of God amongst the English, not merely the high and learned, but likewise the poor and comparatively illiterate.

John de Trevisa said to have translated the Scriptures

It is possible that a careful examination of existing manuscripts would shew that there are more than one old translation extant besides that of Wiclif. It has been positively asserted, that John de Trevisa, a native of Cornwall, who was vicar of Berkley, translated both the Old and New Testaments into English. He was cotemporary with Wiclif, though born some years before him, and also his survivor by some years; it has been supposed that he died in 1399 or the preceding year: Tanner says, in 1412. John de Trevisa was no friend to the then existing state of things in the Church, since he is reported to have said, "Our Saviour sent apostles and priests into the world, but never any monks or begging friars." Whether these were his words or not, they may at least be taken as the expression of his judgment. It is possible that his objection to the friars may have led to a translation of the Scriptures having been attributed to him.

His dislike to the friars

If John de Trevisa did really translate the Old and New Testaments, it is probable that his work was either almost exactly cotemporary or else a little posterior to that of Wiclif; I suppose this from the fact of other works translated by him having been executed about that time: the Polychronicon of Ranulph of Chester was translated by him (to which he himself added a supplement of the events of fifty-five years), and it was finished in April, 1387.

Bale and Caxton's testimony.

Bale attributes a version of the Scriptures to Trevisa, as also Caxton seems to do; whether they had any data for their assertion is not easy to determine.

If Trevisa did translate the Scriptures, his work must have fallen with Wiclif's under the sweeping condemnation of Archbishop Arundel's Oxford Constitutions, and thus unless it were disseminated (like Wiclif's had been previously) by some strenuous efforts, copies of it would necessarily become almost extinct. As the name of John de Trevisa has thus been connected with the English translations of the Scriptures, it will not be amiss to give a few passages of Scripture extracted by Dr. Waterland out of his writings, and published by Lewis:—

Fragments of Scripture in the writings of Trevisa.

Matt. 18: 32. "I forgave the al thy det bycause thou praydest me, wicked servant."
— 22: 18. "The slowe servant hidde his lorde's talent in the erthe."
— 26: 19. "Moche have I suffred by syghte bycause of him."
Luke 11: 45. "my lord taryeth to come" . . . "If a servant begynneth to drink and is dronken, and smiteth and beateth the meyny his lord shall come . . ."
— 19: 13. "The nobleman called his servauntes and bytoke hem ten mnas, and he saide to these servauntes marchaundise with it tyll I come."
— — 16. "Lo, lord, thy mna hath made ten mnas, and his lorde sayde to him, and be thou hauynge power over ten cities."

I know of nothing farther which can be accurately ascertained respecting the claims of John de Trevisa to be regarded as a translator of the Scriptures.

VI.

OPPOSITION TO THE CIRCULATION OF THE SCRIPTURES, AND OTHER CIRCUMSTANCES PREVIOUS TO THE REIGN OF HENRY VIII.

Opposition raised after Wiclif's death.

A bill brought into the House of Lords, 1390

This bill opposed by John of Gaunt

I HAVE yet to speak of the opposition which, after the death of Wiclif, was raised against the spread of the Scriptures in English. I have already adverted to the mention which he himself makes of the enmity which this translation was even in his lifetime exciting. After his death this was carried still farther, for in the year 1390, a bill was brought into the House of Lords in order to suppress this English translation of the Scriptures. John of Gaunt, although he forsook Wiclif when he boldly combated the doctrine of transubstantiation, seems to have always respected both his principles and conduct, and now firmly opposed the enacting of such a law. He spoke thus, "We will not be the dregs of all; seeing other nations have the law of God, which is the law of our faith, written in their own language." He declared that he would support the circulation of the Scriptures in English against those who brought in the bill, whoever they might be. In support of this opposition, it was said, that "if the Gospel by its being translated into English, was the occasion of men's running into error, they might know that more hereticks are to be found among the Latins than among the people of any other language. For that the Decretals reckoned no fewer than sixty-six Latin hereticks, and so the Gospel must not be read in Latin, which yet the opposers of the English translation allowed." The consequence of this opposition appears to have been that there was no legislative prohibition of the Bible in English.

It does not pass

Abp Arundel's testimony respecting Queen Anne, 1394

We have a testimony from one who would perhaps be thought the least likely to give it, of the reception which the English Scriptures received even amongst those in the highest station. Anne of Bohemia, the queen-consort of Richard II., died in 1394, on the 7th of June; her funeral sermon was preached at Westminster by Thomas Arundel, then archbishop of York, and afterwards of Canterbury; in his commendation of "good Queen Anne" he says, that "although she was a stranger, yet she constantly studied the four Gospels in English, and explained by the exposition of the doctors; and in the study of these, and reading of godly books, she was more diligent than even the prelates themselves, though their office and business require this of them" From this it would appear that she had followed the example of her mother-in-law, the princess of Wales and Aquitaine, whose interference on Wiclif's behalf has been already mentioned.

The writings of Wiclif carried to Bohemia

The attendants of this queen, who had accompanied her to England, returned on her decease to Bohemia, conveying with them the writings of Wiclif; whence it was that the light of truth shone forth from Prague, a light which the council of Constance in vain endeavoured to extinguish. We have, I think, in the circumstance of the writings of Wiclif having been thus conveyed into Bohemia, a presumptive evidence that the English Gospels with the exposition of the doctors, was either of his translation, or else one of those which his followers had put forth. There appears to be some connection between the copy of the Scriptures in English used by this princess, and the subsequent dissemination of the works and doctrines of Wiclif by her attendants in Bohemia; for it cannot be questioned that some at least of her household had embraced the doctrines of this reformer. It appears very probable, that Anne of Bohemia herself had received some of his instructions. Wiclif knew something of her, although she came to this country but little more than two years before his death; for he speaks of her as possessing the Gospel written in three languages, Bohemian, German, and Latin; he asks whether to "hereticate her on that account would not be Luciferan folly?" It is possible that she was under some suspicion of holding or favouring the doctrines of Wiclif, and that, for this reason, he inquires respecting her being *hereticated*.

Wiclif's commendation of Queen Anne

The spread of Lollardie

When "Lollardie," as it was termed, was introduced even into the abodes of royalty, it is not surprising that many of every class were also amongst the number of those who had received the doctrine of Scripture Wiclif rejoiced that "many knights favoured the Gospel, and had a mind to read it in English;" among others the following are mentioned as adhering to the doctrines of Wiclif: Sir Lewis Clifford, Sir John Montacute, Sir Reginald Hilton, Sir William Neville, Sir John Peeche, Sir John Clenboun, Sir John Trussel, Sir Richard Sturry, Sir Thomas Latimer, and that faithful martyr of Christ, Sir John Oldcastle, Lord Cobham. Knyghton, as might have been expected, bewailed the *infatuation* of those knights, who preferred the reproach of Christ to the honours of this world.

It is no wonder that the adherents of the Romish doctrine should have been at length thoroughly alarmed, and induced to institute severe proceedings for the suppression of the supposed evil.

Arundel becomes a severe persecutor, 1400

Six years subsequent to his sermon on the death of Queen Anne, namely in the year 1400, Archbishop Arundel, who had before this succeeded Courtney in the see of Canterbury, became the uncompromising persecutor of all who were suspected of "Lollardie." In this year it was that William Sautrè became the first, in England, to yield his life for the truth of God. The archbishop's continued opposition brought other victims into his hands to be either burned or, like Thorp, imprisoned. In the year 1408, we find him taking more determinate measures for hindering the propagation of what he called heresy: the circulation of the Scriptures in English (those Scriptures the reading of which he *once* had commended) was now to be prohibited by any means. A convocation of the province of Canterbury was held at Oxford, and thirteen Constitutions were enacted. The first two of these defined *who* might preach; the third and fourth determined *what* might be preached; the fifth related to what masters might teach their scholars; the sixth was directed against the writings of John Wiclif, by name; while the seventh was nothing short of a prohibition of the Scriptures in English:—"It is a dangerous thing, as St. Jerome assures us, to translate the holy Scripture, it being very difficult in a version to keep close to the sense of the inspired writers: for by the confession of the same father he had mistaken the meaning of several texts. We therefore decree and ordain, that from henceforward no unauthorised person shall translate any part of

1408 A convocation at Oxford

Constitutions Fox, i 597 Collier, iii p. 280

Wiclif's writings condemned

The Scriptures in English prohibited

the holy Scripture into English or any other language, under any form of book or treatise: neither shall any such book, treatise, or version, made either in Wiclif's time or since, be read, either in whole or in part, publicly or privately, under the penalty of the greater excommunication, till the said translation shall be approved either by the bishop of the diocese, or a provincial council as occasion shall require." The six other constitutions relate to the modes of expression in speaking of God; to disputations on points of Romish belief; to the letters dimissory of priests; to the exclusion of "Lollardie" from Oxford; to the deprivation of offenders; and to the process to be employed in dealing with heretics.

Importance of this seventh Constitution

The seventh of these Constitutions, which I have quoted at length, is of great importance, as shewing both the danger which the archbishop supposed would arise from the spread of the Scriptures in English, and also how these things were connected in his mind with *John Wiclif.* Whatever previous versions of particular portions had existed, they had excited no enmity, for they had never been disseminated by the hands of such as Wiclif's "poor priests." So resolute was this prelate in his condemnation, that he perverts and misquotes Jerome to serve his purpose. It is probable that during the thirty years (or thereabouts) which had elapsed between the completion of Wiclif's version and this Oxford convocation, *very many* copies of the English Scriptures had been made, probably the greater part of those of this translation which have come down to us; and it appears likewise that some of the followers of Wiclif had put forth copies in which the translation was either re-wrought or varied, according to what they judged to be simpler English, or less literal in the renderings;—but however much may have been done in this way by others, Wiclif's was still the version which had unlocked the treasures of God's word to the English nation.

Copies of Wiclif's version multiplied.

The circulation of Wiclif's version

Had not the circulation of Wiclif's translation been very wide prior to the enactment of Archbishop Arundel's Constitutions, it is not likely that so many copies would have come down to us; for it was after that time a dangerous thing to possess, or to transcribe them. And yet, in spite of the danger, this was done;—there were those who were willing to face the penalties for heresy, rather than that the word of God should not be circulated: but still we have no reason to suppose that this was done except in comparatively rare instances. The Conventual and Collegiate libraries, too, which were the means of preserving so many of the literary productions of the middle ages, were closed against the writings and translations of Wiclif, unless, indeed, they happened to be buried in unknown obscurity; so that the possession of individuals must have been the means of transmitting them. Perhaps in this way they were more read and prized, while held as dangerous possessions, than they would have been if honoured with a known place in public libraries; and thus they were, I doubt not, the means of secretly instructing many who "sighed and who cried" over the evils which were wrought by those who professed to act in the name of Christ and of his apostles.

Copies of Wiclif's version transmitted through individuals

Such were the attempts made to hinder the circulation of the Scriptures, as well as the original writings of Wiclif, by the archbishop, and very ably were his purposes carried into execution. But the exercise of church authority was not yet fully carried out against Wiclif. In 1406, some of his friends at Oxford appear to have published an instrument, under the University seal, certifying his learning, probity, and godliness; they state that "in his answering, reading, preaching, and determining, he behaved himself laudably, and as a stout and valiant champion of the faith; vanquishing, *by the force of the Scriptures,* all such who by their wilful beggary [the mendicant friars] blasphemed and slandered Christ's religion. Neither was this doctor convicted of any heresy, either burned of our prelates after his burial. God forbid that our prelates should have condemned a man of such honesty for a heretic." This instrument is dated, "At Oxford, in our congregation-house, the 1st day of October, in the year of our Lord, 1406."

1406. The Oxford testimonial in Wiclif's favour. Fox, i 511

This testimonial appears to have drawn forth not a little opposition and anger on the part of the enemies of Wiclif and his doctrines; they tried to represent the document as being false or forged, although they could not deny that the University seal had been affixed thereto. Two years afterwards, as has been stated, Archbishop Arundel's Constitutions, condemning Wiclif and his works, were framed at Oxford. In 1410, the doctrines of Wiclif were condemned in a full congregation at Oxford; a vast number of propositions, as having been taken out of Wiclif's writings, were censured, and the books themselves were publicly burned. Any who maintained the doctrines which were thus censured were to lose their respective degrees. "But, as it happened, these opinions of Wiclif, instead of being stifled, gained ground by this opposition; and his books were more valued than before." Amongst these books, Wiclif's translation of the Scriptures, prohibited two years previously, is apparently to be included. The University of Oxford especially, as well as other parts of that which then was the diocese of Lincoln, was regarded as being "infected" with the

1410 The University of Oxford censures Wiclif's doctrines, and burns his books. Collier, iii. 287

The doctrines of Wiclif still

prevail at Oxford

heresies of Wiclif. This occasioned stringent measures on the part of Archbishop Arundel, in which he was supported by King Henry IV.*

Abp. Arundel applies to the Pope to burn Wiclif's bones, 1411

Amongst other means of dishonouring the memory of Wiclif, Archbishop Arundel wished for papal authority to burn his remains; he solicited the Pope to grant him a Bull, condemning the censured conclusions, and also authorizing this brutal act. It is probable that Arundel could hardly, after the lapse of so many years, proceed to disinter the remains of this servant of Christ unless he were supported by this authority. The Pope, however, condemned the "Conclusions" without sanctioning the burning of his bones.

Council of Constance, 1415

In 1415, however, the council of Constance granted the needful authority for the execution of this indignity: they solemnly condemned him as a heretic, and ordered the removal of his bones far from the burial of any church. Had Archbishop Arundel been alive at this time, the sentence would doubtless have been carried into immediate execution; but his successor, Chicheley, was otherwise occupied than in disturbing the repose of the dead. In 1428, Richard Fleming, bishop of Lincoln, who has been already mentioned as having for a time professed the doctrines of Wiclif, was commanded by Pope Martin V. to execute the decree, which he accordingly did. The bones of Wiclif were dug up and burned, and his ashes were cast into a stream which flows by Lutterworth:—it may seem to be an honour to his memory, that those who were so deeply busied in hindering the spread of the truth of God, and in persecuting those who held it, should have thus treated with indignity the unconscious remains of Wiclif. But strange indeed was it, if those who did it thought they were injuring one whose spirit was at rest in Christ, and whose body (whether mouldered into dust, or destroyed by the folly of man) will be changed and made like the body of Christ himself when he appears in glory.

Wiclif's bones ordered to be dug up

His remains burned, 1428

Throughout the remainder of this century, from time to time, scattered notices are to be found of those who, in spite of the danger, read and circulated the English Scriptures. From the extracts given by Fox, from the register of William Alnwick, bishop of Norwich, a few particulars may be learned relative both to the circulation of the word of God in English, and the danger of so doing. In the year 1429, a charge was made against Richard Fletcher, of Beccles, that he "is a most perfect doctor in that sect [namely, that of the Lollards], and can very well and perfectly expound the Holy Scriptures, and hath *a book of the New Law in English*, which was Sir Hugh Pie's first." This charge shews how completely the possession of the Scriptures in English was one ground on which to accuse a man of heresy.

Register of Alnwick, Bishop of Norwich

Lollards troubled, 1429

R Fletcher Fox, i 755. Charged with possessing the NewTestament in English

The next charge which is mentioned is the following:—"That Nicholas Belward, son of John Belward, dwelling in the parish of Southelam, is one of the same sect, and hath a New Testament, which he bought at London, *for four marks and forty pence* [i. e., £2. 16*s.* 8*d.*], and taught the said William Wright, and Margery his wife, and wrought with them continually by the space of one year, and studied diligently upon the said New Testament."

Nichs Belward charged with buying a New Testament

It was not uncommon to make a part of the charge against certain who were convented before the bishop *that they could read English*, making it at least probable that few of the common people, unless it was from the desire of reading the Scriptures for themselves, were able to do this. Some, who were accused of "Lollardie," had the fact of their possessing, or reading, the word of God in English, alleged in confirmation or aggravation; but some were charged with heresy simply upon this ground alone. For instance, the following is one of the charges:—"Sir Hugh Pie [a priest, who had intercourse with the Lollards] bequeathed to Alice, servant to William White, a New Testament, which they then called the Book of the New Law, and was in the custody of Oswald Godfrey, of Colchester."

Possession of the English New Test a sufficient ground for a charge of heresy

Fox, i 804.

Price of New Testaments in English.

The charge mentioned above against Nicholas Belward, shews us the sum for which a copy of the New Testament in English was at this time sold; Fox, in another part, when speaking of the invention of printing, refers to this circumstance, saying: "*Now* the same price will serve *forty* persons with so many books." It is a *very* moderate computation to suppose that now *four hundred* bound copies of the New Testament can (from the altered value of money and increased facility of production) be purchased for this sum. It is probable that so much was demanded on account of the peculiar danger which at this time attended the circulation of any portion of Scripture in English. In order to form some estimate of the value of four marks and forty pence at that time, it may be stated that this was then a sufficient yearly stipend for a curate.

* A respect for the memory of Wiclif seemed to linger long, or rather, perhaps, to revive, at Oxford; for, in 1564, that University annulled all its statutes against him —Collier, iii 338.

But although the danger in which any were placed who meddled with the English Scriptures did in part increase the price of copies of the word of God, yet it is to be remembered that the *invention of printing* was the great means of causing books to be produced at a moderate price. Few inventions can be so directly ascribed to the providential guidance of God as this may be; would that it had never been used for any end which should militate against his glory! But this, like every other gift of God, has been perverted to evil uses by the blindness of the heart of man. **Invention of printing.**

Fox, after speaking of this invention, under the year 1450, and discussing by whom, and how, it was discovered, speaks thus concerning the invention itself: "Notwithstanding, what man soever was the instrument, without all doubt God Himself was the ordainer and dispenser thereof, no otherwise than He was of the gift of tongues, and that for a singular purpose. And well may this gift of printing be resembled to the gift of tongues: for like as God then spake with many tongues, and yet, all that would not turn the Jews; so now when the Holy Ghost speaketh to the adversaries, in innumerable sorts of books, yet they will not be converted, nor turn to the Gospel." Fox's meaning clearly is, that innumerable sorts of books set forth the doctrine which the Holy Ghost wrote in the Scriptures. **Fox, i. 803.**

"Now, to consider to what end and purpose the Lord hath given this gift of printing to the earth, and to what great utility and necessity it serveth, it is not hard to judge whoso wisely perpendeth both the time of the sending, and the sequel which thereof ensueth."

After speaking of Papal efforts to suppress the truth, he says, "Although, through might, he stopped the mouth of John Hus before, and Jerome, that they might not preach, thinking to make his kingdom sure: yet instead of John Hus, and others, God hath opened the press to preach, whose voice the Pope is never able to stop, with all the puissance of his triple crown. By this printing, as by the gift of tongues, and as by the singular organ of the Holy Ghost, the doctrine of the Gospel soundeth to all nations and countries under heaven, and what God revealeth to one man, is dispersed to many, and what is known in one nation, is opened to all."

The results of Printing, as connected with the diffusion of the English Scriptures, belong, however, to a period subsequent to that in which they were known through the version of John Wiclif. There were many however who, in spite of the imminent peril, did both read the version of Wiclif themselves, and also taught it to others; and these efforts, amongst the poor of this world, continued, especially in the diocese of Lincoln, up to the era usually termed the Reformation. Not a few there were who suffered death on this very account: efforts still went on; and surely it was by the leading Spirit of God, that the word was thus read and prized in secret. **Continued effect of the labours of Wiclif. Martyrs for the word of God.**

The first attempt at giving forth any portion of the Scripture in print in English, is to be found in the Exposition of the Seven Penitential Psalms, by John Fisher, bishop of Rochester, which was published in the year 1505. Reprints of it were made in succeeding years; and from this we may learn that it was both read and circulated. It differs, however, widely from a mere translation; for the exposition is the part to which prominence is principally given; this, being by a Romish prelate, could not, of course, be suspected of any taint of heresy; the episcopacy of the author and translator, would in itself free it from the censure of Archbishop Arundel's constitution. **Bishop Fisher's seven penitential Psalms, 1505.**

PART II.

THE FORMER PART OF THE REIGN OF HENRY VIII.

I.

PERSECUTIONS ON ACCOUNT OF THE WORD OF GOD, 1519—21.

Changed circumstances at the period of the Reformation

A NEW era in the history of the English translations of the Scriptures commences with the Reformation of the sixteenth century. The light which had been struck by Wiclif had not ceased to shine, when the Scriptures were by the labours of others even more purely set forth for the illumination of those who were involved in the papal darkness. In several respects, the circumstances were changed; the Providence of God had brought to light the art of PRINTING, an art which has been an instrument of incalculable blessing in the diffusion of the word of God; books had not now to be multiplied by the slow labours of copyists; there was a new stimulus given to any effort to set forth the Bible in English.

The testimony borne by the remnant of the Lollards has, in several respects, to be distinguished from that which principally commenced with William Tyndale, Thomas Bilney, and George Stafford.

Persecutions on account of the word of God in English

It may be well just to notice the troubles of some who were persecuted but a little while before the time of the printing of the New Testament in English, on account of possessing a portion of the Scripture in their own tongue. This will shew how unchanged was the feeling of opposition which had led to the decree of Archbishop Arundel in 1408.

1521 Diocese of Lincoln. Lollards in Oxfordshire and Buckinghamshire. Fox, ii p. 23. Number and zeal of true professors

High prices paid for portions of Scripture.

Manner in which truth was communicated

The Register of the diocese of Lincoln gives many instances of the sufferings of the servants of Christ; they seem to have been either more numerous or else more active in the counties of Oxford and Buckingham (then both in the diocese of Lincoln,) than in other parts of the kingdom. Fox speaks of "great multitudes which tasted and followed the sweetness of God's holy Word, almost in as ample manner for the number of well-disposed hearts as now [i. e 1563] . . . The secret multitude of true professors was not much unequal: certes the fervent zeal of those Christian dayes seemed much superior to these our days and times, as manifestly may appear by their sitting up all night in reading and hearing; also by their expences and charges in buying of books in English, of whom some gave five Marks [£3. 6*s.* 8*d.*] some more, some less, for a Book: some gave a load of hay for a few Chapters of St. James, or of St. Paul in English. In which rarity of Books and want of Teachers, this one thing I greatly marvel and muse at; to note in the Registers [of the bishops] and to consider how the word of Truth notwithstanding did multiply so exceedingly as it did amongst them. Wherein is to be seen no doubt the marvellous working of God's mighty Power: for so I find and observe in considering the Registers, how one neighbour resorting and conferring with another, eftsoons with a few words of their first or second talk, did win and turn their minds to that wherein they desired to persuade them, touching the truth of God's word and his Sacraments. To see their travels, their earnest seeking, their burning zeals, their readings, their watchings, their sweet assemblies, their love and concord, their godly living, their faithful marrying with the faithful, may make us now in these our days of free profession, to blush for shame."

To understand aright the reason why Fox thus mused and marvelled, it must be remembered how severe the penalties were against any who read or possessed the Scriptures in English.

Dr John Colet Dean of St. Paul's

One of the first who was brought into trouble on this account was Dr. John Colet, dean of St. Paul's (the celebrated founder of St. Paul's school), who died in the year 1519. He was in many respects much in advance of the Romanists of the day in which he lived; and, although it is probable that the thought never crossed his mind of separating from the Romish Communion, yet the measure of truth which he held and preached was such, as both to excite the enmity of zealous Papists, and to attract to his ministry those who saw something of the light of God's truth; so much so, that it was made the ground of a suspicion of heresy that a person had been to hear him.

Bishop Fitzjames, of London, who was a determined enemy of all that was deemed heresy, was, a few years before his death, on the point of proceeding against Dr. Colet, alleging certain reasons for charging him with heretical opinions. This is no wonder, for at Oxford, before he was promoted to the deanery of St. Paul's, he had lectured publicly on the Epistles of St. Paul; and afterwards he was still accustomed to preach and teach Scripture, and not the opinions or writings of the Doctors. But although two bishops joined with Fitzjames in his accusation, the Archbishop of Canterbury, Warham, befriended him, and thus they were unable to injure him. One of the grounds on which they wished to make him appear a heretic, was his having translated the Lord's Prayer into English. This was in itself quite enough to cause a man to be regarded as a *fautor* of heresy, and therefore "violently suspected," so that such an one might be compelled to abjure all heresies, even if no specific crime were to be alleged as to doctrine.

Troubled by Bishop Fitz james

Abp. Warham befriends him

His having translated the Lord's prayer a ground of accusation.

That the Romanists would, at that day, judge a person to be a heretic, and burn him as such, merely on account of his possessing the Scriptures, or any portion thereof, in English, is proved by the fact of seven having been burned at Coventry in the year 1519, on this very account. The charge on which they were taken up by the bishop's officer, was their having taught their children and families the Lord's Prayer and the Ten Commandments in English, and their terrified children were examined to obtain evidence against them. One of them, a widow, was however dismissed by the bishop (probably for want of evidence); and as it was evening, Simon Mourton, the bishop's summoner, offered to go home with her. "Now as he was leading her by the arm, and heard the rattling of a scroll within her sleeve: 'Yea,' saith he, 'what have ye here?' and so took it from her, and espied that it was the Lord's Prayer, the Articles of the Faith, and the Ten Commandments, in English." Mourton, on discovering this evidence against her, said to her, "Ah Sirrah, come, as good now as another time!" and then led her back immediately to the bishop, who at once condemned her to be burned with the six men, who had previously been sentenced. They all suffered together on the fourth of April, 1519, in a place called the Little Park.

Seven martyrs of Coventry, 1519.

They all suffer, April 4th, 1519

There was another person who fled when the others were taken up, or else he would have been treated as they were. He was afterwards taken and burned.

The death of these martyrs appears to have occasioned a considerable excitement at Coventry: it was felt to be at least a strange thing, that they should suffer simply on account of teaching their children some portion of the word of God in English; in consequence of this, the Bishop and his officers industriously spread a report, that the cause of their condemnation to be burned, was not that they had the Lord's Prayer and the Ten Commandments in English, but that they had eaten flesh on Fridays and other fast days. This, however, does not appear to have been objected against them when they were alive.*

False reports spread about them after their death

The grounds of persecution in the diocese of Lincoln, were very similar to those which have just been mentioned as bringing several to the stake at Coventry.

In the year 1521, John Longland, bishop of Lincoln, carried on an active persecution against many of the poor in his diocese, who were suspected of being "*known men*." The manner in which evidence was obtained was this:—a suspected person who was convented before the bishop, was sworn to answer any interrogatories which might be put to him, he was then closely examined as to whom he was acquainted with, who were "known men," together with the circumstances which could be made definite matters of charge against such. Thus it was that relations were compelled, against their wills, to accuse one another, husbands and wives, parents and children, brothers, friends, and every other tie, was cruelly used for the purpose of obtaining ground of accusation against suspected persons. The cruelty of such a proceeding was very great, as great with regard to the unwilling accusers as with regard to the accused, it made them in many cases instrumental in bringing to punishment those who were dearest to them.

1521 Bishop Longland's persecution of "known men"

Manner of obtaining evidence

The results of the persecution of Bishop Longland, in 1521, were set forth in numerous articles

* The execution of these persons has been denied to be a fact, by a writer who offers not a tittle of evidence to disprove this, the direct statement of Fox.—(See Collier, vol. iv. p 27).

concerning doctrine or practice charged against a great many individuals. In Fox's extract from the Register of Lincoln, many particulars of persons and charges, referring distinctly to the circulation of the word of God in English, may be found. See Fox, vol. ii. pp. 23—40.

II.

INTRODUCTORY ACCOUNT OF WILLIAM TYNDALE—HE TRANSLATES THE NEW TESTAMENT.

Wm. Tyndale the first English translator from the Greek

We now come to the labours of those who used the providential advantages of the art of printing, and the spread of the knowledge of Greek and Hebrew, for setting forth the Scriptures in the vernacular tongue. The instrument in the hand of God for translating the New Testament into English, for the first time out of the original language, was William Tyndale, whose memory is on this account to be held in veneration by all who prize the word of God. If the labour of Wiclif was a means of blessing, in giving an English translation from the Latin Vulgate, how much more was that of Tyndale in rendering it *from the original*, and giving it forth *in print*. Wiclif could only draw the water of truth from a stream which was flowing from the fountain; Tyndale could go to the well-spring itself, and give forth the water not sparingly, but with a liberal hand. Had circumstances been reversed, Wiclif would undoubtedly have anticipated the work of Tyndale; but as it is, each occupies his fitting place in the diffusion of the English Scriptures; Wiclif, the first to publish the whole in our tongue, translated from the Latin; Tyndale, the first to publish *in print* the New Testament and a portion of the Old, translated from the original; while Myles Coverdale follows in their steps, as the first to complete and publish in print the *whole Scripture*, translated into English from the original tongues.

Coverdale Tyndale's successor

Tyndale's early life

We know comparatively little respecting the early life of William Tyndale, scarcely indeed more than we do of that of Wiclif; nor can we learn how his mind became first dissatisfied with the state of things then existing in the church:—we know to what this dissatisfaction led in result, but we know not *how* it was that his mind was wrought upon by God.

Born about 1477, in Gloucestershire

Fox, ii 301

Educated at Oxford

At Magdalen Read lectures

His character

The known circumstances of the life of Tyndale previous to his becoming a translator of the Scriptures may be told very briefly. He was born in Gloucestershire about the year 1477: he was "brought up from a child in the University of Oxford, where he, by long continuance, grew up and increased, as well in the knowledge of tongues, and other liberal arts, as especially in the knowledge of the Scriptures, whereunto his mind was singularly addicted; insomuch that he, lying then in Magdalen Hall, read privily to certain students and fellows of Magdalen College some parcel of divinity; instructing them in the knowledge and truth of the Scriptures. Whose manners also and conversation being correspondent to the same, were such that all they that knew him, reputed and esteemed him to be a man of most virtuous disposition and of life unspotted."

The state of learning at Oxford at the time

Tyndale proceeds to Cambridge at a later period

At Oxford, Tyndale had peculiar facilities for the acquirement of those branches of knowledge which he afterwards turned to so good account in the service of God. The introduction of Greek learning by Linacre, had given a new stimulus to study; and it is evident, from the results, that Tyndale profited well by the opportunities thus afforded him. Fox mentions, that after "proceeding in degrees of the schools," he removed to Cambridge: but, as he gives no date, we need not, as I judge, infer that he means that he immediately went to Cambridge after taking his degree at Oxford. Other circumstances, and a lapse of several years, I believe, intervened.

Tyndale's ordination

Offor's memoir, pp 7, 8

March 11, 1502

The next circumstance of Tyndale's life of which we have any account, is his ordination as a priest of the Romish church, which "took place at the conventual church of the priory of St. Bartholomew in Smithfield, on the eleventh day of March, 1502, by Thomas, suffragan bishop of Pavaden, by authority of William Warham, bishop of London, and was ordained priest to the nunnery of Lambley, in the diocese of Carlisle."* He could not have continued in the north of England for many years, since we find him ceasing to be a

* "Will. Tyndale Carliol. dioc ad tit. domus monialium de Lambley, ordinatur presbiter per D Thomam Paraden Ep'um, auctoritate Lond Ep' i xi Martij 1502, *Reg Warham*, Lond Kennett." (Bliss's Wood's Athenæ) I do not know from what place the suffragan styled *Episcopus Paradensis* (or *Pavadensis*) took his title. Qu. may he not have been an Italian, Ep *Patavensis*, and not an English bishop at all?

secular priest, and becoming a regular in 1508. The convent which he joined was that of the Observant Friars, at Greenwich.*

The fact of Tyndale having been a monk, was known from the following memorandum, which was found by the Rev. R. H. Barham, canon of St. Paul's, in a book in the cathedral library; "Charitive orate pro aia Johīs tyndall qui dedit hūc librū cōuentui de grenwych frum minorū de observancia die pfessionis sui filii frts Willmi. Anno 1508."†

He becomes a monk at Greenwich, 1508.

What his motives were in becoming a monk it may not be easy precisely to say; but *perhaps* it was with him as with so many before him; his conscience was aroused, he wished to have peace with God, and he sought, in the observance of a conventual discipline, to attain to the holiness for which he was longing. It may have been so: without direct evidence, it is not possible to penetrate the motives by which Tyndale was actuated; but if it were so, it follows that as yet he was in ignorance of the *finished* work of the Lord Jesus Christ, and the assured salvation through His precious blood to every one that believeth. The seclusion of a cloister, with its routine of observances, might suit one who was going about to establish his own righteousness, but not the soul which really felt the polluting stain of sin, and was conscious of the need of something to put it truly away.

Why did he become a monk?

For several years we know hardly anything of Tyndale: it is probable that he was in his seclusion at Greenwich; all those gifts which he was afterwards to use in God's service being buried for a time in a cloister. And yet so far as he was concerned, this period may have been anything but lost time; he was afterwards to "endure hardness, as a good soldier of Christ," and the process of learning the impotence of all the resources of nature may have been the very means ordered of God, for causing him to rest fully and firmly upon Christ, not only for salvation, but likewise for daily support.

Nothing known of Tyndale for some years

I have before intimated his having spent some time at Cambridge; and I do not doubt but that this must have been subsequent to the time of his becoming a monk by several years. The following are the reasons which lead to this conclusion:—those who have supposed that Tyndale migrated to Cambridge immediately, or at least soon after his taking his degree at Oxford, seem to think that his going thither was connected with a peculiar desire after learning, which was unsatisfied by anything which he could acquire at Oxford; but if this had been his motive, Cambridge, as it then was, would have been the last place to which he would have directed his steps. Indeed, the state of ignorance and even detestation of all real learning which then prevailed at Cambridge, is such as can scarcely now be imagined. Erasmus speaks of one college in Cambridge which, when he published the New Testament in Greek (first edition, 1516) absolutely forbade the use of it.

Sojourn at Cambridge about 1517—21.

Cambridge then not a place for improvement in learning

The testimony of Erasmus.

Thus learning could not have led Tyndale to Cambridge before the time of his becoming first a priest and then a monk; and, just so, there does not appear to have been any interval for him to have made any considerable stay there in the early part of his life. His avocation as a priest took him to the north of England; his noviciate at Greenwich, previous to his profession, occupied some time; and thus he can scarcely be supposed to have passed his recorded residence at that university until a later period of his life; his object, too, appears to have been a far higher one than that of study.

Tyndale's object in going to Cambridge

It was at Cambridge that his intimacy commenced with JOHN FRITH, subsequently his fellow-labourer, and at length his predecessor in becoming a martyr for Christ. Frith was at that time a student at Cambridge, and it would appear, from his acquirements in learning, that he was one who profited by the improvements at the time when that university was beginning, through the efforts of Dr. Barnes and others, to be a place where real learning could be found. Frith was converted by the testimony of Tyndale, "through whose instructions he first received into his heart the seed of the Gospel and sincere godliness." Thus it is evident that Tyndale both knew and preached the Gospel himself before, or at least during, his

John Frith converted by Tyndale

Dr Barnes's efforts to restore learning

Fox, vol ii. p. 250.

* This house was the first which, after Henry's rupture with the Pope, fell under his displeasure. Its inmates were warm opponents of his divorce. This monastery was one of the few which were refounded by Mary

† Previous to this time, he appears to have had his mind directed to the work of translating the Scriptures, or at least some portions of them, into English A Manuscript of some passages of the New Testament thus rendered is in the possession of Mr. Offor. In some places, the initials "W. T" are written, together with the date 1502 If this "W. T" be not William Tyndale, it is difficult to imagine who it could be It is probable that his mind was in some sort aroused to the value and authority of the word of God when at Oxford; and that, in becoming a priest, the object proposed by him was to preach to others some of that truth which he but partially knew himself. The fact of his making any translations from the Scripture shews him to be very different from the generality of those around him. This translation appears to have been from the Greek, which at this time must of course have been in manuscript. In John iii. 3, the Vulgate reads, "nisi quis renatus fuerit denuò;" this passage is translated, "born *from above*," which may be a translation of ἄνωθεν, but cannot be one of *denuò*.—For the examination of this MS., together with many books relative to Tyndale, &c. I am indebted to the kindness of Mr. Offor.

abode at Cambridge. The circumstance of Frith being there as a student during Tyndale's residence, supplies us with some farther proof of the lateness of the period at which he went thither.

Fox, ii. 301.

It appears, from the testimony of Bale, that at the time of Frith's martyrdom, 1533, he was only twenty-six years old; consequently he must have been born in 1507, or the preceding year: he was thus Tyndale's junior by thirty years, and he must have been quite young at Cambridge in 1519 and 1520. Tyndale's residence there could hardly have continued later than this last mentioned year, having probably commenced about 1516 or 1517.

Bilney, Stafford and Tyndale

Fox states that Tyndale became, at Cambridge, "farther ripened in the knowledge of God's word;" and this was not merely to the profit of his own soul, but likewise to that of others. The conversion of Frith through his means has been already mentioned; but there can be but little question that he was also in a great measure the instrument of at least a part of the diffusion of the light of the truth of God which took place at Cambridge at that time. The three persons to whom that university appears to have been especially indebted for instruction in the light of the Gospel were—Thomas Bilney, a faithful preacher, who suffered martyrdom at Norwich in 1531; George Stavert, or Stafford, who commenced lectures on Scripture, and afterwards died of the plague, taken when he was paying a visit of mercy; and William Tyndale. These were the instruments in the enlightening of Cambridge: from Cambridge the Gospel shone into Oxford, as well as into many other places in England.

Commencement of the Reformation at Cambridge, 1516-1517.

Fox, ii 219.

Strype, Mem Ecc. i. 323

The commencement of the Reformation at Cambridge appears to have been in the year 1516, or else the following, which was the very year when Luther published his Theses against indulgences. It was through the reading of Erasmus's Testament when first published (1516) that Bilney learned the Gospel. The passage on which his soul rested was 1 Tim. i. 15; this taught him what peace with God is, and on what it rests. He had, like Luther, sought it in many ways for years. This he began soon to preach to the conversion of many;—it seems to have been about the same time that Tyndale became acquainted with him, and from them others were taught. If their acquaintance commenced then, it is evident that Tyndale's residence at Cambridge began about that time.

Reformation at Cambridge, cotemporaneous with the testimony of Luther.

It is not of much importance to prove that the labours of Tyndale, Bilney, and Stafford at Cambridge were cotemporaneous with those of Luther at Wittemberg; but the fact is very evident. It shews this, however, that the testimony in England was not the consequence of any thing heard or known of a similar movement in Germany. Stafford commenced his lectures on the Scripture at Cambridge about the time when Dr. Colet was troubled for religion. It is absolutely impossible to place this commencement later than the year 1517; probably it was rather earlier. Bilney was the professor of civil law, and he, like Stafford, seems to have been a remarkable exception to the generality of those at Cambridge.

We must carefully bear in mind the distinction between the testimony of the remnant of the Lollards, and that which now commenced in England. The one had been the exposure of various Romish errors, the other brought forward the vital question, "How is a sinner forgiven?" While there was much of godliness in the one, and of the working of the Spirit, there was in the other a life-giving energy which made itself felt. It was indeed the distinctive manner in which the Holy Ghost was testifying to the Lord Jesus Christ.

Tyndale lives in Gloucestershire until 1522

Bliss's Wood's Ath Oxon.

From Cambridge it appears that Tyndale went into Gloucestershire, his native county, to be tutor in the family of a knight named Sir John Welch, at Little Sodbury, twelve or fourteen miles from Bristol. He continued there until about the end of 1522; during which period it is evident that his mind became more opened to the evils existing in the Church, and also to the controversies then pending respecting the Pope and Luther. It is clear that up to this time no public suspicion had attached to his name amongst the persecutors of those who were called heretics; for had this been the case, the diligent inquisitions of Bishop Longland, in his diocese of Lincoln, in 1521, would have been pretty sure to have elicited something against him, seeing that suspected persons were forced to accuse all whom they knew. Still this does not prove but that Tyndale knew something of these "known men" and their tenets. The society into which Tyndale was now thrown is thus described by Fox—"This gentleman, as he kept a good ordinary commonly at his table, there resorted to him many times sundry abbots, deans, archdeacons, with divers other doctors and great beneficed men, who there, together with Master Tindal, sitting at the same table, did use many times to enter communication, and talk of learned men, as of Luther and of Erasmus; also of divers other controversies and questions upon the Scriptures." This gave Tyndale an opportunity of entering into the subjects discussed, and pressing the testimony of the word of God upon those with whom he was thus thrown in contact; a discipline which, no doubt, led him into more close and precise acquaintance

Tyndale's association in Gloucestershire with dignitaries.

with the truth; while at the same time the arguments of Tyndale occasioned the others to bear a grudge against him.

Not long after this, "certain of these great doctors" had an opportunity of freely uttering their sentiments to the knight and lady with whom Tyndale lived, without his being present to reply to the propositions which they advanced; thus "uttering their blindness and ignorance without any resistance or gainsaying." The knight and his lady reported these things to Tyndale, and he replied from the Scriptures to the errors which had been brought forward; this led to his being charged with presumption by the lady, for setting *his* opinion above that of so many learned doctors. But it is humility rather than presumption to adhere to the written testimony of God, and to assert its paramount authority in opposition to all the wise arguments by which men may resist it.

The Doctors express their opinions in Tyndale's absence

Fox

Tyndale replies from Scripture

Tyndale was engaged at this time in translating, from the Latin of Erasmus, "*Enchiridion Militis Christiani;*" which he afterwards gave to Sir John Welch and his lady, who found in it that many of the things stated by Tyndale, were upheld by the testimony of Erasmus. This seems to have decided them that "the doctorly prelates" were wrong, and their own unbeneficed tutor in the right. This incident shews very remarkably, how much more ready the human mind is to bow to the judgment of one who is deemed learned and wise, than to submit to the authority of the word of God.

Tyndale translates "Manual of a Christian Soldier."

This rejection of their teaching rendered the clergy around yet more opposed to Tyndale; so that they were ready to seek any occasion which they could against him: at length they accused him of heresy, and laid their complaint before the Bishop's chancellor. Soon after this, Tyndale, and other priests, were summoned before the chancellor: it does not appear that he was formally cited to answer any given charge, but simply, in common with others, he had notice to attend. But, knowing the temper of the priests whom he would meet there, he expected that they would lay some accusations against him; and thus (as he said himself), "he by the way in going thitherwards, cried in his mind heartily to God, to give him strength fast to stand in the truth of *His word.*" It is important to observe, that the *word of God* and its authority, as coming from God himself, was continually the ground of Tyndale's testimony, and by it he was guided.

He is accused of heresy, and summoned.

At his appearance before the chancellor, it was evident that his adversaries had already prejudiced him against Tyndale; for although no one brought any public complaint against him, yet the chancellor threatened him, and made heavy charges, without however any *ostensible* ground. On this occasion, hard words were the worst that Tyndale received; a very different treatment than what he would have experienced from the bishops of Lincoln and Norwich, Longland and Nix.* After this, Tyndale conferred with an acquaintance of his, an old doctor who had been chancellor to a bishop, from whom he received a private statement of the opinion which he held: that the Pope is Antichrist mentioned in Scripture; but that it was a perilous thing to mention it, seeing that it would endanger any one's life; adding, "I have been an officer of his, but I have given it up, and defie him and all his works." It is most probable that these anti-papal sentiments were much in accordance with those which Tyndale had previously held in his heart. Tyndale, soon after this, was in company with a certain learned theologian; and in an argument this learned doctor, being hard pressed, exclaimed, "We were better to be without God's laws [*i. e.* the Holy Scriptures], than the Pope's [*i. e.* the Decretals]." Tyndale hearing this, burst through what many might deem prudent restraint, exclaiming, "I defy the Pope and all his laws! If God spare me life, ere many years, *I will cause the boy that driveth the plough, to know more of the Scriptures than you do.*" A bold pledge, but nobly redeemed! From this moment we find Tyndale prosecuting the object which was upon his mind twenty years before—the translation and publication of the Scriptures in English.

Tyndale threatened by the bishop's chancellor.

He confers with an old doctor

Tyndale defies the Pope, and pledges himself to translate the Scriptures

Tyndale was evidently at this time a reader of the writings of Erasmus, which (be their deficiencies what they may) contained at least a portion of truth then rarely to be met with. They may probably have known each other at Oxford, for Erasmus was at Magdalen College at the time when Tyndale was at Magdalen Hall. The sentiments of Erasmus may, perhaps, have helped to fix the thoughts of Tyndale on the making of an English version of the New Testament: Erasmus says, "I differ exceedingly from those, who are unwilling that the Divine writings should be translated into the language of the common people, and read by private persons; as if either Christ had taught things so obscure, that they could hardly be understood by a very few theologians; or as if the fortress of the Christian religion be set in this, that it be not known. Perhaps it is more wise to conceal the mysteries of kings, but Christ desires to publish His mysteries as much as possible. I would that all private

Erasmus an advocate for vernacular versions of the Scriptures

Eras Rot. Paraclesis, prefixed to his New Testament, 1519.

* It is not unlikely that Tyndale's freedom from persecution was owing, in part, to the fact that Jerome de Ghinucci, an Italian, residing in Italy, was at this time been bishop of Worcester, in which diocese Gloucestershire then was.

women should read the Gospel and Paul's Epistles. And I wish that they were translated into all languages, that they may be read and known, not only by the Scotch and Irish, but also by the Turks and Saracens. *To know* in what manner soever is certainly the first step. Let it be that many would smile, yet some would receive it. *I would that the husbandman at the plough, should sing something from hence;* that the weaver at his loom should sing something from hence; that the traveller might beguile the weariness of his journey by narrations of this kind. Let all the intercourse of all Christians be of these things; for our daily conversations will be such as we mostly are." It is scarcely possible to doubt that this sentence from Erasmus was in the mind of Tyndale in giving his bold reply; he almost cites it.

The opposition of the clergy increases

The opposition of the clergy around him now increased; heresy of every kind was laid to his charge; while he expressed the moderation of his desires, being willing to live any where on ten pounds a year, if he had but the liberty to teach children and to preach. In preaching, he appears to have been previously very diligent. St. Augustine's Green, Bristol, is mentioned as one of the places which he frequented for this purpose; this was at the time, I suppose, of his residence in Gloucestershire, in the family of Sir John Welch. He now left the situation which he then held, as chaplain and tutor; for it was evident, both to this worthy knight and to himself, that the molestation which he had already received, would be but the prelude to harsher measures.

Tyndale leaves Sir John Welch.

He comes to London about the end of 1522.

Tonstall appointed bishop of London, Oct 22, 1522

He came from Gloucestershire to London about the time that Dr. Cuthbert Tonstall had been appointed bishop of this see. It is probable that this circumstance in part induced him to come to London rather than try to find occupation in the country. It was on October 22, 1522, that Tonstall was appointed bishop of London; and thus it is likely to have been at the end of that year or the beginning of the next that Tyndale came to the metropolis. He had heard of Tonstall by report, and especially through the mention of him by Erasmus, and hence he seemed to expect to find in him a liberal-minded patron of learning and religion. This was to a certain extent the character of Tonstall. Through Sir Henry Guildeford, who was a friend both of Erasmus and of Sir John Welch, Tyndale sent to Bishop Tonstall an oration of Isocrates, translated into English, as a proof of his scholarship; the bishop, however, only returned him a civil answer, that his house was sufficiently filled with chaplains, and that he might probably, without difficulty, find occupation in London. Had the bishop known that Tyndale was only seeking a quiet resting-place, in order to translate the New Testament from Greek into English, it is likely that he would not have let him escape his hands so easily; and had Tyndale been other than a singularly guileless person, he would never have thought that the house of the bishop would be open to one who sought to translate the Scriptures into English.

Bp. Tonstall declines receiving Tyndale.

Humphrey Monmouth meets with Tyndale

Monmouth's account of Tyndale. Strype, Mem Ecc v 116

Some little time had probably elapsed between the arrival of Tyndale in London and his interview with the Bishop; for we find from the examination of a citizen of London named Humphrey Monmouth (in 1528), some particulars of this part of the life of Tyndale. The following is the account given by Monmouth in his petition addressed to Cardinal Wolsey, May 19, the twentieth year of the reign of King Henry VIII. (1528). He was charged with having furnished with money persons suspected of heresy, and with keeping heretical books. To the first of these charges he states in his petition that he had replied:—"I told them that iiij yeres past I did give unto a prieste called Sir William Tyndal, otherwise called Hotchens." . . . . . . "Upon iiij yeres & a half past and more, I herde the foresaid Sir William preach ij or iij sermons at St. Donstones in the West in London; & after that I chaunced to meet with him, & with communication I examyned what lyving he had. He said he had none at all, but he trusted to be with my Lord of London in his service. And therfore I had the better fantasy to him. And afterward he went to my lord & spake to him, as he told me, and my L. of London answered him, that he had chaplaines inough, & he said to him that he would have no more at that tyme. And so the priest came to me again & besought me to help him, & so I took him into my house half a yere, & there he lived like a good priest as methought. He studied most part of the day, & of the night at his book; and he woud eat but sodden meat by his good wil, nor drink but small single beer. I never saw him weare linnin about him in the space he was with me. I did promys him x *l.* sterling, to praie for my father & mother there sowles, and al christen sowles." This last statement shews how much superstition still clung to one who had already learned "the just shall live by faith." Habit and education often cause things to be practised without any consciousness of their inconsistency with the truths which the soul really treasures. The mind of Monmouth seems to have been deeply entangled in Romish errors; before his death, however, he had learned to rejoice in the light of the Gospel; his will gives abundant evidence of this.

Tyndale finds that he cannot translate the

During the time that Tyndale remained in the house of this Humphrey Monmouth, he had sufficient opportunity to make his observations on the state of things in England, and it appears from the account given by Fox that he learned that he could not with safety carry out his intention of translating the Scriptures in any part of this country. On this account, he resolved to leave England, being assisted so to do by some of his friends in London, and he turned his face towards Germany, where now the light of the Gospel which was in England dawning, had begun to shine brightly.

Scriptures safely in England

It must have been about May 1524, that Tyndale left the abode of Humphrey Monmouth; and it appears, from the petition already referred to, that he went almost immediately to Hamburgh. His poverty at this time has been already shewn; but it ought to be mentioned that he stood high in estimation as a scholar; in so much that if the object which was so near his heart had not led him to a foreign land in order to give his own countrymen the Scriptures in their vernacular tongue, he might have obtained a competency in England. The foundation of the College of St. Frideswide at Oxford, by Cardinal Wolsey, has been already mentioned; among others who were intended by Wolsey to be placed there, we find William Tyndale was one. Had this been carried into effect, it would have been an addition of one more to the many Reformers whom Wolsey ignorantly collected and congregated at Oxford.

May 1524, Tyndale leaves England. Sails to Hamburgh. Is in high estimation in England at this time. Cardinal Wolsey wishes to place him at St Frideswide's College Fox, ii 209

Sir Thomas More at a later period thus wrote of the character which Tyndale bore by common report before he left England. "Wyllyam Huchyn,* otherwyse called Mayster Tyndale, ... was (as men say) well knowen or he wente ouer the see, for a man of ryght good lyuyng, studyous and well lerned in scrypture, and in dyuers places in England was very well lyked, and dyd gret good with prechyng."

Sir Thomas More's testimony respecting him

Tyndale sailed from England to Hamburgh, but does not appear to have remained there long; for, having received money from Monmouth, he went into Saxony, where, amongst others, he met with him whose name stands amongst reformers as one of the highest—Martin Luther. There can be no doubt but that the time which Tyndale spent at Wittemberg, and amongst the German reformers in other places, was of no little use to him in opening his mind to many of the portions of popery—such as purgatory—prayers for the dead, and the like, which still adhered to him when he quitted England.

Tyndale goes to Wittemberg and meets with Luther. He learns more truth

But the great object for which Tyndale had become an exile from England, was that which especially engaged his attention. It must have been about the middle of 1524, that he reached Germany; and in less than two years the first edition of his version of the New Testament was printed. Fox mentions that Tyndale had conferred with his friend John Frith, about the value and importance of such a version, and the impossibility which there was of any thing material being accomplished for the dispelling of the ignorance which prevailed so widely in this country, unless this were done; and from this apparently the mistake has arisen that Frith was with Tyndale in Germany, and there assisting in the making of this version. Lewis states this, and others who assert the same have probably only copied from him. Now, the fact simply is, that Frith was, at the time of Tyndale's abode at Wittemberg, first of all at Cambridge, and then removed by Cardinal Wolsey to the new College which he had founded at Oxford, in which University he was incorporated in December 1525; at which place we shall find him getting into trouble on account, not of translating, but of circulating this version, and holding anti-popish principles.

His conference with Frith before leaving England. Frith not with Tyndale at this time. Frith at Oxford Dec 1525 Wood's Fasti.

It does not appear certain in what place the first edition of Tyndale's Testament was printed, but it may have been completed before he left Wittemberg; the number of copies struck off is variously stated, so much so as to make it altogether uncertain how large the impression was. This first edition is a small octavo volume, which appears to have contained merely the text of the New Testament, with a few pages "to the Reder" at the end.† Very shortly after the publication of this octavo edition, another in quarto with marginal glosses was published, and this certainly was one of Tyndale's own, and not one of the editions surreptitiously published by the Dutch printers. From an account given by Cochlæus, (a determined enemy to the Reformation,) we find that this second edition was commenced at Cologne, and, upon the conductors of it being driven from Cologne, it was completed at Worms; we further learn from him that it consisted of three thousand copies. He mentions 'two English *heretics*' who were engaged in getting out this edition; these, doubtless, were Tyndale himself and William Roy who is said also to have been his assistant in making the translation. This Roy was, like Tyndale, one of the Observant Friars of Greenwich, and he either accompanied him in his flight to Wittemberg, or else joined him there. Roy, at length, suffered martyrdom in Portugal in 1531.‡ It was in 1526 that this second edition of Tyndale's Testament was commenced at

1526. Tyndale's Testament, where printed. The first edition, 8vo A second edition 4to. with glosses. William Roy assists Tyndale. Anno 1531. Fox, ii 245

* Tyndale is frequently mentioned under this name: an ancestor of his is said to have assumed it as a disguise during the wars of York and Lancaster Tyndale himself sometimes used it in connection with his own name; "William Tyndale alias William Hitchens"

† This is the edition which was reprinted in 1836.

‡ Roy was a strange character. Tyndale speaks of him as winning friends with wonderful facility, and also as making more enemies than almost any man. Some of the instruments used by Roy against the Romanists were such as cannot be approved of. Satire and ridicule may appeal to the flesh, but can the truth of God be thus advocated? Wolsey received much provocation from some of Roy's verses; and Tyndale was at length obliged to warn others against falling into the same error as Roy had done. What led him to Portugal does not appear.

Cologne, so that we may judge that the first edition had before this been almost entirely sent to England. The two editions differed not only in form and appearance, but likewise in the latter having a prologue and glosses in the margin; it had also probably the Epistles taken from the Old Testament according to the use of Sarum. This I judge because surreptitious Dutch editions have these epistles at the end, and the publishers had no Englishman to correct the press, much less to add any thing else in English. The existence of this second edition seems to have been overlooked by almost every modern writer previous to Mr. Anderson and Mr. Offor, although the mention made of Tyndale's editions by Sir Thomas More and other circumstances might have shown the certainty of its having been printed: its existence is also proved by the fact of the New Testament, both with and without glosses, having been prohibited by Tonstall in this year.

Differences between the first and second edition.

Sir T. More and Bp. Tonstall mention both editions

III.

THE ENGLISH NEW TESTAMENT CIRCULATED IN PRINT,—ITS SUPPRESSION ATTEMPTED.

We have now arrived at an important period in the history of the circulation of the English Scriptures: the first translation of the New Testament from the original language had been made; and it was now actually printed and sent into England. That it was made from the Greek, no one can question who has examined it with care: it will be found continually to leave the readings of the Latin Vulgate, and adhere to the third edition of Erasmus's Greek Testament. Sometimes, indeed, great deference is paid to the critical observations of Erasmus; but still, the translation is made from the Greek and not from his Latin version. When Erasmus departed from the Greek (as he does in several places, apparently through inadvertence), Tyndale does not follow him, but adheres closely to the original. It is true, that Tyndale's first edition bears very evident marks of haste, but still the formation and publication in print of even a hastily executed version was a most important advance.

Tyndale's version made from the Greek Ed 3 Erasmi. 1522.

How was the New Testament received in England? It was almost at once diligently circulated in various parts; we find that not a few of the friends of Tyndale in England earnestly seconded his labours by disposing of these books even at their imminent peril. Some of the copies (probably of the first of the two editions,) reached England early in the year 1526; and it must have been in great secresy that the circulation commenced, for it was not until October 23rd in that year, that Bishop Tonstall issued his formidable prohibition. This, according to Strype, was done at the suggestion of Cardinal Wolsey. The prohibition expressly mentions that the English Testaments which were imported were "some *with glosses* and some without," thus proving that by this time the Cologne quarto edition had reached England. This makes it very probable that the first edition had been almost wholly dispersed in a very short time. All persons were required, within thirty days after the publication of this injunction, to deliver to the Bishop's Vicar General, under pain of excommunication, any copies of this New Testament which they might possess. The prohibition charged Tyndale with having craftily translated the New Testament into English, intermeddling therewith many heretical articles and erroneous opinions, pernicious and offensive, seducing the simple people. This "pestiferous and most pernicious poison" would, (the bishop said,) unless it were speedily foreseen, without doubt contaminate the flock committed to his charge with most deadly poison and heresy. If Tonstall could thus speak of Tyndale's version, the inference almost inevitably follows, that he charges the *Scripture itself* with being heretical. A system which avoids the light of God's truth stands condemned by the word of Christ Himself, John iii. 20.

Reception in England of the New Testament

Its circulation.

Bishop Tonstall's prohibition, Oct 23, 1526

Fox, ii 233 Strype, Ecc. Mem i. 261.

Copies to be given up within thirty days

In the two subsequent years we find many persons convented before their ecclesiastical superiors on charges connected with the possession or circulation of these books; but still, in these proceedings, blind as Bishop Tonstall was in prohibiting the word of God, it must be allowed that he shewed far more mercy to those who were on this account accused of heresy than did many of his cotemporaries.

Tonstall more merciful than many others

Bishop Tonstall not only published his official condemnation of the translation, but he likewise preached against it at Paul's Cross, setting forth to the people that it was a perverted translation, stating that there were in it no fewer than *two thousand* texts falsely translated. But although this assertion was made in order to depreciate the work in the minds of the people, yet it does not appear either to have had that effect, or to have diminished the demand for copies. The following is the account given by John Lambert

Lewis, p. 66.

of the impression which the preaching of Bishop Tonstall against the English New Testament made on him :—" Moreover I was at Paul's Cross, when the New Testament imprinted of late beyond the sea, was first forefended; and truly my heart lamented greatly, to hear a great man preaching against it, which shewed forth certain things that he noted for hideous errors to be in it, that I, yea, and not I, but likewise did many other think to be none. But (alack for pity!) malice cannot say well. God help us all and amend it."

Fox, ii. 348.

We learn some particulars relative to the circulation of this version after its prohibition, from the details of various persecutions for heresy about this time and a little later: by these we see that Oxford, London, and the diocese of Norwich were the parts in which these books were particularly circulated.

IV.

PERSECUTIONS FOR THE NEW TESTAMENT.

During the period which had elapsed between Tyndale's leaving England and the importation of his New Testament, Cardinal Wolsey's college had been set up at Oxford, and many from both universities were removed thither; thus were the doctrines of the Reformation planted in Oxford through that which was done by one, who, of all others, would have peculiarly dreaded such a result. It was thus that the labour bestowed by Tyndale, Stafford, and Bilney, at Cambridge, were transplanted to another soil where again they took root.

The College of St Frideswide founded

Fox, ii

Scholars from Cambridge removed thither, Dec. 1525

Amongst others who circulated the New Testament in English was Thomas Garrett (or Gerard) curate of All Saints, Honey-lane, London, who took many copies with him to Oxford, where he dispersed them amongst the students, but especially amongst Tyndale's Cambridge friends who were now removed to St. Frideswide's. Rumours of these things reached Cardinal Wolsey, and in consequence a search was made to apprehend Garrett; this was in February 1527. Before this time he appears to have circulated a great number of copies not only in Oxford but also in other places. Garrett was at length apprehended and compelled to do penance, by which, however, he did but little satisfy his persecutors, and if he had not escaped he would have got into farther trouble. He was at length burned in 1540.

Thos. Garrett a circulator of the New Testament

Latter part of 1526

A search made to find Garrett Feb 1527

He is apprehended and does penance

In St. Frideswide's college, copies of this prohibited volume were found in the possession of many of Tyndale's former Cambridge friends, who were imprisoned in consequence from February until August, "within a deep cave under the ground of the same college, where their salt fish was laid." John Frith was one of those who were thus confined, another was Cox, who was bishop of Ely in the reign of Queen Elizabeth. Three of these prisoners—Clerk, Sumner, and Bailey, became ill in consequence of having eaten nothing but salt fish from February till the middle of August, and then they all three died in the space of one week; Goodman, another of this company, was so ill when he was liberated that he died shortly after. These were four martyrs for the word of God and his truth; for though they suffered not at the stake, yet did they not love their lives unto the death for the sake of Christ their Lord. After the death of the three in prison, Cardinal Wolsey directed that Frith and the rest who survived should be set at liberty, they were, however, for some time restrained to the distance of ten miles from Oxford: subsequently, Frith left England and joined Tyndale.

Frith, &c imprisoned, Feb to Aug. 1527

Cox, &c.

Frith & others liberated
Frith leaves England

A little after this Bishop Tonstall had no small trouble in his own diocese on account of the circulation of the word of God in English, together with other indications of what was then deemed heresy. How far Tonstall acted, according to his own judgment, in these proceedings, may, perhaps be questioned; he was at this time Cardinal Wolsey's commissary, and he had to act as such. In the autumn of 1527, Bilney was taken up on a charge of heresy; and his recantation seems to have made others more willing to take the same course in order to escape from present suffering. The preaching of Bilney and the New Testament put forth by Tyndale, had, however, done very much for the introduction of the truth of God into London and Essex, as well as other parts. There was, in consequence, a Visitation of the whole of the dioceses of London, for the purpose of purging it of anti-popish books and doctrines. From the account of this visitation given by Strype, it is to be seen that the dispersers of the *printed* New Testament were, many of them, those who had previously been known as Lollards, who circulated manuscript copies of portions of the Scripture. Amongst others who were charged with keeping these forbidden books was Sebastian Herris, curate of Kensington; he had "the New Testament in the vulgar tongue, translated by William Hochyn [Tyndale], priest, and Friar Roy." He was obliged to give up the books, to receive no

Bp Tonstall's proceedings

He visits his diocese

Strype, Mem. Ecc i 114-137

The Lollards circulate the New Test.

Seb. Herris accused, Feb. 24, 1528.

more of them, and leave London for two years, under pain of excommunication; this last-mentioned injunction is stated to be because of London "being so dangerous a place to be infected with heresy." Several persons in Essex, especially at Colchester, were summoned on charges connected with the possession of the New Testament in English. Some of these had written copies, some of them Tyndale's printed version. One of these, named John Pykas, was summoned before the Bishop, March 2, 1527 [1528, according to the present computation, making the year commence Jan. 1, instead of March 25]; he had had certain books of Scripture in English, "one book of Powle's Epistoles" was one of them. "Also, about a two years last past, he bowght in Colchestre, of a Lumbard merchant of London, a New Testament in English, and payd for it foure shillinges. Which New Testament he kept, and read it thorowghly many tymes. And afterward, when he herd that the said N. Testaments were forbaden that no man should keep them, he delyvered it and the book of Powle's Epistoles to his mother agen." In this statement, Pykas speaks of the Testament which he had, as being the one that was *afterwards* prohibited; this marks it as being Tyndale's, although he does not mention that it was printed; and the time at which he received it having been so early, proves that the New Testament must have been circulated in England as soon almost as it was printed. It is probable that the rapid circulation of the first octavo edition, occasioned it to be so speedily followed by the quarto impression, with glosses and prologues.

London, a dangerous place for heresy.

March 2, 1528. John Pykes

Price of a New Testament.

This Testament Tyndale's.

Another who was convented before the bishop during this examination, was Robert Forman, S.T.P., rector of the parish of All Saints, Honey Lane: the principal charge against him was the possession of the books of Luther. It is probable that his sentiments were the same as those of Thomas Garrett, his curate, whose labours in circulating the English Testament at Oxford have been already mentioned.

R Forman convented. Mar 19, 1528

But of those who were apprehended at this time no one appears to have been so extensive a circulator of these books as Robert Necton; the following is a part of his confession:—"He bowght at sondry tymes of Mr. Fyshe,* dwellynge by the Whight Frears, in London, many of the New Testaments in English; that is to say, now v. & now x.; and sometyme mo & sometyme less, to the nombre of xx. or xxx. in the gret volume. The which New Testaments the said Mr. Fyshe had of one Harmond, an English man, beyng beyond see. But how many he had this respondent cannot tell. And this respondent saith, that about a yere & half agon, he fell in acquaintance with Vicar Constantyne, here in London; which shewed this respondent first that the said Mr. Fyshe had New Testaments to sell; & caused this respondent to by some of the said New Testaments of Mr. Fyshe." He afterwards gives an account of some of those to whom he had sold copies. By this confession, we learn more particulars than we otherwise could respecting the manner in which the copies were introduced to England. Fyshe received them from Harmond, or Herman, an English merchant at Antwerp; and then through this Necton, Vicar Constantine, and probably Garrett, as well as others, they were sold in many directions. Necton himself was an itinerant circulator of the word of God; he mentions many places in which he had disposed of copies..... "this respondent saith that about the same tyme he sold fyve of the said New Testaments to Sir William Furboshore, synging-man, in Stowmarket, in Suffolk, for vii. or viii. grotes apece. Also, two of the same New Testaments in Bury St. Edmunds."...."Also he saith, that about Cristmas last, he solde one New Testament to a priste, whose name he cannot tell, dwellyng at Pycknam Wade, in Northfolke."...."Also, one New Testament to William Gibson, merchaunt-man, of the parish of S. Margaret Patens." After mentioning various dealings with Vicar Constantine, he stated, "Also, he sold Sir Richard Bayfell [Bayfield] two New Testaments unbound, about Cristmas last, for the which he payd iij. *s.* iiij. *d.*" He stated that since the preceding Easter he had bought of Geffray Usher, the servant of Mr. Forman, of Honey Lane (already mentioned), eighteen New Testaments, of the smaller volume; "of which New Testaments, since Easter this respondent caryed xv. of them.... to Lynne to sell." These he had left at Lynn, finding a difficulty in selling them, because of the prohibition. "And two of the said New Testaments he hath in his own custodie, with another of the great volume."

Robt Necton convented

Strype Mem Ecc v, 377

Places where the New Testament was sold

Bayfield buys one for 3s 4d

At the preceding Christmas, a Dutchman, who was now in the Fleet, offered Necton two or three hundred copies of the English New Testament for sale; he did not buy them, but sent the man to Fyshe, offering to purchase if Fyshe would do the same; "for the which iij. hundreth he shold have paid xvi *l.* v *s.*, after ix *d.* a pece." [In the price there is some mistake; it should be either "xvi *l.* v *s.*, after xiii *d.* a pece," or else, "xi *l.* v *s.*, after ix *d.* a pece;" the latter, I judge, to be the more probable; but either of these sums would prove that the profits were considerable.]

A Dutchman, in the Fleet, offers New Testaments for sale

It is probable that the Dutchman who offered these copies of the New Testament to Necton for sale was

* Probably this was Simon Fyshe, the author of a remarkable paper entitled, the "Supplication of Beggars;" to which Sir Thomas More replied in his "Supplication of Souls."

John Raymond, who was this year abjured for having caused fifteen hundred copies of Tyndale's New Testament to be printed at Antwerp, of which edition he had brought to England five hundred. *The Dutchman probably John Raymond. Fox, ii. 260*

A considerable number of copies of the New Testament must have been collected in consequence of the prohibition, and the ulterior proceedings connected with the visitation; these seem to have been publicly burned at Paul's Cross, sometime in the year 1528. This burning is alluded to by Sir Thomas More (who defends it as a good deed), as well as by Tyndale himself. Other burnings of these books took place at subsequent periods, which have often been erroneously confounded with what was done in this year. *Many copies of the New Testament collected, and burned, 1528*

This burning of the word of God did not, however, cause the version to be disregarded; it rather led to a suspicion that there was some sinister purpose in thus keeping the Scriptures from the eyes of the people. Tonstall, however, shortly after carried on his zeal in destroying the Scriptures on a larger scale than he had done before.

Another means adopted by Tonstall to crush Tyndale and his translation was by employing the pen of Sir Thomas More to oppose the exiled monk. For this purpose he gave him, on the 7th of March, 1527-8, a licence to read these prohibited books—the New Testament, and some original writings of Tyndale, which had been proscribed by the same injunction. Sir Thomas attacked Tyndale with hearty goodwill in the cause of "holy Church," but in his attacks on the translation he utterly failed; he stated indeed that he found one thousand texts by tale falsely rendered (that is, *one half* the number named by Bishop Tonstall) but in his specification of faults he had but little to say. He had before him two editions, the octavo and the quarto with glosses; the marginal notes of the latter come in for their share of censure. The *distinct charges* against the translation are that "*Priests*," "*Church*," and "*Charity*," are translated "seniours," "congregacyon," and "love;" and also that *grace* was sometimes rendered by *favour*, *penance* by *repentance*, and *a contrite heart* by *a troubled heart*. Such were the trifling reasons assigned for the prohibition and burning of the New Testament. The true one clearly was this, that the same feeling which prompted the constitution of Archbishop Arundel, in 1408, led to similar actions on the part of the popish authorities in the days of Tyndale. *Tonstall engages Sir T More to write against Tyndale. Mar. 7, 1528* *More's Dialogue, book iii ch. 8*

The alleged ground of prohibition, namely, the perversion of meaning in the English translation, had been thus expressed by Bishop Tonstall in his original prohibition in 1526. He stated that certain "blinded through extreme wickedness, wandering from the way of truth, and the catholic faith, craftily have translated the New Testament into our English tongue, intermeddling therewith many heretical articles and erroneous opinions," &c.; now unless it were shewn *what* these offending opinions were, it could not be said whether they were or were not maintained by Tyndale's translation. At all events, before the translation was thus prohibited and the books destroyed as being faulty, the errors or wilful perversions in translating should have been stated. It is no doubt quite true that the version upholds what Tonstall and More called heresy; but this simply results from its *not* being a perversion of the original. *The ground of prohibition*

Meanwhile the Dutch printers were multiplying the copies of the English New Testament; in this they seem to have been simply actuated by the love of *gain*, a clear proof that in spite of strict prohibitions, and the fear of the spiritual authorities, the word of God was making its way among the people. The penalties of heresy (death by burning in case of relapse), would not have been lightly risked had there not been a deep and earnest desire for the possession of the pure word of God in a tongue known by the people. *The Dutch printers multiply copies of this New Testament.*

The first of these Dutch editions appears, from the account given by George Joye, to have been published in 1527, and a second in 1528 or 9. This second must have been taken from Tyndale's quarto edition, because as the Dutch printers had no Englishman to correct the press for them, they could not have added any of the marginal glosses. The following account is given by George Joye of the two surreptitious editions*—"Anon aftir the dwchemen gote a copye, & printed it agen in a small volume adding the kalendare in the beginning, concordances in the margent, & the table in thende. But yet, for that they had no englisshe man to correcte the setting, thei themselues, hauyng not the knowledge of our tongue, were compelled to make many mo fautes then were in the copye, and so corrupted the boke, that the simple reder might ofte tymes be taryed and steek. After this thei printed it agein also without a correctour in a greatter letter & volume, with the figures in thapocalipse, which were therefore miche falser then their firste." It is most probable that the three hundred copies offered for sale to Robert Necton by a Dutchman were of the former of these two editions. The object of the Dutch printers having merely been profit (so entirely so that they did not even employ an English press corrector), *Two Dutch editions, 1527, and 1528.* *Joye's account of these editions.*

* I have to thank Mr Offor for the use of a transcript made *verbatim et literatim* by himself of that very scarce tract "Joye's Apology."

of course *accuracy* was little cared for; the demand for the copies appears to have been such as to make them saleable however carelessly executed. Tyndale meanwhile was busily engaged in publishing other works, urging on the same object which had led him to translate the New Testament. In those which were subsequently written he refers in a very interesting and affecting manner to the treatment with which his translation had been received in England; he says in one place, "Some man wil aske parauenture why I take the laboure to make this worke, in so moch as they will brunne it, seinge they brunt the gospel. I answere in brunninge the Newe Testamente they did none other thinge then I loked for, no more shal they doo if the brunne me also, if it be Gods will it shall be so." Thus was he willing to toil laboriously even if it were in the hope of getting but a few copies of the word of God into circulation in England.

Tyndale's reference to the burning of his books.

The allusions to the burning of the New Testament, which are made by both Sir Thomas More and Tyndale, seem as though they referred to something more definite than the mere burning of the copies which were collected, which could hardly have attracted such peculiar attention. It is most probable that Tonstall succeeded in seizing some of the proscribed books in considerable quantities, and then publicly burned them at Paul's Cross. To this Tyndale seems to refer in the passage just cited, looking forward to his own probable fate; and just so Sir T. More says, "Yt is enough for good cristen men that knowe those things for heresyes, to abhorre and burne vppe his bokes and the lykers of them with them."

Antwerp was the place from which the New Testaments of these four editions were principally exported to England; and therefore any attempt to suppress them in this country must have proved abortive, so long as they continued to be supplied from the Netherlands. Bishop Tonstall had, however, soon an opportunity of doing what he could to prevent their exportation from Antwerp; in 1529 he went thither, probably in company with Sir T. More, on his return from the embassy at the treaty of Cambray; and then he purchased, through one Packington, all the copies of the New Testament which were there for sale; these are mentioned by Halle as having been *all* burned with many other books in St. Paul's Church-yard, in May, 1530. Lord Herbert dates the burning, May 4, 1530. It has been alleged that Tyndale was himself implicated in the sale of these books to the Bishop, but the fact is that he was at Hamburgh at this very time. It is possible that he went thither to avoid the bishop, but at all events his being there proves that he had nothing to do with this sale at Antwerp.*

Tonstall at Antwerp, on his return from Cambray, 1529; buys Testaments

Burning of the New Testament, May 4, 1530.

Tyndale's absence from Antwerp.

So carefully were the distributed copies of the four first editions of Tyndale's Testament collected and destroyed, and so thoroughly did Tonstall procure all that were to be had in Antwerp, that these editions are almost totally extinct. Of the first edition but one perfect copy is in existence (the one from which the reprint of 1836 was executed); of the second (the quarto with glosses) only a fragment appears to be known; while the two Dutch editions have fared scarcely any better. Another edition was published by the Dutch in 1530.

Tyndale did not now confine himself to writing original works: he continued his labours of translation, commencing the Old Testament. Scarcely any thing seems to be known about where he lived, from the time of the publication of his Testament until the year 1529, except that in May, 1528, he was at Malborow (Marpurg) in Hessia, where he published some books. In the early part of this year Fox mentions his having sailed from Antwerp with the intention of going to Hamburgh; he was, however, shipwrecked on the coast of Holland: this makes it not unlikely that he had been mostly at Antwerp, or in the neighbourhood, during the interval, and there had carried on his labours. He continued his voyage, and reached Hamburgh in safety, where he found MYLES COVERDALE, now an exile from England waiting to receive him. It is probable that Coverdale had been known to Tyndale during the abode of the latter at Cambridge.

1529. Tyndale goes to Hamburgh

Shipwrecked.

He meets Coverdale.

Fox says, that "at his appointment Master Coverdale tarried for him, and helped him in the translating of the whole five books of Moses, from Easter till December, in the house of a worshipfull widow, Mistress Margaret Van Emmerson, Anno 1529, a great sweating sickness being the same time in the town."†

* The story, as told by Halle, implies that Tyndale was the seller of the books to Packington; this would hardly have been likely even if Tyndale had been at Antwerp, for it was the Dutch printers who had got out the two latest editions for supplying England. As to the disclosures made by George Constantine, I place little reliance on them: his whole life was such a tissue of duplicity, that it is most probable that, when questioned by Sir Thomas More, he stated whatever he thought most fit at the time. Let it be remembered that Constantine was, in the reign of Edward VI, registrar to Bishop Farrar, of St David's, he seems to have instigated the vexatious proceedings instituted in that reign against the bishop; and in the days of Mary he acted as registrar when Farrar was degraded and given up to be burned.

† The accuracy of this statement as to date, &c, appears from enquiries made at Hamburgh in the autumn of 1840 by Mr. Offor, which he has kindly communicated to me. There was at this time at Hamburgh the widow of a senator, named Van Emmerson, whose proper style would be *worshipfull widow* (ehrwürdige Wittwe), and it was also in this very year, 1529, that the sweating sickness was raging there. The exactness of the date is important, as proving Tyndale's absence from Antwerp.

Part of the Pentateuch published

Strype, Ecc. Mem. i 262

Genesis printed Jan 1530.

At Marpurg, Jan 1530

It was not long after this time that part of the Pentateuch of Tyndale's translation was published. "The chapters of the book of Moses called Genesis," and "The Chapters of the Book of Deuteronomy," are marked by the Bishops as falling under the class of books prohibited by the king's proclamation in 1529. These of course are of Tyndale's translation, and the specification of these two portions of the Pentateuch seems to shew that the other three books were not circulated in England until afterwards. The different books of the Pentateuch, as published by Tyndale, were printed at various places and in various types: Genesis was printed "at Malborow in the land of Hesse .... in the yere of our Lord MCCCCCXXX the XVII daye of January." Thus after he left Hamburgh we find him, in the beginning of the next year, "at Malborow in the land of Hesse," whence probably before long he went to Antwerp.

Proclamation, 1529

Books prohibited. Genesis, Deuteronomy, and the Psalter.

Seven Penitential Psalms

The prohibitory proclamation just referred to, issued in 1529, gives very extended authority to the prelates in proceeding against persons suspected of heresy. A long list of books falling under the description of those forbidden, is subjoined in the bishop's register, the greater part in Latin, but some in English; in this list of condemned publications we find, besides Tyndale's Genesis and Deuteronomy, "David's Psalter in English," and "Seven Psalms;" the former of these must be the English Psalter printed by Francis Foxe at Argentine (Strasburgh), Jan. 16, 1530. Some account of this Psalter will be given at the close of the memorials relative to Tyndale's version and revision. As to the "seven Psalms," it appears as though the seven penitential Psalms translated into English by Bishop Fisher were meant: if so, it shews a determined attempt to suppress the English Scriptures; not only to condemn versions made by one who was deemed a heretic, but likewise that which had been executed by a bishop whose adherence to the doctrines and discipline of Rome was not to be questioned. It is evident that the people were not to be allowed to have the smallest portion of the word of God in their own tongue without incurring danger.

Tyndale's Pentateuch, first portion of the Old Testament made from the original, and printed in English.

This brings another important era in the history of English translations of the Scriptures before us. The Pentateuch of Tyndale was the first portion of the Old Testament which was translated into English out of the Hebrew; and thus the books of this translation, published at separate times, and in different places, claim an honourable precedence as respects the Old Testament, just as Tyndale's octavo edition of 1526 claims with respect to the New. The manner in which the singular volume, Tyndale's Pentateuch, is executed, shews that his must have been a very itinerant life: probably he was often straitened for means; and thus it was only from time to time that he could publish one after another of the books of the Old Testament.

Frith with Tyndale

It is not unlikely that John Frith was Tyndale's assistant in translating this part of the Scripture, since after his escape from England he was with him, and he was apparently at Hamburg at the same time; and this has probably led to the supposition of his having aided Tyndale in the translation of the New Testament, which was published a year and a half, at least, before Frith had quitted Oxford.

Continued enmity in England against Tyndale.

His subordination to authority.

"Obedience of a Christian Man"

Only limit of obedience, Acts iv. 20.

The enmity of the authorities in England against the person of Tyndale and his writings, but especially his translations, still continued unabated; while he, a forlorn exile, seems to have gone on in dependance upon God, and in full resignation to His will. One thing is important, his full recognition of the authority due to his Sovereign as being the ordinance of God: if any thing could have loosed him from this bond it might be thought that persecution for Christ's sake would have done so. In one of his proscribed works, "The Obedience of a Christian Man," he largely states the duty which ought to be cheerfully paid by a Christian to his prince as being the ordinance of God to him for good; thus shewing that he was actuated in making his translation of the Scriptures, not by a feeling of insubordination, but with the spirit of those who, when forbidden to teach or preach in the name of Jesus, replied, "Whether it be right in the sight of God to hearken unto you rather than unto God, judge ye; for we cannot but speak the things which we have seen and heard."

Effect of the testimony of Tyndale

The doctrines and the testimony of Tyndale, gave, perhaps, even more offence than they would have given, had he simply raised his voice against Romish corruptions, because the exposure of evil was the more marked, from the contrast in which it stood to the *truth* which he at the same time presented. The deepest ground of the enmity was clearly his having printed and published, for the first time, the word of God in English.

V.

FURTHER PERSECUTIONS AND EFFORTS FOR THE SUPPRESSION OF THE SCRIPTURES.

Renewed opposition, 1530.

THE continued labours of Tyndale to impart the light of Scripture to his countrymen, were not unnoticed in England. The year after Bishop Tonstall had purchased all the copies he could procure of the Testament at Antwerp, measures yet more stringent were resorted to, in order to prevent the spread of the Scriptures. This argues equally the fear which existed lest the light of God's word should make manifest the surrounding darkness, and the extreme difficulty there was in keeping the people from reading these proscribed books. It may be, that this restraint produced the desire of knowing *what* the prohibited books really contained, and that curiosity led to the procuring and retaining of that forbidden volume; while it is also yet more probable, that comparatively few were bold enough to dare the denounced penalties, unless their hearts had been wrought upon by the Spirit of God, to know and believe the love which God hath to us, and thus to desire to know what is His revealed will.

Restraint excites curiosity.

Bishop Tonstall took, as has been already shewn, the leading part in destroying the copies of the New Testament in English, which either were detected in England, or which were procured elsewhere; but while this temerity, on his part, is mentioned with due reprehension, it is but right to state, that he was far more merciful to the individuals who were brought before him, charged with the crime of possessing the Scriptures, or other grounds of "heresy," than others of the prelates were. Longland, the bishop of Lincoln, was in the habit of sending men to the stake for reading the Scriptures in English, and in this way there was, in his diocese, more of the sufferings of individuals on account of the word of God than in other parts. The burning of the books of the New Testament (apparently those purchased at Antwerp, in 1529) in public, at St. Paul's Church Yard, having taken place May 4, 1530, there was an assembly held in the same month, which seemed to set all the weight of human *authority*, both civil and ecclesiastical, against Tyndale and his translation. A few days after this great burning of the New Testament took place, several of the clergy, Richard Nix, bishop of Norwich, amongst the rest, had made such complaints as should reach the king's ears, concerning the prevalence of the diffusion of Tyndale's Testament; these complaints appear to have led to the publication of a prohibition, on the king's part, of all such books in English.

Public burning of the New Testament, May 4, 1530

Bishop Nix complains of Tyndale's Testament May 14, 1530 Cott. MSS. Cleop E. v. p. 360.

On May 24, 1530, there was an assembly convened by Archbishop Warham, the especial object of which was to examine, and formally to condemn, the books published and circulated by those who were disaffected to the church of Rome. The persons who met on this occasion were, the Lord Chancellor Sir Thomas More, Archbishop Warham, Bishop Tonstall, Stephen Gardiner, (afterwards bishop of Winchester), and several others, apparently delegates from the Universities. The documents drawn up on the occasion are probably from Gardiner's pen, who was the secretary, and one who very fully concurred both with the object of the convention and the measures to be adopted. By the instrument published on the occasion, it appears that the archbishop convened the assembly by direction of the king, who, "hearing that many books in the English tonge, containing many detestable errors and dampnable opinions, prynted in parties beyonde the see, to be brought into diuerse townes and sondrie parties of this his realm in Englande and sawen abrode in the same, to the great decaye of our faithe, and the perylous corrupcion of his people, vnles spedye remedye be brieuelie prouided," his highness, considering also that he, being defender of the faith, would be "full lothe to suffre suche euill sede sowen amongest his people, soo to take roote that it myght ouergrowe the corne of the Catholic fayth," before sprung in the souls of his subjects. After this there followed a vast number of propositions, said to be drawn from the condemned books, each of the propositions is declared to be a heresy, while it is also said that those selected are but samples of the books themselves. But the great object was the proscription of the Scriptures in English; it was not enough to declare Scripture doctrines, such as justification through faith, to be a heresy, the books in which this teaching is found must be restrained if possible; for this reason, the instrument itself concludes thus:—"All whyche great errours and pestylent heresyes beying contagyows and dampnable, wyth all the bookes contenyng the same, *whith the translacyon also of Scrypture corrupted by Wyllyam Tyndall as well in the Olde Testament as yn the New*, and all other bookys yn Inglisshe contenyng suche errours; the Kyngs hyghnes present yn p̄son, by oone hole advyse and assent of the prelattys and clerkys, as well of the unyuersytes as all other, assembled together, determyned vtterly to be expelled reiected and putt away owt of the handys of hys

Assembly for condemning the English Scriptures, &c. May 24, 1530. Collier iv 140.

The original at Lambeth.

Consequences said to result from the books of the reformers.

Tyndale's versions both of the New Testament and the Old condemned.

people, and not to be suffered to go abrode among hys subiects." After a few more similar remarks, there follows a bill in English, which was to be publicly read by certain preachers; the object of this proceeding being to give due information to all, of the solemn condemnation of the books in question.

A bill to be read by preachers

This bill deserves a very particular notice: it appears to be drawn up with peculiar care; and in its statements it is to a great degree guarded; the whole, however, turning upon entirely false premises. It sets forth that in the assembly for the purpose of examining the suspected books, "free lybertye and lycence were graunted vnto euery man to say as hys conscyence and lernyng serued hym; wythowt any reprove or blame to be ymputed or arrected for any thyng to be spoken then, whose p̄son soever yt touched; or any necessytie to agree to the more parte; but only to say that hys owne learnyng and conscyence coulde maynetayne and justyfye after mature delyberacyon and consultacyon had, it was thereby a hole consent, no man repugnyng or aȝen sayng, determyned and agreed, that the bookys now beyng abrode yn thenglysshe tonge, conteynyng false tradycyons and corrupte doctryne farr dyscrepant from the trewe sense of the Gospell and Catholicke vnderstondyng of the Scrypture; only persuadyng pernycyous heresyes to the destruccyon of the sowles of good chrysten men: and that the certentie herof I can reporte to yowe of my owne knowlege beyng oon of the sayd assemble, and hearyng and seyng the sayd opynyons redd declared and examyned, and by the trewe sense and meanyng of goddys lernyng reproued and reiected." Then follows an earnest admonition against both the books and doctrines; after which the bill continues:—

The judgment said to have been unanimous

"Wherfore yow that haue the bookys, called the obedyence of a chrysten man̄, The sume of Scripture, The Reuelacyon of Antichryst, The supplicacyon of Beggars, Māmona iniquitatis, The matrymony of Tyndall,* *The New Testamente in Inglysshe of the translacyon whiche ys nowe prynted*, and suche other bookys yn Englysshe; the auctours wherof other darr not or do not put to ther names, be [they unknowen vnto yow, or els be they suche as haue set forth their]† pnycyouse books, *detest them*, *abhorre them*, kepe them not in yowr handys, delyuer them to the superyours suche as call for them: and yf by redyng of them heretofore, anythyng remayneth yn yor brestys of that techyng; ether *forgett* yt, or by ynformacyon of the trewthe, expell it and purge it, to thentent that ye so purifyed and clensid of that contagyows doctryne, and pestyferows tradycyons may be fyt and apt to receve and reteyne the trewe doctryne and understondyng of christs lawes, to the comforth and edyfycacyon of owr souls: thus I move and exhorte yowe in god to doo, thys ys yowr dewtie to doo thys ye owght to doo, and beyng obstynatt or denyyng and refusyng this to doo, *the prelatys of the church hauyng the cure and charge of your sowles owghte to compel yowe, and your prynce to ponysshe and correct yowe not doyng of the same:* unto whom saynct Paule saythe the sworde ys gyuen by goddys ordince for that purpose."

Titles of prohibited books

The New Testament Books to be given up.

Assertion that the kingly power was given to repress heresy

The document goes on to speak of an opinion engendered "in dyuerse of hys subiectys, that yt ys hys gracys dewtie to cawse the Scripture of God to be translated yn to thenglisshe tonge to be commynycat unto the people; and that the prelats, and also his highnes do wrong in denyying or letting of the same." The citation of this as a common opinion, and its insertion in a document which was to be publicly read by preachers, shews that questionings of this kind were widely prevalent in England; if it had not been so, such doubts would certainly never have been thus promulgated by those in authority; for this would be the readiest way to suggest such questions. The bill continues to speak of the free leave which was given in the assembly to discuss this subject, and how the king promised to conform himself to that which might be approved and confirmed by Scripture and holy doctrine; on this matter there appears to have been much said on both sides;—the question, indeed, was so stated as to lay it open to a great variety of opinions, and this conclusion was arrived at:—"It appered that the having the hole scrypture yn Englysshe ys not necessary to chrystian men; but that wythout hauyng any suche scrypture, endeuoryng themself to doo well, and to applye theire myndys to take and follow suche lessons as the precher techyth them, and so lerne by hys mowth, may aswell edyfy spyrytually yn ther soules as yf they had the same Scrypture yn Englisshe." After this, it is stated that it has sometimes seemed proper for the word of God to be circulated, while at other times it has been deemed needful for this to be restrained, and that the king taking into consideration all circumstances, "thynkyth yn hys conscyence that the dyuulgyng of the Scrypture att thys tyme yn the Englysshe tonge to be comytted to the people . . . . . shulde rather be to ther farther confusyon and destrucyon then the edyfycacyon of ther soules;" also it was said that *all* in the assembly thought that the king and the prelates did well in not suffering the Scriptures in English to be diffused "at this time;" also setting forth that the king promised to have the New Testament faithfully and purely translated into the

Prevalent opinion that the king was bound to provide the Scriptures in English

The king's judgment that the present was an unfit time for the Scriptures to be circulated in English

The New Testament to be

* These prohibited works are mostly those of Tyndale.

† These words within brackets are written in the margin of the document at Lambeth.

given to the people when they should deserve it.

English tongue by learned men, so that he might have it in his hands ready to give to the people when they should deserve it. The people were there exhorted, "That you wyll so detest thes pnycyous bookys, so abhorre thes heresyes and newe opynyons [i. e. the doctrines of the Gospel of the grace of God] so declyne from arrogancy of knowlege and understandyng of scrypture after your fantases; and shewe yourself yn commynyng and reasonyng so sober, quyett, meeke and temperate as all feare of mysusyng the gyft of Scrypture taken away, ye may appere mete yn your prynces eyes, and eyes of your prelattys, as they shall haue no just causse to fear any suche daunger: parsuadyng vnto yowr self yn the mean tyme wout grudgyng or murmuryng the very trowth, whych ys thys; *that we can not requyre or demaund Scrypture to be dyuulged yn the Englissh tonge otherwyse then uppon the discresyons of the superyours*, so as whensoever they thynke yn ther conscyence yt may doo yowe goode, they may & doo well to geve it vnto yowe. *And when so eueryt shalbe seen otherwyse vnto they doo amyss yn suffering yow to haue yt.*"

The judgment of superiors to be implicitly received

I have been the more particular to give an ample account of this prohibition, because it is of especial importance in connection with the restraints laid in England upon the circulation of the Scriptures; it is likewise important, as being a record that it was a discussed question whether the king ought to give the people the Scriptures in English; the question would, however, have come home more closely, if it had been—Ought the king to restrain the people from possessing and using the Scriptures, which they already have in their hands? The last cited paragraph runs very counter to the paramount authority of God; for the statement is equivalent to this—God has no right to speak to men in His word, except when and how "the superiors" see fit. The question however is not Has man a *right* to read the word of God? but Has God paramount right for His word to be heard? The document in question answers this in the negative. At the end of it are given the names of the persons who were present at the assembly.

Ought the king to restrain the people from having the Scriptures?

It is stated in the document that the condemnation of the prohibited books, and the withholding of the Scriptures were agreed to with the unanimous consent of those who were present; we shall, however, find shortly, good cause to question the accuracy of this statement with regard to one individual at least—Hugh Latimer.

Hugh Latimer a dissentient

Proclamation, May 9, 1530

The king followed up these proceedings by a proclamation issued in the ensuing month, in which he calls upon his subjects to banish Tyndale's translation of the Scriptures, as well as "all *other* bokes of heresie," promising to cause the Scriptures to be translated for the use of the people, when it should seem convenient. The proclamation farther holds out the severest threatenings against any one who might read any portion of the Scripture, either in writing or in print, in English, French, or Dutch.

Reading the Scriptures in English, French, and Dutch, prohibited

Latimer writes to the king, Dec. 1, 1530

These severe measures were not without their results; persons were apprehended for possessing books of Scripture, and in consequence of these circumstances, on the 1st of December, Hugh Latimer, afterwards bishop of Worcester, whose name appears at the end of the prohibition of May 24th preceding, wrote to the king, freely expostulating with him respecting the prohibitions which were laid upon the circulation of the Scriptures. This alone proves that the document in question did not really express the sentiments of all who were present in the assembly. Latimer intimates that those who disobeyed the mandate took it more as proceeding from the prelates than from the king. He even indirectly defends the New Testament as translated by Tyndale, speaking of its having been "meekly offered to every man that could and would, to amend it if there were any fault."

He defends the version of Tyndale.

He refers to the differing judgments in the assembly of May 24.

And not only does it appear that some of those in the assembly of the 24th of May, 1530, were dissentients *in heart*, but it is evident that their judgments likewise were *expressed;* for Latimer plainly tells the king—"But as concerning this matter, *other men have shewed your grace their minds, how necessary it is to have the Scriptures in English.* The which thing also your grace hath promised by your last proclamation; the which promise I pray God your gracious highness may shortly perform, even to-day before to-morrow." Farther on in the letter, Latimer says—"And so as concerning your last proclamation prohibiting such books, the very true cause of it and chief counsellors (as men say, and of likelihood it should be) were they whose evil living and cloaked hypocrisy, those books uttered and disclosed. And *howbeit there were three or four, that would have had the Scripture go forth in English*, yet it happened there [i. e. in the assembly of May 24], as it is evermore seen, that the most part overcometh the better; and so it might be that these men [i. e. those who had been taken into custody for retaining the Scriptures] did not take the proclamation as yours, but as theirs set forth in your name."

Number of the dissentients three or four

The proclamation not taken as the king's.

Latimer fully exculpated from the charge of opposing the Scriptures

These extracts, from this interesting letter of Latimer, suffice to prove that *he* cannot be charged with having joined in the attempts which were made at this time to crush Tyndale, and hinder the light of God's truth. The charge would never have been brought against him, had it not been that the document before referred to, having his name amongst others, as present at its issue, was contemplated alone, without the letter to the king having been taken into consideration at the same time. It was Latimer's misfortune that a document, containing direct falsehood, was approved by a large majority, and the few dissentients had sentiments thus put forth in their names which they both abhorred in their hearts, and against which they had borne their testimony.

The alleged unanimity, a direct falsehood against Latimer

The following is the conclusion of Latimer's letter to Henry VIII.:—"Take heed of their worldly wisdom, which is foolishness before God, that you may do that God commandeth, and not that seemeth good in your own sight without the word of God; that your grace may be found acceptable in his sight, and one of the members of his church, and according unto the office which he hath called your grace unto, you may be found a faithful minister of his gifts, and not a defender of his faith, for he will not have it defended by man or man's power, but by *his word* only; by the which he hath evermore defended it, and that by a way far above man's power or reason, as all the stories of the Bible make mention.

Latimer's faithful exhortation to the king

"Wherefore, gracious King, pity yourself, have mercy upon your soul, and think that the day is even at hand when you shall give account of your office and of the blood that hath been shed with your sword. In the which day, that your grace may stand stedfastly, and not be ashamed, but be clear and ready in your reckoning, and to have (as they say) your *Quietus est*, sealed with the blood of our Saviour Christ, which only serveth at that day, is my daily prayer to him that suffered death for our sins, which also prayeth to his Father for grace for us continually. The Spirit of God preserve your grace. *Anno Domini*, 1530. 1 *die Decembris*."

Latimer refers to those who suffered martyrdom

If it be asked *who* were the principal movers in these solemn proceedings for the suppression of the Scriptures, I believe that there can be very little doubt or question that it was the same who had previously done what they could to prevent their circulation in English, and to crush the translator; the previous efforts of Bishop Tonstall and Sir Thomas More having been so thoroughly unavailing to these ends, they seem now to have tried something yet more formidable, by adding the weight of the king's authority to their endeavours. It is pleasant to find that there was with them such a faithful witness for God and his word as Hugh Latimer.

Sir. T More and Tonstall, the principal actors in the convention

---

VI.

TYNDALE'S LIFE IN EXILE.—ATTEMPTS TO ALLURE HIM TO ENGLAND.

THUS while in England the whole weight of authority was opposed to Tyndale and his godly labour of translating the Scriptures, he was himself in Antwerp or the vicinity, having just (as has been already said) completed the Pentateuch, a work the printing of which was evidently accomplished in the midst of many wanderings. It is not unlikely that even before this time attempts had been made to seize Tyndale's person, and that the changes in his place of abode were in part consequent upon this. But still it is deeply interesting to mark the steadiness of purpose with which he was prosecuting his godly design; and to this end the little separate pamphlets, in which he printed and began to reprint the Pentateuch, have great value. Wiclif was enabled, by the orderings of God's providence, to continue his labours with comparative tranquillity, there were even some of the great in this world who had befriended him, while with Tyndale it was altogether different. He lived a most precarious life, and was in continual danger of being arrested to receive the punishment which was then so commonly awarded to the faithful servants of Christ.

During a part of the time of his sojournings in various places he had the company of his friend John Frith, from whose testimony we learn a little of the life which Tyndale led. He says, in his answer to Sir Thomas More in 1533:—

"And Tyndale I trust lyueth well contente with such pore Apostlesi lyfe as God gave hys Sonne Christ, and hys faythfull mynysters in thys worlde, whych is not sure of so many mytes as you be yearely of many poundes; altho' I am sure that for hys learnynge and iudgement in the Scripture, he were more worthye to be promoted then all the Bishoppes in Englande. I receyued a letter from hym whych was wrytten sens Christmas, wherin amonge other matters he wryteth thus:—'I call God to recorde agaynst the daye we shall appeare before oure Lorde Jesus to geue reckonynge of our doinges that I neuer altered one syllable of Godes worde agaynst my conscyence, nor wolde do thys daye, yf all that is in Earth, whether it be honoure, pleasure, or ryches might be geuen me.

Tyndale's motives in translating the Scriptures

"'Moreouer, I take God Almyghty to recorde to my conscience that I desyre of God to my selfe in thys worlde no more then that without which I cannot keep his Lawes,'" &c. "Judge, good Christen reader, whether these wordes be not spoken of a faythfull, clene, and innocent herte. And as for hys behauyoure is suche that I am sure no man can reproue him of any synne, howbeit no man is innocent before God whych beholdeth the herte"

This testimony of Frith concerning his friend and brother in Christ, William Tyndale, was given not long before he himself was called to lay down his life for Christ's sake, which took place on the fourth of July, 1533. It is introduced in this place, because the manner of Tyndale's life of hardship had continued much the same for some years, and it was to the period from 1528 to 1531 that Frith referred, as concerning which he had had personal experience; he having for that time been often the companion of Tyndale.

The circulation of the Scriptures hindered

No edition of the New Testament in English from 1530 till 1534

It is probable that the severities resorted to had in a great degree hindered the importation of copies of the New Testament into England, especially after the burning of Bayfield, for there does not appear to have been any edition printed from the year 1530 until 1534, whereas there had been from 1526 to 1530 no less than five editions, two of Tyndale's own, the one without glosses—the other with them, and three published by the Dutch printers. The difference in the issues of these New Testaments is at least remarkable, and can scarcely be attributed to any other cause than the severe proscription by the English authorities.

Why no farther portion of the Old Testament was published in English, except Jonah.

It is not only, however, the translation of the New Testament by Tyndale which was prohibited by the king's proclamation, the portions of the Old which were already executed fell under the same sweeping condemnation; this may account for the fact that no portion of the Old Testament was published by Tyndale beyond the Pentateuch, excepting the book of Jonah; the Pentateuch itself, however, does not, in Tyndale's life-time, appear to have been reprinted farther than the book of Genesis.

The prophecy of Jonah was the last portion of the Old Testament which Tyndale lived to publish; he was, however, engaged in the succeeding years of his life in translating the historical books as far as the end of the second of Chronicles, which translation appears to have remained in the hands of some of his friends—very probably in the possession of John Rogers, afterwards himself in part a translator or reviser of the Scriptures, and ultimately a martyr for Christ;—and thus at length, in the year 1537, the whole of the portions of Scripture which had been translated by the labour of Tyndale, were published together in the Bible which bears the name of Thomas Matthew: in this Bible, those books which had not been translated by Tyndale were supplied out of the version of Myles Coverdale.

The whole of Tyndale's translations published in 1537, in Matthew's Bible.

Efforts of Tyndale's enemies to entice him to England, 1530

Stephen Vaughan the king's agent

His letter concerning Tyndale, Jan. 26, 1530. Cott MSS. Galba, B x p 42

The enemies of the truth in England were not content with proscribing equally the translations and the writings of Tyndale, for they sought to have his person also in their power. How soon these attempts commenced we have no evidence, but it is certain that early in the year 1530, efforts were made to induce him to return to England. Part of a letter from Stephen Vaughan, the agent of Henry VIII. in the Netherlands, is among the Cotton MSS. This letter is dated from Barrough, near Antwerp, Jan. 26, 1530, and is addressed to the king himself. He says, "I have written three sondry letters vnto Wylliam Tyndale, and the same sent for the more suretie to iij several places, to Frankforde, Hamborough, and Marleborough." This proves that Vaughan had some information respecting the places in which Tyndale had been sojourning about that time; for he had spent a considerable part of the preceding year at Hamburgh, and was a few days before the date of this letter (namely, on the 17th of January 1530) at Malborow, where and when he printed his translation of Genesis. Vaughan goes on to speak of the inducements which he had held out to Tyndale, to persuade him to return to England. One thing this letter proves indubitably—the importance which in the eyes of Henry was attached to getting Tyndale in his own power; for not only does Vaughan speak of his own exertions, but also of "some other person whom your magestie commanded to persuade by like meanys;" he enclosed to the king the letters which he had received from Tyndale, as well as his reply to this other emissary. The exact object which was sought in getting Tyndale to England does not transpire; it may be that ultimate proceedings in the matter were not arranged even in the mind of Henry himself.

The inducements held out to Tyndale.

Vaughan's letter to Cromwell

Vaughan wrote a letter to Cromwell accompanying the one to the king: in this he says, "It is vnlikely to get Tyndale into England when he dayly hereth so many thinges from thense whiche feareth hym. After his booke answering my Lord Chancellor's book be put fourth, I think he wyll wryte no more. The man is of a gretter knowlege then the Kynge Highnes doth take him for, which well appereth by his workes. Wolde God he were in Englande."

Tyndale goes

It is not unlikely that the letters of Vaughan were in part the means of leading his steps from Marl-

from Marleborough to Antwerp

Tyndale reaches Antwerp before April 18, 1531.

borow to Antwerp or the neighbourhood; and we may judge from the letters of Vaughan which are extant, how much he urged his return to England—a step which, if taken, would have been of fatal consequences to him. A part of a letter from one of the king's agents is extant, which must have been written not long after that to which I have just referred; it shews that Tyndale had now come to Antwerp. This letter gives an interesting account of an interview which the writer of it had with Tyndale on the day preceding, close to the city of Antwerp.* He says,—

Vaughan's interview with Tyndale, April 17, 1531. Cott MSS Titus, B.i p 67.

Their conversation.

Tyndale's fidelity to the king

Tyndale's privations

His previous warnings to the king

The Scriptures prohibited.

"The day before the date hereof, I spake with Tyndall withowt the town of Andwerp, and by this meanes He sent a certeyne person to seke me, whom he had advysed to say that a certeyne frend of myne vnknowen to the messenger, was very desirows to speke with me; praying me to take paynes to go vnto him to suche place as he should bryng me Then I to the messenger, what is your fryend and where is he? His name I know not, said he, but if it be your pleasure to go where he is, I wilbe glad thider to bryng you: thus dobtfull what this matter ment, I concluded to go with hym, and folowed hym till he browght me withowt the gate of Andwerp into a feld lying nyghe unto the streme, where was abidyng me this said Tyndall At our metyng, do you not knowe me? said this Tyndale I do not well remember you, said I to hym; my name, said he, is Tyndall But Tyndall, said I, fortunate be our metyng Then Tyndall: Sir, I have bene excedyng desirous to speke with you And I with you; what is your mynd. Sir, said he, I am enformed that the Kynge's grace taketh great displesure with me for puttyng furthe of certaine bokes which I lately maid in these partes, but specially for the boke namyd the Practise of Prelates, whereof I have no littell marvaill consideryng that, in it I did but warne his grace of the subtyle demeanor of the Clargy of his Realme towardes his person & of the shamefull abusions by them practised, not a littell threatnyng the displeasure of his grace and weale of his Realme In which doyng, I shewed and declared the harte of a trew subiect which sowght the saluegard of his Riall person and weale of his commons, to thentent that his grace thereoff warnyd mygh in dewe tyme prepare his remedies against the subtyle dreames Yf for my paynes theirin takyn Yf for my pouertye Yf for myn exille out of myn naturall contrey, and beyng absent from my fryndes Yf for my hongar—my thurst—my cold—the great danger wherewith I am every where compasyd—and fynally yf for innumerable other hard and sharp sicknesses whiche I indure, not yet feellyng theyre asperitie be reson I hopyd with my labors to doo honor to God—trew service to my prynce, and plesure to his commons, how ys yt that his grace this consyderyng may ether by hymselfe thyncke or by the perswasions of wother, be browght to thyncke, that in this doyng I schold not schow a pure mynd, a trew and incorrupt zeale, and effeccyon to his grace Was there in me any suche mynde when I warned hys grace to beware of his cardinall, whose iniquyte he schortly after approvyd accordyng to my writyng? Doth this deserve hatered? Ageyne, may his grace, beyng a crysten prynce be so vnkynd to God, whiche hathe commaundyd his word to be spredde thorowgh owght the world; to geve more faythe to the wykkyd perswasions of men, whiche presumyng above Goddes wyssdom and contrary to that which Cryst expressly comandeth in his testament dare saye, thatt yt is not lefull for the pepoll to have the same in a tonge that they understond, because the puritie thereof schold opyn mens ies to se ther wyckydnes!! Is there more danger in the kinges subgects then in the subgectes of all other princes, which in every of their tongges have the same under pryveleage of their sufferaynse, as I now am very deth ware more pleasaunt to me then lyffe consyderyng mans nature to be suche as can bare no trewethe This, after a long communycation had between us."

Tyndale's objections to come to England.

Vaughan apologizes for not having pursued Tyndale

Dangers of Tyndale's life.

The remainder of this letter speaks of the objections made by Tyndale as to his coming into England; he not feeling at all secure, whatever promises might be made him by the king, knowing the power which spiritual censures exerted against any one accused or suspected of heresy. The writer also makes a kind of apology for not having *pursued* Tyndale; this proves that the agents of the king had orders to arrest Tyndale, if they had the opportunity, and likewise that they had at least permission so to do from the authorities at Antwerp; well might Frith then call the life which Tyndale led "a poor apostle's life," for he had to suffer, not only from extreme poverty and privation, but also from the continual danger of his liberty and life. If we value the labour which he bestowed upon the version of the Scriptures which he sought to give his countrymen, our estimate of the pains which he took will greatly increase, when we consider his circumstances at the time.

Tyndale's "Practise of Prelates" His opposition to Henry's divorce

This letter, from which the citation has just been made, shews how intensely the mind of Tyndale was directed to the free introduction of the Scriptures into England; it seems to have been in order to urge that point that Tyndale sought this remarkable interview. For the right understanding of the reference which Tyndale made to his book, "The Practise of Prelates," it may be needful to state that in it he had freely spoken against the divorce of Henry, tracing up the religious scruples which it was said that the king was acting, to insinuations which had been brought into his mind to serve certain ambitious ends.

* This letter is imperfect, and has neither date nor writer's name, but it may be constructively shewn to have been also written by Sir Stephen Vaughan (though the defective copy in existence is a transcript by another hand), and the date to be April 18, 1531

Tyndale spoke what he believed to be the truth of God in the matter, not dreading the displeasure of his sovereign, referring in justification of his conduct to the rebuke which John the Baptist had given to Herod. Nothing could have shewn less guile than the conduct of Tyndale in thus giving to the king advice so unpalatable.

S Vaughan writes to the king, May 20, 1531. Cott MSS Galba B x p 5

In another letter from the agent of the king, mention is made of Tyndale, as well as of his friend Frith, who was yet absent from England. Sir Stephen Vaughan wrote to the king on May 20, 1531; the latter part of his letter related principally to these two exiles. Vaughan speaks in terms of high commendation of Frith, whilst mentioning, at the same time, his poverty, which he is disposed to regard as having partly induced him to marry; this he thinks may hinder his endeavours to induce him to come to England. As to Tyndale, he speaks of an interview which he had had with him, and the effect which the reading of a clause in a letter of Cromwell's, which spoke of the king's kindness and compassion to those who would be converted and amend.

An interview with Tyndale mentioned.

Tyndale much moved by part of a letter from Cromwell His willingness to suffer that the Scriptures might be circulated in English.

"And as I thought so it cam to passe For after sight therof, I perceyued the man to be excedinge altered, and to take the same very nere vnto his hearte, *in suche wise that water stode in his yees.* And answered what gracious wordes are these. I assure youe, sayed he, *If it wolde stande withe the kinge most gracious plaisur to graunte only a bare text of the scripture to be put forthe emonge his people,* like as is put forthe emonge the subgectes of the emperour in these parties, and of other cristen princes, *be it of the translation of what person soever shall please his magestie,* I shall ymedyatlye make faithfull promyse neuer to write more, ne abide two dayes in these parties after the same: but ymedyatly to repayre into his realme, and there most humbly submytt myselfe at the fete of his roiall magestie, *offerynge my bodye to suffer what payne or tortures, ye what dethe his grace will,* so that this be obteyned And tyll that tyme, I will abide th aspect of all chaunses what so euer shall come, and indure my lyfe in as many paynes, as it is able to bere and suffer. And as concernynge my reconsiliacion his grace may be assured that what soeuer I haue sayed or written in all my life ageynst thonour of Goddes worde, and so proved; the same shall I before his magestie and all the worlde, vtterly renownce and forsake And with most humble and meke mynde imbrace the truthe, abhorringe all errour souer at the most gracious and benygne request of his royall magestie, of whose wisdome, prudence and lernynge I hear so greate prayse and commendation, then of any other creature lyuyng. *But if those thinges whiche I haue written be true, and stand with Goddes worde, why shulde his magestie hauynge so excellent a guyft of knowlege in the scriptures, moue me to do any thinge agenst my conscience.*"

Vaughan goes on to tell the king, that if he had a distinct promise from him to Tyndale, that he would be much more likely to succeed in inducing him to return to England.

Value of the testimony of this letter.

This letter is valuable, as shewing how thoroughly the mind of Tyndale was bent upon his work of service to God—namely, the giving of the Scriptures to his countrymen in their own tongue. It was now nearly thirty years since his mind had been turned to this subject (some of the manuscript translations which appear to be his are dated 1502), and now in poverty, exile, sickness, and danger; this was to him the object for which he sought to live. It was not for name or credit that he toiled,—let the Scriptures be given forth in English, be the translation whose it might, so long as it was the true word of God, he was willing to write no more, and even to obey the orders of the king, by giving himself up, even knowing the certain consequence to be death by burning.

Cromwell's letter to Vaughan in reply to his of April 18, 1531: Cott MSS Galba B. x p. 338

There is extant the draught of a letter from Cromwell to Vaughan, to which no date appears; but it would seem, from the contents, to have been written about the same time as the letter from Vaughan, an extract from which has just been given. This draught of a reply, must have been written before the king received the letter of Vaughan, dated May 20, 1531; while, at the same time, it is pretty evident that Vaughan had not received this letter when he wrote on that date. The draught of the reply to Vaughan's letter was corrected and interlined by the king himself, and the kind of alterations which are made, proves how the mind of Henry was bent upon opposing or destroying Tyndale. The diligence of Vaughan in procuring the book in reply to More is commended, yet very great apprehension is expressed lest Vaughan himself had not become too friendly with Tyndale, his letters being judged to shew much affection towards him.

The king himself corrects this draught

Fear expressed lest Vaughan should be influenced by Tyndale

The king's animosity against Tyndale increases

The king clearly dreaded the influence which Tyndale might have over Vaughan, and was also much offended by the reply to Sir Thomas More. The letter running in Cromwell's name, but corrected by the king, contains this sentence: ". . . . I myght well perceyue that he thought that ye have moche affection towardes the saide Tyndale, whom in his maners, & knowledge in woordly thinges, ye vndoubtedlie in your letters do moche allowe and commende, who's workes being replete with abhominable sclaunders and lyes, imagened and onelye fayned to enfecte the peopull, declareth him to lake grace,

Vaughan's commendation of Tyndale reproved

native lerning, godly discrecyon, and all other good qualities, nothing else pretending in all his workes but evedente dyssaite, that ye in such wise, by your letters prayse, set forth, and avaunce hym, which nothing else pretendyth but disquiet and sowe sedytyon among the peopull of this realme. His highnes, therfore, hathe commaunded me to aduertise you that his pleasure is to wryte that ye shoulde desyste, and leve eny ferther to persuade or attempte the sayde Tyndale to cum into this realme. Alledging that he perceyuing the malycyous, perverse, vncharitable mynde and judgment of the said Tyndale, is in maner without hope of reconcylyacyon in hym, and is veray joiyous to haue his realme destytute of such a person." The letter goes on to speak of the danger which might arise from the presence of Tyndale if he were to return to England; and how he might *corrupt* the whole realm to its great injury. What then was Tyndale's offence? He had put forth the New Testament in English,* and had defended his having done so against the foolish and frivolous charges brought against it by More. This was the true ground of the efforts of Henry and his emissaries; and so soon as it was manifest that the honest simplicity of Tyndale touched the heart of Henry's agent, the object which had been sought was abandoned, and Tyndale was to be no more solicited to return. **Fear expressed lest Tyndale if in England might corrupt the whole realm.**

If Vaughan's former letter had given offence, that of May 20th must have greatly increased it, so that it is not to be wondered at, that we find but little further mention of Tyndale in any of the proceedings in England. **Offence occasioned by Vaughan's letters**

The latter part of the letter to Vaughan mentions Frith, whom he was still to seek to allure to England; the king not having any such direct grounds of displeasure against him as he had against Tyndale, Frith did return to England, probably about the time of Lambert's arrest, fully expecting, it would seem, that the promises made to him would be kept, and that he would be unmolested for the faith of Christ; the result has been already told, he was taken up, committed to the tower, and after a long imprisonment and repeated examinations, was condemned by Bishop Stokesly, and suffered death in Smithfield, July 4, 1533. He had married while abroad: his wife had remained in the Netherlands; but she appears, from one of the letters of Tyndale to Frith, to have been able to give up her husband to suffer for the Lord's sake without repining, being able to look onward to the glory which is reserved for those who have washed their robes, and made them white in the blood of the Lamb. Fox, in the very interesting account which he gives of the sufferings of this faithful martyr of the Lord Jesus, speaks of the narrative as being the most affecting of any of those relating to the martyrs who laid down their lives in the days of Henry VIII. **Frith, still solicited to return to England, complies.** **Committed to the tower Condemned by Bp. Stokesly Put to death July 4, 1533**

The letters of Tyndale to Frith while he was in the Tower, are very interesting, for they shew how his heart was stayed upon the Lord, and how earnestly he desired that Frith might in all things witness a good confession. He earnestly cautions him against saving his life by an abjuration, warning him how Bilney did this by the advice of false friends, and then had no ease in his conscience until he again gave himself up to suffer death, urging upon him the exceeding importance of consistent and faithful testimony. **Tyndale's letters to Frith**

"Dearly beloved, be of good courage, and comfort your soul with the hope of this high reward, and bear the image of Christ in your mortal body, *that it may at his coming be made like to his immortal*, and follow the example of all your other dear brethren, which choose to suffer in hope of a better resurrection. Keep your conscience pure and undefiled, and say against that nothing Stick at necessary things, and remember the blasphemies of the enemies of Christ, saying, they find none but will abjure rather than suffer the extremity. Moreover, the death of them that come again after they have once denied, though it be accepted with God and all that believe, yet it is not glorious; for the hypocrites say, he must needs die, denying helpeth not. But might it have holpen they would have denied five hundred times, but seeing it would not help them, therefore, of pure pride and mere malice together, they speak with their mouths that their conscience knoweth to be false. If you give your self, cast your self, yield your self, commit your self wholly and only to your loving Father, then shall his power be in you and make you strong, and that so strong, that you shall feel no pain, which should be to another present death; and His Spirit shall speak in you and teach you what to answer according to His promise" **The hope of the Christian** **The resurrection.**

In another letter Tyndale tells Frith, "Your wife is well content with the will of God, and would not for her sake have the glory of God hindered." These letters appear, from their contents, to have been written **Frith's wife mentioned by Tyndale.**

* It is singular, that in a very short time after this, Cromwell became one of the most earnest promoters of the circulation of the Scriptures in English. It is probable that, even at this time, he was acting as the instrument of Henry, as unhappily he often did afterwards. He was probably very willing that attempts to take Tyndale were to cease

shortly before Frith was burned; and from them we may learn with what steadiness of purpose Tyndale looked on to the expected close of his own earthly pilgrimage. In another of his letters to Frith, written apparently some time previously to those from which the above extracts are taken, he exhorts him, if he has opportunity, to "thrust in that the Scripture may be in the mother tongue;" this great object being never kept out of sight by Tyndale.

Frith to use his influence for the Scriptures in English.

VII.

TYNDALE REVISES HIS NEW TESTAMENT—HIS IMPRISONMENT AND MARTYRDOM—COTEMPORARY VERSIONS.

TYNDALE'S "poor Apostle's life" was now drawing to a close; his occupation had been for some time continuing to translate the books of the Old Testament, which he accomplished up to the end of the Second of Chronicles. When his circumstances are considered, it is really wonderful that he could have done so much. In the early part of 1534, he appears to have had a little comparative repose, becoming an inmate in the family of Thomas Pointz, an English merchant, at Antwerp.* This period seems to have been employed in revising his translation of the New Testament—of this book he had not himself published an edition since the two of 1526, and it was now four years since the Dutch printers had published their third edition. In his labour of revision, Tyndale bestowed great pains; a comparison of the original with the revised edition proves this; not many verses can be found together in which he had not made some alterations (often but slight), in order more accurately to express the sense of the Greek. The Dutch printers seem to have tried to forestall Tyndale, by getting out another edition before his was ready; they procured the aid of an English refugee, named George Joye, who had previously published, in 1531, a translation of Isaiah from the Latin, and was at this very time engaged in publishing and translating Jeremiah and the Psalter. It was this circumstance probably that gave rise to the proposal on the part of the Dutch publishers, that Joye would aid them in their attempt to publish an English New Testament: he seems to have been a man of a very unsober mind, very earnest against the Church of Rome, but not particularly sound in Christian doctrine. The copy used by the Dutch printers, owing to its having been three times printed without the aid of an English press-corrector, had become so inaccurate that (by Joye's account) it was in not a few places unintelligible, so that his toil in correcting the press was considerable. Sometimes, also, he says, the text was in such a state that he was obliged to take his Latin Bible and re-render the passage, so as to give some meaning to the words which had become corrupted. But this was not all, for he made, in one respect at least, a strange alteration, expunging the word "resurrection," and substituting "the life after this;" a translation which, if it meant anything, was a cloke for some unsoundness in doctrine; and for this end it was intended by Joye, as we shall see from the manner in which the subject is alluded to by Tyndale. This corrupted edition of Tyndale's New Testament was published in August, 1534.

Early part of 1534, Tyndale has a little repose, in the house of Pointz, at Antwerp

George Joye aids the Dutch printers

Joye's alteration of the word "resurrection"

This corrupted edition published Aug 1534

In the following November, Tyndale published his own revised, or third, edition (the seventh in all); in this, besides amending the version, he also did much to remodel the language, so as to give the whole in more idiomatic English; for although this had been done with a considerable degree of success eight years before, yet Tyndale had then no opportunity to examine the whole so as to make it what he could wish. He took advantage, in his revision, of the faults which had been found with his version as first published, and thus made such changes as substituting "elder" for "senior," which he had previously given as the rendering of πρεσβύτερος; this, it may be remembered, was one of the great faults found by Sir T. More in the previous editions. In speaking of the editions of Tyndale's version, this his revision stands in the first place as exhibiting him as a translator. The two editions, octavo and quarto, of 1526, are precious as samples of the earliest endeavours of this holy servant of Christ to give the word of God to his countrymen. But the edition of 1534 is the one which should be taken into account when his accuracy as a translator is examined.

Tyndale's corrected edition, Nov 1534

Πρεσβύτερος newly rendered.

Tyndale's revision

* Fox mentions (ed. 1, p. 513), that Sir John Welch married a daughter of Sir Robert Pointz; this Thomas Pointz may have been one of the same family, and this may have connected him with Tyndale.

¶ The Ne=we Testament, dylygently corrected and compared with the Greke by Willyam Tindale: and fynesshed in the yere of oure Lorde God. A. M. D. & xxxiiij. in the moneth of Nouember.

The title of this edition, copied in the margin, expresses that care had been bestowed in the revision. After this follows, " W. T. vnto the Reader. Here thou hast (moost deare reader) the New Testament or covenaunt made wyth us of God in Christes bloude. Which I have looked over agayne (now at the last) with all dylygence, and compared it vnto the Greke, and have weded oute of it many fautes, which lacke of helpe at the begynninge and oversyght dyd sowe therin." The principal part of this prologue is occupied with a statement of the right use of Scripture, and a description of the obedience which accompanies true faith in Christ; part of this might be misunderstood, were we not to bear in mind that the Romanists perverted every thing which was said about justification by faith, as though faith meant a mere assent to the narrative of the four gospels. This Tyndale combats, shewing that the fulfilment of the will of God is attendant on that faith which truly justifies.

The title of the revised edition

The prologue

The revision of the version

The right use of Scripture

After this, a few lines are occupied with an explanation of the term "Elders," which in this edition was used as the more correct expression of what had been at first termed by Tyndale "Seniours."

Elders defined

Then follows, "A prologe into the iiii. Euangelystes;" this is succeeded by a notice of an erratum, namely, in the twenty-third of Matthew. By mistake there had been printed, "Clense first the *outside* of the cup and platter;" for this he tells the reader to substitute "ynneside."

Tyndale had heard of Joye's edition of the New Testament in English; but although he was surprised at his attempt to supplant him, he took no particular notice, though it was in itself particularly ungenerous to publish an edition in Tyndale's name at the very time when his genuine edition corrected was expected to appear; but when the printing of this edition was almost finished, a copy was brought to him of Joye's edition, and many places were pointed out in which strange alterations had been made. In consequence of this, Tyndale prefixed another prologue * to this edition, stating that the changes which had been published under his name were not really his; for that instead of a copy which was so treated deserving the name of being diligently corrected, it was really grievously corrupted. Tyndale says, "thorow oute Mat. Mark & Luke perpetually: and ofte in the Actees, & sometyme in John, and also in the Hebrues, where he fyndeth this worde Ressurrection, he chaungeth it into the lyfe after this lyfe, or verie lyfe, and soche lyke, as one that abhorred the name of the resurrection." He goes on to say, that if this change be "a dylygent correccion then must my translacion be fautie in those places, and saynt Jeromes, and all the translatours that euer I heard of in what tonge so euer it be." Tyndale might well express his surprise at such a rendering having been adopted,—a rendering which seems as though it were only meant to take away the true hope of Christians, that as Christ arose, so shall they arise—they having in His resurrection the earnest and the exemplification of theirs. But it pained Tyndale that Joye had so acted as to make him seem responsible for this heretical perversion.

Tyndale remarks on Joye's edition

The corruption as to the word "resurrection" noticed

This New Testament altered by Joye, on which Tyndale animadverted, was the first attempt in English to pervert the word of God, for the purpose of upholding false doctrine; happily, this has been done but rarely, and those versions in which this dishonest mode of procedure has been adopted have never obtained much acceptance, or come into general use. Tyndale expressed much indignation at this conduct of Joye; but the offence was great:—1st. He had daringly corrupted the word of God. 2nd. He had done this in order to introduce and disseminate his own heretical doctrine. 3rd. He had done this in such a way as to cause his errors to be ascribed to Tyndale, as though Tyndale had been guilty of this gross dishonesty in translating, and as if he held these erroneous doctrines.

Joye's the first attempt in English to pervert the word of God

A short extract from the prologue, too interesting to be omitted, shews us what were Tyndale's feelings in giving out his own translation. He says, "As concerning all I have translated or other wise written, I beseeche all men to reade it, for that purpose I wrote it: even to bringe them to the knowledge of the scripture. And as farre as the scripture approveth it, so farre to alowe it, & if in anye place the worde of God dysalow it, there to refuse it, as I do before oure savyour Christ & his congregacion. And where they fynde fautes, let them shew it me, if they be nye, or wryte to me if they be farre of: or wryte openly agaynst it & improve it, & I promyse them, if I shall perceave that there reasons conclude I will confesse myne ignorance openly."

A few months (Feb. 27 1535) after Tyndale had thus disclaimed all participation in the heretical

Joye's Apology published

* From Joye's Apology, it would seem that this prologue had been circulated previous to the completion of the New Testament, to which it was afterwards prefixed.

perversions made by George Joye, the latter published an Apology for the New Testament with which he had been connected; in this Apology he represents his whole connection with regard to the surreptitious edition, as though it were one merely of a pecuniary nature on his part in undertaking the correction of the press of the New Testament in English; but he makes no real defence of himself with regard to the alteration of the word *resurrection*, and allowing this change to be attributed to Tyndale himself. He also, by implication, charges Tyndale with indolence in not having edited an impression of his New Testament for so many years, and with covetousness because of the sum said to have been given him by the printer for the copyright of his corrected version. Joye might have known that Tyndale instead of being indolent had been laboriously engaged in many works in the midst of danger, privation, and sickness; and as to the charge of covetousness, it applies very badly to one who was willing to live upon ten pounds a year, so that he might teach children and preach the gospel.

He charges Tyndale with indolence

Joye's statements respecting resurrection

Joye asserts that Tyndale had not spoken correctly in charging him with holding heretical doctrine relative to the resurrection; he allows that in some places it really does signify the rising again of the body; but he maintains (whether from ignorance or perverseness) that in others it means simply the state of the separate spirit in happiness with the Lord. It is not easy to gather what his doctrine really was on this point, for he seems to contradict himself; alleging that "they that are in their graves" in John v. does not mean the body but the soul; if so what could the resurrection be?

His charge of false doctrine against Tyndale

He charges Tyndale with maintaining that the spirit is in a state of sleep from the time of its departure from the body until the resurrection; an assertion which appears from Tyndale's own previous statements to be utterly groundless. The Apology of Joye proves his scholarship to have been but limited, and also that he could but little appreciate Tyndale's learning.

The Dutch imitation of Tyndale's revision

The Dutch printers probably found that the sale of the edition edited by Joye was hindered by the publication of Tyndale's revision three months after; and thus they published an edition which is an evident *imitation* of Tyndale's revised edition; indeed there can hardly be a doubt but that it was intended to pass for the genuine edition, for it is even dated as being finished in 1534, *in November*, just like the genuine book, which of course cannot be the true date.

Tyndales apprehension

The completion of the revision and printing of Tyndale's third edition brings us to the time of his apprehension and imprisonment.

The account of the betrayal and martyrdom of Tyndale was communicated to Fox by Thomas Pointz, who had been his host for the previous nine months, it appears that one Henry Philips made acquaintance with Tyndale, so that he at length became an inmate in Pointz's house. After some time Philips went to Brussels, where he appears to have charged Tyndale with heresy, so that some of the officers of the emperor were sent to Antwerp to apprehend him. Shortly after this, Pointz had occasion to be absent for a few days from Antwerp, and Philips took the opportunity to put Tyndale into the hands of those who were sent to apprehend him. He was taken to the castle of Vilvoord or Filford, near Brussels; at which place he remained until his martyrdom, nearly two years afterwards. Great efforts were made by Pointz and others to procure his discharge, but all was ineffectual. Pointz procured letters from England in favour of Tyndale, and it appears probable that he would have obtained Tyndale's liberty, had not Philips, being resolved not to be baffled, charged Pointz likewise with heresy. On this account he also was arrested, and was subjected to a severe examination, as well as imprisonment for a considerable time. At length, having an opportunity he escaped, and again renewed his efforts to liberate Tyndale; the testimony which Pointz gives, concerning the character and conduct of Tyndale, in a letter addressed to his brother (dated Aug. 25, 1535), is highly interesting and valuable; he speaks of him in the highest terms.

Henry Philips accuses Tyndale at Brussels

He betrays him

Tyndale taken to Vilvoord Castle Nov 1534

Pointz arrested

Cott MSS Galba B x p 60

It is difficult even to surmise who were the instigators of Philips in this matter. Henry had little or no influence in the Netherlands at this time, for his having divorced the aunt of the Emperor, Catherine of Arragon, was the occasion of almost an open rupture. Philips apparently belonged to that party amongst the English, who wished still to uphold the authority of the Pope, and who, therefore, condemned the divorce, else he would have been little likely to have gained any favour with the authorities at Brussels; but, however this may be, it was rather a strange proceeding to condemn Tyndale at such a time in the Emperor's dominions, he being known to be an opposer of the divorce, holding that the marriage having been made ought to be kept.

The king of England not desirous of Tyndale's liberation.

Of one thing we may be very certain, that Henry had no desire to procure Tyndale's liberation; it has been already shewn that Henry had a strong personal dislike to him, as well as to his proceedings; and although his rupture with the Pope might make him look with a more favourable eye upon some of the "Gospellers," yet Tyndale had no reason to expect any kindness from the king, seeing that to express a judgment in opposition to his divorce from Catherine had become the surest way to excite his displeasure. It was on this account that Fisher, the aged Bishop of Rochester, and Tyndale's antagonist, Sir Thomas More, were beheaded in 1535. Hopes were entertained by many that his imprisonment might terminate, not by his martyrdom, but by his liberation: they made strenuous efforts to this end; and in the Prologue of Coverdale to his Bible, he also exhorts the reader to pray that this might be brought about.

In 1536, when Tyndale suffered, Henry VIII. and the Emperor were again on good terms; which may have been the reason of his being put to death, even though Henry had nothing to do with his apprehension. If Henry had chosen, he might now have interfered to save him.

Changes in England in the latter part of Tyndale's life

During the latter years of Tyndale's life, subsequent to his having taken up his abode in the neighbourhood of Antwerp, great changes were going on in England: the authority of the Pope had been denied; many things connected with popery were abolished; and these events, humanly speaking, had led to the attainment of that which Tyndale so ardently desired, namely, the circulation of the word of God in English. We have no means of knowing whether he had heard before his death that the Scriptures of Coverdale's translation were printed. If Tyndale did know this, it must have been no small consolation to him; for all his sufferings were for the sake of the diffusion of the word of God. But whether Tyndale was or was not aware of it, it shews how graciously the Lord was favouring that work which his imprisoned servant had begun, carrying it on in His own way almost beyond the utmost expectations which Tyndale himself could have entertained. In the years 1535 and 1536 there were *at least* four editions of Tyndale's New Testament printed, that is, twelve editions altogether; this proves an increased demand for them, which, if known to the imprisoned translator, must have greatly encouraged him. It was proof that his labours had not been bestowed in vain.

Coverdale's translation.

Four editions of Tyndale's New Testament, 1535 and 1536

Lewis, p. 85

Offor, p 81

Tyndale's correspondence with the divines of Louvain

His imprisonment appears to have been occupied with keeping up a continual correspondence with the ecclesiastical authorities at Louvain, who plyed him with interrogatories to which he was compelled to reply; his English writings being ransacked, and passages translated which could be made the groundwork of charges against him.

Tyndale's martyrdom, Sept 1536

It was in September 1536, that the martyrdom of Tyndale took place. We know far fewer particulars of him at that time than we do concerning many of the servants of the Lord Jesus who suffered in this country; but the letters which he had written a few years previously to Frith shew on what his mind was stayed in the anticipation of such an event: the topics which he had suggested to his friend were, doubtless, those by which his own soul was now upheld. These letters may be taken as supplying to us the thoughts, feelings, and confidence of Tyndale himself under similar circumstances: he was willing to give his body to suffer for Christ's sake, knowing that at his coming it would be made like unto His glorious body, he was willing to suffer in hope of the promised resurrection. He was first strangled and then burned, meeting in this respect with more mercy in the *manner* of his death than he would have met with in England. His dying prayer was, "Lord, ope the king of England's eyes!"

His dying prayer

Thus died, about the sixtieth year of his age, this faithful servant of God and martyr of Christ, whose labours for his Lord had led him into paths of suffering here; but who will, according to the promise on which his soul was stayed, appear with Christ at His coming, bearing His image. Vainly did his enemies shew their hatred in burning his lifeless body, it was but a testimony that his service to Christ had drawn forth the enmity of Satan; and though his scattered ashes had no place of burial, yet He who has promised to change our vile body to make it like unto His own glorious body—can as well guard unto that day the scattered ashes of his martyred servants, as he can the mouldering bodies of those who lie in their graves until He shall come, when they "shall have their perfect consummation and bliss in His eternal and everlasting kingdom."

Tyndale's life the introduction of the English Scriptures in print

The life of Tyndale is in all its circumstances the history of the introduction of the Scriptures in English into England; without knowing who and what Tyndale was, we never could understand by what instrumentality God was pleased to work in bringing this blessing to pass. A poor exiled monk, wandering from country to country, was thus made by God the means of incalculable blessing to his ignorant countrymen: in vain did the authority of all England, civil and ecclesiastical and moral, strive to crush him; he went on stedfast in his purpose, not in any strength of his own, but in the power of the Spirit of God. And when, at length, his weary wanderings ended in imprisonment he had this joy, that he had been labouring in the service of a master who both could and would reward his every toil. Death was not that which could affright him, for he knew what the apostle meant when he said, "We had the sentence of death in ourselves, that we should not trust in ourselves *but in God that raiseth the dead*." He knew that when his enemies had done their worst, they could but take his mortal life, and then his spirit would

2 Cor i 9

Phil i. 23. "depart and be with Christ which is far better," while the *resurrection* was the joyful point of expectation, which placed him both in body and in spirit beyond the power of death. The account of the labours of Tyndale closes the period in which the Scriptures in English were a proscribed book: from this time and onward more or less liberty was given for their possession and use:—all this must be looked on as a blessed result which the Lord was pleased to vouchsafe to the service and the prayers of Tyndale. Martyrs have suffered in various causes; Christian martyrs have laid down their lives for very many precious *portions* of God's truth, but William Tyndale was emphatically A MARTYR FOR THE WORD OF GOD.

Besides the translations from the original tongues of the New Testament and part of the Old published by Tyndale, there were likewise versions of a few books of the Old Testament executed from the Latin, and printed between the years 1530 and 1534.

The Argentine English Psalter, 1529-30.

The first of these translations is the Argentine English Psalter (to which allusion has already been made), the translator of which calls himself by the designation of *Johan Aleph;** this Psalter was published in 1530, and it bears the following title:—"The Psalter of David in English, purely and faithfully translated after the text of Feline, every Psalm havyng his argument before declarynge brefly thentente and substance of the wholl Psalme."

From the "text of Feline"

This translation has been already mentioned as having been prohibited soon after its publication: little, however, seems to be known respecting its reception and circulation in England. The date at the end is January 16, 1530; it was thus the first whole book of the Old Testament which was printed in English, the completion of Tyndale's Genesis having been *one day* subsequent.

Joye's translation of Isaiah, 1531

Joye accused of heresy, 1527

He escapes.

In the year 1531, there was published a translation of the prophet Isaiah by George Joye, the same who has already been mentioned as having superintended an edition of Tyndale's New Testament with strange alterations. Joye had been a fellow of Peterhouse College at Cambridge, but being accused of heresy in 1527, and finding himself in danger he escaped to the continent—the common place of refuge for those who fled from persecution in England. Joye's learning does not seem to have been great; he indirectly shews that he knew little or nothing of Greek or Hebrew, for he made his translations of portions of the Old Testament from the Latin; and as to the New he himself says, that in correcting the press of the edition of Tyndale's Testament which he altered—"where I founde a worde falsely printed I mended it; and when I came to some derke sentences that no reason coude be gathered of them, whether it was by the ignorance of the first translatour or of the prynter, I had *the latyne text* by me, and made it playne: and where any sentence was imperfite or clene left oute, I restored it agene, and gave many wordis their pure and native signification in their places which they had not before." It can scarcely be imagined that Joye would have taken the Latin text as his standard, if it were not that he was ignorant of the Greek.

His translations made from the Latin

Joye contemplates the publication of an English Bible

Shortly after this George Joye appears to have contemplated the publication of the whole Bible in English. This is to be gathered from what Tyndale says in another of his letters to Frith, written towards the middle of 1533.

Joye's translation of Jeremiah, May, 1534

In May, 1534, Joye published an English translation of the prophet Jeremiah; "The song of Moses is added in the ende to magnifie our Lorde for the fall of Pharao, the Bisshop of Rome." The fall of the bishop of Rome here spoken of in this title meant, I suppose, the extinction of his supremacy in England by the authority of Henry and his parliament; however, the application of Exod. xv. to this event is using Scripture without much regard to analogy.

Joye's translation of the Psalms, Aug 1534

A translation of the book of Psalms was published by Joye in the month of August in the same year, 1534; this was in the title professed to be "diligently and faithfully translated;" the Latin text which he used is stated by Lewis to be that of Friar Felix;—a revised edition, I suppose, of one of the five Latin Psalters then commonly received and used in the Church services.† Joye's English Psalter was published in the same month that his unwarrantable edition of Tyndale's Testament was completed.

* And yet it is *possible* that this was the real name of a translator; a Sir John Aileph was one of the sheriffs of London not many years subsequent to this period, and this may have been edited by one of the same family

† See Stephens's Psalterium Quincuplex

PART III.

THE LATTER PORTION OF THE REIGN OF HENRY VIII.

I.

MYLES COVERDALE PREVIOUS TO HIS TRANSLATING THE BIBLE.—PROCEEDINGS IN ENGLAND RELATIVE TO THE SCRIPTURES.

THE history of the translation and publication of the New Testament and of a portion of the Old by William Tyndale has been that of a kind of struggle between light and darkness; *authority* of every kind being used to repress the knowledge of the word of God. But during the imprisonment of Tyndale, times and circumstances were strangely changing, and thus, although it was not even tacitly permitted that his translation should be possessed or used, yet that of another was actually completed, and about to be circulated by the king's permission. Thus before Tyndale had laid down his life for the sake of Christ, the desire of his heart was on the point of being granted, though it is probable without his knowing it. The Scriptures in English were soon about to be placed in the hands of every one. How earnestly Tyndale had desired this is manifested by his own words,—"If it wolde stande withe the kinge most gracious plaisur to graunte only a bare text of the Scripture to be put forth emonge his people ... *be it of the translation of what person soever shall please his magestie,* I shall ... most humbly submytt myselfe at the fete of his roiall magestie, offerynge my bodye to suffer what payne or tortures, ye what dethe his grace will, *so that this be obteyned.*" If such were Tyndale's expressions when at liberty, what may we not judge were his feelings when he was a prisoner for the word of God? I doubt not that, during his confinement, his PRAYERS were earnest in this matter to Him who hath all hearts under his control, even, as we know, that he prayed for this at the time of his execution, and that the unlooked for permission that the Scriptures should be freely circulated in English, was, in part, the answer of the Lord to the petition of His servant.

Change of circumstances in England during Tyndale's imprisonment

The desire of his heart

His prayers

The translator, whose labours were thus permitted to be possessed and read, was MYLES COVERDALE, the first who translated the whole Bible into English from the original languages. The history of Coverdale is, as we shall find, intimately connected with translations of the Scriptures into English for a space of nearly thirty years.

Myles Coverdale.

The period passed at Hamburgh by Coverdale, in company with Tyndale, his predecessor in biblical translation, has been already noticed. This is an interesting point in his history; it is one in fact which seems to have had a continued influence upon his future course. But before speaking of the labours of Coverdale, in connection with the translation of the Scriptures, it will be well to notice the few facts that are known of his previous life and conduct, and the circumstances which made him an exile for the faith of Christ his Lord.

Coverdale at Hamburgh with Tyndale.

Myles Coverdale * was born in the year 1488 about eleven years after the birth of Tyndale. He was

Coverdale's

* In many of the circumstances relative to Myles Coverdale, the "Memorials of Coverdale," 8vo 1838, have furnished much with regard to authorities and investigated facts, for which otherwise it would have been necessary to search: and my labour in comparing authorities has thus been much lessened. It is true that some facts have been ascertained which the author of the "Memorials" has not noticed, but I owe much to his work. *Inferences* I have of course drawn for myself, for which the author of the "Memorials" must not be supposed to be responsible He has my hearty thanks for the aid afforded by his careful researches

birth, 1488, in Yorkshire.

probably a native of the district of Coverdale in Yorkshire, from which it is most likely that he received his name: Coverdale is more likely to have been a personal than a family surname. He was brought up at Cambridge in the Augustine monastery, of which he afterwards became a monk. I have already, in speaking of Tyndale's visit to Cambridge, adverted to the state of that University during the greater part of the first quarter of the sixteenth century.

Brought up at Cambridge, Mem Cov p. 3

Becomes a monk

It was in the days in which Cambridge was yet enwrapped in ignorance, both spiritual and mental, that Coverdale studied there: and it was when some beginnings were made in the acquisition of knowledge, that he was one of the first to take some means of obtaining more learning than he had obtained from his hitherto limited education.

Coverdale receives priest's orders

Tanner

He received priest's orders at Norwich, from John, bishop of Chalcedon. This may have been some years before the time at which he gave himself diligently to the study of the Scriptures; and it is almost the only definite fact relating to the early part of the life of Coverdale, except his becoming a monk, of which we have any particular account.*

He becomes a diligent student of Scripture

His letter to Cromwell Mem. Cov p 193 Chap Ho. West Bund C

At some period between this and the open avowal of the doctrines of the Reformation made by Barnes and others at Cambridge, we find Coverdale diligently addicting himself to the study of the Scriptures; this is manifested by an interesting letter addressed to Thomas Cromwell, afterwards Earl of Essex, who seems, from what Coverdale says, to have made him some promise, or held out to him some hope of assistance in obtaining books for his studies. He says,—"I am the booldyr of your goodnesse in thys my rude style, yf yt lyke your favour, to revocate to your memory the godly communication which, your Mastyrschype had with me, your oratour, in Mastyr Moorys howse, upon Easter Eve," . . . . . He then asks Cromwell's help, informing him, "Now I begyne to taste of Holy Schryptures; now (honour be to God) I am sett to the most swete smell of holy lettyres, with the godly savour of holy and awncyent Doctoures, unto whose knowlege I can not attayne, without dyversyte of bookys, as is not unknowne to your most excellent wysdome Nothyng in the world I desyre, but bookys, as concernyng my leinyng; they onse had, I do not dowte, but Allmyghty God schall perfourme that in me, whych He, of Hys most plentyfull favour and grace, haith begone." This letter is subscribed, "Your chyld and beedman in Jesu Chryst, Frere Myles Cov'dale."†

Soliciting books

Dr Barnes the prior of the Augustines Fox ii p 453

The prior of the Augustines, the house to which Coverdale belonged, was Dr. Robert Barnes, who had studied at Louvain, and whose attainments were far greater than those of most others at Cambridge. It was probably through Barnes, that Coverdale began, as he says, to taste of Holy Scripture. It does not seem at all certain what the period was at which Barnes commenced his labours for the encouragement of learning at Cambridge; but it could hardly have been previous to the year 1517, and perhaps even later by a few years. About the time of this revival of learning at Cambridge, the Gospel began to be preached there by Thomas Bilney, who afterwards was burned at Norwich. Among others who were converted by this means was Barnes himself, who, though he had been diligent in studying the word of God, and in instructing others, as well as in preaching against hypocrisy of every kind, had hitherto never fully known what the Gospel of the grace of God meant.

He encourages learning at Cambridge

The Gospel preached at Cambridge

Barnes converted

The conversion of Barnes was an event of some importance in its results, as connected with the reformation. He stood at this time unrivalled in literary eminence at Cambridge, and yet had to learn the lesson so humbling to the pride of man, that "no flesh shall glory" in the presence of God. The energy and influence of Barnes received a direction which was felt by others; and thus his instructions became important auxiliaries of the efforts of those who were already labouring in setting forth from Scripture the Gospel of the *grace* of God. At a later period we find Barnes amongst those who laboured in other places, and who also aided in the distribution of the Scriptures.

Tyndale at Cambridge.

About the same time, William Tyndale, being at Cambridge, was the means of the conversion of *John Frith*, afterwards his friend and fellow-labourer. About the same period, or perhaps earlier, likewise

* The author of the "Memorials of Coverdale" assigns the date of this circumstance to the year 1514 In his note he cites Tanner as his authority, saying, "He gives the date MDXCIV but the C is evidently an error of the printer" That there is a mistake in the passage is evident, but whether the "C" ought to be wholly expunged, as the author of "Memorials of Coverdale" has done, or whether it ought to be changed into an "X," it would be difficult to determine; nor do I see at all whether it is the more probable to suppose that Coverdale became a priest in 1514 or in 1524

† It is, perhaps, impossible to assign a date to this letter: the author of "Memorials of Coverdale" thinks that it was written before the year 1514 This, I believe, is much too early; for it would make Coverdale exceedingly in advance of his fellows at Cambridge in having a "taste of Holy Schryptures" It was after 1516 (when the New Testament of Erasmus was first published) that the mind of Bilney was enlightened; and it was not till some time after this that Barnes was converted to Christ by Bilney Whether Coverdale had a taste or desire for the truth of God at any previous period may be questioned

George Stafford lectures on divinity

George Stafford (or Stavert) of Pembroke Hall, first gave lectures in divinity at Cambridge; this appears to have been one of the means through which the light of God's truth became known there.

Scripture especially the object of Coverdale's study

It is interesting in the midst of all that was going on at Cambridge, to find that the mind of Coverdale especially rested upon the study of Holy Scripture. It seems as though even then God had been fitting him for that work which in subsequent years he was to accomplish—the completion of the first English translation of the Scriptures from the original languages.

Progress of the Gospel at Cambridge

Fox ii 434

The preaching of the Gospel had continued some time both at Cambridge and in the neighbouring counties, but without any direct attack being made upon the authority or the doctrines of Rome. The Gospel was the means in England, as well as in other countries, of bringing to some souls the knowledge of peace with God; and this often went on for a considerable time without causing any decided collision with the ecclesiastical powers: but those who see what the finished work of Christ means, learn at length how it is denied by the doctrines of Rome; and thus, not only truth is held, but error is decidedly opposed and renounced. On the other hand, although the Romish authorities may not at first shew their displeasure, so long as they are not directly opposed, yet they soon feel the contradiction which exists between the doctrine of the free grace of God and the whole of the system of Rome. It was thus in England: Bilney and his companion Arthur at length attracted the attention of Cardinal Wolsey, and were brought into trouble in the year 1527. This was the signal for others, either to shrink back from the open profession of the Gospel, or to go forward at all hazards. Barnes and others at Cambridge chose the latter alternative. On the Sunday before Christmas-day, in the year 1527,* Dr. Barnes preached at St. Edward's Church, belonging to Trinity Hall: he took for his subject the Epistle for the day (the third Sunday in Advent), Phil. iv. 4—7, and *postilled*† it so as to form a resolute attack upon the Romish authorities, making Cardinal Wolsey the direct object of part of his assault; in this he may, perhaps have gone whither his zeal, rather than the spirit of a sound mind, led him. Barnes's sermon excited, as it might be expected, considerable attention; "he was immediately accused of heresy by two fellows of the King's Hall." From the subsequent examination of Barnes before Cardinal Wolsey, we learn how he had treated a part of his subject; it was probably from the words, "Let your moderation be known unto all men, the Lord is at hand,"—that he spoke of the grandeur of churchmen as forming a contrast to that which ought to characterise the disciples of Christ. The giving of alms, according to the command of the Lord, was set in contrast with all this worldly glory, and one point urged was, how much better it would be for all the superfluity of worldly glory to be sold, in order that the poor might be aided. It is no wonder that a discourse like this should have excited considerable attention, as well as the resolute opposition of those who upheld the pomp and authority of Rome's priests.

Bilney and Arthur arrested, 1527.

Bold stand of the "Gospellers" at Cambridge.

Barnes's sermon, 1527 Phil iv 4—7

His attack on Wolsey.

Barnes accused of heresy.

Proceedings from Christmas, 1527, to Lent, 1528.

The proceedings at Cambridge lasted for some weeks, from Christmas, 1527, until "within six days of Shrovetide; in the following year;" so that the upholders of Barnes must have almost wondered at the non-interference of the ecclesiastical authorities. They were not, however, unmindful of these proceedings,

* There can, I think, be no doubt that these occurrences at Cambridge took place almost immediately after the lamentable abjuration of Bilney (Dec 7, 1527) The author of "Memorials of Coverdale," places it earlier: he says, "Fox does not mention the date of this circumstance, but he intimates, in his History of Wolsey, that it was about the year 1526." At first sight it would seem from the manner in which the circumstances are stated by Fox (ii p. 206), that the submission of Bilney had been subsequent to that of Barnes: but there are many reasons for holding a contrary opinion; for instance, Bayfield was charged amongst other things, with having (Sep 13, 1527) spoken well of Bilney and Arthur, then imprisoned by Cardinal Wolsey (Fox, ii 269), and yet, after Bayfield had been imprisoned, Barnes was still at liberty, and exerting himself to procure his liberation: this alone is decisive as to the order of the events. But farther, although Fox does intimate loosely that it was *about* 1526 that Barnes was troubled, yet he mentions synchronous events which prove that it must have been in February, 1528 When Fox states a *date*, he often does it very loosely, or else his printer has made very numerous errors, but he frequently gives *notes of time* which serve to correct the erroneous date. He states expressly, that it was "as the ambassadors were thus travelling to Rome to promote the cardinal to be Pope, although the Pope was not yet dead, *in the mean time* the cardinal played the popish persecutor here in England," &c. These words, "in the mean time," give a synchronism which makes the time of the occurrence clear. *When* were these intrigues for the Popedom going on at Rome? The date of his letter to Sir Gregory Cassaley on the subject is February 6, 1528, and it was only a little while before, that Pope Clement had become ill, and not very long after that he recovered This agrees exactly with the dates which Fox gives in another place; so that the end of 1527 may be confidently recorded as the period of the preaching of Barnes against the pomp of the cardinal

† To *postill* or to *postillate*, is to take a portion of Scripture, and, after reading it through, to expound in order the topics mentioned This was done without excluding a large exposition of some one or more parts; the term is derived from *post illa;* that is, after a certain portion of text, a comment or exposition introduced Nicolaus Lyranus formed his commentary in this manner, and several, Wiclif for one, followed the same plan in their preaching

Another mode of preaching or teaching was called "declaring;" this was going through the Scriptures which spoke of a particular subject, and giving a combined view of their testimony when seen in connection The modern plan of taking a few words and forming a discourse upon them, stands in marked contrast to both these modes of teaching, while it altogether loses the distinctive value of each. *Postillation* taught the import of the text with the context, thus leading to an exact knowledge of the Scriptures; while *declaring* led on to a comprehensive view of the range of truth revealed by God

Barnes arrested publicly.

Books searched for

for on the day above-mentioned, Dr. Barnes was arrested by a sergeant-at-arms, who had come down from London; this was done "openly in the convocation house, to make all others afraid." Nor was this all, for a search was likewise made, about the same time, for prohibited books, in the rooms of about thirty suspected individuals. The search at this time was occasioned by the fact of prohibited books in Latin and English having become very numerous since the latter part of the year 1526. However, not a single prohibited book was seized; for Dr. Farman, of Queen's College, heard that this search was likely to take place, and thus had time to warn the others, to conceal or carry away those that they possessed.

Barnes taken to London
Coverdale accompanies him.
Barnes adjudged a heretic
He is resolved to suffer, but is persuaded by his friends to recant

Dr. Barnes was taken as a prisoner to London. Coverdale accompanied him, and lent him his aid in writing for him, and giving him what assistance he could in replying to the articles objected to him. After various examinations Barnes was adjudged a heretic, and thus the only alternative left for him was to suffer death by burning, or recant. His own resolve was to lay down his life for the testimony of the truth; but, alas! he was overpersuaded by the suggestions of some of his friends, of whom, however, it is clear that Coverdale was not one, who used the argument which so often prevails in emboldening individuals to tamper with conscience; "they persuaded him rather to abjure than to burn, because (they said) he should do more good in time to come, and divers other persuasions which were mighty in the sight of reason and foolish flesh." How many have, since Barnes, done those things which they knew to be evil before the Lord, from the *desire of usefulness;* as though any supposed or hoped-for future good could justify the commission of present evil, however slight.

Coverdale's zeal in preaching.

When Barnes consented to abjure, Coverdale probably left him; if he returned to Cambridge, he could have continued there but a short time, for almost immediately we find him preaching the Gospel in Essex. He is mentioned by Bishop Bale, as having been particularly active in this labour; he says of Coverdale, that while " others dedicated themselves in part only, he gave himself wholly up to propagating the truth of the gospel." This was a course which required a heart fully resting upon the knowledge of that heavenly inheritance which through the blood of Christ belongs to those who believe; he had seen in Barnes the consequences of testimony against Romish corruption of doctrine, but still he went on steadily in his course. So long as Barnes was at Cambridge as his prior, he had been comparatively safe; and now, that he was deprived of his encouragement, and Cambridge was a peculiarly dangerous place for those who favoured the reformed doctrines, he laid aside his monk's habit, and either left or did not return to his convent, and became an itinerant preacher, having assumed the habit of a secular priest.

Coverdale preaches at Bumsteed on the fourth Sunday in Lent, 1528
Fox, ii 267
Thomas Topley's confession
He recants.
Coverdale opposes image worship and auricular confession.

About four weeks after Coverdale had been in London with Dr. Barnes, he was at Bumsteed (or Steeple Bumsteed) in Essex, a parish of which Richard Fox, a favourer of the Reformation, was the curate. We learn this from the confession of Thomas Topley, an Augustine friar of Stoke Clare, who was induced, partly by reading certain books, partly by the instructions which he received from Coverdale and Richard Fox, to renounce both his order and his habit, and, like Coverdale, to appear simply as a secular priest. Topley was brought before Bishop Tonstall on this account, when, like others, he recanted the doctrines which he had received. We learn from his confession, that on the fourth Sunday in Lent, Coverdale had preached that images were not to be worshipped, that auricular confession to a priest was not necessary to the forgiveness of sins, and that transubstantiation was contrary to the word of God. In this last mentioned point he was probably in advance of Barnes.

Coverdale at Hamburgh, Easter to Christmas, 1529.

The next place in which we find Coverdale is at Hamburgh, about a year subsequent to this sermon which he had preached at Bumsteed. Where he had been in the interim, or how he had escaped to the Continent, are circumstances concerning which we have no information. It is, however, scarcely to be doubted, that after the information received from Topley, it was altogether unsafe for him to remain in England. The search for heretics which was then made in the diocese of London was very strict, as it was also in that of Lincoln (then much more extensive than it is at present), and Cambridge also could be no safe abode for him. He must have remained concealed if in England; and in escaping, it must have been with considerable difficulty and danger.

Coverdale and Tyndale together at Hamburgh, Easter to December, 1529.

Fox, in his account of Tyndale, says that he, having finished the translation of the book of Deuteronomy, wished to print it at Hamburgh, and that in his voyage thither he was shipwrecked, and then "he came in another ship to Hamborough, where at his appointment Master Coverdale tarried for him, and helped him in the translating of the whole five books of Moses, from Easter till December, in the house of a worshipful widow, Mistress Margaret Van Emmerson, Anno 1529, a great sweating sickness being the same time in the town."

It is *probable*, from this account, that Hamburgh was the place to which Coverdale had escaped from

England, and that previous to his departure from this country he had some intercourse with Tyndale, so as for them to appoint to meet one another at Hamburgh.

It is interesting to find these two laborious exiles thus brought together in a foreign land; the one having been obliged to quit England on account of his desire that the word of God should be circulated in English, the other on account of the opposition existing between the Gospel and the doctrines of Rome. It has been questioned how Tyndale became acquainted with Coverdale;* but when it is remembered that Tyndale had been for some time at Cambridge but a few years previous, that his being there was intimately connected with the introduction of the Gospel amongst those who lived there, and that Coverdale was one of those who very early upheld the truth at Cambridge, there can, I think, be but little doubt that the friendship of Tyndale for Coverdale as well as for Frith commenced at Cambridge.

With respect to *what portion* of the Pentateuch was translated conjointly by these two exiles, it has been doubted whether it was merely a retranslation of the book of Deuteronomy, or whether they retranslated together the whole of the five books: but whichever it be, we find Coverdale now using the "taste of Holy Schrypture" which he had received, and the Scriptural learning which he had acquired, to make known to his countrymen the word of God in their own tongue. The work of Tyndale and Coverdale together.

We find Coverdale at Hamburgh from Easter till December, 1529, subsequently at Antwerp, previous to the end of 1534, and at some time during his exile in Denmark. Where he was at the time of the betrayal and imprisonment of Tyndale we do not know; but it is not unlikely that the same habits of itinerant preaching which had previously, as well as subsequently characterized him, led him at this period to various places. As yet, he had not begun to be a Bible translator independently of Tyndale; nor did he commence his labours until after the imprisonment of his predecessor. Had Tyndale lived, he would doubtless have continued his work, so as to have translated the whole of the Scriptures. To this point he was striving: if it had been so, Coverdale would not have laid aside for a time his itinerant life, in order to become a translator; but it is probable that the work on which he was engaged with Tyndale at Hamburgh, suggested to him the first thought of carrying on the complete labour of translating the Scriptures. Coverdale an itinerant preacher

Two leaves of Genesis were printed by George Joye, in February 1533: this circumstance, as we learn from Tyndale's letter to Frith, occasioned a rumour respecting a new Bible: "Out of this is sprung the noise of the new Bible; and out of this is the great seeking for English books at all printers and bookbinders in Antwerp, and for an English priest that should print." The rumour that such a Bible was to be published seems, from Tyndale's account, to have spread pretty widely. It is clear that such a work was wished for, and this desire may have led to the report being credited. Lewis says, "On the 17th of March, 1533, the convocation of the province of Canterbury met. Among other things done by it, it was decreed, that the Holy Scriptures should be translated into the vulgar tongue, and the laity prohibited contending about articles of the faith and the Holy Scripture; but I do not find, that the former part of this decree was executed at this time." It is questioned whether this be not altogether a mistake of Lewis's; and it is doubtful whence he took the statement. It is most certain that the convocation met as he describes, but that it decreed a translation of the Scriptures to be made, seems quite unfounded. Now it is clear, from what Tyndale wrote to Frith, that in this very year, and in the same part of it, there was "a noise about a new Bible," it is probable that some account connected with this rumour was the basis of Lewis's statement,—a statement which anticipated the proceedings of the convocation which met at the close of the following year. George Joye publishes two leaves of Genesis The rumour of a new English Bible Meeting of the convocation Lewis, p 78. A translation of the Scripture decreed

It will be well for a while to leave Coverdale, and the circumstances in which he was, to look at the events which had passed in England during the time of his absence on the Continent,—events which led on to the most important results, as it regards this country.

During the time in which proceedings had been carried on for the entire suppression and extinction of the Scriptures in English, a change gradually took place in the relations in which Henry VIII. stood towards the Pope. This change, although it was brought about simply for worldly and selfish ends, was at length instrumental in giving free permission in England to possess and use the Scriptures. Henry's rupture with the Pope

No monarch of Europe possessed so absolute a sway as Henry: he governed, through Wolsey, the clergy of England as entirely as he did the laity; and when Clement VIII., during his imprisonment, The power and authority of Henry

* The author of "Memorials of Coverdale" suggests, that "through the means of Barnes, or his own reputation for learning and letters, he was favourably esteemed by Tyndal;" —as to Barnes having recommended Coverdale to the notice of Tyndale, it is disproved by the fact that Barnes was yet in prison, so that Coverdale must have found his way to the continent the first of the two.

appointed Wolsey his vicar-general for England, Henry virtually held in his own hands an authority which none of his predecessors had wielded. He possessed even then, virtually, that ecclesiastical supremacy which he afterwards claimed formally. On the downfall of Wolsey, Henry's passions seem to have been directed against the clergy; and thus they were compelled, as an atonement for having acknowledged Wolsey's legative authority, to assent to the title of the king as being supreme head of the Church of England, so far as is permitted by the law of Christ. This, it is to be observed, was not intended as a direct renunciation of the papal authority, neither did it have that effect: other circumstances, which were in course of occurrence at the same time, led to this.

Henry's case of divorce. The question at issue

These circumstances were connected with the divorce of Henry from his first wife, Catherine of Arragon, the widow of his elder brother Arthur. The question of the lawfulness of the king's marriage was one on which the minds of Papists and Protestants were alike divided. The matter was argued (so far as it was referred to Scripture) upon the injunctions of the law of Moses, the principal question being this: Does the prohibition of Lev. xx. 21, extend universally? or, Is it limited by the directions of Deut. xxiv. respecting the marrying of a brother's widow? Some held that the directions of Deut. xxiv. were limited to the Israelites, while those in Lev. xx. were binding upon all men. Then, amongst Romanists, there was this farther question,—If the marriage be forbidden by the law of God, can the Pope's sanction render it valid? So that *if it were assumed* that the marriage were essentially prohibited, the question would be—Can the Pope set aside the commands of God? Both these questions were long debated, so that it was not until the divorce of Henry had been pending six years that it was concluded; and then (1533) it was done by virtue of his own absolute authority.

Lev xx

Deut xxiv

Henry at length divorced, 1533

Tyndale and Coverdale of opposite opinions on the question

To shew how very divided the minds even of the friends of the Reformation were on this subject, it will suffice to state that Tyndale condemned the divorce, while Coverdale approved it. It is thus a great mistake to suppose that this was made at the time in any sense a party question by the Reformers, and that they had unanimously favoured that step which led to such remarkable and (in the end) beneficial effects in England. This step of Henry brought about fully that rupture with the Pope and the discarding of his authority, which introduced the free circulation of the Scriptures in our native tongue. Truly, it is wonderful to mark the means by which God accomplishes His own gracious purposes!

Cranmer consecrated archbishop of Canterbury, March 30, 1533

The king's marriage with Anne Boleyn, Nov 14, 1532. Sentence of divorce from Catherine, May 22, 1533

Dr. Thomas Cranmer was consecrated archbishop of Canterbury, March 30, 1533: he was nominated to the archbishopric by Henry; and the appointment was confirmed by the Pope, who sent the necessary bulls. It is probable that the Pope was not unacquainted with the character and sentiments of Cranmer; but it was not the time for him to question the appointment which Henry had made, unless indeed he wished to hasten the open rupture which was already threatening. In this appointment of Cranmer, the king found one who was fully prepared to help him through his difficulty in the affair of the divorce, as well as to confirm his marriage with Anne Boleyn, which had taken place Nov. 14, 1532. The sentence of nullity concerning Henry's previous marriage was not given by Cranmer until May 23, 1533, more than half a year after.

There were now three persons who were so connected with Henry as to have a peculiar influence over him; and all of them were in a certain measure favourable to the Reformation; so far, at least, as to uphold the publishing of the Scriptures in English: these persons were Anne, the new queen, Cranmer, and Cromwell, Henry's minister.

Henry freed from obligation to the Pope

It is probable that it was his having some knowledge of this combination of circumstances, that induced George Joye to send to the king and queen the two leaves which he had printed of Genesis; but Henry was not yet prepared to sanction such an undertaking. However, one great hindrance was now removed; for the king had no longer any occasion to seek to stand well with the Pope. So long as he had been a suitor in the Papal Court, he had sought to do this; but his entire rupture with Rome left him wholly unshackled in that quarter.

Desire for the Scriptures in English

Meeting of the convocation, Dec 19, 1534

Certain resolutions agreed

Through the latter part of the year 1533, and the whole of 1534, the publication of the Scriptures in English seems to have been freely spoken of—especially among the clergy. This may be attributed to two causes,—1st. the desire on the part of Cranmer, Latimer, and others, that the Scriptures should be permitted in English; and 2nd. the difficulty which was found by the clergy to suppress the prohibited version of Tyndale, which could hardly be accomplished; and therefore it might be judged best to give the people an approved translation in the hope of thereby suppressing that which was forbidden. Thus when the convocation of the clergy of the province of Canterbury met in the close of 1534, there were certain resolutions agreed to unanimously; their purport being, that the archbishop of Canterbury should make instance to the king, in the name of the convocation—1. That he would please to decree and command that all who had any prohibited books in their possession, whether printed in England or abroad, should, within three months, deliver them up to such persons as the king might name, upon such penalties in case of non-compliance as the king might see fit to declare. 2. That the king would vouchsafe to decree *that a translation of the Scriptures into English should be made* by certain honest and learned men whom the king should nominate; and that the Scriptures so translated should be delivered to the people according to their learning. 3. That the king would prohibit, on certain penalties, that any laymen should contend publicly concerning the Catholic faith, or articles of faith, or the sacred Scripture, or its meaning.

to respecting the Scriptures Strype's Cran p 34

These resolutions appear to be a kind of compromise; the people might have the Scriptures if they could be prevented from disputes about doctrines to be believed, and if they would hold in their possession none except a permitted translation.

These resolutions a kind of compromise.

It may require some explanation why such matters should have been referred to the king. Now it occurred in the month preceding these resolutions of the convocation (namely, in Nov. 1534), that an act of parliament raised the claim of the king's supremacy so high, as to make him not merely the supreme ruler of all estates ecclesiastical as well as civil, but actually to put all church discipline into his hands. He was declared to have full authority to visit, order and reform all heresies, abuses, &c. which by any manner of spiritual authority or jurisdiction, may lawfully be ordered or reformed. This threw all ecclesiastical discipline completely into the hands of the king and those commissioned by him, making the convocation itself to be almost powerless. Previous to the passing of this act, there was no need for them to have petitioned the king respecting a version; for, by the constitution of Archbishop Arundel, in 1408 (to which an appeal had been made by More but about five years previously), the convocation possessed full power to authorise a translation of the Scriptures, or even a single bishop might have done this within his own diocese.

An act of parliament sets the king's supremacy very high, Nov. 1534 Collier iv. 251

The convocation almost powerless

The convocation, in agreeing upon this petition to the king, seem to have so framed their requests, that nothing should be gained except in appearance, by those who favoured the Reformation. To let the people have the Scriptures, and to hinder them from knowing what the Scriptures taught, was certainly a rather ingenious device. It is probable also that, if the king were to have nominated several of the superior clergy to this task of translating the Scriptures, care would be taken by them, that the version, when complete, should not even seem to uphold the doctrines which Tyndale and Frith taught.

Nothing as yet gained save an appearance by the friends of the Reformation

There does not appear to be any thing known respecting the manner in which Henry received this petition. This much is certain, that Cranmer, Cromwell, and the queen, would by no means uphold the whole of what was solicited; and, at the same time, it is plain from the conditional promise made by the king in 1530, that he was not altogether averse to a translation of the Scriptures into English: *he*, however, was inclined to clog the concession much in the same way as it had been done by the convocation.

That some results followed immediately from the petition is, I think, most probable, although the connection cannot be directly traced: certain facts, however, relating to identity of *time*, &c. make it almost certain that the first complete English Bible translated from the original languages, is owing indirectly in some measure to the proceedings of this convocation. It is probable that the report of this petition to the king spread widely; and to those who longed for the Scriptures in English, it must have been no small encouragement thus to see even the prelates willing upon certain conditions to circulate them.

The indirect cause of Coverdale's translation.

To return to Myles Coverdale: the place of his sojourn at this period—the close of 1534—is not certainly known. He had been at Antwerp, but he had probably gone elsewhere before this time, indeed, the arrest of Tyndale in the preceding month, would in itself shew him the insecurity of that city for an English exile; and thus he would probably have then gone elsewhere, even if he had remained there with Tyndale and Rogers up to this time.

Coverdale at the close of 1534.

II.

COVERDALE'S TRANSLATION—ITS RECEPTION IN ENGLAND.

We now come to regard Myles Coverdale as a *Bible translator*, a capacity in which he had been previously engaged, when he had at Hamburgh aided Tyndale in the translation of part of the Pentateuch. It is from the dedication to King Henry VIII., and from the prologue to the reader, which Coverdale prefixed to his version of the Scriptures, that we learn some particulars as to the motives which induced him to take

Coverdale as a Bible translator.

Reference to Tyndale's imprisonment.

the work in hand, together with other circumstances in connection with its history. It is evident that when Coverdale speaks, in this prologue, of the adversity of those who had commenced the work of translating the Scriptures, he refers to the imprisonment of Tyndale, his former fellow-labourer. Up to the very time of his apprehension, Tyndale had laboured in this field—the last work in which he had been engaged having been the careful revision of his version of the New Testament.

Date of Coverdale's commencement of his version, close of 1534.

From this we learn *when* it was that Coverdale first undertook this work of translation, namely, at some period subsequent to the imprisonment of Tyndale, in Nov. 1534.

The cost undertaken by others Mem Cov., p 49. Barnes again in London.

In his dedication, he says that "as the holy goost moued other men to do the cost herof, so was I boldened in god to laboure in the same." The author of "Memorials of Coverdale" conjectures that it was Cromwell who, principally, if not wholly, bore the cost of the printing. This is not impossible; especially when we remember that Cromwell had, some years previously, patronised Coverdale, when he "began to taste of Holy Schrypture." Dr. Robert Barnes was also again in London, the patronage of Queen Anne making him safe for the time; and it is very likely that he was not at this period unmindful of his friend, who had at his own peril given him his support; he may indeed have urged Cromwell to move in the matter. It will be observed how remarkably the date which Coverdale incidentally states as that at which he commenced his translation, agrees with that of the address of the convocation to Henry VIII., respecting a new translation of the Scriptures. Tyndale was imprisoned in Nov. 1534; the address of the Convocation was in the very next month. Coverdale gives a further proof of the date of his beginning to translate: he speaks of his having been aided by five sundry interpreters in the Dutch [German] and Latin languages. Now what can these five have been? In the Old Testament he may have had, 1st. the Vulgate; 2nd. Paguinus' version; 3rd. Luther's German translation; 4th. Leo Juda's German-Swiss version; but, as for a fifth, until the year 1534, there was no other, unless, indeed, versions taken from the Vulgate were meant: but this could not be the case, because he never could have considered the Vulgate, and a version made from it, as distinct aids.* Thus, at no period previous to the year 1534, could he have these aids. In this year, the first volume of Sebastian Munster's folio Hebrew Bible was published *with a Latin version*, and this must have been Coverdale's *fifth* subsidiary translation. In the prologue to the edition of Coverdale's version which was printed in 1550, he speaks expressly of the time when he was first moved to take this work in hand: he says—"For the which cause (accordinge as I was desyred Anno 15.34.) I toke the more upon me, to set forth this specyall translation, not as a checker, not as a reprouer or despiser of other mens translacions," &c.; so thus we have the most conclusive evidence as to the year in which the work was begun, and also what part of the year in which it must have been.

Proofs of the date when Coverdale commenced his version.

The translations by which he was aided.

Coverdale's prologue, 1550

Motives which led to the making of this version

The resolutions of the convocation neglected.

This version could not have been undertaken in direct compliance with the resolution of the convocation. Coverdale clearly was not appointed to the work by the king: had he been so, some intimation would certainly have been found in his dedication; and besides no steps were taken by Henry to comply with the other things requested in the resolutions. The truth was this, I should judge;—it was seen by some of those about the king that such a translation, if completed, would not be disagreeable to him; and thus they proposed it to Coverdale, offering pecuniary aid for the printing. Coverdale was unwilling to undertake it, questioning his own competency, and not wishing even to seem to interfere with the labours of Tyndale; but from the fact of the latter being imprisoned, all hopes being at an end that he would at present complete the version which he had commenced, Coverdale was willing to do his best to supply the immediate need by making a new version, which might serve as a temporary expedient, until Tyndale himself, if liberated, or else others more skilful than himself, might complete a translation of the Scriptures. Such appear to me to have been the motives and encouragements of Coverdale in commencing his work.

Coverdale's opinion of the benefit of various translations. Prologue

Coverdale thought that many and diverse translations were rather helpful than otherwise; because thus a reader who could not consult the original texts might have a better opportunity of obtaining a knowledge of the true meaning of the Scriptures; and thus his "specyall translacyon" would at least be helpful to this end. He says, "Now, where as the most famous interpreters of all geue sondrye iudgmentes of the texte (so farre as it is done by ye sprete of knowlege in the holy goost) me thynke noman shulde be offended there at, for they referre theyr doinges in mekenes to the sprete of trueth in the congregacyon of God: & *sure I am, that there commeth more knowlege and vnderstondinge of the scripture by theyr sondrie translacyons, than by all the*

* Whitaker, in his "Enquiry into the Interpretation of the Hebrew Scriptures," supposes that Coverdale did this; had he, however, paid a more deliberate attention to the statements made by Coverdale himself, and the whole bearing of the connected facts and dates, he would, I think, have come to a different conclusion. Whitaker overlooks the possibility of Coverdale having used Sebastian Munster's Latin translation, and he seems to have forgotten Leo Juda's Swiss version

gloses of our sophisticall doctours." It is probable that most who have considered the subject would agree with the judgment which Coverdale thus expressed.

The completion of the work, Oct. 4, 1535

The period of the completion of Coverdale's version is marked by a subscription at the close of the volume, "Prynted in the yeare of our LORDE, MDXXXV., and fynished the fourth daye of October." I have already shewn that the translation could not have been commenced before November, 1534, and probably it was not until the following month; thus, the longest time that Coverdale could have had for the completion both of the translation and of the printing, was *eleven months;* and if his work did in any way result from the resolutions of the convocation (Dec. 19, 1534), then the whole was executed in the short space of *nine months and a half.* The time when he began was certainly not previous to Nov. 1534, the date of the completion is found in the book itself; so that, however difficult it is to believe that it was actually accomplished in the limited time stated, the fact cannot be reasonably called in question.

Time occupied by the translation

Coverdale's extraordinary zeal and diligence

Coverdale's intense earnestness in giving the Scriptures to the people in English, as well as his unwearied diligence and assiduity are thus fully proved; without these, together with the blessing of God upon his labours, Coverdale's Bible would never have been the translation that it is: when the circumstances are taken into consideration, it certainly is one of the most astonishing performances ever executed.*

Reasons why he did not simply adopt the versions already executed by Tyndale

It might be thought that as time pressed so much when this translation was commenced, the simple course for Coverdale would have been to have taken Tyndale's Pentateuch and New Testament, just as they were, to have procured likewise those books (Joshua to Chronicles inclusive) which he had translated, but which remained unpublished, and then to have merely supplied the books which still remained untranslated: this would at least have diminished his labour not a little. Three reasons appear, however, to have hindered him from taking such a course:—1st. By so doing, he might in some measure interfere with Tyndale's own labours, and seem as though he intended to supplant him;—2nd. It was the firm conviction of Coverdale that many translations in a vernacular tongue are a help to the understanding of Scripture;—and 3rd. He had to bear in mind that Tyndale's translations, both in the Old Testament and in the New, were already prohibited in England; so that he would have made his book condemned before it was published, had he adopted the versions of Tyndale as a commencement. I have already adverted to the probability that there is of Coverdale's having good reason to believe, even when he commenced his version, that such a translation would not be altogether unacceptable to the king. Now it is clear, that the version itself should be such as the king would not be displeased with, which would most probably have been the case, if the offensive translation of Tyndale had been presented as a considerable part of this new Bible.

Coverdale's Old Test and Apoc. a new translation

The Old Testament and the Apocrypha are thus a new translation; the Pentateuch bearing in some parts a strong resemblance to Tyndale's, but still it is a new translation. The New Testament appears to be in part a revision of Tyndale's, in which Coverdale took much care, and availed himself both of the original edition (1526) and the amended one (1534). He sometimes accords with one of these, sometimes with the other, but not unfrequently makes an entirely new version of a whole passage. If it be asked, why in the New Testament Tyndale was followed so much more than in the Old, I think it might thus be accounted for:—it is evident from the dedication to the king, that Coverdale knew before it was completed that it would probably receive the royal permission for its circulation, and that there had been some communication about the matter between Coverdale or some of his friends in England (such as Cromwell or Barnes) with the king. He may have thus learned, that even if a considerable part of the New Testament did follow Tyndale's version, it would not be made a ground of objection, provided it were revised throughout. Such a consideration as this, may account for the circumstance in question. It is not, however, to be understood, that Coverdale, even in the New Testament, is a servile follower of his predecessor,—far from it, but he uses Tyndale as his *basis*, just as King James's translators took the Elizabethan Version, or Bishop's Bible, for theirs.

The New Test partly a revision of Tyndale's

Coverdale's dedication

The dedication to King Henry VIII. which is prefixed to Coverdale's Bible, shews that it was at length a privilege permitted by Henry to his subjects to have the Scriptures in their own language. This change in Henry's conduct is stated by Coverdale in express terms. He commences his dedication with a comparison of the high priest Caiaphas and the Pope, in that each had declared that of which he himself knew not the true meaning; Caiaphas, in prophesying that one man should die for the people; the Pope, in

Coverdale's comparison of Caiaphas and the Pope

* In the year 1837, the parishioners of St Magnus the Martyr, erected a monument to the memory of Coverdale In the inscription, it is stated that he "spent *many years* in preparing a translation of the Scriptures This statement, however, is not quite correct; for though it is true that Coverdale spent many years in labours connected with the translation of the Scriptures, yet the period occupied by the work under notice was really less than *one year* What deserves to be known, is the *shortness* of the period in which his intense assiduity completed his labour.

The title, "Defender of the Faith," given to Henry

conferring the title of "Defender of the Faith" upon Henry. After speaking of Caiaphas, he says, "Even after the same maner y[e] blynde bysshoppe of Rome (that blynde Baalam I say), not vnderstondynge what he dyd, gaue vnto your grace this tytle: *defendour of the fayth*, onely by cause your hyghnes suffred your bysshoppes to burne God's worde the rote of fayth, and to persecute the louers and mynisters of y[e] same, where in very dede the blynde bysshoppe (though he knewe not what he dyd) prophecied, that by the ryghteous admynistracyon and continuall diligence of your grace, the fayth shulde so be defended, *that God's worde the mother of Fayth with the frutes therof, shulde haue his fre course thorowe out all Christendome, but specyally in your realme.*" This is a very express testimony. Coverdale recites, with strong reprehension, the king's former conduct in keeping the Scriptures from the people, and punishing those who circulated them; and speaks in commendation of the altered course which the king had now commenced.

Coverdale's estimate of the king's conduct

To the same purport, he says, a little farther on:—"And the trueth of Baalam's prophecie is, y[t] your grace in very dede shulde defende the Fayth, yee euen the true fayth of Christ, no dreames, no fables, no heresie, no papisticall inuencions, but the vncorrupte fayth of God's most holy worde, which to set forth (preysed be the goodness of God, and increase youre gracyous purpose) your hyghnes with youre most honorable councell, applyeth all his studye and endeuoure." We learn, I think, from this dedication, the circumstances in which Coverdale completed his version, just as we learn from the prologue the events which led to its commencement. At first he had been urged to undertake the work, the king being apparently not directly hostile; but before it was completed the king was become actually friendly.

Circumstances in which Coverdale's version was completed.

Coverdale does not put the king's authority as being paramount in spiritual things; God, *and His word*, he speaks of as being superior; and, by his plain statements respecting Henry's previous conduct, he shews that he would not flatter the king, in order to procure his sanction for the circulation of his version of the Bible.

Josiah used as a comparison.

Farther on, in the dedication, he speaks of Josiah, and his pious care in restoring the law of God; and then he compares the altered conduct of Henry with the reformations of that Jewish king. This may *now* seem a strange comparison; but Coverdale could then only judge of the king's *actions*, and from them he deemed that the grace of God was truly in the heart of Henry; and that this had led him to consent that the Scriptures might be circulated in English.

Intention of Henry to suffer the Scriptures in English.

Coverdale rests upon this intention of Henry, to let his subjects have the Scriptures in English, as being *a known fact;* and thus, towards the conclusion of the dedication, he commits his translation to the king's hands, "to correcte it, to amende it, to improue it, yee & cleane to reiecte it, yf youre godly wysdome shall thynke necessary. And as I do with all humblenes submitte myne vnderstondynge and my poore translacyon vnto the spirite of trueth in your grace [it has been before shown that Coverdale clearly regarded that Henry had now been converted to Christ, and thus he speaks on this supposition;], so I make this protestacyon (hauyng God to recorde in my conscience) that I haue nether wrested nor altered so moch as one worde for the mayntenance of any maner of secte: but haue with a cleare conscience purely & faythfully translated this out of fyue sundry interpreters [it has before been shown what these five were, and how they were used], hauyng onely the manyfest trueth of the scripture before myne eyes."

Coverdale's faithful purpose in translating

Coverdale's disinterestedness resembles that of Tyndale.

Coverdale's willingness that his translation should be suppressed if the king saw fit, and that some other might supply its place, resembles the expression of Tyndale's desire: "If it wolde stande with the kinge most gracious plaisur to graunte only a bare text of the Scripture to be put forthe emonge his people..... *be it if the translation of what person soever shall please his magestie*," &c. Both of these translators sought to meet the need of their countrymen; and so long as they might freely have the Scriptures, they were satisfied, their object being very different from that of those who sought to establish their own credit as translators. Tyndale and Coverdale both sought the glory that cometh of God.

The notices which this prologue and dedication afford us, are of considerable interest: they let us know how some of the links of the chain of English Scripture translations were wrought.

Zurich, Frankfort, and Cologne all mentioned as probable places for the printing of this Bible. Mem. of Tyndale, p. 77, see note.

It would appear from the difference of the type, &c., in which this Bible itself was printed, from that of the introductory pieces, as though these latter had been printed in England, and then prefixed; the book having probably been transmitted in sheets from the place in which it was printed: *where* this may have been is much disputed. The places to which it has been attributed are Zurich, Frankfort, and Cologne. The first of these was supposed by Mr. Wanley, from the resemblance of the type to that used by Christopher Forschover. Frankfort has been named from the *wood cuts* resembling some used there, while Mr. Offor ascribes it to Cologne.* Other cities have also been named as the place at which this was printed. If this

* There is this difficulty, however:—Would the printing of heretical books have been allowed there at this time?

could be ascertained, it would tell us where Coverdale himself was from the end of 1534 until the latter part of 1535.

This Bible, after it had been printed and sent to England, remained for several months before it was circulated. This has occasioned two alterations to be made in some of the copies—the one is a change in the introductory part of the dedication, which had at first mentioned "Queen Anne" as being the consort of Henry; this was changed into "Queen Jane," subsequent, of course, to May 20, 1536, the day of Henry's marriage with Jane Seymour:—the other alteration was the reprinting of the title-page, with the date of 1535 changed into 1536.

This Bible not circulated for many months.

Anne Boleyn beheaded, May 19.

Jane Seymour mar. to Henry, May 20, 1536.

The cause of the delay respecting this Bible was stated by Coverdale himself, in a sermon preached at Paul's Cross. This sermon is thus alluded to by Fulke, in his reply to Gregory Martin.

"Now if some of our Translators or they all have not attained to the best and most proper expressing of the nature of all words and phrases of the Hebrew and Greeke tongues in English, it is not the matter that I will stand to defend, nor the translators them selues, I am well assured, if they were all liuing. But that the Scriptures are not impudently falsified, or wilfully corrupted by them, to maintaine any hereticall opinion, as the adversarie chargeth us, that is the thing that I will (by God's grace) stand to defend against all the Papists in the world ......I myself, and so did many hundreds beside mee, heare that reuerend Father M Doctor Couerdale of holy and learned memorie in a sermon at Pauls Crosse, vpon occasion of some slanderous reports that then were raised against his translation, declare his faithfull purpose in doing the same, which, after it was finished, and presented to king Henry the eight, of famous memorie, and by him committed to divers Bishops of that time, to peruse, of which (as I remember) Steuen Gardiner was one: after they had kept it long in their hands, and the king was diuers times sued vnto for the publication thereof, at the last being called for by the King himselfe, they redeliuered the booke: and being demanded by the King, what was their iudgement of the translation, they answered that there were many faults therein. Well (said the King) but are there any heresies maintained thereby? They answered, that there were no heresies that they could finde maintained thereby. If there be no heresies (said the King) then in God's name let it goe abroad among our people According to this iudgement of the King and of the Bishops, M. Couerdale defended his translation, confessing that he did now himselfe espie some faults, which if he might reuiew it once ouer againe, as hee had done twice before, hee doubted not but to amend: but for anie heresie, hee was sure there was none maintained by his translation After the same manner I doubt not (by God's helpe) so to defend all our translations .. . that not one shall be found of purpose to maintain any hereticall opinion, and not many errours committed through negligence ignorance or humane frailtie.

Fulke does not say when it was that Coverdale preached the sermon in question at Paul's Cross; but there can be very little doubt, I should think, that it must have been during some part of the reign of Edward VI., after his translation had been reprinted, in 1550.

It has been supposed that Queen Anne Boleyn's influence led to Henry's permission that the Bible should be read in English. This is probable, and seems confirmed by what that Queen herself wrote—a MS. manual of Devotions (quoted by Lewis), in which God is thanked for having put it into the king's heart to let his people have the Scriptures; but although this permission appears to have been obtained through Anne's request, or, at all events, in her life, yet the Bible clearly was not circulated in English until after she was beheaded (May 19, 1536). The reason of this appears to be that the bishops to whom Coverdale's translation was delivered, had not returned it to the king.

Anne Boleyn's influence

Her prayer. Lewis, p 97

The English Bible not circulated in her life

A few days after the execution of Queen Anne, June 9, the convocation agreed upon a form of petition to be presented to the king, that he would graciously indulge unto his subjects of the laity the reading of the Bible in the English tongue, and that a new translation might be made for that end and purpose. This petition proves that Coverdale's translation was not yet circulated, and that it did not altogether please those to whom it was given in order to be overlooked. Perhaps this objection may have partly arisen from its not having been executed in precise accordance with their petition, in Dec. 1534, when they requested that the king would name certain honest and learned men for the purpose of making a translation.

June 9, 1536 The convocation petition for a new translation

Heylin, quoted by Lewis, p 102

Coverdale's translation not yet circulated

However, it was very clear that the king was resolved that the people should have the Scriptures in English: and we find this shewn in a copy of certain injunctions issued by Cromwell, in the year 1536, as they stand in Fox. The seventh of these runs thus:—"*Item.* That every parson, or proprietary of any parish church within this realm, shall on this side the feast of St. Peter, ad vincula [i. e. Aug. 1], next coming, provide a book of the whole Bible in Latin, *and also in English*, and lay the same in the quire *for every man that will to look and read thereon*, and shall discourage no man from the reading of any part of the Bible, either in Latin or English, but rather comfort, exhort and admonish every man to read the same, as the very word of God, and the spiritual food of man's soul, whereby they may the better know their duties to God, to their Sovereign Lord the King, and their neighbour; ever gently and charitably exhorting

The king resolved that the people should have the Scriptures

Cromwell's injunctions, 1536 Fox, ii, p 324

them, that using a sober and modest behaviour in the reading and inquisition of the true sense of the same, they do in no wise stiffly or eagerly contend or strive one with another about the same, but refer the declaration of those places that be in controversie to the judgment of them that be better learned."

This injunction must relate to Coverdale's Bible. The intention of Henry thus shewn. This clause omitted in Cranmer's register. Inquiry into the cause of this discrepancy

That this injunction, as it stands in Fox, must relate to Coverdale's Bible is clear, because there was then no other complete version printed; so that we see what the intention of Henry was in the matter; I say *intention*, because this never seems to have been carried into execution; and, in the copy of these injunctions, in Cranmer's register, this clause is altogether omitted. How is this discrepancy to be accounted for? It is owing, I suppose, to one of three causes,—either to the death and disgrace of Queen Anne causing the king for a time to change his mind; or else, because the convocation requested a new translation, and Cromwell was unwilling to issue injunctions directly opposed, in this respect, to the wishes of the prelates and clergy; or else, the copies put into the hands of the bishops by the king, were not yet returned; and thus it would be contradictory to command a copy to be in every parish church by a certain day, when, in fact, no copies could be obtained for carrying into effect the injunction. It is clear, from the copy in Cranmer's register, that when these injunctions of Cromwell were actually published, the clause in question was omitted.

Coverdale's version gets into circulation

But although this first printed English Bible was not set in every parish church, as had been at first intended; yet, before the close of the year 1536, it had found its way into circulation, rather as a version *permitted* by royal authority than enjoined. The specific proof that it was, at least, at the close of the year 1536, that the English Bible, translated by Coverdale, was allowed to be circulated, is to be found in the fact of two reprints having been executed in the very next year. This would certainly not have been done, had not the copies been previously exhausted.

In proof that this version was permitted by the king, and did not merely get into circulation without any such permission, we have—1st, the statement of Coverdale, in his sermon at Paul's Cross; and, 2nd, the thanks which he gives the king, in the dedication of the Latin and English Testament, published by Nicholson, in 1538, for his kindness and favour respecting the Bible which he had dedicated to the king.

More editions of Tyndale's Testament.

Tyndale's Testament probably now tacitly permitted

It is also to be borne in mind, that in this same year, in which Coverdale's Bible was permitted to be read without peril, there were, at least, three or four editions of Tyndale's New Testament printed: this shews that they must have had an increasing sale in this country; for in no preceding year had there been, apparently, such a number of editions. It is true, that in 1534, there were three impressions; but one of these was Joye's corrupted text, and one of the others a surreptitious edition of Tyndale's own revision of his version. Thus we may conclude, that though the prohibition was not formally abrogated which made it penal to possess Tyndale's Testament, yet that virtually this was tacitly permitted, at least, during this year.

Uncertain where Coverdale was. Probable that he returned to England before the close of 1536

Bibl. Suss. vol. ii

In all this time it does not seem to be certainly known where Coverdale was: we have not been able to trace his movements from the time that he was at Antwerp with Tyndale and Rogers. However, it appears on several grounds most probable, that he had come to England before the close of the year 1536. It is beyond a question that Coverdale was in England at the early part of the year 1538; at which time he addressed certain letters from Newbury to Cromwell: these letters prove that he was not in this country as a person in danger, but standing in Cromwell's favour. He was probably in England pretty soon after the arrival of the copies; and the alteration made in the title page (the date being changed, and the words "out of Douche and Latyn" omitted) were probably done by himself. We find, from one of his letters to Cromwell (without date), that he was in some way connected with Nicholson the printer; and this, as well as other circumstances, makes it probable that the Southwark reprints were executed under his own eye, and that the editions of 1537 formed one of the recensions of his translation to which he referred in his sermon at Paul's Cross.

And now I must leave Coverdale for a while, in order to advert to the publication of all the translations of William Tyndale, which were in this same year (1537) collected and printed.

III.

"MATTHEW'S BIBLE" PUBLISHED AND CIRCULATED.

It has already been shewn, how the intention of Tyndale to complete a translation of the Bible was frustrated, by his imprisonment and subsequent martyrdom. It is probable, that his revised New Testament was intended as a portion of such a complete version. The books of the Old Testament from the Chronicles and onwards, were (with the exception of Jonah) left untranslated at the time of his imprisonment; and even after that period, it was the hope of Coverdale, and others of his friends, that he would be set at liberty, and thus be able to complete his undertaking. He left, in manuscript, a translation of the books from Joshua to Chronicles, inclusive, which either remained with his friends at Antwerp, at the time of his arrest, or else was transmitted by him to some of them from Vilvoord. On the morning of his martyrdom, he is stated by Fox to have sent to his friend Pointz a pacquet of papers: it is not improbable that it contained part of this version. But however obtained, the translation was, after his death, in the hands of some of his friends; and now that the circulation of the Scriptures in English was tolerated, they were not long before all that had been executed by Tyndale came forth in print.

Tyndale's intentions frustrated

The books from Joshua to Chronicles left in MS.

His friends publish his version

In 1537, the year of the two reprints in England of Coverdale's Bible, the translations of Tyndale were published in a collected form, the portion of the Scriptures and the Apocryphal books which had not been translated by Tyndale being supplied out of the version of Coverdale. This Bible bears the name of MATTHEW'S BIBLE, from the name of Thomas Matthew being given on the title page and at the end of the dedication, as though he had been the translator or editor, or else publisher.

1537. Matthew's Bible.

It appears to have been commonly assumed, that Thomas Matthew was a name wholly fictitious, and that no such person was concerned in any way in connection with the publication of the Bible. It *may* be so; but it has, I think, been too hastily taken for granted. It is certain that there was at this time a person named Thomas Matthew, of Colchester, one of those who were convented on March 2, 1527, before Bishop Tonstall, on charges of heresy. This, at least, shews that there was one of the name amongst the favourers of the Reformation; and I judge it to be far more probable that he was in some way connected with this Bible, than that it was attributed to a wholly fictitious person of the same name. The Essex *Lollards* appear to have been well and closely acquainted with each other. Now Coverdale had, it is clear, laboured much amongst some of them: indeed, his notoriety in that county appears to have led to his becoming a voluntary exile; and thus, it is not improbable, that some of those who had been troubled on account of religion in that part, might, like him, have sought a refuge on the Continent. It is to be borne in mind, that Colchester, the abode of this Thomas Matthew, was one of the places to which Tyndale's Testaments were brought from the continent: Bayfield, who suffered martyrdom, had imported them thither. It is not impossible, from the connection of Bayfield with Tyndale, that the latter might continue to have some intercourse with the favourers of the word of God in that place: this *may* have led in some manner to this Thomas Matthew having in his possession the MS. of Tyndale, from which the Bible in question was subsequently printed. I would merely suggest the connection of Tyndale with Colchester, as having possibly something to do with the name affixed to this Bible; for, after all, it is to be remembered, that we have no record of the transactions which led to the publication of this Bible.

Thomas Matthew perhaps a fictitious name

Thos Matthew of Colchester.

Doubtless there were, at this time, others of the name of Thomas Matthew. One of this name seems to have been a few years later a person of some consideration amongst the favourers of the Reformation; for, in the reign of Mary, he was one of the members of the House of Commons who withdrew (Jan. 12, 1555), after certain proceedings for the setting up of Popery were sanctioned.

Another Thos Matthew

Strype Mem. Ecc iv p 272.

If any real person of the name of Thomas Matthew were connected with this Bible, it is clear that he was not the translator (the dedicator does not speak of himself as such), since it is taken out of Tyndale and Coverdale; nor yet does he seem to have been the editor, for this office is stated to have been occupied by JOHN ROGERS, an individual intimately connected with the publication and revision of the Bible in English. To this edition was prefixed, An Exhortation to the Study of Holy Scriptures, beneath which stand J. R. the initials of his name. This may, I think, be regarded as a proof that Thomas Matthew was not merely a fictitious name assumed by John Rogers; for had this been the case, the Exhortation would probably have been signed T. M. instead of J. R.

Thos. Matthew not the translator

John Rogers the editor of this Bible

This Bible appears to have been printed at the expense of Richard Grafton and Edward Whitchurch, who, at a subsequent period, became printers themselves; and through whose means, in this manner, many editions of the English Scriptures were published. Their initials appear at the beginning of the Prophets; perhaps the part of the expense which they defrayed commenced there. Thomas Matthew may actually have been the person at whose cost the preceding part was printed. Whether or not Archbishop Cranmer had any thing to do with the actual publishing of this Bible, does not appear to be clearly known, he did, however, patronize it warmly when it actually was published.*

Questioned where this Bible was printed. Fox says it was at Hamburgh, ii p 434.

It has been questioned, as in the case of Coverdale's Bible, *where* this was printed. In the absence of any certain proof, there appears no sufficient reason for discrediting the statement of Fox, who mentions Hamburgh as the place; although it may be remarked, he knew so little about this edition, that his account is in some respects wholly inaccurate; events and records were the things with which he had to do, and not the history of books. Mr. Offor thinks it was at Lübeck.

Fox. iii Lewis p. 223. [E. Coll T. Baker S T B] Rogers educated at Cambridge At Antwerp Goes to Wittemberg Returns to England Goes again to the continent. Collier, p. 103

John Rogers, the editor of this Bible, was brought to a knowledge of the truth at Antwerp by Tyndale and Coverdale. He had been educated at Cambridge. Subsequently he became the chaplain to the English company of merchant adventurers at Antwerp. After he saw the errors of popery, he is mentioned as having been for some time at Wittemberg. He may have gone thither at some period between 1531 and 1535; but when it was, or for what length of time, there does not appear to be evidence. He must afterwards have returned to England, as he is said to have again gone to the Continent about the time of the commencement of the printing of Matthew's Bible. Collier says, "When Tindal was executed for religion, Rogers being apprehensive of hard usage in England, under King Henry VIII., retired to Wittemberg in Germany, where, learning the language of the country, he had the charge of a parish." It seems, however, like an anticipation for a parochial charge to be spoken of as being given to Rogers thus early: it is pretty evident that *this* visit to Wittemberg must have been subsequent to the year 1540.

Superintends Tyndale's version

However, it is clear that he was on the Continent about, or a little after, the time of the martyrdom of Tyndale; but it is more probable, I should judge, that he went to superintend the publication of the translation which had been executed by that faithful martyr of Christ. This Bible has the character of *Tyndale's* labours so stamped upon it as clearly to shew that the undertakers of it were not ashamed of its being marked, as being (at least, in a considerable part) his version; some of his prologues and notes are retained: at the end, likewise, of the Old Testament, the letters W. T. are printed in *very* large text capitals curiously flourished. Thus, if the name of Thomas Matthew were a device to conceal the real translator, it was indeed a very transparent veil, and one but little fitted to serve the object proposed, while the book itself contained so many proofs of its true origin.

Matthew's Bible reaches England before Aug 1537 Cranmer writes to Cromwell, Aug 4 State Papers vol i pt. 2, no xciv. The Abp 's judgment that the version was very well done.

This Bible was completed and had reached England by August, 1537, for, on the 4th of that month, Cranmer wrote to Cromwell about it, requesting him to exhibit it to the king, to whom it had been dedicated, and, if possible, to procure the king's license for its being read and sold by all without any danger from any acts, ordinances, or proclamations, to the contrary: this refers, I suppose, to the prohibition, on May 28, 1530, of every portion of Scripture which had been published by Tyndale, to the penalties of which many might have thought themselves exposed, if they were to circulate copies without such a license being given by the king. The archbishop gave his judgment of the version that it was very well done. The license was requested as one that should be in force until the bishops should put forth a translation, which Cranmer thought would not be "till a day after Domesday;" this shews how the prelates opposed the Scriptures being freely circulated among the people. Those among them who desired this, such as Cranmer, Latimer, and Fox, must have found their path a very difficult one.

Cranmer writes to Cromwell again, Aug. 13 Cotton MSS. Cleop. E v p 329 b Strype's Cran 82 Cott MSS Cleop E v p. 292

On the 13th of the same month (August) Cranmer wrote again to Cromwell: he speaks of his having heard that the Bible had been exhibited to the King, and also that the King had licensed it. He expresses his hearty thanks for this service, not questioning that God would reward him for his diligent care in thus exerting himself towards the setting forth of the word of God in English; and that for this, his name would be handed down to posterity. A few days afterwards (the 28th) in writing to Cromwell, he again adverts to the same thing.

First expressly sanctioned

It is rather remarkable that the first edition of the Scriptures in English, which received an express sanction from the king, was this, of which the New Testament and the Pentateuch had been but seven

* Strype says (Mem. Cran) that after Cranmer had put the Bible into the hands of several to correct portions of it, and had obtained the king's leave for its publication, "he could not see his desire effected by these men, till it was happily done by other hands"; referring to the publication of Matthew's Bible. This might seem to decide the matter, that Cranmer was not a curator of the edition which bears the name of Matthew; but it may be, that Cranmer, as he could not get his own design complied with, aided by his support the publication of this Bible, as well as giving it his patronage when actually printed

years before so strictly prohibited. The version had been condemned as faulty: it was said to be filled with heresy; to be corrupted in order to maintain heretical doctrines and the like; and yet this very version of Tyndale was thus set forth at length with all the sanction which the king's license could give it. This seems indeed like an answer to the dying prayer of Tyndale. Here was the version, about which he had laboured so long and so laboriously—to execute which he had become an exile from England—the version which, when first sent to England, had been condemned and burned, and in consequence of which some who read it were burned likewise—the version which all men were prohibited to read, possess, or circulate—now, in less than a year after the translator's martyrdom, "set forth by the king's most gracious license."

English edition contains parts previously prohibited

An apparent answer to Tyndale's dying prayer.

Much is due to Rogers as the editor of this edition, of which a great part was only in manuscript when it passed into his hands; he seems to have acted both as desiring to give his countrymen a Bible as correct as possible, and likewise to perpetuate the labours of his friend and instructor in the truth of the gospel. Rogers clearly had nothing to do with the pecuniary concerns connected with this Bible; probably, in making any arrangement with Grafton and others, he only sought to get the book printed as well as he could, while *his* business was to care for the accuracy of the impression. Fox gives the following account of the effect which this edition of the Bible produced,—"The setting forth of this book did not a little offend the clergy, namely, the bishops aforesaid, both for the prologues, and especially because in the same book there was one special table collected of the common places in the Bible, and the Scriptures, for the approbation of the same, and chiefly about the Supper of the Lord, and Marriage of Priests, and the Mass which there was said not to be found in the Scripture." It is no wonder that such topics as these should give offence; it is also probable that the doctrinal statements of the New Testament, and those contained in the prologues of Tyndale were little calculated to make this translation acceptable with the greater part of the church authorities.

Editorial care of Rogers.

He had nothing to do with the pecuniary concerns of this edition

Fox. vol. ii. p. 453.

The bishops offended with Matthew's Bible

But this was quite the *popular* translation: the New Testament of Tyndale had been circulated for eleven years, and had quite a hold on the affections of the people. *This* was sufficient to make Matthew's Bible more acceptable than Coverdale's: indeed, this Bible, in various editions, was one which continued to be much used for many years, while that of Coverdale (highly valuable as being the first complete printed version of the Scriptures) had but one edition, after the appearance of Matthew's Bible, until its modern republication in 1838; and this one reprint was not until the year 1550. Coverdale's *New Testament* was, however, reprinted many times in the reigns of Henry VIII. and Edward VI. Coverdale does not seem to have wished in any way to rival Tyndale as a translator; and thus, although he made Tyndale's version of the New Testament in a great measure the basis of his own, yet it is clear, from his prologue, that nothing was farther from his thoughts than the idea of superseding it.

The popularity of this translation.

It should be added that the edition of Tyndale's Testament, from which that part of Matthew's Bible was taken, was that of the year 1534, which had been carefully revised with the Greek, completing it just before his apprehension and imprisonment. The version being one that had thus been revised *may* have been one reason why the king did not refuse to license this Bible, for it might be *said*, that the heresy was expunged in the revision; although it would be hard for any one who objected to the edition of the year 1526, to find any improvement in that respect in the one published eight years later.

New Test of Matthew's Bible taken from Tyndale's revised Testament, 1534.

IV.

PREPARATIONS FOR THE "GREAT BIBLE"—COVERDALE TRANSLATES THE NEW TESTAMENT FROM THE LATIN.

THE measures which had been taken in England before the end of the year 1537, for the licensing of the Bible in English were, as has been shewn, very pleasing to Cranmer. He appears to have exerted himself, previously as well as subsequently, for some years to this end, both amongst the prelates in the convocation, and in the use which he made of the influence which he possessed over the king. At length he obtained, by the aid of Cromwell, permission from the king that the Bible might be translated into English and printed. "The care of the translation lay wholly upon him; assigning little portions of this holy book to

Cranmer's efforts for the Bible in English

Strype, Cran. p. 81.

Part of the N.

Test. distributed for revision.

divers bishops and learned men to do; and being dispatched, to be sent back to him." *When* this occurred does not precisely appear; but it is evident that the endeavours of Cranmer to procure a new translation were made between the middle of 1535, and the middle of 1537. It is thus, very likely, that the proceedings of Cranmer for the making of this translation were in reference to the resolution either of the convocation, Dec. 19, 1534; or else, which seems more probable, that of the convocation of June 9, 1536. The proof that these measures of Cranmer belong to the interval which I have thus assigned to them is this:—Strype speaks of their being "not long after" Cranmer's visitation of the diocese of London, in 1535; and he says expressly that these endeavours had been made previous to the publication of Matthew's Bible, by which they were at least for a time superseded.

Strype, Cran. p 48, 81.

The manner in which Cranmer proceeded to obtain a revision of the Bible in English, is narrated in Fox's Manuscript preserved by Strype:—

"—— The archbishop whose mind ran very much upon bringing in the free use of the holy scripture in English among the people, put on vigorously a translation of it And, that it might not come to be prohibited, as it had been, upon pretence of the ignorance or unfaithfulness of the translators, he proceeded in this method.—First; he began with the translation of the New Testament; taking an old English translation thereof, which he divided into nine or ten parts, causing each part to be written at large in a paper book, and then to be sent to the best learned Bishops, and others, to the intent they should make a perfect correction thereof And when they had done, he required them to send back their parts, so corrected, unto him at Lambeth, by a day limited for that purpose: and the same course no question he took with the Old Testament It chanced that the Acts of the Apostles was sent to Bishop Stokesly to oversee and correct When the day came, every man had sent to Lambeth their parts corrected, only Stokesly's portion was wanting. My Lord of Canterbury wrote to the Bishop a letter for his part, requiring him to deliver them unto the bringer, his secretary. He received the Archbishop's letter at Fulham: unto which he made this answer; 'I marvel what my Lord of Canterbury meaneth, that thus abuseth the people, in giving them liberty to read the Scriptures: which doth nothing else but infect them with heresy. I have bestowed never an hour upon my portion, nor never will. And therefore my Lord shall have this book again, for I will never be guilty of leading the simple people into error.' My Lord of Canterbury's servant took the book, and brought the same to Lambeth unto my Lord, declaring my Lord of London's answer. When the Archbishop had perceived that the Bishop had done nothing therein, 'I marvel,' said he, 'that my Lord of London is so froward that he will not do as other men do.' One Mr. Thomas Lawney stood by; and hearing my Lord speak so much of the Bishop's untowardness, said, 'I can tell your Grace why my Lord of London will not bestow any labour or pains this way. Your Grace knoweth well, that his portion is a piece of New Testament. But he being persuaded that Christ had bequeathed him nothing in his Testament, thought it mere madness to bestow any labour or pain, where no gain was to be gotten And besides this, it is the Acts of the Apostles; which were simple poor fellows, and therefore my Lord of London disdained to have to do with any of them' Whereat my Lord of Canterbury and others that stood by could not forbear from laughter."

The book of Acts sent to Bp Stokesly.

His refusal to translate

Lawney's remarks on him.

Bp Stokesly a great enemy to the Gospel

It is to be remembered that Bishop Stokesly was particularly marked as an enemy of the Gospel: he had been the persecutor of Frith and many others who suffered for the alleged crime of heresy. Lawney, who made such free remarks upon him and his conduct, had been a companion of Frith at the college of St. Frideswide, where he likewise was one of the sharers of his imprisonment, on account of suspected books and doctrines.

Lewis, p 90, Mem Cov. p 47

The date of these events

This account of Strype (or rather perhaps of Fox), requires a few observations. Lewis, and the author of "Memorials of Coverdale," speak of this narration, as though there were no clue to the period to which it belongs. Accordingly they place it rather before the time to which, according to the very words of Strype, it must be referred: they speak of it as though it might have taken place in 1534, although Strype says it was "not long after" the middle of 1535. The latter writer suggests in a note that this translation might have taken place some years later in connection with the Great Bible, which was published in 1539. If he means that these things might have happened, then he brings them to a period too late, for this must have been (as has been already shewn) prior to July or August, 1537. I should not have thought it so needful to clear up the point as to the date of these events, had not a degree of needless uncertainty been thrown over them, which would have been altogether avoided, had the account given by Strype been observed in all its particulars.

Tyndale's translation used by Cranmer as a basis.

The "old translation" taken by Cranmer was, I suppose, a copy of Tyndale's: this might be called "old," in the sense of having been one previously made, not as having existed for many years. The transcription of it into paper books was probably done that the revisers might have space for their corrections to be fairly written, and also lest any should object to bestow their labour upon a book which had been already condemned.

Although it be said, in the above account, that "the same course, no question, he took with the Old Testament," yet I think that this is very doubtful. It seems merely to be a surmise either of Strype or of Fox, drawn from the fact of the New Testament having been thus revised. If he did proceed in this manner with the Old Testament, what translation should he take? Tyndale had only published the Pentateuch and Jonah; and the version of Coverdale, though printed in October, 1535, was not published for some time: indeed, it might at this very period be yet in the hands of the bishops appointed by the king to examine it. I believe that there is no sufficient ground for supposing that more was accomplished in this revision than the New Testament by nine or ten bishops and others. It must have been in reference to this undertaking, that Gardiner wrote to Cromwell: "Nevertheless, I have as gret cause as any man, to desire rest and quiet, for the helth of my body: wherunto I thought to have entended, and to absteyne from bookes and wrytyng, having finished the translation of Saynt Luke and Saynt John, wherin I have spent a gret labour." This letter, of which the exact date is uncertain, shews that in some respects Cranmer had authority to require the prelates, who so greatly opposed the reformed doctrines, to aid in this work, and thus Stokesly was a singular instance of opposition.

Bp Gardiner's letter to Cromwell MS chap Copy Westm. Bundl C. Mem Cov, p 48.

It is probable, that the offence which was taken at the notes and prologues of the Bible which bears the name of Thomas Matthew, led the projectors of it, as well as the friends of the circulation of the word of God, to think of publishing a less obnoxious edition; an edition which should contain the text, but no annotations which might give needless offence. This appears to have been represented to the king, who committed the care of the matter to Cromwell. The parties employed by Cromwell for carrying this into execution were Richard Grafton and Edward Whitchurch, the same who had borne the expense of Matthew's Bible. It may be that this was done as an act of justice, as a compensation for the superseding of their Bible by the new one, which was about to be printed.

Grafton and Whitchurch employed.

With these, as corrector of the press and editor, Myles Coverdale was joined, who was at this time in England, and had been employed by Cromwell in various services. I have already noticed the fact which has been so commonly overlooked, that Coverdale returned from the continent about the year 1536: this in itself shews the reason he was now employed on this service by Cromwell. In the early part of the year 1538, Coverdale was at Newbury, in Berkshire, employed in searching out popish books, and carrying out the commands of the king, that Thomas Becket should be no longer honoured as a saint. He was there on the 7th of February; on which day, as well as the following, he wrote to Cromwell, and he continued there at least till the 5th of March, when he again wrote to him. How long before this he went to Newbury does not appear.*

Coverdale at Newbury, 1538

He writes to Cromwell, Feb. 7, and Feb. 8, 1538

In his letter of February 7, Coverdale tells Cromwell that for want of diligent care many books were circulated which upheld the papal power, or were "against the king's lawful object concerning Thomas Becket." He had required the curate of Newbury to call for such; in consequence of which, in two or three days a great number were brought to him. He seeks for Cromwell's authority for this, and that he may collect such books wherever he may find them. This letter was sent to Cromwell by Coverdale's servant. It would seem that Coverdale had been but a few days at Newbury when he wrote this letter; for, in another written the very next day, he mentions as a thing which he had just discovered, that the matin books in the church at Newbury set forth the Pope's authority, just the same as had been before the papal authority had been abolished in England. This appears to have troubled Coverdale greatly, supposing that the same might exist similarly elsewhere; and that thus many of the priests were under the penalty of a *præmunire:* this fear he mentioned to Cromwell only, not letting even the bearer of the letter, "good Mr. Wynchcombe," know what he had written.

The third letter from Newbury, dated March 5, complains of certain things at Henley-upon-Thames, such as Thomas Becket's martyrdom in a window, and persons excluding from their houses those who favoured the Gospel. These things he attributed to the bishop of Lincoln (of whose diocese Henley was a part): and

He writes again, March 5

* These letters published by Mr Pettigrew (Bibliotheca Sussexiana), prove incontestably, the return of Coverdale to England. I had formed my own judgment that he did so return, before I knew any thing of the contents of the letters in question, on the following grounds:—

1st The statement of Bishop Bale as to the length of Coverdale's exile, shewing him to have been in England about 1539 or 40

2nd The reprints of Coverdale's Bible at Southwark, in 1537, which must have been supervised by himself.

3rd. The fact that the books which Coverdale wrote about this time were printed in England; which would probably not have been the case, had not Coverdale himself returned.

The letters of Coverdale published by Mr. Pettigrew, are without any date, as to the year in which they were written; but, from the mention of Prince Edward in them, it is evident that they belong to the early part of 1538, and not to the previous years.

when it is remembered that this bishop was Longland, the persecutor of the Lollards in 1521, we need not wonder at Coverdale's surmise.

Coverdale's occupations, while in England, may be properly adverted to before his steps are traced to Paris. Besides the employment at Newbury, and perhaps elsewhere, on which he seems to have been sent by Cromwell, he made about this time another version of the New Testament, using as his basis the Latin Vulgate. His judgment was decidedly in favour of many translations being used, in order that the English reader might have the opportunity of examining into the meaning of the Scripture, without being limited to the translation of any one man, or one body of translators. It may be asked, Why should he take the trouble to re-translate the New Testament himself? It may be, that, in his editions of the Bible, he had more closely followed the version of Tyndale than he had wished, and that pressure for time had induced him to make the New Testament much less of a new translation than those portions of the Old had been, which Tyndale also had rendered into English. It may be, that he wished, now that he had comparative leisure to re-translate the New Testament, to add one more version to the apparatus with which the vernacular reader was furnished for the understanding of the Scriptures. But whatever his motives may have been, he made at this time a new version of the New Testament, differing more from the translation contained in his Bible than that had done from Tyndale's.

Coverdale translates the New Test. from the Latin.

This translation seems to have been printed in the beginning of 1538; and it became the basis of subsequent impressions of Coverdale's New Testament.* In the Lent of 1538, there was printed in Southwark, by James Nicholson, a New Testament of this version, together with the Latin text. Coverdale was not the corrector of it; and the only part for which he was responsible was the dedication to the king. Some one else appears to have prefixed a Preface to the Reader; and the execution of the whole book was clearly done with great carelessness, not at all answering the hopes of Coverdale respecting Nicholson's attention. He seems to have given him free leave to print it, having arranged the plan of the work, and written the dedication, and then personally to have ended his connection with this edition. With regard to what time in Lent it was published, it is evident that Coverdale was at Newbury during a good portion, at least, of that time, and then appears to have gone to Paris, while the book was yet in the press; so that the publication could have been but a little before Easter. This, in itself, explains what might now, after a lapse of more than three hundred years, have seemed difficult to account for; namely, why Coverdale should have written the dedication to the king, and then have left the book without bestowing any further trouble upon it: for the needful care in printing, he seems wholly to have relied upon the printer Nicholson. From the dedication to the king which was prefixed, we learn what the motives were which induced Coverdale to plan a New Testament in English and Latin on the same page. He commences his dedication thus:—

This translation printed beginning of 1538.

Mem. Cov, p 95

Eng and Latin Testament, Lent, 1538.

Dedication written by Coverdale.

Coverdale's motive in his Duoglott Test.

"Consyderynge (moost gracious Soueraigne) how louyngly, how fauourably, and how tenderly your hyghnesse hath taken myne infancy & rudenesse in dedicatynge the whole bible in English to your moost noble grace. And hauynge sure experience also how benynge and gracious a mynde your hyghnes doth euer beare to all them that in theyr callyng are wyllynge to do theyr beste: It doth euen animate & encorage me now lykewyse to vse the same audacite towarde your grace." After this, he speaks of the reproach and ill-will which the enemies of the word of God manifested toward those who sought to circulate the Scriptures in English. He says that they "seke out new occasions, how they may depraue & synistrally interprete our wel doynges. And where as wth all faythfulnes we go about to make our brethren (youre graces louynge subiectes) participante of the frutes of oure good wylles, they yet not regardynge what profite we wolde be glad to do them, reporte euell of vs, sklaunder vs; and saye the worste of vs: *Yee they are not ashamed to affirme, that we intende to peruerte the Scripture, and to condemne the commune translacion in Latyn, whych costumably is red in the church:* where as we purpose the cleane contrary."

This made it very desirable that the English text should be printed by the side of the Latin, so as to exhibit to all who were capable of forming a judgment, that there was no purpose in the minds of the translators, either to contemn the Latin version which had been used in the West for a thousand years, or to corrupt the Scripture. Coverdale had likewise other objects in procuring this Duoglott Testament to be

* I conclude that the 16mo. Testament mentioned in Memorials of Coverdale, p. 225 (out of Herbert), as published by Coverdale, was of this version. The following are my reasons:—The New Testament, English and Latin, printed in Lent of this year, by Nicholson, in Southwark, follows Coverdale's second translation, although carelessly printed so as to abound with errors. Of this edition by Nicholson, Coverdale said, that it was disagreeable to his former translation in English; by which he appears to have meant, that his translation was not accurately given: however, he himself, in printing an edition at Paris (to supersede the inaccurate edition printed at Southwark), adopts the same translation which had been in the Southwark edition, correcting the typographical and other errors This shews that he did not complain of the translation itself, for it must have been his own; and the "former translation" referred to, cannot be that of his Bible, but his new translation, which had, before this time, been printed. If it had not, Nicholson could not have printed a negligent impression of it.

set forth: he says, that it was done, "not so much for the clamourous importunyte of euell speakers, as to satisfye the iust request of certayne your graces faythfull subiectes. And specially to induce and instruct such as can but Englishe, & are not learned in the Latin, that in comparynge these two textes together, they maye the better vnderstonde the one by y[e] other. And I doute not but such ignoraunte bodies as (hauynge cure and charge of soules) are very vnlearned in the Latyn tunge, shall trough thys smal laboure be occasioned to atteyn vnto more knowlege, and at the leest be constrayned to say well of the thynge, whyche here tofore they haue blasphemed." This second translation of the New Testament made by Coverdale, appears to have been in a great measure *adapted* to the Vulgate Latin, so as to shew that he did not at all despise that translation, and likewise, in order to help the English reader the more effectually to the understanding of the Latin text by the side. This accounts for many of the variations between the version in his Bible, and this which was published separately.

Difference between this and Coverdale's previous version

Farther on Coverdale says, "For as much as in our other translacions, we do not followe thys olde Latyn texte word for word, they cry out vpon vs: As though al were not as nye the truth to translate the scripture out of other languages, as to turne it out of the Latyn. Or as though the holy goost were not the authoure of his scripture as well in the Hebrue, Greke, French, Dutche, and in Englysh, as in Latyn. The Scripture & worde of God is truly to euery Christen man of lyke worthynesse and authoritie, in what language so euer the holy goost speaketh it. And therefore am I, and wyl be whyle I lyue (vnder youre moost gracious fauoure and correction) alwaye wyllynge and ready to do my best aswel in one translation, as in another."

The incorrectness of the common Latin copies noticed

He makes some observations (as he very well might) on the inaccuracy of the Latin copies which were at that time commonly circulated; an inaccuracy which was before long acknowledged as freely by Romanists as by the advocates of the Reformation. Coverdale tells us, in the dedication to Cromwell, prefixed to the corrected Paris edition of the same year, that this dedication to the king had been written in the preceding Lent. I now for a while leave this edition, to which Coverdale's attention was again called, after he was at Paris engaged in the correcting of the Great Bible.

Coverdale translates some of the Psalms into metre

During Coverdale's stay in England, in 1537 or 1538, he appears to have published certain Psalms and other portions of Scripture turned into English metre, which seems to be the first attempt of the kind in the English language: and however quaint and rugged it may seem to modern ears, it may be regarded as being as much the precursor of the Hymns in which Christians join in "giving thanks unto the Father which hath made us meet to be partakers of the inheritance of the saints in light," just as Coverdale's Bible has ushered in the version, in which we now read the record of the Holy Ghost concerning the love of the Father in the gift of the Son. The proof that this book of Psalms was published before the latter part of 1538, is found in the fact, that it was prohibited amongst other books at that time, and also it was printed in England, which shews that Coverdale had probably not as yet left for Paris.

Col i 12

Coverdale's movements when in England unknown

Works attributed to him

We do not know where Coverdale was during any part of his stay in England, except at Newbury; but he mentions in his dedication to Cromwell (prefixed to the Latin and English Testament, printed at Paris in the latter part of this year), that he had "not long agoo" been thirty miles from the place at which "a right famous man's sermon" was printed, which was falsely said to have been "depraved" by him, although he had never set pen thereto, although he had been desired to do so. This refers, I suppose, to the sermon of Osiander, "How and whither a Christen man ought to flye the horrible plage of the Pestilence," which bears the name of Myles Coverdale on the title-page; but as I suppose, from what he himself says, he was not really the translator, but was thirty miles away at the time when it was done. This was in 1537; so that Coverdale must have been at some place thirty miles from London (where the book was printed) before he was sent by Cromwell to Newbury. It is not at all improbable, that he was employed on similar business at various places in England; and letters may be discovered throwing some farther light upon the circumstances of Coverdale's stay in England.

The Bible to be published without notes or prologues

Cranmer's recension of the New Testament probably used

To return to the edition of the Bible which Cromwell was about to cause to be published. It has been already said that this was to be an edition without notes or prologues, such as had given offence in Matthew's Bible. What translation was ordered to be used does not appear; and with regard to the New Testament, it is, I think, most probable, that the recension which Cranmer had caused to be made a little while before, was now used: if not, it would seem strange for Cranmer to have obtained leave to procure a translation to be made, and to have it printed; and yet for no use to be actually made of the permission so obtained. If this were not the work which Cranmer had thus laboured to procure, we neither know what became of that recension, nor yet by whom or how the text of this Bible was formed. It may further be remarked, that this New Testament agrees very accurately with the account which is given of the recension directed by Cranmer: it is the text of the translation of Tyndale, revised throughout, more or less. Some, also, of the alterations are such as have crept in, from the revisers having the Vulgate in their minds. To take an instance: in John x. 16, Tyndale had rendered the Greek thus:—"and other shepe I have, which are not of this *folde*. Them also must I bringe, that they maye heare my voyce, and that ther maye be one *flocke* and one shephearde." In this translation the distinction between αὐλή and ποιμνή is rightly observed; but in the "Great Bible," of which I am now speaking, the verse is rendered, "and other shepe I haue, which are not of this *fold*. Them also must I bring, and they shall heare my voyce, and ther shall be one *folde* and one shepeherde." In this version, no distinction is made between the two words, the Latin being followed (in sense, at least), in which they are alike translated "*ovile*." Coverdale was right, like Tyndale, but the reviser (Gardiner appears to have had this portion sent to him) has introduced an inaccurate rendering, which has continued through various versions, and is retained to this day. The great difference in the sense of the passage, which is occasioned by this variation, I need hardly point out: in fact, the whole interpretation of this part of the chapter would be influenced by the rendering of this verse.

Tyndale's New Testament the basis.

John x 16. αὐλή & ποιμνή

Gardiner the reviser of this part

Bishop Stokesly's portion, the Acts of the Apostles, was probably revised, in some measure, by some one else for this edition; but it does not appear much changed from the translation of Tyndale.

With regard to the Old Testament in this edition, but little seems to be known. Many writers seem to have regarded this as but a reprint of Matthew's Bible; and thus many of the things which they have said regarding that edition, may really belong to this. There can be no question that Matthew's Bible (i. e. Tyndale's translation, in part, and Coverdale's, in part) was the basis of the Old Testament in this edition; but by whom the revision was made, and who translated the book of Psalms, and other parts which are actually re-wrought, does not appear to be stated. The title-page simply informs us, that it was "truly translated after the veryte of the Hebrue and Greke textes by the dylygent studye of dyuerse excellent learned men, expert in the forsayde tonges." Now there is an individual, whose name has not, as far as I can see, been connected with this edition, who seems to me to have strong claims to be considered one of the "dyuerse excellent learned men" who were engaged in this version or recension; this individual is John Rogers, the editor of Matthew's Bible, who has often been regarded as though he were, at least in part, the translator of that book; of which, however, he could not be, as it consists wholly of the version of Tyndale, with the parts which he did not execute, supplied out of Coverdale's translation.

Matthew's Bible the basis of the "Great Bible"

Psalms newly translated.

Bale attributes to Rogers the translating of the whole of the Scriptures, from Genesis to Revelation, and that in this he had recourse to copies in Hebrew, Greek, Latin, German, and English. This work he connects with the publication of Matthew's Bible. In this he is plainly in error; but still, there is no reason why the whole statement should be incorrect; it may refer to this edition, although it could not to that. Rogers returned to England between the publication of Matthew's Bible and the year 1540; which is proved by his then escaping on account of the penalties imposed by the act of the Six Articles, to which he, having married abroad about the year 1537, was exposed. It is likely that he was in England at this time; and being already connected with Grafton in the publication of the Bible, this may have led to his introduction to Cranmer's notice, as a fit person to be engaged on the literary labour of the New Bible. Of course, in a case like this, probabilities alone can be brought forward: but the case is simply this;—there is a recension of the Old Testament, to which no author is assigned: Rogers is asserted to have made a translation of the Bible, which does not appear, unless this be it; so that I think the conclusion to be strongly probable that the Old Testament of this Bible (at least, in a great part) was really the work of Rogers. This portion, although in many places it is verbatim the same as Matthew's Bible, is in others so entirely different as to be a new version: the Psalms, especially, in the "Great Bible" are far superior to Coverdale's translation, which had been adopted in Matthew's.

Rogers returns to England

Rogers's claim stated.

The Bible which was to be printed, appears to have been prepared in England for the press; and then the care of the impression was confided by Cromwell to Grafton and Whitchurch, while the work of correcting the press was given to Myles Coverdale: this was done probably on account of his known competency and learning. Coverdale does not appear to have been in any way employed in the translation itself. This he probably would have been, had the preparation of the work been Cromwell's province, instead of Cranmer's. It does not clearly appear at whose suggestion it was, that this Bible was determined to be printed at Paris; whether it was the device of Cromwell for the procuring of better workmanship, or whether (as Strype suggests) it was the idea of Grafton himself.

The Great Bible prepared for the press in England

The only intimation that I can find of the exact time at which Grafton and Coverdale went to Paris, in order to superintend the printing of this Bible, is drawn from what Coverdale says in the dedication of his Latin and English Testament, in this year, to Cromwell: he mentions there the edition already spoken of, the dedication of which he had written "this last lent;" then, after speaking of his not having superintended the edition himself, he says, "trustinge, that *though I were absent & out of the lande*, yet all shulde be well." This implies that Coverdale left England in Lent, 1538; that is to say, soon after his letter of March 5th, to Cromwell. The first intimation of their being actually at Paris, is found in a letter which they wrote jointly to Cromwell, on the 23rd of June; by which time they were already engaged in their work. It is probable that they had been for some time in Paris; for the manner in which they had settled to their work, implies that they had arranged all their plans of proceeding; while, at the same time, by their informing Cromwell what their plans were, it shews that they had not been devised in England. They say:—

Coverdale goes to Paris, Lent. 1538

Coverdale and Grafton write to Cromwell from Paris. Chap.Ho.West. Bundle C State Papers, i 575

"After moost humble and hartie commendacions to your good Lordship Pleaseth the same to understand, that we be entred into your worke of the Byble, wherof (accordynge to our moost bounden dutie) we have here sent unto your Lordship 2 ensamples; one, in parchement, wherein we entende to prynt one for the Kynges Grace, and another for your Lordship; and the second, in paper, wherof all the rest shalbe made; trustynge, that it shalbe not onlye to the glorye of God, but a synguler pleasure, also, to your good Lordship the causer therof, and a generall edefyenge of the Kinges subjectes, accordynge to your Lordshipes moost godlye request. For we folowe not only a standyng texte of the Hebrue, with the interpretacion of the Caldee, and the Greke, but we set, also, in a pryvate table, the dyversite of redinges of all textes, with such annotacions, in another table, as shall doubtles delucidate and clear the same; as well without any singularyte of opinions as all checkinges and reprofes."

Critical care

By this account of the editorial care which this edition received in going through the press, it appears that Coverdale (for this was his department) compared the revised version with the Greek and Latin texts, marking and making a list of the variations. These passages when they contained any word or sentence in the Latin or Greek which was not in the Hebrew, we shall find that they afterwards inserted in the text itself, in a smaller type and within marks of parenthesis. The "standing text of the Hebrew with the Chaldee and Greek interpretation" can only indicate, I should imagine, the Complutensian Polyglott, which Coverdale, in his editorial care, may have used: certainly no other edition of the Scriptures which had at this time been printed suits the description.

Passages inserted from the Vulgate

They afterwards speak of the mechanical execution, materials, and expense:—"The prynt, no doubt, shall please your good Lordship. The paper is of the beste sorte in France. The charge certainly is great." In the latter part of the letter they speak of their danger on account of the work in which they were engaged. They say that they hope "to be defended from the Papistes by your Lordshippes favourable letters; which we most humbly desyer to have (by this berer Wyllyam Graye), ether to the Bysshop of Wynchester [Gardiner], or to some other, whom your Lordship shall thinke moost expedyent. We be dayly threatened, and looke ever to be spoken withall, as this berer can farther enforme your Lordship; but how they will use us, as yet we knowe not."

The print and paper

Danger threatens

It is evident, from this letter, that they had not as yet obtained any permission to proceed with their work in France, and that they found the opposition to be much greater than they had expected. The bishop of Winchester, Gardiner, to whom they requested that letters might be sent in their behalf, was at this time the English ambassador at the Court of France. A little while after this he was recalled; and Edmund Bonner, archdeacon of Leicester, who had previously been employed as ambassador to the Emperor Charles V., was sent to Paris in his room. In consequence of the application of Grafton and Coverdale to Cromwell, Henry VIII. wrote to Francis to request him "to permit and license a subject of his to imprint the Bible in English within the University of Paris, because Paper was there more meet and apt to be had for the doing thereof, than in the Realm of England, and also that there were more store of good workmen for the ready dispatch of the same."

Bonner succeeds Gardiner as ambassador

Fox, ii 434

Henry's application to Francis

Bonner was directed likewise to give all the assistance that he could to those who were engaged in the printing of the Bible, so that they might be unmolested in the prosecution of their work; and that the needful license might be obtained for them to go on with safety. In this Bonner acted with promptitude, which indeed was ever one of his characteristics; and the needful permission from King Francis was obtained. This must have been procured after Coverdale had seen the faulty Southwark edition of his Latin and English Testament (which was some time in July), for the printing of this again at Paris was certainly contemplated in the permission which was obtained from Francis. This permission was addressed to Richard Grafton and Edward Whitchurch. It set forth that Francis had heard, on sufficient authority, that Henry had given them permission "to print and cause to be printed, and to be brought and transferred

Francis gives permission

Cott MSS Cleop E v 326 b

into his kingdom, the Holy Bible both in Latin and in British or English;" and that as they "both for the sake of paper and other honest considerations" wished to perform their work at Paris, he gave them free leave so to do without any molestation or hindrance, whether to the printing or to the conveying of the books to England when printed. There was, however, this proviso, that the books should be printed sincerely and purely, so far as in them lay, without any private or unlawful opinions.

A proviso made

This license having been obtained through the exertions of Bonner, the work appears to have gone on for some time without any hindrance. They continued to print the Great Bible, and also another edition of Coverdale's Latin and English Testament: which is said to have been done, partly at least, at the instance of Bonner, who shewed great zeal for the publication of the Scriptures in English.

V.

THE PRINTING OF COVERDALE'S LATIN AND ENGLISH TESTAMENT AT PARIS.—THE COMPLETION OF THE "GREAT BIBLE."

Coverdale's Eng & Lat Test

IT will be well here to give a brief account of the second edition of Coverdale's English and Latin Testament, seeing that it was printed during the time that the "Great Bible" was in hand, and was completed before that was finished. It is probable that Bonner procured the insertion of the Scriptures in *Latin* as well as in English, in the license of Francis, in order that he might attain his desire of getting this book printed. This Paris edition does not appear to have had any very great attention paid to its execution, Coverdale's time and mind were pretty well occupied with the work connected with the "Great Bible." However, it pleased Bonner, who was very anxious that it should be printed, and who "himself took a great many of them, and payed for them, and gave them to his friends." This New Testament was completed by the beginning of December, at which time Grafton mentions it in a letter to Cromwell. He complains greatly of the Southwark edition, and speaks of it as though Coverdale had himself had nothing whatever to do with it, whereas, in fact, he had permitted Nicholson to print it, and had written the dedication to the king. By his account, it seems to have been reprinted at Paris, in order to supersede the former inaccurate impression; although the other work, which they had upon their hands, was such that they had "enough to do besides."

Fox ii 434

Cotton MSS Cleop. E v 328

Grafton's letter to Cromwell, Dec 1, 1538

Coverdale dedicated this edition to Cromwell; and, in so doing, he enters into the history of the preceding impression, thus supplying many of those particulars which are known respecting it. He commences his dedication thus:—

"I was neuer so wyllinge to laboure and trauayll for the edifyeng of my brethren (right honorable and my singular good lorde) but I am and purpose to be while I lyue, by gods grace, euen as readye to amende and redresse anye maner of thynge, that I can espye to be ether synistrally prynted, or negligently correcte And no lesse do I esteme it my dewtye to amende other mens fautes, then yf they were myne awne Trueth it is, that this last lent I dyd with all humblenesse directe an Epistle vnto the kynges most noble grace; trustinge, that the boke (wher vnto it was prefixed) shulde afterwarde haue been aswell correcte, as other bokes be. And because I coulde not be present my selfe by the reason of sondrye notable impedimentes) therfore in asmoch as the new testament, which I had set forth in English before, doth so agree with the latyn, I was hartely well content that the latyn and it shulde be set together Prouyded allwaye, that the correctour shulde followe the true copye of the latyn in anye wyse, and to kepe the true and right Englishe of the same. And so doynge I was content to set my name to it And euen so I dyd: trustinge, that though I were absent and out of the lande, yet all shulde be well: And (as God is my recorde) I knew none other, till this last Julye, that it was my chaunce here in these parties at a straungers hande, to come by a copye of the sayde prynte Which whan I had perused I founde, that as it was disagreable to my former translacion in English, so was not the true copye of the latyn texte obserued, nether the english so correspondent to the same, as it ought to be: but in many places both base, insensyble, and cleane contrary, not onely to the phrase of oure language, but also from the vnderstondyng of the texte in latyn."

He mentions Nicholson's edition

This edition first seen by Coverdale on July 1538

The translation mentioned in the above extract, which he had set forth in English, agreeing with the Latin, must, I suppose, mean (as has been already intimated) the New Testament, which had been published this same year, with the words, "Search the Scriptures," at the top of the title.

In an address to the reader, he states that this book "hath not bene set forth vnto the heretofore so exactly, and in all poyntes so perfectly as myght haue bene, I praye thee conster all to the best, and blame neyther the prynter ner me, consydering that we beare no worse mynde vnto the then thou doest to thy selfe." He exhorts the reader that he will so use the scripture, "that . . . thou wylt so embrace it, folowe it, and practise it in thy daylie lyuinge, that thou euen marye thy selfe to the frutes of the holy goost therin: And so vse it, that thou be sober in the knowlege therof, not onely avoyding all contencion and strife; But also wyth all humblenesse, & under correction to requyre of them (that be lerned in scripture) the true sense and vnderstonding of soch places, as vnto the be yet darke and obscure."

Coverdale makes some remarks upon the state of the Latin text: "There be in it many & sondrye sentences, wherof, some be more then the Greke, some lesse then the Greke, some in maner repugnaunt to the Greke, some contrary to the rules of the latyn tonge and to the right order therof, (as thou mayest easely perceaue, yf thou compare the diuersyte of the interpreters together)." Yet he did not think that it was his place as a private individual to revise the Latin text, except, however, in one place, namely, in the Lord's Prayer in Luke xi., he inserted all the petitions in the Latin, although the common copies of the Vulgate omit two of them. This edition was, in the title, stated to be printed "in Paris, by Fraunces Regnault, M. ccccc. xxxviii. in Nouembre. Prynted for Richard Grafton and Edward Whitchurch, cytezens of London." State of the Latin text

The Southwark edition having been thus condemned for its inaccuracy, Nicholson the printer got out another edition, which was stated in the title to be "Faythfullye translated by Johan Hollybushe." It has often been said, that Coverdale published it under the assumed name of John Hollybush; but not only does there appear to have been no reason why he should assume the disguise of so grotesque a name, but it is farther evident that it was simply a device of Nicholson's. His edition of *Coverdale's* Latin and English New Testament was known to be grievously inaccurate, he wished in some way to cover the loss he had incurred; and to this end he printed another edition, which he chose to ascribe to a fictitious person, John Hollybush, to distinguish it from his previous edition, so that its sale might not be hindered by the appearance of Coverdale's name. Nicholson's other edition

It is probable that Nicholson, hearing that Coverdale's Latin and English Testament was either about to be reprinted, or else was in course of reprinting at Paris, with more attention to accuracy, printed the one bearing the name of Hollybush without delay, in order to anticipate the Paris edition. I conclude that it was printed before the Paris edition was completed; otherwise it would probably have followed its text, which it does not. In the places in which it varies from the former inaccurate edition, it often differs equally from that printed at Paris: when it varies from the Paris edition, it appears commonly to agree with that which Nicholson had previously printed.

The publication of these various editions manifests the continued circulation of the word of God in England. A few years previously, all the weight of authority was opposed to the diffusion of the Scriptures; but now, through the good providence of God, the ruling powers in England were bending their efforts to this very end. It may be, that the motives of some of those who sought this were very low and selfish; but still God was pleased to overrule the whole;—while others, such as *Cranmer* and *Cromwell* were unquestionably influenced in this matter by far higher motives. Coverdale must, indeed, have rejoiced at the occupation in which he was engaged: he had laboured to give his countrymen the word of God in their own tongue, with an intensity of earnestness which has rarely been equalled, and (I may confidently affirm) never has been exceeded. And now he was sent by the king's vice-gerent to care for the publication and correction of an edition which was to be freely read and circulated, with all the sanction that the king's authority could confer. Previously editions had been printed abroad; and all the difficulty and danger had been connected with their introduction into England; but now things were so entirely changed, that the only danger was connected with the printing of the books in a foreign land. Continued circulation of the Scriptures in England Motives of Cranmer and Cromwell

The printing of Coverdale's Duoglott Testament did not prevent the "Great Bible" from continuing at press; on the 9th of August, 1538, Coverdale, Grafton, and Gray wrote to Cromwell, giving some account of their proceedings with the Bible. They say:— Coverdale, Grafton, and Gray write to Cromwell, Aug 9, 1538 Chap. Ho West. Bundle C State papers, i 578

"After moost humble and due salutacion to your good Lordship. Pleaseth the same to understand, that your worke going forward, we thought it oure moost bounden dutie to sende unto your Lordship certayne leaves therof, specially seynge we had so good occasyon, by the returnynge of your beloved servaunt, Sebastian. And as they are done so will we sende your Lordship the residue, from tyme to tyme As touchynge the maner and order that we kepe in the same worke pleaseth your good Lordship to be advertised that the merke ☞ in the text signifieth, that upon the same (in the later ende of the booke) there is some notable annotacion . . . . This marke ✢ betokeneth, that upon the same texte there is diversitie of redynge, amonge the Hebrues, Caldees, and Grekes, and Latenystes; as in a table, at the Stenographic marks used in the Great Bible ende of the booke, shalbe declared This marke ✠ sheweth that the sentence written in small letters, is not in the Hebrue, or Caldee, but in the Latyn, and seldome in the Greke; and that we, neverthelesse, wolde not have it extinct, but higlye accept yt, for the more explanacion of the text This token †, in the Olde Testament, geueth to understand, that the same text, which foloweth it, is also alledged of Christ, or of some Apostle in the New Testament"

At the time when they wrote this letter they do not appear to have been in any apprehension of being disturbed or hindered in their labour, for they make no allusion to any thing of the kind. They probably judged that the license of the king made them fully secure.

Bonner appointed Bp of Hereford

Fox, ii 434

During the time that the printing was going on, Edward Fox, bishop of Hereford died. Bonner was appointed his successor, but still continued at Paris as ambassador, and shewed his friendship in every way, apparently, to all who were concerned in the printing of the Bible. Fox says of him, "The which Bishop outwardly shewed great friendship unto the merchants that were the imprinters of the same, and moreover did divers and sundry times call and command the said persons to be in manner daily at his table both dinner & supper, and so much rejoiced in the workmanship of the said Bibles, that he himself would visit the Imprinter's house, where the same Bibles were printed, and also would take part of such dinners as the Englishmen there had, and that to his cost, which as it seemed he little weighed." There can be very little doubt but that all this conduct on the part of Bishop Bonner was affected in order that he might stand well with Cromwell; it has been even supposed that his assiduity in aiding the work of the "Great Bible" was one reason, both of his being made bishop of Hereford, and likewise in the following year, on the death of Stokesly, of his subsequent translation to the see of London.

Bonner seeks Cromwell's favour

Coverdale and Grafton write to Cromwell, Sept 12, 1538 Chap Ho West. Bundle C State papers, i 588

There is another letter extant in the handwriting of Coverdale, sent jointly by himself and Grafton to Cromwell, in favour of the printer of the Bible, whom they here call Fraunces Reynold. This letter states that he had been long a printer of English books, and that he had then by him a large number of primers and others, which he was hindered from selling by the Company of Booksellers [Stationers]. The request made is that he may, under certain provisos, be allowed to sell those which he had in stock already printed; if this were granted, he engaged in future to have an Englishman as press-corrector. They conclude the letter, adverting thus to the printing of the Bible:—"Thus are we bolde to wryte unto your Lordshippe, in his cause, (as doth also my Lord Elect of Herfford) beseching your Lordshippe to pardon oure boldnesse, and to be good lorde unto this honest man, whose servant shall geve attendaunce upon your Lordshippes most favorable answer. Yf your Lordshippe shew him this benefyte, we schall not fare the worsse in the readynesse and due expedicion of this your Lordshippes work of the Bible, which goeth well forwarde, and, within few monethes, will drawe to an ende by the grace of Allmightie God."

Coverdale's letter to Cromwell, Oct. 30, 1538, Bibl. Suss

The work thus progressed without the conductors having any present apprehensions of danger. In a letter of Coverdale's to Cromwell, dated October 30th, he does not even mention it; his object in writing being to endeavour to nullify certain injurious reports which had been spread respecting a Mr. Beckynall, an Englishman studying at Paris, who had been reported to have continued to uphold the authority of the Pope. This Mr. Beckynall appears from this letter to have lodged with the Englishmen who were superintending the work of printing the "Great Bible."

Coverdale's Duoglott New Test completed, Nov 1538

In the following month (November), Coverdale's Duoglott New Testament was completed at press, and at once was put into circulation through the assiduity of Bonner. This may probably have led on to the catastrophe which soon after occurred. It appears likely that the Inquisition took the alarm at the publication of this book; and they feared to what the doings of the English superintendents of the press might lead.

Fox, ii 434

Coverdale's letter to Cromwell, Dec. 13, 1538 Harl MSS Cod 604. p 98.

By the 13th of December they had just reached the end of the printing of the "Great Bible." Fox says that "the Printer went forward, and printed forth the book even to the last part, and then was the quarrel picked with the Printer." Coverdale's letter to Cromwell, dated Dec. 13 [1538], speaks of the seizure of which they were apprehensive, and very plainly shews that the printing of the Bible itself was just completed. Coverdale commences his letter with inquiries respecting the annotations to the Bible expository of the passages marked with a hand ☞: from this it seems clear that the only question now was, whether those additions should be appended to this edition or not; and by this it is intimated that the book itself had been completed. The supplementary tables of the Epistles, Gospels, &c., at the end of which is given the date, April, 1539, begin on the same page as the Revelation concludes. The book is printed in *gatherings* or *quires* of eight leaves, the folio pages being so printed that they lie inside one another, like those of an octavo volume. The *signatures* also run like those of an octavo; thus the last part of the New Testament could not be actually printed off, until it were known what was to come at the end, whether it should be the proposed annotations, or whether the volume should simply conclude with a table. To ascertain this appears to be one of the objects of Coverdale's letter. He says:—

"Right honorable and my syngular good lorde (after all dew salutacions) I humbly beseche youre lordshippe, y[t] by my lorde electe of herdforde, I maye knowe youre pleasure, concernyng the Annotacions of this byble, whether I shall proceade therein or no —Pitie it were, y[t] the darck places of y[e] text (vpon y[e] which I haue allwaye set a hande ☞) shulde so passe vndeclared As for anye pryuate opynion or contencious words, as I wyll utterly avoyde all soche, so wyll I offre y[e] annotacions first to my sayde lord of herdforde; to ye intent y[t] he shall so examen y[e] same, afore they be put in prynte, yf it be y[r] lordshippes good pleasure y[t] I shall so do"

This may *now* seem to have been a strange work for Bonner to be employed about at this time. He was shewing as much zeal and earnestness for the setting forth of the Bible, as either Cromwell or Coverdale: it was therefore but natural that Coverdale should wish to submit the annotations which he might make to the approval of Bonner, as being a person with whom he might consult about their propriety.

Coverdale next adverts to his Duoglott New Testament, which had been dedicated to Cromwell:—"As concernyng y[e] new Testaments in english & latyn, wherof yo[r] good lordshippe receaued lately a boke by yo[r] seruaunt Sebastian y[e] cooke, I besech yo[r] l. to consydre y[e] greness therof which (for lack of tyme) can not as yet be so apte to be bounde, as it shulde be." From the manner in which he then mentions the work of the Bible, it appears that not only had they, from time to time, sent "certayne leaves therof" (as they mention in their letter, Aug. 9), but that now they sent some considerable quantity of sheets: they were apprehensive of a seizure, and thus they employed the same means which conveyed this letter for transmitting to Cromwell's keeping and care a certain portion of the impression; as much, it is probable, as could be sent by the opportunity whatever that might be. Coverdale says:—"And whereas my sayde lord of hardford is so good vnto us as to convaye this moch of y[e] Bible to yo[r] good lordshippe, I humbly beseche y[e] same, to be y[e] defender & keper therof: To y[e] intent y[t] yf these men proceade in their cruelnesse agaynst us & confiscate the rest, yet this at y[e] leest may be safe by y[e] meanes of youre lordshippe." This desire that what was sent might be in safety, plainly shews that it was not merely a copy, or even a few copies, that was transmitted to Cromwell, but a part of the impression, which was dispatched for further safety.

Sheets of the "Great Bible" sent to Cromwell

It is clear that before this letter was written they had had some intimations of what the proceedings of the Inquisition were likely to be, and thus they must have found that the royal permission given by Francis would avail them very little. It can hardly be thought that the Inquisitors would have proceeded in direct defiance of the license of the king, unless there was either some technical objection which they could raise against the instrument itself, or else something done by those so licensed which rendered void the permission which they had received: *both* of these grounds of objection might, I believe, have been raised: the latter, in that the Latin and English New Testaments had been circulated by Bonner at Paris, instead of being at once conveyed to England, according to the terms of the license. Many things, likewise, in the dedication and preface might be made grounds of accusation, so that the license might be judged to be forfeited, in consequence of "private and unlawful opinions" being maintained in the books printed. And then, as to the Instrument, it appears to have been regarded as in itself void, as having been granted for a purpose which only tended to the furtherance of heretical pravity.

The proceedings of the Inquisition

Four days after Coverdale had warily transmitted to Cromwell, by the aid of Bonner, a portion of the impression: the dreaded interference of the ecclesiastical authorities actually took place. On the 17th of December, Henry Garvais, S.T.D, "Prior of the Convent of the Preaching Friars at Paris, & Vicar-general of the Venerable father Friar Matthew Ory, of the same order & D D. Inquisitor-general of heretical pravity in the whole kingdom of France, by apostolical & regal authority especially deputed," issued an instrument setting forth, "That since from the translation of the Sacred Scriptures, as well of the Old Testament as New, into the mother tongue, which cometh to the hands of the simple, it is found in these last days that some have taken occasion of error in the faith; and that it is provided by edicts of the supreme court of parliament, that none should print the Old & New Testament in his mother tongue or sell it being printed." After thus stating the grounds of the proceedings, it is stated that one Francis Regnault printed the Bible "in the vulgar Brittanic or English language, by reason of which scandals & errors might arise in the Church;" in consequence of this, all priests, vicars, and curates are called upon to summon the said F. Regnault, "and all other whom it might concern," to answer to the charges. They were also prohibited, under canonical pains, to print the said Bible, or to remove or conceal the sheets already printed, without

The instrument of the Inquisition. Dec 17, 1538 Cotton MSS. Cleop.E v.320

The printer summoned or a charge of heresy

their being seen by the Inquisitor's vicar-general. It will be observed, that Grafton and Coverdale were only mentioned by implication in this document; this may have been done to prevent any direct collision with the secular powers.

The subsequent transactions are thus narrated by Fox:—

Fox, ii 434

Coverdale and Grafton leave Paris

The Bibles seized, and burned

Four dry-fats of them sold

"Then were sent for the English men that were at the cost and charge thereof, and also such as had the correction of the same, which was Miles Coverdale: but having some warning what would follow, the said English men posted away as fast as they could to save themselves, leaving behind them all their Bibles, which were to the number of two thousand five hundred, called the Bibles of the great volume, and never recovered any of them, saving that the Lieutenant Criminal having them delivered unto him to burn in a place of Paris (like Smithfield) called Malbert place, was somewhat moved with covetousness, and sold four great dry-fats of them to a Haberdasher to lap Caps in, and those were bought again, but the rest were burned to the great and importunate loss of those that bare the charge of them"

The copies which were "bought again," must, from what Fox says a little farther on, have continued for a considerable time in the hands of those who bought them of the "Lieutenant Criminal;" it was not until about a year, at least, subsequently, that Grafton recovered them.

This was the conclusion of the attempt to print at Paris an English Bible, which, for accuracy and execution, should surpass those which had preceded it. The history continues:—

The English-men get the printing presses, &c

The Bible completed in London

"But notwithstanding the said loss, after they had recovered some part of the foresaid books, and were comforted and encouraged by the Lord Cromwell, the said English men went again to Paris & there got the Presses, letters & servants of the foresaid printer, and brought them to London, and there they became Printers themselves (which before they never intended) and printed out the said Bible in London, and after that printed out sundry impressions of them; but yet not without great trouble & loss, for the hatred of the Bishops, namely St Gardiner & his fellows, who mightily did stomack and malign the printing thereof"

Part of this edition published April, 1539

The transactions connected with the procuring of the presses, types, &c. must have occupied some time; for it was not until April, 1539, that this edition of the Bible (or, at least, that portion of it which Coverdale had sent to Cromwell) was published. Fox says, in the above extract, that they printed it out in London, although he had said before, that the printing of the Bible was complete, even to the last part of it, before the Inquisition interfered. By this we may understand, that the table to find the Epistles and Gospels, and the table of the Epistles and Gospels for various saints' days, were, with the conclusion of the book, printed at the date, which is afterwards given, "The ende of the new Testament and of the whole Byble, Fynisshed in Apryll, Anno M. CCCCC. XXXIX. A dn̄o factū est istud." It is thus evident that these supplementary pieces were printed several months later than the greater part of the Bible itself; and it is probable that the printers had not made any formal conclusion of their book, because they did not as yet know whether the proposed annotations by Coverdale, upon the passages marked with a hand, ☞, would be allowed to be appended, and these would then have commenced upon the page on which the Revelation ends.

"Cranmer's Bible"

Cranmer's prologue, 1540

This Bible is very commonly called "Cranmer's Bible." It is doubtful whence the name has arisen, whether from some of the copies having Cranmer's Prologue in them, or from some other cause. This Prologue is supposed, on good grounds, to belong really to the folio Bible of the year 1540, and to be inserted in some of the copies of this edition. How this came to pass may, I think, be easily explained. The name of "Cranmer's Bible" may belong to it, on account of the New Testament having been the recension which the archbishop had caused to be executed a few years before.

Close of 1539

It could not be till the close of this year, 1539, that Grafton and his colleagues obtained the "four dry-fats full" of Bibles which had been preserved from the fire. Fox says, "After the Imprinters had lost their Bibles, they continued suitors to Bonner, as is aforesaid, to be a mean to obtain of the French King their Books again; but so long they continued suitors, and Bonner ever fed them with fair words, promising them much, but did nothing for them, till at the last Bonner was discharged from his Embassade, and returned home." Bonner is not to be blamed for his want of success in obtaining the interference of Francis for the recovery of the unburned copies. He had, before this, offended Francis, by his bluntness with regard to some diplomatic negociations, about which he was employed. On his being translated from the see of Hereford, of which he was bishop elect, to that of London, vacant by the death of Stokesly, he sent for Grafton, who was then in Paris (this must have been when he went to try to procure his Bibles, for the date does not accord with the time of the printing). When Grafton came to him, Bonner said to him:—

Bonner recalled

Translated to London

His speech to Grafton

"Master Grafton, so it is that the King's most excellent majisty hath by his gracious gift presented me to the Bishoprick of London, for the which I am sorry, for if it would have pleased his Grace, I could have been well content to have kept mine old Bishoprick of Hereford" Then, said Grafton, "I am right glad to hear of it, & so I am sure will be a great number of the city of London; for though they yet know you not, yet they have heard so much goodness of you from hence, as no doubt they will be glad of your placing " Then said Bonner, "I pray God I may do that may content them " After this, he said, adverting to his predecessor, "The greatest fault that ever I found in Stokesly was, for vexing and troubling of poor men, as Lobley the book-binder and other, for having the Scripture in English; and, God willing, he did not so much hinder it, but I will as much further it, and I will have of your Bibles set up in the Church of Pauls, at least in sundry places, six of them, and I will pay you honestly for them, and give hearty thanks " He blames Stokesly

How little did it then seem that Bonner would himself so far outdo Stokesly as a persecutor of the saints of God, that his predecessor's name is scarcely known for cruelty in comparison with his own. But to be earnest for the circulation of the word of God in English, was the pathway to favour, so long as Cromwell continued at the head of affairs in England; and this had doubtless much to do with Bonner's zeal, though he may, indeed, have thought himself sincere; so little does the heart often know the motives by which it is actually influenced. The contrast of Bonner's subsequent conduct

Grafton appears to have been more successful, after the recall of Bonner, in procuring the portion of the books which the haberdasher had bought, than he had been before; for Fox says, expressly, that Grafton bought them, and that while Bonner continued ambassador at Paris, he did not succeed in so doing. These copies, obtained about the latter part of the year 1539, were, I expect, completed with the same additional pieces as those which had been issued in the preceding April, and their apparent date would be the same; these rescued copies are, I suspect, those to which Cranmer's preface is prefixed.* This preface appears to have been written in the latter part of 1539; for on the 14th of November (in this year it is almost certain) Cranmer wrote to Cromwell, asking if the king had seen and allowed the preface which he had written to the Bible, that it might be given to the printer to print. Now, at this time, this preface could not be wanted in haste for any Bible which was to be published in the following year; and I think it is most probable that this preface was first printed at this time, to be prefixed to the second issue of the Paris printed Bible. If, therefore, the name of Cranmer's Bible be supposed to belong rightly to the edition of 1540, on account of its having his prologue, the re-issue of this prior impression appears to deserve it on precisely similar grounds. Enough copies may have been printed off to serve both for this issue and for the forthcoming impression. The copies bought and completed Cranmer's preface written, end of 1539 Chap Ho West Bundle C Mem Cov p 92

The publishers of this edition, in a short preface which they have prefixed, inform the reader what was intended by the marks which are placed in various parts of the book.

"First, where as often tyme ye shall fynde a small letter in the texte, it sygnifyeth that so moche as is in the small lettre doth abounde and is more in the common translacyon in Latyn, then is founde ether in the Hebrue or in the Greke, whych wordes and sentences we have added, not only to manyfest the same vnto you, but also to satisfye and content those, that here before tyme, hath myssed soche sentences in the Bybles and new testaments before set forth Moreover whereas ye find this sign ☙, it betokeneth a dyuersyte and difference of readynge betwene the Hebrues and the Chaldees in the same place, which diuersytes of readinges we were purposed to haue set forth perticulerly vnto you: But for so moch as they are very longe and tedyous, and thys volume is very greate and houge allreadye, we haue therfore at tyme left them oute, trustynge herafter to set them forth in some lytle volume by them selues We haue also (as ye maye se) added many handes both in the mergent of thys volume and also in the texte, vpon the which, we purposed to haue made in the ende of the Byble (in a table by them selues) certen godly annotacions: but for so moche as yet there hath not bene suffycient tyme minystred to the Kynges moost honorable councell, for the ouersyght and correcyon of the sayde annotacyons, we will therfore omyt them, tyll their more conuenient leysour " The variations omitted

The title-page of this Bible is very remarkable for the engraving with which it is surrounded. In the upper part of the page above the title, Henry VIII. appears seated on his throne, with bishops and other ecclesiastics on his right hand, the Lord Cromwell and other lords on his left; he is delivering the Bible on each side, and from his mouth proceed labels containing portions of Scripture. Above this, in the Title-page described

* Various copies, which all appear as if they belonged to this Paris printed edition, have in them minor variations; they contain the same matter, folio for folio, but in the initial letters, &c there are many variations This singular fact may be in part accounted for, by supposing that the copies sent by Coverdale to Cromwell, as well as the recovered copies, were in some, or many of the sheets, partially defective, and that thus the printers re-composed some of the sheets, working the impressions which were needed to complete the sets

Lewis speaks of the tome containing the Apocrypha in this Bible, as concluding on folio lxi Now it is the fact, with regard to certain of the copies (the splendid one, for instance, which belongs to the Baptist College at Bristol, from which the version contained in the present work is printed), but the lxi is an erratum for lxxx; the preceding folio is numbered quite right Other copies which have the same concluding date, have the true numbering of this folio; so that it is clear that that leaf was either reprinted, or else corrected while in course of printing; this is the greatest discrepancy which has been alleged with regard to the several copies Some of the editions of 1540 are said to be those of the year 1539, continued in the same way, namely, by fresh sheets being printed to make up for deficiencies. All these issues of the Bible being alike, folio answering to folio, the pages of them have become much intermixed

back ground, Christ appears in the clouds, and the king is kneeling on one side, with his crown placed on the ground. In the parts of the page on each side of the title, are two representations: on the one side, Cranmer appears mitred, delivering the Bible to the clergy, with an admonition to the exercise of their functions; and, on the other side, Cromwell gives it to the laity. At the feet of the two figures of Cranmer and Cromwell, their arms are exhibited within a circle. The lower part of the page is occupied by a preacher and a congregation. Out of the preacher's mouth proceeds a label, on which is inscribed 1 Tim. ii. 1, &c.; and the congregation respond to the exhortation to pray for kings and all that are in authority with the cry of "Vivat Rex," which proceeds from their mouths: some have "God save the King," but it is the general arrangement of the composition that the labels should be in Latin. In one corner of the representation of the preacher and the congregation there is a prison, at the bars of which some prisoners are to be seen, and they alone do not join in the acclamation: this was, I suppose, intended to intimate that this punishment awaited all undutiful subjects.

¶ The Byble in Englyshe, that is to saye the content of all the holy scrypture bothe of yᵉ olde and newe testament, truly translated after the veryte of the Hebrue and Greke textes, by yᵉ dylygent studye of dyuerse excellent learned men, expert in the forsayde tonges.
¶ Prynted by Rychard Grafton & Edward Whitchurch.
Cum priuilegio ad imprimendum solum.
1539.

The title itself is copied in the margin. The table of "subjects contained in the Bible" which had been published in Matthew's Bible, was omitted in this edition; but the "exhortation to the study of the Bible," and "The summe and content of all the holy Scripture" were retained. This continued, with slight alterations, to be the authorised English version of the Bible (except, of course, during the revival of popery in Mary's reign) until, in 1568, it was superseded by the version which bears the name of "the Bishop's Bible:" it has, therefore, an importance, so far as permanence is concerned, to which no previous version is in any way entitled. The Psalms of this translation are still well known, from their having been retained as the version used in the Liturgy of the Established Church. The translation of this book, I suppose (as I have already intimated) to be the work of John Rogers.

The Psalms still retained in the Prayer-book

The copies of this edition in circulation could not have been very numerous, so that this recension could not have come into general use until the re-impression in the year 1540. The prologue of Cranmer contained an exhortation to the reading of the Scripture, together with a setting forth of the uses for which it is profitable: the writing of this prologue was apparently connected with the setting up of the Bible in all churches, which was at this time directed, in order that the people might resort thither and read, and thus have the opportunity of knowing for themselves what was revealed in the Scriptures.

Cranmer's Prologue

This prologue contains also an interesting allusion to the fact that although many in England at that time regarded the unfolding of the word of God to the people in their vernacular tongue as a strange innovation, yet that in truth the innovation had consisted in the withholding of the Scriptures.

The withholding the Scriptures an innovation.

"And yet if the matter should bee tryed by custome, wee might also too alledge custome for the reading of the Scripture in the vulgar tongue, and prescribe the more auntient custome For it is not much above one hundred years agoe, since Scripture hath not been accustomed to bee read in the vulgar tongue within this realm: and many hundred years before that it was translated and read in the Saxons tongue, which at that time was our mother tongue: whereof there remain yet divers copies, found lately in old abbies, of such antique maner of writing and speaking, that few men now been able to read and understand them And when this language waned old, and out of common usage, because folk should not lack the fruit of reading, it was again translated into the newer lenguage, whereof many copies remain, & bee daily found"

After thus discussing the question of innovation, he takes up the subject on the ground of its own merits,—"Let us here discuss, what it availeth, Scripture to bee had and read of the lay & vulgar people." On this matter Cranmer contents himself with quoting from Chrysostom, in a condensed form, certain earnest exhortations addressed to his hearers, that they would at home consider and read in the Scriptures those things concerning which they heard sermons. In these quotations, the various objections which different persons might raise against the reading of Scripture being necessary for them, are briefly answered. After the citations from Chrysostom, Cranmer speaks of the uses of Scripture, and then in the latter part of the prologue treats of the misuse which unholy men might make of the liberty of reading the word of God; against which abuse he earnestly cautions the readers.

This appeared to be the fittest place for noticing the prologue of Cranmer, since copies of it are sometimes found prefixed to the "Great Bible" of 1539, and since it appears it was for the second issue of that impression that it was printed at first.

V.

MEASURES TAKEN FOR THE CIRCULATION OF THE SCRIPTURES—TAVERNER'S BIBLE PUBLISHED.

THE care of Cromwell was not confined to the printing and publishing of the Bible in English, he also took measures for causing it to be circulated and read. The position of vicar-general and vice-gerent of Henry, which he occupied in his newly acquired ecclesiastical supremacy, was certainly a strange and anomalous one. It is not improbable that the idea of such an office had been suggested to the mind of the king from the circumstance of Pope Clement having, during his captivity, appointed Wolsey to the office of vicar-general under him for the kingdom of England. But although the office of Cromwell was strange and anomalous, yet it must be conceded that in one respect it was used for good. No one seems to have exceeded him in zeal and earnestness for the diffusion of the Scriptures: in this he was used as a providential instrument in the hands of God for bringing about great blessing. How little could this conduct have been looked for from Cromwell, when it is remembered that a very few years before he had joined in the fruitless attempts that were made by Henry to entrap Tyndale on account of the publication of the English Scriptures.

The measures which Cromwell adopted are to be found in the injunctions to the clergy which he published in September, 1538, while the "Great Bible" was in the press at Paris. The second and third of these injunctions ran thus:— Injunctions, Sept. 1538

"*Item,* that ye shall provyde on this side the feast of —— next commyng, one boke of the whole Bible of the largest volume in Englyshe, and the same sett up in summe convenyent place within the said churche that ye have the cure of, whereat your parishners may most commodiouslye resort to the same and rede yt; the charges of whiche boke shal be ratablie born between you the parson, and the parishners aforsaid, that ys to say, the one half by yowe, and th'other half by them Fox, ii. 525 Mem. Cov p 107 The Bible to be set up in every parish church

"*Item,* that ye shall discorage no man pryvely or apertly from the readinge or hearinge of the same Bible, but shall expresslye provoke, stere, and exhorte every parsone to rede the same, as that whyche ys the verye lively worde of God, that every christen man ys bownde to embrace, beleve, and folowe, yf he loke to be saved; admonyshinge them neverthelesse, to avoid all contention and altercation therin, and to use an honest sobretye in the inquisition of the true sense of the same, and referre th'explication of obscure places to men of higher jugement in Scripture" To be freely read

It is to be remembered, that in the year 1536 an injunction, somewhat similar to the former of these, had been intended to be issued, although (as is shewn by Cranmer's register) it was afterwards withdrawn. It is probable that the objections which were made to the notes and prologues of Matthew's Bible prevented the intended injunction from being revived until this time, when a new edition was about to appear, which was regarded as clear of all such objectionable matter.* A similar injunction intended in 1536

The remainder of the injunctions issued by Cromwell at this time, refer to the teaching of the people the Lord's Prayer, &c., in English, the abolition of certain parts of popish idolatry which had been accustomed, the abrogation of Thomas Becket's day, and other similar subjects. Probably the abolition of many of these things gave less offence to the priests who received the injunctions, than did the setting forth the Bible in English.

The king also published a declaration to be read by all curates upon the publication of the Bible, the date of which is supposed to be about this time, probably a little later than the actual distribution of the copies of the Bible in various parishes: this distribution must have taken some considerable time, for as the number of copies of the "Great Bible" which were preserved was comparatively small, it was impossible for by far the larger number of parishes to be supplied with copies, unless indeed they were permitted to use, by way of a temporary provision, the translations which had been previously published. In the "declaration" which was thus to be read, the people were informed that the king "for a declaratyon of the A declaration to be read Cott MS Cleop E v 327

* It has been said (Mem Cov p 107), that it "cannot be ascertained whether these injunctions referred to Matthew's Bible, or to the one which was then printing at Paris;" now I believe, that it is very certain and clear that the injunction was purposely so worded as to exclude Matthew's Bible; "the whole Bible of the *largest volume*," seems expressly intended to apply to the forthcoming edition, to the exclusion of all that had preceded The day not being named need not lead to any uncertainty about which Bible it was, because, if the book had been already printed and in England, why should any such blank have been left at all? In the injunctions which were framed after the printing of Coverdale's Bible, the day is mentioned against which the book was to be provided; and so surely would it have been in this case, if the book itself had been completed.

The king's sanction expressly stated

greate zeale he bereth to the setting furth of Gods woorde," had permitted and commanded that the Bible, being translated into English, should be sincerely taught by the curates, and laid in every parish church, that all by reading and hearing might learn their duty to God, &c. This preamble was probably intended to meet the gainsaying of those who would not believe that the king had permitted the Scriptures to be thus read and taught. The declaration continues:—

"His Majestie hath willed and commanded this to be declared unto youe, that his Graces pleasure and hiegh commandment is, that in the reading and hering thereof, first most humbly and reverently using and addressing your selfes unto it, you shall have alwayes in your remembrance and memoryes, that all things conteyned in this booke is the undoubted Wyll, Lawe, and Comaundement of Almighty God, thonly and streit meane to knowe the goodnes and benefyt of God towards us, and the true duty of every christen man to serve him accordingly And that therefore reading this book with such mind and firm feyth, as is aforesaid, you shall first endeavour yourselfes to conforme your owne lyvings and conversation to the contents of the same: and so by your good and vertuouse example to encourage your wifes children, and servants, to live-wel and christienly according to the rule therof"

The authority of Scripture set forth

The latter part of this declaration is very singular: it principally relates to what should be done by those in whose minds any diversity of opinion should arise in the reading of Scripture. They are directed not to have open reasoning on the subject in taverns or alehouses; but to have recourse to learned men, to whose judgments they were quietly to submit themselves. It is most certain, that taverns and alehouses are very unfit places for the discussion of questions as to what the word of God teaches; but the proposed remedy savours much of human policy. It might be well for those who were in doubt to confer with others who might be able the better to instruct them; but for them to be allowed to read the Scriptures, and yet to be bound to receive the interpretation which men, however wise or learned, might choose to impose thereon, was causing them, at least, in some measure, to receive the truth of God as though it had been the tradition of man. If any interpretation of Scripture be *authoritatively* imposed, it makes the judgment of man to be received as being of equal weight with the word of God.

Alehouses not to be used for disputing on Scripture

It is not that every man has a *right* to judge for himself as to what the truth of God is, but that every man is *responsible* to God for hearing and taking heed to whatever God is pleased to declare. It is thus the Scriptures are presented to us; and no one can transfer his own responsibility to another.

How little the curates, to whom the injunctions of the vicar-general and the direction of the king were sent, liked them, or cared to comply with them, we shall soon have cause to see.

Fox, ii. 369 Mem. Cov p. 111. Cott MS Cleop E v fol 340, b

The king also issued certain regulations respecting the importation and printing of the Scriptures in English. Certain injunctions, the date of which appears to be November, 1538, contain, amongst other things, a prohibition of the importation of English books printed abroad; also a prohibition of the printing of any book in English, unless it were first allowed by some of the king's privy council, and others whom he might appoint, and then the words "Cum privilegio Regali," were to be put with the addition of "ad imprimendum solum." No English books of Scripture were to be printed, or imported from abroad, with any annotations in the margin, or any prologue or additions in the calendar or table, unless such annotations or additions were first examined and allowed by the king, or by those whom he might appoint. Every book of Scripture that was printed, was to have the plain name of the translator affixed to it. No person within the realm was to print any book of Scripture, unless it had been examined by the king, or by one of the privy council, or by a bishop, whose name was to be expressed. These various particulars are enjoined under heavy penalties. The other parts of the injunctions show, even more plainly than the above, that they were framed with a spirit very hostile to the Reformation. They were probably the suggestions of Gardiner; and they seem to have been intended to hamper the circulation even of the "Great Bible," which was then at press in Paris.

On the 14th of November, 1539, the king issued his letters patent, prohibiting any one from printing any English Bible for the space of five years, unless he were licensed by Cromwell. This was done to avoid the inconveniences which might proceed from the use of a variety of translations.

Taverner's recension, 1539

In the year 1539, besides the "Great Bible," there was a recension of Matthew's Bible, executed by Richard Taverner. This edition is a sort of revision; the text being, for the most part, the same, except in minor particulars. It seems as though the object of Taverner had been to correct the translation in every place where he had observed any error, or what seemed to him to be such.

Richard Taverner, the editor of this Bible, was born in the year 1505, in the county of Norfolk. He was educated at Ben'et College Cambridge; afterwards, he removed to Oxford, where, at the College of St. Frideswide's, he was admitted a junior canon; and, in the year 1527, he took his degree of bachelor of arts.

After this, he returned to Cambridge, where he took his master's degree; and, coming to London, began to study law; first, at Staire Inn, otherwise called Strond Inn (which stood upon part of the site now occupied by Somerset House): from thence he removed to the Inner Temple, where he accustomed himself to make rather a singular and pedantic use of his knowledge of Greek, by quoting the law in that tongue whenever he had occasion.

Studies law

In 1534, Taverner was taken into the employ of Cromwell; through whose interest, three years afterwards, he was made one of the clerks of the signet in ordinary; a situation which he retained till the accession of Queen Mary, in 1553. It was while thus standing in the favour both of the king and of Cromwell, that he published his "Recognition" of the Bible. He also published some other works about this time. After the fall of Cromwell, in 1540, Taverner was for some time committed prisoner to the Tower: this has been variously represented, some supposing that it was on account of the Bible which he had edited, while others have attributed it to his having slandered Anne of Cleves, Henry's fourth wife. Be that as it may, he was soon liberated, and continued in favour with the king.

Taken into Cromwell's employ, 1534

Sent to the Tower, 1540

In the reign of Edward VI., in consequence of the great scarcity of godly preachers to set forth the Gospel, Taverner, although a layman, received from the king a license to preach throughout the kingdom. However strange the mention of this may now appear, it was not without some kind of precedent at that time. Sir Thomas More, after he was called to the bar, read a public lecture in the church of St. Laurence, Old Jewry; these lectures were attended by the more learned of the city of London. They were not, it is true, upon the Scripture, but upon St. Augustin *De Civitate Dei;* but still the thing itself bore a strong resemblance in kind to Taverner's license.

Licenced to preach, 1552

Sir T More a lecturer in St Laurence's church

The license granted to Taverner runs thus:—

The license to Taverner

"Whereas ye people are ignorant through the slackness of pastors, to ye intent y^t^ people may learne how to use themselves toward God & us Having knowledge of ye learning & honest conversation of our servant Rich Taverner sometimes student in Oxenford & Cambridge, & M^r^ of arts, wee have authorized him to preach in all places of our dominions, commanding all Bps & officers of ye clergy & laity to permitt him freely to preach & to apprehend all y^t^ shall interrupt him, &c

"Gevven under our hand and seale the 13 May in ye year of our raigne"

The year of this instrument (although omitted in the date) was 1552. Accordingly, he preached both at court before the king as well as in other places. His habit appears to have been studiously unclerical, for he preached in a velvet bonnet, a damask gown, and with a gold chain about his neck; he often preached thus attired in the beginning, at St. Mary's, Oxford, in the reign of Elizabeth.

He preaches before the king and in other places

During the reign of Mary, Taverner retired to his house, Norbiton Hall, in the county of Surrey, where he mostly continued during the whole of her reign. On the accession of Elizabeth he presented her with a congratulatory epistle, upon which she offered him the honour of knighthood, which he declined, probably, in part, on account of his income being too limited for him to support this dignity. He was, a little after this, unable to lend 100*l.* to the queen, who had required from him this sum.

At Norbiton Hall in the reign of Mary

Elizabeth offers to knight him

He continued to preach for several years, and was also put into the commission of the peace for the county of Oxford, of which he served the office of High Sheriff in the year 1569. In this year he preached before the University, but in a style which, however it might have been pleasing to pedantic scholars, did not much savour of Christian simplicity; it is not unlikely, however, that he accommodated himself in some measure to his audience. On this occasion, in addition to his other habiliments, he wore a sword at his side.

High Sheriff of Oxfordshire, 1569

He died in the year 1575, 14th July, at his house, Wood-Eaton, near Oxford, aged seventy years.

His death, 1575

Although Taverner holds a far from conspicuous place amongst the English Reformers of the sixteenth century, yet his zeal and care in seeking more purely and accurately to give forth the word of God in English, was a work which, doubtless, helped on the knowledge of the Gospel. The numerous editions through which it almost immediately went, prove that its circulation was considerable; and this too was without its being set forth by any authority as a translation which was to be set in the parish churches: the translation with which this had to compete in circulation was the "Great Bible," and it is very probable that many, who could not afford so large a volume, found Taverner's edition a book which more suited their means. It is to be observed, that they were private readers alone who used this book in its various editions, as it was never, even for a time, publicly made an "authorized" version.

The circulation of Taverner's Bible considerable.

The New Testament of Taverner's "Recognition of the Bible," is not to be confounded with that which he also published separately: this last mentioned has almost to be regarded as a distinct work. It was also published in 1539.

Taverner's New Test

State of the English Reformation

A brief glance at the state in which things were in England, as regards the Reformation, at the time of the first publication of the "Great Bible" (namely, in April, 1539), together with a retrospective view of some events, will be fitting at this point.

Little opposition made in England to the casting off of papal supremacy

The hopes of reformers

The fabric of Romish doctrine had received a severe shock in England, in the separation of this country from the communion of the see of Rome. This measure, if regarded in itself, was evidently popular in England. There was amongst the far greater part of the people, an earnest clinging to every jot of ceremonial superstition delivered to them by tradition; but their attachment to the see of Rome was far from strong. Thus it was, that the transfer of the ecclesiastical supremacy from the Pope to the crown, took place with scarcely a struggle. The consequences of this step were, however, momentous; and in the issue (through the overruling providence of God), productive of results replete with blessing. Those who had for years secretly longed for the free circulation of the Scriptures, and the unhindered preaching of the Gospel, were encouraged by the hope that the separation from Rome would become so wide, that nothing might hinder the introduction of better things; many sanguinely expecting the immediate result to be the full shining of the light of the Reformation.

Mistaken

In this hope they were greatly mistaken: they seem little to have borne in mind how multiform error is, and that, although the authority of Rome was cast off, yet that that negative step was no pledge of would next be done.

Apprehensions of the upholders of Romish doctrine

Henry's inclinations and interests

On the other hand, those who wished doctrines, ceremonies, &c., to remain just where they had been, were filled with apprehensions lest the casting off of the papal authority might lead to farther departures from the doctrines and practices hitherto received. Thus, Henry with his title of "Supreme Head of the Church and Congregation of England," was placed between two widely opposing parties, the one urging on, the other retarding, the Reformation. But, besides these external influences, there were other motives which impelled him in contrary directions: his *inclination,* all other considerations aside, was decidedly and strongly in favour of popish doctrine and ceremonial, while, on the contrary, his interest led him into a course of opposition. Again, his desire of appropriating to himself the Abbies, and other foundations of a similar kind, led him to make deep inroads upon the received doctrines. Purgatory, as then held, was not to be an obstacle to the grasp of the royal prerogative: and besides this, after his rupture with the Pope, he had taken a position in which it was necessary to entrench himself, if he would keep his people clear of papal influence.

To the operation of these conflicting elements in the mind of the king, as well as around him, we may attribute much of his otherwise extraordinary conduct. He went a certain distance according to the counsel of Cromwell, Cranmer, and others; but, after a while, his end was answered, and the fear of too great innovation, together with the counsels of Gardiner, and of the great majority of others who were thoroughly papists in every thing except that of the supremacy, prevailed, and this caused him to take gradually retrograding measures.

The overruling providence of God with regard to the Scriptures

But one great event, which was brought to pass by the sovereign and overruling hand of God, was the giving forth of the Scriptures in English: true it is, that they were afterwards restrained, but a deed was done which could not be undone; the truth of God was brought to bear upon the consciences of men—the light had shone forth, which Satan and his emissaries might strive in vain to extinguish.

The "Gospellers" could appeal to the Bible in the hands of the people

More results from the reading of the word than from preaching

And now that the Bible was in the hands of the people, there was that to which the "Gospellers" might appeal in support of the message which they bore; while, at the same time, the placing of one copy of the Bible in every parish church, for the free perusal of the people, led to this,—that even when there was no preacher to bear the glad tidings of God's grace, the book of God contained the message within itself. Thus the consciences of some were aroused by the reading of the word. The poorest and the most illiterate might hear it read; and those who could read, and possessed the means, might have the word of God in their own houses for their free use. The preaching of Latimer, Barnes, and others, may have done much; but the Spirit of God, working in the hearts of those who read and heard the word of God, did far more.

The form and appearance of the Scriptures as now printed, indicates the change which had taken place. When Tyndale first published the English New Testament in print, he did it, as he himself says, with the full expectation of its being burned by those of the ecclesiastical authorities into whose hands it might come. It was printed in a small volume, as were almost all the other impressions for several years. The portion of the Old Testament which Tyndale published in English, was likewise very small in size. The reason of this is obvious; it was a perilous thing for any one to possess any such books, and they were therefore made such as should attract very little observation. Thus, those whose hearts knew something of the preciousness of the word of God, retained their volumes of Scripture without the same probability of detection. But now it seemed as though it were sought to make the Scriptures as conspicuous as might be; the size both of the volume and the type being amply enlarged. The latter of these changes was one which must have greatly increased the facility of reading the Scriptures, to those who had but little learning.

There is one class of persons who must have regarded the change concerning the free use of the Scriptures in English with peculiar joy; those who had been so severely persecuted a few years before by Bishop Longland, on account either of possessing, knowing, or teaching, some portion of Scripture, however small it might be. Well might the "Great Bible" close with the citation from Psalm cxviii. "This is the Lord's doing:" and indeed it might have been added, "and it is marvellous in our eyes."

Joy of those who had been persecuted, at now possessing the Scriptures freely.

But although in the free circulation of the Scriptures much was done, yet still the fabric of Romanism in a great measure remained; and there was still an abundant opportunity for the enemies of the truth to oppose themselves, in such a way, as to cause the destruction of some of those who held and prized it. This was soon done, and the advantage was not relinquished until the word of God was again attacked, and the effort made to consign it to oblivion. In fact, unless the word of God were again to have been taken away, the opposers of the truth could never have been sure of their victory, because in the Scripture was found that revelation of God, by which the Spirit of truth dispels every array of false doctrine which man may have set up.

Efforts of the enemies

It is, indeed, wonderful to see how God used the most unlikely means (as man might judge) for the introduction of His word and truth, and how He graciously wrought for the maintenance of what He had thus brought in.

VI.

EFFORTS OF THE OPPOSERS OF THE REFORMATION.—EXECUTION OF CROMWELL AND OTHERS.

THE visible progress of the Reformation in England had, in the early part of the year 1539, advanced farther than at any previous time. The efforts which had been made for so many years, seemed now to be crowned with success; and that which had now to be looked for, was the renunciation of the many portions of Romanism which still practically acted as so many denials of the Gospel of the grace of God. There were two means in operation for the accomplishment of this end: the one, the preaching of the Gospel, the other, the reading of the Scriptures. The latter was the instrument by far the most widely diffused of the two; for although there were several holy and faithful men, who set forth the Gospel of Christ in its simplicity, they were few indeed when compared with the length and breadth of England, and fewer still when compared with the numbers of those who were strenuously upholding the very things which the advocates of the Gospel sought to bring down.

Visible progress of the Reformation at the beginning of 1539.

But earnest as the friends of the reformed doctrine were, the opposers of the truth in England, with Gardiner, bishop of Winchester at their head, were not idle: the point to which they directed their efforts being the maintenance of such anti-scriptural tenets for doctrines, to be held under pain of suffering death, as should make the farther progress of Reformation a thing almost hopeless to its advocates.

Opposition to the truth by Gardiner and others.

In all these proceedings, the power and grace of God is wonderfully shewn out, while the counter workings of Satan are also very plainly to be traced. The one had been shewn by the manner in which the Scripture had, at length, in spite of all opposition, become circulated through England: the other was now to be displayed in the subsequent hindrances which were introduced.

The Act of the Six Articles, which was passed in this year, was a decided step for setting a limit to the Reformation; a limit which should make the casting off of the papal authority the only difference between England and any Roman Catholic country.

The Act of the Six Articles

A little before, it appears that Cranmer had laid before the king certain considerations tending to a farther reformation: these considerations set up the authority of Scripture, and the impropriety of any thing being decreed in matters of religion except according to its warrant. Various doctrines, such as purgatory, invocation of saints, and "unwritten verities," in general are taken up, and the point is urged whether they ought to be required to be held or not. One thing to which these considerations particularly refer is, the marriage of priests, a matter which had been forbidden by the king's injunctions of November, 1538 (probably through the instigation of Gardiner); and Cranmer, being himself married, felt it exceedingly. He requests the king not to pronounce the marriage of priests to be against Scripture; but if it

Cranmer addresses the king for farther reformation.

Collier, v. 33 Cott MSS Cleop E v 50

Marriage of priests referred to.

cannot be expressly permitted, to forbid either party to discuss the question under a penalty. If this could not be granted, he requests that the subject may, under certain regulations, be disputed in both Universities, offering that if the asserters of the lawfulness of the marriage of priests should fail in the argument they should be put to death: on the other hand, if they proved their point thus, that such marriages should be allowed.

Date of address.

Many circumstances shew that this document must be referred to about this time; and advantage appears to have been taken of it by the opponents of the Reformation to bring about the Act of the Six Articles.

Proceedings in the House of Lords, May 5, 1539

In the House of Lords, on the 5th of May in this year, Lord Audley, the chancellor, informed the House that the king had commanded him to move that a committee be appointed for the drawing up of articles for agreement in religion, which they were to report to the House. Accordingly a committee was appointed

A committee for articles of religion

consisting of Cromwell, Cranmer, and the bishops of Worcester and Ely, together with five other prelates of entirely opposite sentiments. The consequence was that such a committee, after debating for eleven

The Duke of Norfolk proposes Six Articles

days, came to no conclusion. Upon this the duke of Norfolk informed the House that no progress had been made, and he himself proposed Six Articles for the consideration of the Lords, which, when concluded on, might be made the basis of a law. It is probable that Gardiner suggested this measure.

The first of these articles was, Whether there be the real presence in the Lord's supper, with or without transubstantiation; the second, Whether the laity ought to receive the Lord's supper in both kinds; the third, Whether, by the law of God, priests might marry; the fourth, Whether vows of chastity (i.e. monastic vows) ought to be observed; the fifth, Whether private masses ought to be celebrated; the sixth, Whether auricular confession ought to be continued.

The king interferes

Cranmer argued for three days together against these articles: but by the direct interposition of the king's authority, they were all determined according to the popish doctrines. Strange indeed for human *authority* to undertake to determine that such or such a thing is or is not according to the word of God; and yet so it is, the authority of God is pleaded, even when the revelation of the Holy Ghost is the most disregarded.

The Act of the Six Articles passed

An act was at once passed, imposing the penalty of death for offences against the determination with regard to the articles. To oppose the first, namely, transubstantiation, was declared to be heresy; and this additional provision was made, that there was no liberty allowed of abjuration. The other five articles were established under the penalties of felony. One reason which probably influenced the king in causing this law to be made was, in order that the suppression of the monasteries might be more palatable to the popishly-affected part of the people. In these articles a limit was declared, beyond which the king would

Cromwell's dislike to the act

Latimer and Shaxton resign their bishoprics

not go. Cromwell did not venture publicly to oppose the king's will with regard to this act, although he did afterwards what in him lay to hinder the penalties imposed from being enforced. Latimer resigned his bishopric of Worcester, and was imprisoned, as was also Shaxton, who resigned the bishopric of Salisbury: the latter, however, afterwards conformed, and was liberated.

The Bible not placed in many parish churches. Strype, Cran p 99

Thus there were these two things tending in different directions: the spread of the Scriptures, and new laws of persecution. It is not surprising, that under such circumstances, the injunctions with regard to setting copies of the Bible in the parish churches, were not much regarded in many places.

"The parsons, vicars, and curates did read confusedly the word of God and the king's injunctions, lately set forth, and commanded by them to be read: humming and hawking therat, that almost no man could understand the meaning of the injunction And they secretly suborned certain spreaders of rumours and false tales in corners, who interpreted the injunctions to a false sense......And they bade their parishioners, notwithstanding what they read, being compelled so to do, that they should do as they did in times past, to live as their fathers; and that the old fashion is the best: and other crafty and seditious parables they gave out among them"

But although the priests made this opposition, and in many places kept the people in ignorance of the fact that they had free leave to read the word of God in English, yet we find that in many places there was much joy manifested by those who, for the first time, received the Scripture in their own tongue.

"It was wonderful to see with what joy this book of God was received, not only among the learneder sort and those that were noted for lovers of the Reformation, but generally all England over by the vulgar and common people; and with what greediness God's word was read, and what resort to places where the reading of it was Every body that could, bought the book, or busily read it; or got others to read it to them, if they could not themselves; and divers more elderly people learned to read on purpose And even little boys flocked among the rest to hear portions of the holy Scriptures read"

The Bible read aloud

It is to be remembered that the Bible, chained in the parish church, might there be perused by the parishioners, when and as was convenient to them; this reading was (often, at least) aloud, so those who could not read themselves had often the advantage of hearing what was in the word of God. The description just given applies, of course, to those places where the king's injunctions were read, and where, in compliance with them, the Bible had been obtained.

But although the word of God was by the law of the land now permitted to be read, yet there were obstacles still existing, arising from the strong predilection in the hearts of many for all things which had been a part of their old superstition. Thus, although persecution on this account had ceased for a while, yet *household persecution* was still an instrument by which those who loved the truth could be troubled: the word of our Lord has in this respect ever been found to be true, "a man's foes shall be they of his own household." One of those who, at this time, had to "endure grief, suffering wrongfully" at the hands of his own kindred, was a lad about fifteen years old, named William Maldon, of Chelmsford. Immediately that the king had permitted the Bible to be set in all the churches to be read by the people, several poor men of that town bought the New Testament, and used on Sundays to sit reading it together in the lower end of the church. This attracted others to listen to what was read, and amongst them this William Maldon, who came every Sunday to listen to the message of the Gospel.

Popery in the hearts of many

Wm Maldon persecuted by his relatives

Strype Cran p 91

He hears the Bible read

His father, who was deeply attached to the belief and worship of Rome, having observed it, fetched him away, that he might say the Latin Matins with him: this grieved him; and when he went at other times to hear the Scriptures read, his father still persisted in taking him away. At length, he resolved to learn to read English so that he might peruse the Scriptures without being dependent on the aid of some one else who might be reading aloud; and when he had acquired this knowledge, he and his father's apprentice succeeded in purchasing together a copy of the New Testament. To conceal it, they hid it under their bed-straw, and when they had opportunity they perused it. One night after his father was asleep, he and his mother began to converse concerning the crucifix, and kneeling down to it; the knocking on the breast which was then used; the holding up of the hands to it when it was carried by in a procession: all this he told his mother was contrary to the commandment of Him who had said, "Thou shalt not make any graven image, nor bow down to it, nor worship it." This enraged his mother, who said to him, "Wilt thou not worship the cross, which was about thee when thou wert christened, and must be laid upon thee when thou art dead?" Upon this both the son and the mother went to their beds. The latter soon told her husband what had passed; whereupon, in great fury against his son for denying that the cross should be worshipped, he went to the room where he slept, and "taking him hold by the hair with both hands," he pulled him out of bed and whipped him unmercifully. This severe beating was borne by the lad with cheerfulness, inasmuch as he could truly regard it as being for Christ's sake. His constancy in enduring this treatment without even shedding a tear enraged his father the more; so that he ran and fetched a halter and put it about his neck, saying, that he would hang him. At last, after much intreaty from the mother and the brother of the sufferer, he left him almost dead. Such was the enmity which was manifested against those who held the truth of the Gospel,—an enmity, in fact, which ever exists in the unregenerate heart, although at times it may be so concealed as to seem as though it were not there. Doubtless, the case of William Maldon was far from being solitary, and many who were sheltered from the legal penalties which they would have suffered seven years previously, found enough to endure from those with whom they were most closely connected.

His father's opposition

He learns to read and procures a New Testament

The 2nd commandment

Maldon's father ill treats him.

But the energies of the opposers of the Reformation were not directed simply to hinder persons from reading the Scriptures, or to make them suffer for what they learned from thence; but, just as they had in the year 1539 procured the passing of the Act of the Six Articles, so, in the following year, they succeeded in working the downfall both of Cromwell, who had protected to the utmost of his power those who were liable to the penalties of that act, and of Barnes and others who were the most prominent as preachers of the Gospel. The dissolution of the abbies had rendered Cromwell unpopular: many of his acts had been harsh and oppressive; and those who opposed the Reformation had deep cause of hatred against him, on the ground of his having been the chief mover in procuring the free circulation of the Bible: what the particular ground of offence was, which the king had against him, is not so easy to discover. It may be that, as he had listened to the suggestions of those who adhered to "the old learning" with regard to the Six Articles, so he did with regard to the destruction of Cromwell. It has been supposed that Cromwell's connection with Barnes was in part, at least, the cause of the king's altered feelings towards him; this is made the more probable, from the circumstance that Barnes and two others, Hierome and Garret, (the same who had in 1527 been troubled for circulating the Scriptures) were put to death almost immediately after the fall of Cromwell.

Cromwell's downfall

The ground of Henry's offence

His connection with Barnes

Cromwell had but just reached the highest pitch of earthly greatness to which he ever attained. On the

Cromwell created Earl of Essex, Ap 18, 1540

His arrest, June 9

Attainted in parliament

18th of April he was created Earl of Essex, and he was also appointed Lord Chamberlain. Nothing from this time till the 9th of June, seemed to intimate the change which awaited him. On that day, after having attended in his place in the House of Lords, he was arrested at the council board on a charge of high treason; and, a few days afterwards, a bill of attainder was read against him. He was allowed no opportunity of making any defence, or of meeting the charges which were laid against him: these charges were of heresy and treason, the former on account of his having favoured those who were now deemed heretical preachers, the latter on account of various acts done by him as vicar-general. The bill was read a second and third time in the House of Lords on the 19th of June, and on the 29th it came back from the Commons, having passed that house.

Beheaded, July 28

Cranmer intercedes for him

On the 28th of July, Cromwell was beheaded on Tower-hill, in pursuance of the act of attainder passed against him. He had, during his imprisonment in the Tower, sought to move the king to compassion, but in vain: he was doomed to die without knowing who were his accusers, or what were the definite grounds of his condemnation. Cranmer, too, sought to procure for him the mercy and favour of the king; but his interposition was altogether fruitless.

I shall not pretend even to sketch Cromwell's career: he holds a place in this account as having been the great instrument, in the hands of God, to cause that the Scriptures should be unrestrainedly read and known in this land. His actions, which cannot be spoken of with commendation, have often been set forth against his memory; and yet it is, I think, impossible for any one, who himself knows the mercy of God in the blood of Jesus Christ, to read the account of his death, without believing him to have been a sinner saved through grace.

His conduct on the scaffold

When he was brought upon the scaffold, in addressing the spectators, he told them that he was not come thither to clear or exculpate himself, as some had thought that he would. He confessed himself to have been a great sinner, for which he asked the forgiveness of God; he called all present to witness that he died not doubting any article of the faith; he exhorted all to pray for the king and Prince Edward, and for himself that, while life remained, he might not waver in his faith. Then kneeling down, he commended himself to the Lord Jesus, the Almighty Saviour of sinners:—

His prayer. Fox ii 433

"O Lord Jesus, which art the only health of all men living, and the everlasting life of them which die in thee; I wretched sinner do submit myself wholly unto thy most blessed will, and being sure that the thing cannot perish, which is committed unto thy mercy, willingly now I leave this frail and wicked flesh, in sure hope that thou wilt in better wise restore it to me again at the last day in the resurrection of the just I beseech thee, most merciful Lord Jesus Christ, that thou wilt by thy grace make strong my soul against all temptations, and defend me with the buckler of thy mercy against all the assaults of the devil I see and knowledge that there is in myself no hope of salvation, but all my confidence, hope, and trust, is in thy most merciful goodness. I have no merits or good works which I may alledge before thee. Of sins and evil works (alas!) I see a great heap; but yet through thy mercy I trust to be in the number of them to whom thou wilt not impute their sins; but wilt take and accept me for righteous and just, and to be the inheritor of everlasting life. Thou, merciful Lord, wert born for my sake, thou didst suffer both hunger and thirst for my sake; thou didst teach, pray, and fast, for my sake; all thy holy works and actions thou wroughtest for my sake, thou suffredst most grievous pains and torments for my sake; finally thou gavest thy most precious body, and thy blood to be shed on the cross for my sake. Now, most merciful Saviour, let all these things profit me, which hast given thyself also for me. Let thy blood cleanse away the spots and foulness of my sins Let thy righteousness hide and cover my unrighteousness Let the merits of thy passion and bloodshedding be satisfaction for my sins. Give me, Lord, thy grace that the faith of my salvation in thy blood waver not in me, but may ever be firm and constant That the hope of thy mercy and life everlasting in thy blood never decay in me, that love wax not cold in me Finally, that the weakness of my flesh be not overcome with the fear of death. Grant me, merciful Saviour, that when death hath shut up the eyes of my body, yet the eyes of my soul may still behold and look upon thee; and when death hath taken away the use of my tongue, yet my heart may cry and say unto thee, Lord, into thy hands I commend my soul, Lord Jesus receive my spirit. Amen."

His execution

He then gave himself into the hands of the executioner, and "patiently suffered the stroke of the axe."

Had Cromwell held a more humble station, had he not sought the power, wealth, and honours of this world, he might have adorned the doctrine of God in his life. His zeal for the Reformation might have led to his suffering death for the confession of the doctrine of Christ; but this would have been a very different thing to his being compelled to lay down his life on questionable charges.

Want of learning has been frequently objected against Cromwell. Amongst other things, it has been said, that his acquirements consisted only in knowing the New Testament in Latin by heart: if this be true, it shews at least some knowledge of that learning which is of value in the sight of God—of the holy Scriptures, which are able to make wise unto salvation through faith, which is in Christ Jesus.

Barnes, Garrett, and Hierome burned, July 30

Two days after the execution of Cromwell, Dr. Robert Barnes, Thomas Garrett, and William Hierome, were burned in Smithfield. Barnes, after his escape from Northampton to Antwerp, had gone to Wittemberg; and, remaining there for some time, he became established in the grace and knowledge of Christ. Soon after, he was sent to England on a mission by the king of Denmark, when Sir Thomas More would have entrapped him, had not the king prevented him. In 1533, he returned again to England unmolested, and was employed by the king in several affairs. He now became one of the most diligent and zealous preachers of the Gospel in London; and this at length, through the contriving of Gardiner, led to his martyrdom.

Barnes's escape

His return, 1533

Garrett.

Wm Hierome, vicar of Stepney

Garrett, who had been troubled on account of circulating Tyndale's New Testament at Oxford, was now become also one of the preachers of the Gospel in the city, as also was William Hierome, vicar of Stepney. It was in consequence of their preaching the Gospel fully, and that the flesh is altogether evil, so that "whatsoever is not of faith is sin," that Gardiner opposed them. One of the articles maintained by Gardiner against Barnes was, "I may do well by the gift of God, before I am justified towards the attainment of justification." Another was, "A man being in deadly sin, may have grace to do the works of penance, whereby he may attain to his justification." Barnes, Hierome, and Garrett, were required at the Easter sermon at St. Mary Spital, to recant what they had taught at Paul's Cross concerning justification by faith: accordingly, Barnes read what might seem a recantation, and then preached precisely the same doctrine as before. Hierome and Garrett did exactly the same. For this they were all three sent to the Tower, where they remained until the 30th of July following, when, without having ever been called to an answer, they were taken to Smithfield and burned as heretics.

Gardiner opposes them

They are called on to recant

Sent to the Tower

Burned July 30, without being called in to answer

These three men were most truly martyrs for the Gospel of Christ. It was no collateral question that was made the ground of their death, but simply their having set forth that Gospel which Paul preached.

A bill of attainder against them

They were proceeded against by a bill of attainder, and condemned to be burned or to suffer whatever death the king might see fit they should suffer. They were brought to Smithfield, together with three papists, who were condemned to suffer the penalties of treason for denying the king's supremacy; so that here was a most extraordinary spectacle, persons of the most opposite doctrines put to death in different manners, according to the matter in which their belief was discrepant from that of the king.

The protestation of Barnes

In Smithfield, Barnes made a protestation to the persons who were present, concerning the doctrine which he had taught.

Hierome earnestly exhorted the spectators who were there present; and Garrett made a profession of the Christian doctrine which he had preached.

Two of these, Barnes and Garrett, had been persons very conspicuous, the one at Cambridge and the other at Oxford, in the early setting forth of the Reformed doctrines: both of them had previously shrunk back from resisting unto blood, so that now they might indeed regard it as being of the grace of that Lord in whom they had believed they were honoured thus, in the manner of their death, with bearing testimony to the doctrines which they had preached and the Scriptures which they had circulated.

VII.

PROCEEDINGS RELATIVE TO THE SCRIPTURES.—A NEW VERSION PROPOSED.

Anomalous state of things in England

THE state of things, as regards religion in England, was now increasingly anomalous. The Gospel was not to be preached under the pain of suffering as heretics. Many doctrines were enjoined, on pain of death, to be received as being in Scripture; and yet the Bible, in which not a word was said about some of these very doctrines, was not only allowed to be circulated, but the injunctions which had been before made with regard to its being placed in every parish church, were repeated and enforced. This new proclamation was dated May 6, 1541: it recited, that the king had set forth certain injunctions requiring the Bible to be placed in every parish church, to the intent that all his subjects might read it: and, in order that the right end might be answered by this, the proclamation enjoined that none should read the Bibles with

The king's injunctions, May 6, 1541

Cott MSS Cleop E v 337

a loud voice during the time of mass, or other divine service; that no layman reading it should dispute or argue, but only reverently peruse it for his own edification.

By this it seems as though the Bibles had, in some places, been actually read aloud, while the Latin service was going on. The injunction seems to contemplate its still being read at such times, but only restrains the manner in which this should be done.

As to laymen being forbidden to dispute about Scripture, the Act of the Six Articles seems to have been already sufficiently stringent upon that point; for the things there defined were enough to make not laymen only but all others fear to hold lightly any disputation as to what the Bible actually contained.

Many parishes yet destitute of Bibles

Penalty

Price of Bibles

This proclamation farther sets forth that the king had heard that, in spite of his former injunctions, there were many parishes destitute of Bibles; at which he marvelled not a little, enjoining that a Bible should be speedily procured for every parish church: the time limited for this was the next All Saints' day, (Nov. 1, 1541,) after which a penalty of 40*s.* a month was to be imposed where one was not obtained. The price likewise of the Bibles of the largest volume was fixed at 12*s.* well bound and clasped, and 10*s.* unbound.

Bibles printed, 1541

It is not improbable that the knowledge of the king's intention to fix the price of copies so low may have led to the inferiority, both as it regards paper and press-work of the Bibles printed this year, to those which had been executed at Paris, and completed and perfected in London The Bible published in the year 1541 has the title as copied in our margin: other copies have the name of Richard Grafton as the printer.

Bps Tonstall and Heath oversee this edition

¶ The Byble in Englyshe of the largest and greatest volume, auctorysed and apoynted by the commaundement of oure moost redoubted Prynce, and soueraygne Lorde Kynge Henrye the .viii. supreme heade of this his churche and Realme of Englande: to be frequented and vsed in euery churche wᵗin this his sayd realme, accordynge to the tenour of his former Injunctions geuen in that behalfe.

¶ Ouersene and perused at the cōmaundemēt of the kynges hyghnes, by the ryghte reuerende fathers in God Cuthbert bysshop of Duresme, and Nicolas bishop of Rochester.

¶ Printed by Edwarde Whitchurch.
Cum privilegio ad imprimendum solum
1541

This was probably stated to be overseen by two bishops, in consequence of the king's injunctions in November, 1538, which required that all books of Scripture should be examined and allowed by the king, or by a privy councellor, or by some one bishop whose name was to be expressed. It is not unlikely that these were specially appointed by the king for this service, because it was by some said that the Bible had only been of Cromwell's setting forth: and they, therefore, did not allow that the king wished it; for it would only be carrying out the actions of one who had been declared a traitor. This was met by the statement of the title, that these two bishops had overseen and perused it *at the king's command.* The wood engraving which had been before used was still retained, only that the Arms of Cromwell which had been under his feet in the original engraving, were now removed. This was done with respect to all the Bibles of the previous year which had been issued subsequent to his attainder.

Some account of Bp Tonstall

The two bishops by whom this edition was overseen and perused were persons of no small celebrity and learning. Cuthbert, bishop of Durham, was the same Bishop Tonstall, who, when diocesan of London, had shewn so much zeal for the destruction of Tyndale's New Testaments. It is rather remarkable that the version of the Great Bible, thus perused and overseen by him, is in its *ground-work* the very version which he fifteen years before had condemned as being full of heresy. Tonstall was deprived of his bishopric towards the end of the reign of Edward VI., but restored at the accession of Mary; during whose reign, although he was always very popish in doctrine, yet he avoided the work of persecution: in particular, he protected his relative, Bernard Gilpin, who, although he conformed to all the ceremonies and ritual of Popery, continued by a strange inconsistency to preach the Gospel of Christ; and for this he became obnoxious to the ruling powers.

Deprived and restored

His death, 1559, aged 86

On the accession of Elizabeth, Tonstall was again deprived for refusing to admit her supremacy; a very few months after which he died, in the year 1559, aged eighty-six.

Some account of Bp Heath.

The other of these two prelates was Nicholas Heath, then bishop of Rochester; who had, in the latter part of the year 1535, accompanied Edward Fox, bishop of Hereford, and Dr. Barnes, to Smalcald, for the concluding of a league between Henry and certain of the Protestant princes of Germany. He was then archdeacon of Stafford; and, as "Heath, the archdeacon," he was spoken of highly by Melancthon.

Bp of Rochester, 1540.

In 1540, he was made bishop of Rochester; and was supposed, at the time, to be in some measure a favourer of the Reformation, standing high in Cranmer's favour. However, he subsequently shewed strongly his attachment to "the old learning." He was translated from the see of Rochester to that of Worcester; of which, however, he was deprived in the reign of Edward VI. After the accession of Mary, he became archbishop of York; and, subsequently, Lord Chancellor. During this reign he was one who was leniently disposed towards Protestants. However, it may be questioned whether, if he had chosen, he might not have exerted himself in their behalf, considering the situations which he held. After the death of Mary, he was deprived both of his situation of Lord Chancellor, and of his archbishopric, and continued the rest of his life in a private station.

Bp. of Worcester. Deprived. Abp. of York. Lord Chancellor. Deprived

It is not to be supposed, that two men of learning, such as these were, would have authorised an edition of a version which was corrupt, or palpably inaccurate: they were both of them competent scholars of the original languages of Scripture; and thus their public testimony is of some value.

Both these bishops competent scholars

Lewis says, "In this edition are omitted the hands pointing, and the mark ❦; but there is no difference in the text." The first of these remarks is correct, for the "hands" are omitted; the second is altogether inaccurate, for the mark is retained throughout the book; and the third is not quite correct, for there are some variations (although very few) in the text itself. For instance, in Isaiah lvii. 5, the "Great Bible" of 1539 had followed Coverdale, reading the verse, "Ye take your pleasure vnder the okes, and vnder all grene trees, the chylde beynge slayne in the valleys, and dennes of stone." This was now altered into, "Ye make your fyre vnder the okes, and vnder all grene trees, and ye offre children in the valleies and dennes of stone." This proves that some persons had had discretionary power of altering the version, if they had seen fit to use it: perhaps they showed their judgment in allowing the text to remain almost unaltered. The orthography of this Bible resembles modern spelling much less than that of 1539; this may perhaps be accounted for by the fact, that Bishop Heath was remarkable for the little attention that he paid to orthography. It was even a subject of surprise when he was in Germany, in 1535. It is probable that the actual editorship devolved principally on him, as being so much younger than his coadjutor Tonstall.

Lewis's remarks on this edition, p 141. Variations in the text. Defects of this Bible in orthography

Some of the Bibles which appear to be of this impression are dated at the end, May, 1541, while others have November, 1540: the latest of these two dates is probably that at which the greater part of them were issued. It is probable that Bonner had long before complied with the king's injunctions by setting up a copy of the Bible in St. Paul's; however, this year he fulfilled the promise which he had made to Grafton, on his being appointed bishop of London, by setting six copies of the Bible of this edition in St. Paul's, that the people might resort thither and read them. It appears that at this time Bonner's chief aim was to ingratiate himself with the king, by obeying his commands most thoroughly. It can hardly be supposed that he had any real desire to promote the Reformation; and yet this seemed to be the case until the attainder of Cromwell. He had shewn it by appointing, in 1540, Barnes, Hierome, and Garrett, as three Lent preachers at Paul's Cross; and it was this very appointment that caused their collision with Gardiner, in consequence of which they were burned. But still as long as the king upheld the circulation of the Bible, so long Bonner went along with him in it.

Bonner sets six copies in St Paul's. Collier, v 84. Strype Chron 120

The six copies placed in St. Paul's were chained to six pillars, to each of which an admonition was fastened. In this Bonner reminds them of the dispositions which they ought to bring with them when coming to read the word of God; directing them that they were not to make any expositions on the text, but simply what is declared in the book itself; they were "not to read aloud nor in time of divine service or sermon" [this means, I suppose, that according to the king's injunction, they were not to read aloud at the time of divine service or sermon, so as to disturb]. They were not to meet together in great numbers, so as to make a multitude; nor were they to fall into disputes, or clashing one with another; they were warned, that if they continued their *former misbehaviour*, and did not comply with these instructions, he would be forced, against his will, to remove the occasion, by taking the Bibles out of the church.

Bonner's admonition to those who read the Bible. Collier, v p. 84

From the mention of "former misbehaviour" in these injunctions, it appears that they had previously assembled in great numbers, and had likewise created disturbance by disputations while they read. It is not unlikely that six copies were placed in different parts of the Cathedral, in order to remedy this inconvenience, so that many might read without too great a concourse being in any one place. The threat at the end of Bonner's admonition was but too indicative of the measures which were likely to be adopted.

Persecution for the Six Articles

It is to be remembered, that persecution on account of the Act of the Six Articles was at this time going on with much violence. This had been the case ever since the attainder of Cromwell; so that for the people to have the Scriptures in their possession at all seemed wonderful, considering how they were the

The last public act in favour of the circulation of the Scriptures in Henry's reign

means, through the grace of God, of enlightening them in matters of religion. But although the king had set forth his proclamation on the 6th of May, 1541, for the effectual observance of his previous injunctions, with regard to the placing of the Scriptures in the churches, and although a penalty was declared against those who dared to disobey, yet this was the last public act of this reign which seemed favourable to the circulation of the Scriptures. Six years (from 1535 to 1541), is the utmost limit of the time during which the king's mind was favourable to the unhindered diffusion of the Scriptures. Throughout the remainder of this reign, we shall find restriction after restriction imposed both upon the reading and also upon the printing of them.

Charges relative to Scripture Fox, ii 452.

Bonner a persecutor.

Lord Audley interferes

During the time that persecution was going on, in consequence of the Act of the Six Articles, many also had charges laid against them on account of the word of God. Some were charged with reading it in service time, so as to make a "brabling"; others, with collecting a crowd by reading; others, with disputing about it, or giving an exposition. In these proceedings Bonner was very active, completely frustrating the hopes which had been formed of him. A very large number of persons were taken into custody by him and others in London, on account of offences against the Six Articles, or for reading the Scriptures; so many that there was no room in the prisons for them to be lodged. Bonner was for resorting to severe measures, which probably would have been adopted, had not Lord Audley, the lord chancellor, boldly and generously interfered. Permission was obtained from the king, that the prisoners might become sureties one for another; and thus they were all discharged from custody: they were bound to appear in the Star Chamber on the morrow of the feast of All Souls, then next ensuing, to answer, if they were called on: and with this all further proceedings against them were dropped.

John Porter persecuted. Fox, ii 452.

His death

A little after these circumstances, a young man, named John Porter, began to read the Bible aloud in St. Paul's, and many used to resort to hear him; for he could read well, and had a loud voice. Bonner at length took offence at this; and, sending for Porter, he rebuked him very sharply for his reading. Porter defended his conduct, as being according to law, and therefore what he might do without giving offence. Bonner then charged him with making expositions on the text, and gathering great multitudes about him: to this he replied that he trusted that he should not be proved to be guilty of a disturbance. At length, Bonner sent him to Newgate, where he was treated with extreme cruelty. His friends having afterwards paid the gaoler to let him be placed with the other prisoners, he took the opportunity of reproving their wickedness and blasphemy, and gave them such instructions as he had learned out of the Scriptures. Such offence was taken at this, that he was placed in the lowest dungeon of the gaol, and there so loaded with irons, and treated, in other respects, so severely, that he died in about a week.

The translations censured before the king.

The influence under which Henry was in this part of his reign, being almost entirely opposed to the work of the Reformation (and thus, doctrinally in accordance with his own natural inclinations), it is not to be wondered at, that he should have given heed to accusations which were made against the translation of the Scriptures which was now in use. Gardiner, who was at the head of this party, appears to have loaded it with all the accusations that he could, although it is probable that St. Luke and St. John were revised by himself. In this he was seconded by others; and thus both the version itself was depreciated, and the consequences resulting from the reading of it were represented as being very grievous.

Attempts to suppress the version in use

The object which was sought to be effected was the suppression of the version already circulated, it being supposed that not only some considerable time must elapse before a new one could be executed, but, it might not be impossible so to hamper the business, as altogether to prevent its being finally accomplished.

A new version proposed

The convocation, Feb. 16, 1542

Fuller, b 5, p 237.

It is probable that the king's mind had been directed to the preparation of a new version, one which might be framed with the greatest care and circumspection; for he directed Cranmer to require the bishops and clergy, who met in convocation, February 16, 1542, to revise the translation of the New Testament. The intention probably was that the Old should be undertaken in the same manner, after the New had been completed.

Parts of the New Test distributed to bishops

In the third session of the convocation, a plan was arranged for the execution of the revision; a distinct portion being allotted to each bishop. The arrangements were thus proposed:—St. Matthew's Gospel, to Thomas Cranmer, archbishop of Canterbury; St. Mark's Gospel, to John Longland, bishop of Lincoln; St. Luke's Gospel, to Stephen Gardiner, bishop of Winchester; St. John's Gospel, to Thomas Goodrick, bishop of Ely; the Acts of the Apostles, to Nicholas Heath, bishop of Rochester; the Epistle to the Romans, to Richard Sampson, bishop of Chichester; I. and II. Corinthians, to John Capon, bishop of Salisbury; Galatians, Ephesians, Philippians, and Colossians, to William Barlow, bishop of St. David's; I. and II. Thessalonians, to John Bell, bishop of Worcester; I. and II. Timothy, Titus, and Philemon, to Robert Parfew, bishop of St. Asaph; I. and II. Peter, to Robert Holgate, bishop of Llandaff; Hebrews, to John Skip, bishop of Hereford; James, John I., II. and III. and Jude, to Thomas Thirlby, bishop of Westminster; Revelations, to John Wakeman, bishop of Gloucester, and John Chambers, bishop of Peterborough.

Bonner omitted

It is rather remarkable that a prelate ranking so high as Bonner did at this time, was altogether omitted in the distribution of the parts of the New Testament.

These revisers delay the business

Points in the translation debated:—

Our Lord or *The Lord*; *Church* or *Congregation*; *Charity* or *Love*

The greater part of those who were thus appointed were thoroughly opposed to the circulation of the Scriptures; and to this end they sought to delay the matter as much as possible, by debating trifling questions connected with the work; such for instance as whether the expression *The Lord* or *Our Lord* should be constantly used; as if this had not depended upon what the original might be in each distinct case. They debated whether *Ecclesia* should be rendered *Congregation* or *Church;* and here, indeed, they had much greater reason for coming to a definite understanding with one another: the versions made from the Greek having adopted the word *Congregation,* which had indeed been made a charge against Tyndale. Another word which was made a matter of debate was *Charitas,* about which it was questioned whether it should always be translated *Charity* or *Love;* Tyndale had given offence by the latter rendering, which, however, is much more accurate than the other. It would have been convenient if in every version one or the other had been uniformly adopted, as the equivalent of the Greek term.

Gardiner proposes to add to the second Commandment

Another proposition made by Gardiner and his adherents, was marked with peculiar boldness: it was suggested, that in the Second Commandment, after the words "Thou shalt not make to thyself any graven image," there should be added, "*with a design to perform divine worship to it.*" How hopeless must have been the thought of obtaining a new *translation* at the hands of those who were so bent on blasphemous *perversion.* What could Gardiner and his party have thought of the Scripture, and of the Holy Ghost, who is the author of Scripture? Did they suppose themselves to be competent to mend the revelation of God?

The Old Testament to have been revised as well as the New

The Latin taken as a basis

Ninety-nine terms proposed to be left untranslated

From the Second Commandment having been thus mentioned, as needing, in Gardiner's mind, an emendation, it is clear, that if the revision of the New Testament had been completed, the Old was likewise to pass through the hands of the Convocation. It also appears, that they did not think of taking the Greek Text for their basis, but the Latin Vulgate; this is shewn by the words of which the manner of translation was debated, having been cited from that version. This is yet more clearly shewn by the fact that, in their sixth session, Gardiner read a catalogue of *ninety-nine* Latin words and phrases, which he proposed should be left untranslated, or else Englished with as little alteration as possible. This was proposed, on account, it was said, of their genuine and native meaning, and the majesty of the matter signified by them. It is, however, evident enough, that his design was so to hamper the matter, as to make the version, if ever it should be completed, not very intelligible to the poor and illiterate.*

Cranmer proposes that the work should be confided to the Universities

The king assents

It thus became very clear that no aid could be expected in this work from the bishops of "the old learning:" they were willing enough to find fault with the versions hitherto made; but they were for throwing every hindrance in their power in the way of making a new one. Upon this, Cranmer seems to have proposed to the king, that the matter should be taken out of the hands of the Convocation, and be given to the two Universities. This the king directed should be done; and Cranmer acquainted the upper House of Convocation with this determination of the king. They were much surprised; and all, except the

* It will be well to give Gardiner's list of *majestic* words, which he would have had left untranslated: the reader will at once see that a great part of them are very simple terms, and others have an English equivalent formed from, and nearly resembling, the Latin.

Ecclesia.
Pœnitentia
Pontifex
Ancilla
Contritus.
Holocausta
Justitia
Justificare
Idiota
Elementa.
Baptizare
Martyr
Adorare
Dignus.

Sandalium
Simplex
Tetrarcha
Sacramentum
Simulachrum.
Gloria.
Conflictationes
Ceremonia
Mysterium
Religio.
Spiritus Sanctus
Spiritus
Merces.
Confiteor tibi Pater

Panis propositionis
Communio.
Perseverare.
Dilectus
Sapientia
Pietas.
Presbyter.
Lites.
Servus
Opera.
Sacrificium
Benedictus
Humilis
Humilitas

Scientia
Gentilis.
Synagoga
Ejicere
Misericordia
Complacui
Increpare
Distribueretur Orbis
Inculpatus
Senior.
Apocalypsis
Satisfactio
Contentio.
Conscientia
Peccatum.
Peccator
Idolum.
Prudentia
Prudenter

Parabola
Magnifico
Oriens
Subditus.
Didrachma
Hospitalitas
Episcopus.
Gratia
Charitas
Tyrannus
Concupiscentia
Sicera.
Apostolus
Apostolatus
Egenus
Stater.
Societas
Zizania
Christus.

Conversari
Profiteor
Impositio manuum
Idololatria
Dominus
Sanctus.
Confessio
Imitator
Pascha
Innumerabilis
Inenarrabilis
Infidelis
Paganus
Commilito
Virtutes
Dominationes.
Throni.
Potestates
Hostia

bishops of St. David's and Ely (Barlow and Goodrick), protested against such a measure. They spoke of both the Universities as being in a very degenerate condition, and that the chief learning in the land was to be found in the Convocation. The archbishop, however, adhered to the determination of the king, that the existing translation of the Old and New Testaments should be examined by the universities. Thus ended the proceedings of the Convocation relative to a translation of the Scriptures; but the councillors by whose advice Henry was now principally guided, took good care that nothing should be done towards the proposed revision by the universities.

Grafton summoned before the council

Other measures were now set on foot to hinder the printing and publishing of the Bible. Grafton was summoned before the council, and first charged with the printing of Matthew's Bible, against which objections had been made on account of the introductory pieces and the marginal notes. Grafton, in fear, made excuses for himself in all things. He was afterwards examined relative to the "Great Bible," as to what notes had been intended to be affixed to it, to which the (hands) ☞ in the text and margin referred: to this he said, that he knew of none; but that his intention had been to have employed learned men to have made the notes; but when he saw the king and the clergy not willing to have any, he proceeded no farther. Grafton's excuses and answers were not deemed satisfactory; and he was sent for six weeks to the Fleet, and was not liberated until he had given security in the sum of three hundred pounds, that he would neither sell, print, nor cause to be printed, any more Bibles, until the king and the clergy could agree on a translation.

Sent to the Fleet

Privilege to print the Bible for four years granted to Marlar, March 12, 1542

On the 12th of March in this year, the king granted an exclusive privilege to Anthony Marlar, of London, haberdasher, to print the Bible for the ensuing four years. He does not appear, however, to have acted on this patent right himself, or to have employed others to do so for him, the only object in giving him the exclusive privilege was probably to prevent the Bible being printed. This Anthony Marlar had presented the king with a splendid copy on vellum of the Bible published 1540.

VIII.

THE ENGLISH SCRIPTURES PROHIBITED.

Parliament meets, Jan 22, 1543

The opposition to the diffusion of the Scriptures increased amongst those in authority; and thus, when parliament met on the 22nd of January, 1543, complaints were made of the injury which had been done by the circulation of the Scriptures through the false glosses and interpretations which had been put upon them: accordingly there were certain proceedings, both in parliament and in the Convocation, for remedying these disorders. What the evils were, which had arisen from the reading of Scripture, is not distinctly specified; but one thing is clear, that darkness ever deems light an evil thing and shuns its approach.

The Scriptures complained of

Proceedings of the Parliament and the convocation

The proceedings in parliament were directed to the hindering of certain translations from being circulated, and to the limiting of the perusal of Scripture to persons of particular ranks. The proceedings in the Convocation seem to have been intended as a kind of substitute for the liberty thus taken away. Did we regard exclusively the proceedings of the Convocation, it would have seemed as though the nature of that body had been changed in the past year; but the whole looks like a compromise. The parliament passed an act in consequence of the representations that were made to it, in which, after reciting that a great diversity of opinion had sprung up in consequence of the reading of Scripture, &c., it enacted, that all manner of books of the Old and New Testament, being of the crafty, false, and untrue translation of Tyndale, and all books which should contain doctrines contrary to those set forth, or to be set forth by the king, should be abolished, extinguished, and forbidden to be kept and used in this realm, or any where else in the king's dominions. The penalty for disobedience was a fine of ten pounds for the first offence for every book, together with three months' imprisonment; while an offender was liable for a second offence to forfeit all his goods, and be imprisoned perpetually.

Tyndale's translations prohibited.

Other Bibles still allowed.

All Bibles or New Testaments, however, which were not of Tyndale's translation were to remain in use; but if any preambles or annotations were found in any of them, then the owners should cut or blot them out, so as to make them illegible: this was under a penalty of 40*s.* for every Bible. Summaries of chapters, however, were to be allowed to remain. The act set forth, that although the higher classes had made a good use of the king's permission to read the Bible, yet the lower classes had, on the contrary, abused the privilege. It was, therefore, enacted, that, after the following 1st of October, no one should read the Bible aloud publicly, in a church or elsewhere, unless he were appointed so to do by the Ordinary of the place (certain exceptions are then made to this clause); the penalty for an offence was to be a month's imprisonment. It was farther enacted (and this was the severest part of the whole), that no women, artificers, apprentices, journeymen, servingmen (of the degree of yeomen or under), husbandmen or labourers, should read to themselves or any other the Bible or New Testament in English. Permission was then expressly given for all who did not belong to the classes already named, and also for every noblewoman and gentlewoman, to read the Bible in private. These exceptions are said to have been obtained by Cranmer, and that not without strenuous exertions.

Many prohibited from reading the Bible.

The effect of this, it is to be observed, was that all who had the ability of reading the Scriptures in Latin might do so also in English; that is, the Scripture in English was allowed to those who could not be prevented from using it in another tongue, while those who were unlearned might remain without the liberty of reading God's word in any language at all.

The proceedings in the Convocation, to which reference was made, were these. On February the 21st, 1543, it was ordered, that on every Sunday and holiday throughout the year, the curate of the parish should, after the Te Deum and the Magnificat, read to the people, one chapter in the New Testament in English, without exposition; and when the New Testament had thus been read through, they should then begin the Old. What a poor substitute this must have been for the free permission of reading for themselves which the people had previously possessed! No doubt, it seemed like an important grant that the priest should himself read the Scripture to the people in English: but at the rate at which this was to be done, it would be a work of many years to go through the whole Bible; if any one heard something read, and wished to recall what it was, he would have had to wait for *seventeen years* or thereabout before it could again be read in course. Happily the state of things changed before there was even the opportunity of once reading through the Bible at the rate proposed; and before one seventeen years had passed, that liberty of reading the word of God for ourselves without hindrance, was so granted by the gracious providence of God, that no effort of Satan or his servants has as yet prevailed in taking from the inhabitants of this land the important privilege. Do we sufficiently remember our responsibility in this matter?

One chapter to be read in church every Sunday Feb 21, 1543

Not long after these proceedings in Parliament and in the Convocation, the book which the king had employed several to compile during the preceding three years, was published under the title of "A Necessary Doctrine and Erudition for any Cristen Man;" in the preface the king speaks in defence of the limitations and restraints which were now imposed upon the reading of God's word. He thus addresses his subjects:—

The Necessary Erudition published

"We, by the helpe of God and his worde, haue trauayled to purge and clense our realme from the apparent enormities of superstition wherein by openyng of goddes trueth, with settyng furth and publishyng of the scriptures, our labours (thankes be to god) haue not ben void and frustrate"

The king then speaks of there being two classes of persons, those who teach and those who are taught; for the former of these,

"the hauing, reading, and studynge of holy scripture, is not only conuenient but also necessary; But for the other part of the churche ordeined to be taught, it ought to be demed certainly that the reading of the olde and new testament is not so necessary for al those folkes, that of duty they ought and be bound to read it, but as the prince and the policy of the realme shal thinke conuenient, so to be tollerated or taken from it"

Restraints on the Scripture defended

Let us consider this dogma of the king for a moment before continuing the quotation:—the Scripture is only to be read by the people at large, as the prince and policy of the realm think convenient. Suppose that at the time when the Apostle Paul wrote to the Thessalonians the governing powers had thought fit that that church should not read what he sent them, how would this have consisted with the apostle's inspired injunction, "I charge you by the Lord that this epistle be read unto *all* the holy brethren." In short, the argument of the king rests upon a false foundation; if the authority of God be not greater than that of Kings who are ordained of Him, then the ground which Henry takes is defensible, *but not else.*

The king's dogma considered

1 Thess v

The king goes on to say:—

"Consonant whervnto the politike law of our realme hath now restrained it [sc the reading of the Scriptures] from a great meyny, esteming it sufficient for those so restrained, to here & truly bere away the doctrine of scripture taught by the preachers, and so imprint the lessons of the same, that they may obserue and kepe them inwardly in their hart, and as occasion serueth, expresse them in their dedes outwardly"

Tyndale's the only version forbidden by name

The only translation which was forbidden by name was Tyndale's; and it seems strange why that should be singled out for prohibition, and all others allowed still to be used. It is not known how this specification was construed, because it might seem to comprehend every version of the New Testament hitherto printed, except that one which Coverdale had made in conformity with the Latin Vulgate. The New Testament in Matthew's Bible, is simply Tyndale's reprinted. A great part of the New Testament in Coverdale's Bible, is simply a recension of Tyndale's; while in the "Great Bible" the same thing is evidently and emphatically true. Were all these then to be deemed the false crafty and untrue translation of Tyndale, or were they any thing better? It would indeed be difficult to draw a distinction, and call the New Testament of the "Great Bible" a sincere and genuine version, and yet condemn that of Tyndale. In proscribing this one version, it seemed as though every printed copy of the Scriptures was placed at the mercy of those who would have to administer the enactment.

No more editions of the Bible in Henry's reign

It is not to be wondered at that there should have been no more editions of the Bible during the reign of Henry. The copies which were in circulation may have afforded a supply which sufficed for those who were willing to retain the Scriptures at all hazards, like the "known men," or Lollards, who had been troubled on that very account in the earlier part of this reign. The only impressions of any portions of the word of God which were subsequently printed, appear to have been the Pentateuch, in 1544, and an edition of the Epistles and Gospels for the Sundays, which was printed afterwards; together with one of the New Testaments according to the text of the "Great Bible." To these, Joye's Book of Daniel (1545) should be added.

The copies in circulation

The number of copies in circulation at this time must, however, have been very considerable. Besides the editions of Cranmer's (or the "Great Bible"), which were intended for the parish churches, and were probably mostly appropriated to them; and besides Matthew's Bible, which may be supposed to have been particularly prohibited by the act of Parliament,—there were three editions of Coverdale's Bible, and the same number of Taverner's. If we suppose that these editions were in number, an average between that of Matthew's Bible and the "Great Bible," as printed at Paris, they must altogether have consisted of about twelve thousand copies; while the various versions and recensions of the New Testament which were in circulation, must, at the same rate, have amounted to about fourteen thousand copies. Thus, exclusive of the supply for the parish churches, there were about twenty-six thousand copies of a considerable portion of the Scriptures still in the hands of the people; a large part of which, especially of the editions of the New Testament, was most probably in the hands of the classes who were now prohibited to use them.*

The copies proscribed

The number of Bibles which were distinctly proscribed by this act (the two editions of Matthew's) may have been about three thousand. The number of copies of the New Testament must have been much more considerable; because, besides the twelve separate editions which had been printed since Tyndale's revision of his version in 1534, there might probably be many even of the earlier Dutch editions in the hands of some: these copies probably amounted in number to fourteen thousand. If we suppose all the parish churches supplied with Bibles, or even enough copies of the "Great Bible" printed for a supply, this would make about twelve thousand copies more; so that the total number of printed Bibles in use may be estimated to have been about twenty-seven thousand, and the copies of the New Testament about twenty-eight thousand, besides various editions of portions of the Scriptures.

The Scriptures retained in spite of the penalties

It is probable (or rather almost certain) that those who possessed copies which were of a proscribed translation, did not very easily or willingly part with them; and also it is not to be supposed that those who knew the value of the word of God in their own tongue, would be more ready to refrain from reading it for themselves, than had been the case when only written copies were obtainable, or when Tyndale's New Testament had first been printed. Such an act of parliament might hinder printers, such as Grafton, from endangering themselves by printing Bibles or New Testaments, but it could not be much regarded by those who indeed knew the Scriptures to be the word of God.

In some instances great severities were resorted to, in consequence of the word of God being found in the possession of those who had, by the act of parliament, been prohibited to read it. Some who were very zealous for the "old learning," went beyond the law altogether in their persecutions.

Bp Longland causes T Bernard and J. Morton to be burned

It is not to be supposed that John Longland, bishop of Lincoln, would be the last in any thing of this kind. About this time he caused two men to be burned on the same day: the one named Thomas Bernard, for teaching the

* In the above estimate I merely take *undoubted* editions; I should not be surprised if the actual number of copies were nearly double what is stated above Editions which are page for page the same, are often found, when closely examined, to be of different impressions

Lord's prayer in English (which was expressly permitted by the law); and the other named James Morton, for keeping the Epistle of St. James in English in his possession. This was completely in character with the persecution which Longland had carried on in 1522; and it shews how unchanged was his enmity against the word and truth of God. Fox, ii 453

The measures which the king had taken to hinder the Scriptures from being so read as to lead persons to discuss its doctrines, appear to have been so thoroughly ineffectual that some new measures were resorted to, in order if possible to keep the consciences of the people in subjection, not to God and his word, but to the imperious will of the king. In 1542, the attempt to keep the people from freely reading the Bible had commenced; and by the beginning of 1543, this had been so far carried into effect, as could be done by an act of parliament. Nearly three years after, however, the same things were complained of by the king as before. In proroguing the Parliament, on the 24th of December, 1545, the king took occasion to address them on this subject:—

The king's address to the Parliament, Dec. 25, 1545.

"And although you be permitted to reade holy scripture, and to haue the worde of God in your mother toungue, you must vnderstande that it is licensed you so to doo, onely to informe your awne conscience, and to instruct your children and famely, & not to dispute and make scripture a railyng and a tauntyng stocke against Priests and Preachers (*as many light persones do*). I am very sory to knowe and here, how vnreuerendly that most precious iuell the worde of God is disputed, rimed, sang, and iangeled in euery Alehouse and Tauerne, contrary to the true meanyng and doctryne of the same And yet I am euen asmuche sory, that the readers of the same, folow it in dooyng so faintly and coldly. For of this I am sure that charitie was neuer so faint amongst you, and virtuous and godly liuyng was neuer less used, nor was God himself amongst Christians euer less reuerenced, honoured, or serued"

This last sentence appears like a reflection upon the Lords and Commons whom the king was addressing, for they belonged to the classes who were allowed to read all versions, except that which had been prohibited: those who were said to have disputed about Scripture, may be supposed to have belonged to the classes who were now forbidden to read for themselves.

Another prohibition of the Scriptures, July 6, 1546

In the following year, the king published a more stringent prohibition of books of Scripture, and others which contained matter that might be deemed offensive or heretical. This proclamation, which is dated July 6th, 1546, sets forth—

"The king's most excellent majesty understanding how, under the pretence of expounding and declaring the truth of God's Scripture, divers lewd and evil disposed persons have taken upon them to utter and sow abroad, by Books imprinted in the English tongue, sundry pernicious and detestable errors & heresies, not only contrary to the laws of this realm, but also repugnant to the true sense of God's law & his word, by reason whereof certain men of late, to the destruction of their own bodies and souls, and to the evil example of others, have attempted, arrogantly and maliciously to impugn the truth, and therewith trouble the sober, quiet, and godly religion, united and established under the King's majesty in this his realm; his Highness minding to foresee the dangers that might ensue of the said books, is enforced to use his general Prohibition, Commandment, and Proclamation, as followeth"

The first thing enjoined is,

Tyndale and Coverdale's versions forbidden.

"That from henceforth no man, woman, or person, of what estate, condition, or degree soever he or they be, shall after the last day of August next ensuing, receive, have, take or keep in his or their possession, the Text of the New Testament of Tyndale or Coverdale's translation into English, nor any other than is permitted by the Act of Parliament made in the Session of the Parliament holden at Westminster, in the four and thirtieth and five and thirtieth year of his Majesty's most noble reign"

The act here referred to, is that which has been already mentioned as having passed in 1543, by which Tyndale's translation was prohibited. It does not expressly permit any particular version, but leaves all except Tyndale's in the same condition that they were in before: this proclamation appears to extend the prohibition to Coverdale's New Testament, leaving whatever was not Tyndale's or Coverdale's without any condemnation.

Books of certain authors prohibited

The proclamation goes on to prohibit the receiving or possessing of any books printed, or which might afterwards be printed, in English, in the names of Frith, Tyndale, Wiclif, Joye, Roy, Basil, Bale, Barnes, Coverdale, Turner, Tracy, or any of them; together with all books which might contain anything contrary to the act of parliament before referred to. All such books were to be delivered up to persons appointed for the purpose, before the last day of August, in order that they might be burned. The king published his forgiveness of those who still retained prohibited books, on this condition; namely, that they should now be given up in the manner provided; and those who were appointed to receive the books were forbidden to be curious in examining who the persons might be who brought them; all that they had to do was to receive them and burn them.

Forgiveness for past offences if prohibited books were given up

Penalties

The penalty for disobedience of this proclamation was imprisonment at the king's pleasure, and also "such fine and ransome" as the king or four of his council might impose upon the offender. The same penalty, together with the king's extreme indignation, was denounced against all who should import from abroad any books concerning the Christian religion, without having first obtained the king's licence.

The prohibition of Coverdale's Testament, as well as that of Tyndale, was an extremely sweeping censure: it left comparatively few copies of any sort which were allowed to be read even by the privileged classes. It is clear, I think, that this proclamation intended some version or recension to remain as an allowed book; this must have been that of Cranmer (or the "Great Bible,") which was distinctly regarded as not being Coverdale's, although he had the charge of it while it was passing through the press. The fact of this being the one permitted version of the New Testament was probably the occasion of an edition of it being printed this year. There probably would be some considerable demand for it if those of Coverdale's translation were destroyed in any considerable numbers.

The "Great Bible" still unprohibited

A shepherd's memorandum

It is probable that the prohibitory act of parliament had been in many places but little attended to, until this proclamation was issued. The following memorandum was written in this year by a shepherd on Sunbury Hill in Middlesex: it stands on a spare leaf of Polydore Vergil's Invention of Arts abridged in English:—"On the invention of things, at Oxford, the yere 1546 browt down to Seynbury by John Darbye, price 14d. When I kepe Mr Letymers shype I bout thys boke when the Testament was abergatyn, that sheperdys might not red hit: I prey God amende that blyndnes. Wryt by Robert Wyllyams, keppynge shepe vppon Seynbury Hill." This shepherd must have retained his Testament until this year; and it would seem, from this memorandum, that it was then that he dated the prohibition for those in the lower classes to read the Scriptures. It is not too much to suppose that in other places the state of things in this respect was similar.

Destruction of English Bibles

The destruction of the copies of the Scriptures must have been carried on with great diligence; and it is probably owing to the care with which this was done, that so few copies of the three editions of Coverdale's Bible have come down to us. Only about four copies appear to be known of the two editions (taken together) of the year 1537. The destruction must have been almost as complete as that of the two first editions of Tyndale's New Testament.

But although the king carried on his arbitrary proceedings, and shewed the bent of his inclination in thus suppressing the Scriptures, there was not wanting a faithful monitor to testify to him, even as Latimer done in 1530.

Supplication of the Poor Commons
Strype, Mem Ecc i 633

In this year, a few months apparently after the proclamation had been published, a book appeared addressed to the king, entitled, "A Supplication of the Poor Commons." It set out with a complaint concerning the state in which England was, through the conduct of the priests, &c. Speaking of their teaching, it is said:—

Priests complained of Their teaching

The prohibition on reading the Bible

"They tell us, that vice, uncharitableness, lack of mercy, diversity of opinions, and other like enormities, have reigned in England ever since men had the Scriptures in English They say, it sufficeth a layman to believe as they teach, and not to meddle with the interpretation of Scripture . They cannot abide this name, the *Word of God;* but they would have the Scriptures called, the *Commandments of God*. They have procured a law that none shall be so hardy as to have the Scriptures in his house unless he may spend 10*l* by year And what meaneth this, but that they would famish the souls of the residue, withholding their food from them? We appeal to your highness's judgment in this behalf, whether this would be indifferent or no; if none should be allowed meat in your highness's house, but such as were clothed in velvet, with chains of gold about their necks? What servants would your majesty have shortly? What starvelings would your servants be of all other? For no man within your realm may refuse to do you service Hath God put immortal souls in none other, but such as be possessioners of this world? Did not Christ send word to John the Baptist, that the poor received the Gospel? Why do these men disable them from reading the Scriptures, that are not endued with possessions of this world? , Because they are the very same that shut up the kingdom of heaven before men They enter not in themselves, nor suffer they them to enter that would."

The writer then speaks of the argument which might be used, that, as it was Parliament which had made the law, so it was in effect the act of the whole people:—

"Whereunto we answer, that if we have given it over from us to the possessioners of this world, we may well be likened to the Gadarenes (Mark v), which desired Christ to depart from their country. . If we have rejected this merciful proffer of our most merciful Father (to have the Scriptures the declaration of God's will), when He used your highness as His instrument to publish and set forth His most lively word; let us fall down prostrate with repentance of this contempt of His most merciful gift: most humbly beseeching Him to behold the dolours of our hearts, and to forget our obstinacy therein, giving your highness such desire of our salvation, that you will as favourably restore unto us the Scripture in our English tongue, as you did at the first translation thereof set it abroad Let not the adversary take occasion to say, the Bible was of a traitor's setting forth, and not of your highness own doing For so they report that Thomas Cromwell, late Earl of Essex, was the chief doer, and not your highness, but as led by him.

The writer, after this, speaks of the manner in which the king's former injunction had been abused by the bishops and clergy:—

"When your highness gave commandment that they should see that there was in every parish church, one Bible at the least, set at liberty: so that every man might freely come to it, and read therein such things as should be for his consolation; many of this wicked generation, as well priests as others their faithful adherents, would pluck it other into the quire, other else into some pew, where poor men durst not presume to come; yea, there is no small number of churches that hath no Bible at all And yet not sufficed with the withholding it from the poor of their own parishes, they never rested till they had a commandment from your highness, that no man of what degree soever he were, should read the Bible in the time of God's service as they call it. As though the hearing of their Latin lies, and conjuring of water & salt, were rather the service of God, than the study of His most holy word, This was their diligence in setting forth the Bible at your highness commandment" The Bishops, &c oppose the Scriptures

The zeal with which the late proclamation against Tyndale's and Coverdale's versions had been carried out is next adverted to, shewing how the letter of the king's orders had been even overstepped:—"But when your highness had devised a proclamation, for the burning of certain translations of the New Testament, they were so bold to burn *the whole Bible*, because they were of those men's translation."

After this, the proceedings relative to the making of a new translation are thus spoken of:—

"We heard say that they proffered your highness that if you would please to call in the Bible again, forasmuch as it was not faithfully translated in all parts, they would oversee it: and within seven years set it forth again . Your bishops .. if they might have gotten in the Bible for seven years, they would have trusted, that by that time, either your highness should have been dead, or the Bible forgotten; or else they themselves out of your highness' reach; so that you should not have had like power over them, as you have now." Their unwillingness to set forth a version

The writer next speaks of the Bible which had been overseen and perused at the king's command, by Bishops Tonstall and Heath:—"When your Majesty appointed two of them to overlook the translation of the Bible, they said, they had done your highness' commandment therein: yea they set their names thereunto. But when they saw the world somewhat like to wring on the other side; they denied it and said, they never meddled therewith: causing the printer to take out their names which were erst set before the Bible, to certify to all men that they had diligently perused it according as your highness had commanded."

These notices of events then recent, relative to the circulation of the Scriptures, are highly interesting. It is to be observed, that in this "supplication," facts are arranged without any regard to the actual order of time. The writer speaks at considerable length of the sufferings of the poor, through the conduct of the priests; and he earnestly entreats the aid of the king. He thus presses upon him the responsibility under which he was:—

"If you suffer Christ's poor members to be thus opprest, look for none other than the rightful judgment of God, for your negligence in your office and ministry. For the blood of all them that by your negligence shall perish, shall be required at your hands Be merciful therefore unto yourself, and unto us your most obeissant subjects .... Remember that your hoar hairs are a token that nature maketh haste to absolve the course of your life." The king's responsibility

The king's end was probably much nearer than the writer of this supplication thought. He did not survive his proclamation for widely suppressing the Scriptures more than a few months; he died on the 28th of January, 1547, in the fifty-sixth year of his age, and the thirty-eighth of his reign. Thus the effects of that proclamation passed away in a very short time. The death of Henry, Jan 28, 1547

It was now about one and twenty years since the first copies of the English New Testament in print had been circulated; the consequences of this had been momentous: the earnest desire after the knowledge of the revelation of God had been excited; and it would have been impossible to have thwarted it. Many would probably have suffered, for they had learned the value of the revelation of God, and that it is worth retaining at all hazards. Every effort had at first been made to crush the Scriptures in English; but, through the blessing of God, those efforts failed; the opposers afterwards lent a helping hand, and became, for a time, the instruments of their diffusion. At length, they again hindered the spread of God's word; but just when these hindrances were endeavoured to be greatly increased, the whole scene changed, and the restrictions vanished away. In tracing out these events, how much there is to manifest the overruling power and grace of God in bringing such mighty results to pass, through the labours of two of His servants, William Tyndale and Myles Coverdale.

The knowledge of the Gospel accompanies the spread of the Scriptures

It is very evident, in reviewing the events of the preceding twenty years, that just as the Scriptures spread in England, so did the knowledge of that Gospel which had been so long obscured; namely, that God accounts sinners righteous for the sake of that work which Christ has finished; and that, through His blood, all who believe have forgiveness of sins as their present and continuing blessing.

IX.

REIGN OF EDWARD VI.—SCRIPTURES AGAIN CIRCULATED.

State of things at the commencement of the reign of Edward VI

Unfavourable as the close of Henry's reign had appeared to the circulation of the Scriptures, it was the prelude to better things. The restraint which had been laid upon the Scriptures in English, by the suppression of Tyndale's and Coverdale's translations, must have been very effectual in withdrawing from ostensible circulation the greater part of the copies of the whole Bible which had been printed, and *all* those of the New Testament, as a separate volume; until, in the same year in which this restraint was imposed, Grafton printed an edition of the New Testament, according to the "Great Bible," to meet the demand for the word of God which might yet exist amongst the privileged classes.

Thus, at the commencement of the reign of Edward VI., the Scriptures were almost entirely withdrawn from circulation; the mass of the people were forbidden to read them; and one chapter, read by the priest every week, was the only permitted manner for the people at large to obtain any knowledge of the revelation of God.

It is to be observed, that whatever liberty had been granted at times, in the reign of Henry, to the preaching of the Gospel, no steps of any importance had been taken to get clear of the ritual of Rome. Even those who held any post in the established church (such as it then was), were thorough conformists, in action, to the services of the Roman Missal; every thing relating to the Pope's jurisdiction had been weeded out, but the book was essentially the same. Some practices, which were full of idolatry and superstition, had been abrogated; and a few attempts had been made towards the introduction of English prayers, in the stead of those in Latin. In fact, the state of things, at the close of Henry's reign, was such, that a retrogradation to the owning of the Pope's authority *seemed* much more probable, than a steady advance in the doctrine of the Reformation.

But still, much had been done. The silent testimony of the word of God had gone forth; and, although that word had again become a volume withheld from the many, yet the seed sown in their hearts could not be so easily uprooted. Results, in the following reign, manifested that the seed which had been thus already sown, had not been wasted.

Romish ritual combined with the Gospel

It is to be observed, that frequently, educational habit leads men into inconsistencies of conduct which seem almost inexplicable. This is found to be the case even with those who make the profession of the name and the Gospel of Christ; and thus it is that the routine of a false system is adhered to, long after the system itself has been seen to be evil. This in part explains how, in the reign of Henry VIII., even those who wished to further the Gospel of Christ, continued the usage of ceremonies which, when analysed, are found to be utterly subversive of the true doctrine of the grace of God. Thus, in England, it was long before the use of a false service was really felt to be an evil thing. The questions which occupied the minds of those who thought about righteousness and peace with God, were those which related to individual salvation, far more than those which had to do with the rectitude, or the reverse, of any particular prayer, system, or ceremony. Let this be borne in mind; and we shall understand how gradually, even after the death of Henry, the external framework of Romanism was thrown aside.

Somerset, the Protector, a helper of the Reformation

At the accession of King Edward, the actual weight of government fell at the first upon his uncle, who was now created Duke of Somerset, and made Lord Protector. Somerset was an instrument in the hand of God, for carrying on the Reformation in England, very much in the same way in which Cromwell had been ten years before. Among the early acts of this reign, was the reversing of the restrictions which had been laid on the circulation and the reading of the Scriptures.

The Scriptures again permitted

In May, 1547, there were certain injunctions drawn up; which, in the following September, were published, and circulated by the king's visitors, who were appointed to visit and to preach in every diocese of the kingdom. Amongst other things required by these injunctions, were the following:— Injunctions circulated, Sept, 1547. Collier, v 199 Fox, b 9, p 5

"Within three months after this visitation, the Bible of the larger volume in English, and within twelve months Erasmus, his Paraphrase on the Gospel was to be provided, and conveniently placed in the church for the use of the people," that they "might reverently, without any argument or contention, read and hear the same at such times as they listed, and not be inhibited therefrom by the parson and curate, but rather to be the more encouraged and provoked thereto"

"And that every ecclesiastical person under the degree of a bachelor of divinity, shall provide for himself the New Testament, in Latin and English, with Erasmus's Paraphrase And that the bishops and their officers shall examine the parochial clergy in the study of Holy Scriptures"

The clergy were to "examine such as come to confession in Lent, whether they can repeat the Creed, the Lord's Prayer, and Ten Commandments, in English And that unless they are thus far acquainted with the fundamentals of religion, they ought not to be admitted to the blessed sacrament of the altar"

"And that in the time of high mass, he that says or sings the same, shall read the Epistle and Gospel in English, and one chapter at matins, immediately after the lessons; and at even song, after Magnificat, one chapter of the Old Testament And that when nine lessons are to be read in the church [sc Latin lessons], three of them shall be omitted, with the responds; and at even song the responds, with all the memories [i e commemorations of persons deceased], shall be likewise omitted"

A form of "bidding" prayer was at the same time set forth, and prescribed to be used, the conclusion of it ran thus:—

"You shall pray for all them that be departed out of this world, in the faith of Christ, that they with us, and we with them, at the day of judgment, may rest both body and soul with Abraham, Isaac, and Jacob, in the kingdom of heaven"

These extracts from the instructions contain what was now ordered with regard to the word of God in English: they likewise shew how little had been done to innovate upon the service of Rome; in fact, the things which but a little while after were so strenuously and rightly condemned by the Homilies, were still in the most part remaining, only the light of the word of God was introduced amongst them: and this light soon began to manifest the darkness around. Means taken that the word of God in English should be known

It seems probable from these injunctions that in the latter part of the preceding reign, the Bibles had been removed from some of the churches: and indeed, when they might no longer be freely read by the people, no good reason seems to have remained for their continuing where they had been so set; since their being placed there was for that object and no other. These injunctions put matters relative to the circulation of the Scriptures in precisely the same position as they had been in the year 1541; this, however, was added,—the reading of some portions of them in public, which had commenced when they were prohibited to be read by the people in general. In other respects also the greater part of the observances were retained which had been upheld in the preceding reign. It is true that in some places there were those who had a zeal for the truth of God which led them without any warrant from the government to destroy various emblems of idolatry. The cessation of persecution upon the Act of the Six Articles, may have emboldened them in these proceedings. Strype says, "From the beginning of King Edward's reign, hitherto, the old way of worship, and the rites and ceremonies continued as they had done in the former reign, without, or but small, variation:" the reason of this, he states to have been that the meeting of a Parliament was waited for before any such innovations should be made. Boldness of some reformers Strype, Mem Ecc ii 56

It is probable that the copies of the "Great Bible," which had been printed between the years 1538 and 1541, were still undestroyed and preserved; for if this had not been the case, the injunctions could not have been complied with. No edition of the Bible was published in this reign previous to the year 1549, although in the year in which the injunctions were issued, an edition of the New Testament, English and Latin, was published; and in the following year several editions in English. Copies of the Bible yet in existence. Cotton's list The Paraphrase of Erasmus on the Gospels completed Jan 1548

The Paraphrase of Erasmus upon the Gospels, which was enjoined to be procured within twelve months after the issuing of the injunctions, was not yet printed. It was, however, completed in the ensuing January. The translation of this paraphrase from the Latin had been in a great part executed before the death of Henry VIII., through the instrumentality of the queen, Catherine Parr, his last wife. Queen Catherine Parr causes the translation to be made

Myles Coverdale had been on the continent during the latter years of the reign of Henry: he appears Coverdale during the latter part of Henry's reign. His second exile, 1540

to have returned to England after the seizure of the Bibles at Paris, and to have left it again either on the passing of the Act of the Six Articles, or else soon after; probably before the trouble of Barnes and his companions. Bale says that his return, on the accession of King Edward, was after an exile of seven years. The places of his abode during the time when he had thus become, for the second time, a voluntary exile from his native land, cannot be traced with any exactness; some of them are, however, known; and these shew that his was a very wandering life. It must indeed, in many respects, have resembled "the poor Apostle's life" of Tyndale, of which Frith made mention. One of the places at which he sojourned for some time was the University of Tübingen, where the degree of Doctor of Divinity was conferred upon him. He earned his livelihood during the time partly by teaching young children. It is not unlikely that some of his pupils were persons of more advanced age.

His wanderings. At Tübingen made D D. His means of subsistence

At Augsburg, May, 1545. Nuremburg, Oct 1545

From the dates and places at which certain of his books were printed, while he was abroad, we may, I think, gather, that, in May, 1545, he was at Augsburg; and that, at the end of the following October, he was at Nuremburg. Where he had been, besides Tübingen, during the time preceding, does not appear.

His long residence in Germany had made him a complete master of the language; and thus, although no longer able to continue to preach to his own countrymen, he was not hindered from labouring as an evangelist abroad. He must have been occupied in this manner during some of his wanderings, for the Duke of Deux-Ponts presented him, in consequence, with the benefice of Bergzabern, in his duchy, three leagues south-west of Landau. This must have occurred during the latter part of his exile; for he is said to have retained it until the accession of Edward VI., when the persecution on account of the Six Articles having been stayed, he was able to return to England in safety.

Appointed minister at Bergzabern

His marriage

He was now a married man. When he became so is uncertain—whether during his previous exile, or during this period of banishment: if the former, then most probably that circumstance alone sufficed to hinder him from being in England after the Act of the Six Articles was passed. His wife was born, it is said, "either in Germany or Denmark:" the latter, perhaps, is the country intended;* her name was Elizabeth. She was one of two sisters, of whom Johannes Macchabæus Alpinus, a Scotchman, holding a high situation in the employ of the King of Denmark, married the other. This makes it probable that Coverdale was himself married while in Denmark, which must have been, I believe, between the years 1531 and 1534. Very little is known of his wife, except that she was "a most sober, chast, and godlie matrone," and that she was still alive while Coverdale was bishop of Exeter.

Strype, Mem Ecc iii 346

Hoker, Mem Cov p 139

Coverdale's return to England. Appointed almoner to the Q Dowager. The queen's death, Sept 1548

Coverdale must have returned to England very soon after the accession of King Edward. He returned, says Bale, "poor in this world, but rich in the grace of Christ." Soon after this, Catherine Parr, the Queen Dowager, who had married the king's uncle, Thomas, Lord Seymour of Sudely, appointed him her almoner. This it was, probably, that caused him to be connected with the translation of part of the second volume of the Paraphrase of Erasmus. The first volume of this was published in January, 1548. In the following September, the queen, who had patronized the work, died at the seat of her husband, Sudely Castle, in Gloucestershire. She was buried in the chapel belonging to Sudely Castle; and Coverdale preached her funeral sermon, warning the persons who were present, that none of the funeral ceremonies were performed with the view of benefiting the deceased queen; in order that in so doing, he might clearly avoid the Popish abuses which had universally prevailed. It is to be observed, that, as yet, the dead were prayed for in the services of the church; so that Coverdale, in boldly stating the truth on this subject, was going beyond what might be styled the existing state of the English Reformation.

Her funeral sermon preached by Coverdale. MS Coll of Arms Mem Cov p 141

Parliament, Nov 1547

In November, 1547, the Parliament and the Convocation both met, the latter on the 5th, the former on the preceding day. This Parliament enacted legally many of those things which the Protector had previously done by proclamation; for instance, the Act of the Six Articles was wholly repealed; all statutes for the punishment of Lollards were likewise repealed; as also was the act which had been passed in the preceding reign, by which the reading of the Scriptures was restricted. Thus there was now, not only legal permission for all to read the word of God without any hindrance, but likewise there was a repeal of those laws by which any might have been punished on account of the truth which they might learn. To the end of this reign, no restriction was imposed upon the use and diffusion of the Scriptures: editions multiplied; and the many things in which the rites of popery were thrown off, prove that the fruit of the circulation of the Scriptures was (through the blessing of God) abundantly ample. The instrument to whom the people of England were indebted for this blessing, was the king's uncle, the Protector Somerset.

Act of the Six Articles repealed. Other changes. Circulation of the Scriptures

* Strype says, "He lived long in Germany and Denmark; where he had a benefice, and married a sober woman, named Elizabeth, born in those parts" This is not very definite

It was declared that the Lord's supper ought to be received according to the institution of Christ under both kinds, bread and wine, and likewise, that the priest ought not to receive alone, without the people.

The Convocation.

The Convocation likewise, at the same time, agreed that the Lord's supper ought to be received under both kinds, and that priests might marry; the ground on which both these decisions rested was, the testimony of God in His word. The successive steps which were taken in the succeeding convocations by Cranmer, Ridley, and others, in opposition to transubstantiation, the Latin service, and other ceremonies and doctrines of Rome, cannot be recounted here.

X.

OCCURRENCES CONNECTED WITH COVERDALE AND OTHERS, IN THE REIGN OF EDWARD VI.

The word of God misused.

OTHER matters of interest relative to Coverdale remain to be mentioned, as occurring in the reign of Edward VI. Many made an evil use of the liberty which was accorded them, of freely reading the word of God: this led to harsh measures towards certain of them. Those who received the reformed doctrines had yet to learn, both that the excision of heretics was not their province, and that varying judgments as to many points need not hinder the exercise of Christian love. Many are spoken of at this period as having given trouble from their holding, some Anabaptist,* and some Arian doctrines. Certain of the former were tried on the 27th of April, 1549, before Archbishop Cranmer, and others at St. Paul's; and on the Sunday after their next meeting, one of the said Anabaptists, named John Champneys, of Stratford-le-Bow, did penance at Paul's Cross, on which occasion Coverdale preached. This is the first intimation as to where he was after he had left Sudely Castle upon the death of Queen Catherine Parr.

Anabaptists and Arians

Anabaptists tried, April 27, 1549

John Champneys does penance

Coverdale preaches. Mem. Cov. p 142

Strype Cran. p 254

The proceedings which were carried on in this reign, for reformation in religion, were, of course, unpopular with those who clung to "the old learning;" while, at the same time, such a thing as toleration appears never to have entered the minds of those who were in authority. These circumstances occasioned a great deal of commotion in England in the summer of 1549: insurrections broke out in various parts of the country, of which the most considerable was in Devonshire and Cornwall. This commenced in the month of June; soon after which, they sent their demands to the king, embodied in seven articles. To these a reply was sent in the king's name, which had, however, no effect in causing them to disperse, and they in return sent a supplication to the king. But although they took the place of suppliants, they were very far from thinking themselves to be merely such; for their articles are couched in a peculiarly dictatorial strain, and nothing would suffice them but a punctual compliance. The Lord Privy Seal, Lord Russell (afterwards Earl of Bedford), was sent against them; and he offering to receive their complaints, they gave him their demands, which were now increased to fifteen articles. They referred principally as before, to the re-establishment of popery, only now their demands were greater and more definite; they required that all ancient councils should be observed, that the law of the Six Articles should be re-enacted, that the Latin Mass should be restored, that all who would not worship the Sacrament should die as heretics, and other matters of a similar kind. Their tenth article is remarkable:—"We wil haue the Bible, and al books of Scripture in English, to be called in again. For we be informed that otherwise the clergy shal not of long time confound the heretics." This was an ingenuous confession, it shewed how ill all that which was of man's devising, and to which his heart so fondly clung, could bear the introduction of the light of God's pure word.

Commotions in England Summer 1549

Devon and Cornwall

The demands of the rebels

Lord Russell sent against them.

Farther demands of the rebels.

Their opposition to the Scripture

* It is right to state most explicitly, that those who are called by writers of this period "Anabaptists," are not to be confounded as regards either doctrine or practice with those Christians who now reject the doctrine of infant baptism.

If any ask, "What did the Anabaptists of this period hold?" It may suffice to refer such to the examination of the Anabaptists above mentioned They held that "the elect sinned not, and could not sin; that they that be regenerate never fall away from godly love [this was a different doctrine from that of the salvation of every justified person]; and that the elect have ***a right to take*** so much of the things of the world as may supply their necessities" That these were not misrepresentations, was proved by the confession and abjuration of John Champneys, above mentioned.

However, let the errors be grievous as they may, we no where in the New Testament find the church authorised to punish those who err, except in excluding them from the communion of God's people.

Other measures were taken besides the Lords Russell and Gray having been sent against the rebels; various preachers were sent into the West on this occasion, but none seem to have shewn much willingness to undertake so dangerous a work, except Myles Coverdale. This was spoken of several years afterwards, as being greatly to his commendation.

Preachers sent to the West.

Coverdale goes thither

The rebels, headed by Humphrey Arundel and Henry Bray, mayor of Bodmin, had laid siege to Exeter; and, after all attempts at a negociation had failed, Lord Russell attacked and routed part of their men. This was in the latter part of July: the siege of Exeter had continued several weeks, and the inhabitants were nearly starved into a surrender. In spite of a partial repulse, the rebels continued their siege, which was ended by their being totally routed on the 5th of August, by a second attack of Lord Russell. Four thousand men were killed or taken prisoners: they had at this time maintained the siege for six weeks.

Siege of Exeter

Rebels routed, Aug 5, 1549

Coverdale having been sent into the West on this occasion, preached in various places; this was as much needed there as in any part of England, or perhaps more so. He preached a thanksgiving sermon after the victory at Exeter. The council had guaranteed to requite the preachers who undertook the service on which they were employed in this matter; accordingly, we find in the following year (July 20), a reward of forty pounds given to him from the king.

Coverdale preaches in various places

Where Coverdale was during the period which had elapsed after the victory at Exeter until the following July (almost a year) does not appear. He may have continued in the West for some considerable time, which is rendered probable from the date of the king's donation to him; or he may have gone abroad; which is rendered not improbable, from the fact of an edition of his Bible having been published this year (1550) which is said to have been printed at Zurich. If he were present himself at the place at which it was printed, he could not have remained until it was completed, which was not until the 16th of August, 1550. This edition of his Bible is clearly one of the two revisions which he mentioned in his sermon at Paul's Cross, in which he defended his version; and this circumstance makes it seem likely that he was himself present at the place where the printing was executed.*

An edition of Coverdale's Bible printed, 1550

On the 18th of January, 1551, Coverdale is mentioned as one who was appointed a commissioner, with Cranmer and others, for the searching out and examining of Anabaptists and other heretics. The powers given to these commissioners was very great. Under this commission, (the second of the kind which there had been in this reign,) an Arian, named George Van Paris, was condemned as an obstinate heretic: the warrant for his execution by burning was made out by the lord chancellor in April this year. It is needful to mention this circumstance, because Coverdale belonged to this commission; although it does not appear that he was concerned in the affair, and whether he acted at all as a commissioner cannot be ascertained. Arianism is a most awful and blasphemous heresy, nearly approaching to that of Socinianism (that resort of those who are too cowardly to avow themselves infidels); but that is no ground for the putting of such to death; and the deed is to be reprehended by whomsoever it be sanctioned.

Coverdale a commissioner for examining heretics, Jan 18, 1551.

Van Paris condemned.

Coverdale was in favour at this time with the ruling powers.† He had been for some time spoken of as likely to succeed to the bishopric of Exeter: such a supposition was mentioned in June, 1550, by Peter Martyr, who highly commended Coverdale, expressing his opinion that nothing could tend more to the restoring of true religion in England, than for men such as Coverdale to be generally entrusted with the administration of the Church.

Coverdale proposed as Bishop of Exeter

P Martyr's commendation of Coverdale

Veysey, the bishop of Exeter at this time, was an old man who was commonly absent from his diocese, and who was altogether opposed to the Reformation. It was therefore looked on as sound policy to endeavour to induce him to resign. This was negociated in some manner which does not seem very clear; the ground assigned in his resignation is that of old age and infirmities. Such measures as these gave an opportunity, throughout the reign of Edward VI., for rapacious courtiers to enrich themselves, by getting possession of the estates which had previously belonged to the various bishoprics. It was so in this case; for one of the arrangements of Veysey's resignation was, that the alienation on his part of the property of the see would be connived at. The property of the see was pretty well reduced by these alienations; for whereas, in 1534, the estimated annual value of this bishopric was more than fifteen hundred pounds, it was now reduced to one-third part of that sum.

Bp Veysey induced to resign

He alienates the lands of the bishopric Reveue, £1566:14:7½

* A re-issue of this edition in 1553 had a new title page printed for it

† The following notice of him occurs about this time:—"On the 7th of March, 1551, Lord Wentworth, who had been Lord Chamberlain to the king, was buried at Westminster in an honourable manner, and Coverdale preached the funeral sermon"—Mem Cov. p 145

Coverdale was nominated to the vacant see, August 14th, 1551. The next day the royal letters were directed to Archbishop Cranmer, informing him of the appointment, and desiring him to consecrate him. A delay, however, occurred: Coverdale was too poor to pay his "first fruits" to the king; he therefore had to wait at court in order to get himself excused this payment, and also to do homage on his appointment. He found, however, nothing but delays; and this apparently from secret hinderers of the Gospel, so that he was obliged at last to obtain the interference of Cranmer to help on the business. Cranmer accordingly wrote to Cecil, the secretary, for Coverdale, entreating that no delays might be made, and stating the need that there was of him in his diocese.

Coverdale's nomination, Aug 14, 1551

This apparently brought matters to a point, and he was consecrated on the 30th of August, by Archbishop Cranmer, assisted by Nicholas Ridley, bishop of London, and John Hodgkin, suffragan of Bedford. Scory was consecrated bishop of Rochester at the same time.

His consecration, Aug 30 1551

A few days after, he received his license to preach, which was, in those days, needed even by Bishops; such a fear was there of popish doctrine being preached. On the 10th of September he also had a license for himself and Elizabeth his wife, with any five or six guests who might be with them, to eat flesh upon the days which had been appropriated to fasting or abstinence.

Coverdale's name occurs about this time in the king's commission, for revising and recompiling the Ecclesiastical Laws. This commission is dated October 6, 1551: it is probable, however, that Coverdale was in his diocese, and so did not act upon the commission.

Coverdale appointed a Commissioner for revising Ecc Laws

As Bishop of Exeter, Coverdale's diligence has been highly commended; he was especially remarked for what was then so much needed,—frequent preaching. This he attended to upon every holyday, as well as lecturing, at some one of the many churches in Exeter, twice every week. His godliness and uprightness of life seem to have procured for him general respect; and farther, they may have commended the Gospel to the consciences of some of those who thus saw its fruits. His care over his own house was likewise highly commended; which indeed is a thing most needful in any one who has the care of the Church of God: "If a man know not how to rule his own house, *how shall he* take care of the church of God?"

Coverdale's diligence

1 Tim iii 5.

He does not appear to have been skilful in civil or canon law; and thus, he was glad to procure the services of Dr. Robert Weston, to whom he committed the charge of his ecclesiastical jurisdiction.

Dr Robt Weston, his chancellor

Coverdale, however, had enemies: and surely it must be so, according to the teaching of the Apostle: "Yea, all that will live godly in Christ Jesus shall suffer persecution." The grounds of objection to him were these: that he was a preacher of the Gospel, an enemy of papistry, and a married man. Many attempts were made by his enemies to bring him into some snare, but in vain: other attempts were likewise made to kill him by poison; but, through the merciful care of his God and Father, this was frustrated. The Lord had service for him yet; and he whom *He* preserves is safe, let Satan rage as he will. It is probable, that Coverdale continued mostly in his diocese, during the two years that he retained his episcopal function. The only thing which is known to have called him away, was his attendance in parliament: in this, as in other things, punctuality and diligence were his characteristics. The first assembling of parliament after he was made bishop of Exeter, was on January 23, 1552: this session continued until the dissolution on the 5th of April following. During this session, there were but two days on which he was absent. Another parliament met in March, 1553: it assembled on the first day of the month, and was prorogued on the last; from this Coverdale was absent but one day.

Coverdale's enemies.

2 Tim iii 12

Efforts of his enemies

His attendance in Parliament

This brings the narrative of the known events relative to Coverdale, down to the close of the reign of Edward VI.; a period at which (as we shall see), not only his circumstances were changed, but his liberty and life endangered.

To return to the circumstances relative to the circulation and translation of the Scriptures. It is not to be expected that, in a reign like that of Edward VI., many incidents would occur relative to this subject. The circulation of the Scriptures now went on smoothly and quietly, without being subject to those various fluctuations which had taken place in the preceding reign. The even course of the current caused its progress to be less marked, than had been the case when its surface was continually rippled.

Free circulation of the Scriptures in the reign of Edward

Many editions of the Bible and New Testament were printed; some being reprints of Matthew's Bible, some of Cranmer's, or the "Great Bible," and some of Taverner's revision. Those who were in power were avowed favourers of the Gospel; and thus, of course, no attempts were made to abridge the free permission with regard to the Scriptures, which had been granted in the beginning of this reign. In this

Many editions

Labours of Gospellers

time of quiet, there was much likewise done, through the labours of diligent Gospellers; and by the two-fold testimony—the word of God in the hands of the people, and the preaching of the true Gospel—many souls were converted.

Some mention of the duke of Somerset

The duke of Somerset has been already mentioned as having been, in the early part of the reign of his nephew, the principal instrument in altering the whole of that course of proceeding which had been adopted in the latter part of the reign of Henry VIII.

His actions in his high and perilous station of Lord Protector, do not belong to this place: it may suffice to say, that he shewed himself to be a favourer both of the Gospel and of those who preached it; and it was his endeavour, so far as he could, to appoint such men to be bishops as might be helpers forward of the truth.

His power of short duration

His power and authority were, however, but of short duration. He was much beloved by the people at large; but amongst the nobility there were many who envied his authority. In consequence of this, they took occasion a little after the various insurrections, in the year 1549, to accuse him of many things connected with the administration of affairs, and thus they succeeded in depriving him of his offices, and of a considerable portion of his property. The king was now almost entirely in the hands of Dudley, earl of Warwick (afterwards duke of Northumberland), who had principally exerted himself for the deprivation of Somerset. After this, the enemies of the Reformation seem to have taken courage, hoping that the deeds of Somerset would be as transient as his power had been short-lived. They likewise hoped that the earl of Warwick would exert himself to undo what the Protector had done.

The earl of Warwick,

Collier, v 375

"Those who were averse to the Reformation made their court to the earl of Warwick, expecting his inclination lay for their purpose; but this nobleman, being more concerned for his own greatness than for any systems of religion, disappointed their hopes He found the abetting the Reformation was the most effectual way to recommend him to the king Thus he appeared in a new disguise, and appeared strongly in his master's sentiment"

The Reformation continues

Thus, although Somerset was no longer able to use his power and influence, the work of Reformation went on. It is true, that the chief power was in the hands of a wicked man, but still policy made him act as the king desired; and farther, the wholesale appropriations which the courtiers made of lands which had belonged to abbies or bishoprics, could only be kept up by an apparent zeal for the farther progress of Reformation.

Somerset a prisoner

After the duke of Somerset had been deprived by his enemies, who conspired against him, of his office of Protector, he was kept for a little while a prisoner in the Tower: his enemies, however, were unable to compass his death at this time; and, accordingly, he was set at liberty again. Two years afterwards, they appear to have been apprehensive lest he should recover his former station of Protector; and for that reason they concerted measures for his destruction. He was committed to the Tower, October the 16th, 1551, and on the first of the following December, he was tried in Westminster Hall. He was charged on several counts with high treason and felony. No evidence was brought against him except *written depositions*: the lords, who took the most prominent part in his trial, were his principal enemies; and yet so notoriously were the charges devoid of proof, that they could do no other than acquit him of the heavier charges of treason, although they convicted him of felony; this, however, was done without evidence which could warrant such a verdict. The people heard of his acquittal; and, without being aware that he was convicted on another charge, were loud in their acclamations: when, however, they knew the real state of the case, they gave full proof of their vexation.

Soon liberated

Re-committed to the Tower, Oct. 16, 1551

Tried, Dec. 1

Convicted of felony

Beheaded, Jan 22, 1552

He remained a prisoner in the Tower until the 22nd of January, 1552, on which day he was beheaded upon Tower Hill. After having prayed, he addressed the people who were there assembled, reminding them of obedience to the laws, and speaking of his willingness to die. He afterwards spoke of the progress of the Reformation:—

Fox, book ix

"Moreover, dearly beloved friends, there is yet somewhat that I must put you in mind of, as touching Christian Religion, which, so long as I was in authority, I always diligently set forth and furthered to my power Neither do I repent me of my doings, but rejoice therein, sith that now the state of Christian Religion cometh most near unto the form and order of the Primitive Church Which thing I esteem as a great benefit given of God, both unto you and me Most heartily exhorting you all, that this which is most purely set forth among you, you will with like thankfulness accept and embrace, and set out the same in your living Which thing, if you do not, without doubt greater mischief and calamity will follow"

When he had proceeded thus far in his speech, there was a considerable disturbance among the people; and it was said that a messenger was bringing the king's pardon for the duke: this made them loud in their vociferation and acclamations; but the duke, well knowing how fully his enemies had planned his destruction, beckoned to the people to be quiet, and then continued to speak to them. He informed them that they were mistaken in the thought of a pardon being sent him, and asked them to join with him in prayer for the king, to whom he said he had ever shewn himself to be a faithful and true subject, diligent in his affairs, and in seeking the common profit of the kingdom. To this the people heartily responded, exclaiming that this was most true. He then prayed for the king, and exhorted the people to obedience; after which he thus concluded his speech:—

"Moreover, forsomuch as heretofore I have had oftentimes affairs with divers men, & hard it is to please every man, therefore if there be any that hath been offended and injured by me, I most humbly require and ask him forgiveness, but especially Allmighty God, whom throughout all my life I have most grievously offended; and all other whatsoever they be that have offended me, I do with my whole heart forgive them Now I once again require you, dearly beloved in the Lord, that you will keep yourselves quiet and still, lest through your tumult you might trouble me For albeit the spirit be willing and ready, the flesh is frail and wavering, and through your quietness I shall be much more quieter Moreover, I desire you all to bear me witness that I die here in the faith of Jesus Christ; desiring you to help me with your prayers, that I may persevere constant in the same unto my life's end" His dying profession.

After he had again prayed, he prepared himself with very great composure for execution; binding a handkerchief over his own face, and laying himself upon the block.

"Thus this most meek and gentle duke lying along and looking for the stroke, because his doublet covered his neck he was commanded to rise up and put it off; and then laying himself down again upon the block, and calling thrice upon the name of Jesus, saying, *Lord Jesus, save me!* as he was the third time repeating the same, even as the name of Jesus was in uttering, in a moment he was bereft both of head and life, and slept in the Lord Jesus, being taken away from all dangers & evils of this life, and resting now in the peace of God; in the preferment of whose truth and gospel he always shewed himself an excellent instrument and member, and therefore hath received the reward of his labours" Fox, book ix

"Whatsoever his other vices and virtues were, this is certain, that his end (the Lord so working with him) was constant in Christ's truth, as his life was before a great maintainer of the same"

It is not a little remarkable that the two great instruments in setting forth the Scriptures to be read without danger, Cromwell and Somerset, should both have similarly suffered. The latter was by far the most unblemished as to his public administration of affairs, but Cromwell was placed in a yet more difficult position than that which Somerset afterwards held. Each, doubtless, was injured by ambition, and thus their devotedness to Christ and his glory was greatly hindered. Somerset had far greater opportunities than Cromwell for carrying on the work of Reformation, and it must be granted that he used them: if the means to which he resorted were not always such as can now be approved, it must ever be borne in mind that, although in some it is more discernible than in others, the work and service of every saint on earth is hindered and marred by imperfections. The only ground which either Somerset or Cromwell could take before God is that upon which alone any will join that innumerable multitude out of every tongue, who shall be gathered before the throne, namely, *the blood of the Lamb*, the unfailing resource provided by God for sinners. Cromwell and Somerset

Although there was, in this reign, perfect liberty as regards the use and circulation of the Scriptures, yet it is not a little remarkable, that no new translation or recension was published.* This shews, I think, that the proceedings in 1542 in the convocation, however much helped on by Cranmer, in the hope that a translation might be produced to which objections could not well be made by those who were popishly inclined, did in no way prove that he much objected to the version or revision then in use, which commonly bears his name. Throughout the reign of Edward, this was the version publicly used in the parish churches; and, indeed, the Psalms taken from it are, even at the present day, read in the services of the Established Church. No new version made in the reign of Edward

There appears, however, to have been a project for a new translation of the Bible into English, in which it is said that Martin Bucer was principally to have aided. Bucer and Paulus Fagius had been invited into England by the Protector Somerset, and Cranmer; after their arrival, they were appointed to be professors at Cambridge, the former of divinity, the latter of Hebrew. They had arrived in England in April, 1549, and for about three months had been Cranmer's guests. It was apparently during this interval Project for a new translation Bucer and Fagius arrive in England, April, 1549

* The Bible published by Beck, can scarcely be called a new recension, for it is almost the same as Matthew's Bible

that the idea struck Cranmer that these two learned foreigners might be fitly employed in making a revision of the English Bible.

Strype's Cran. 281

Intended to be employed as translators

"As it had been a great while his pious and most earnest desire, that the holy Bible should come abroad in the greatest exactness and true agreement with the original text, so he laid this work upon these two learned men. First, that they should give a clear, plain, and succinct interpretation of the Scripture, according to the propriety of the language. And, secondly, illustrate difficult and obscure places, and reconcile those that seemed repugnant to one another And it was his will and advice, that to this end and purpose their public readings should tend. This pious and good work, by the Archbishop assigned to them, they most gladly and readily undertook. For their more regular carrying on this business, they allotted to each other, by consent, their distinct tasks Fagius, because his talent lay in the Hebrew learning, was to undertake the Old Testament; and Bucer the New"

Both taken ill

This proposed arrangement was presently frustrated by the illness with which both Fagius and Bucer were seized. The former wished, if possible, to get to Cambridge, to commence, if he could, his appointed lectures; he hoped, likewise, that the change thither might benefit his health. He left Bucer behind him, still sick, and unable to travel; Fagius, continuing ill, earnestly wished to be joined at Cambridge by Bucer, who arrived on the 5th November, 1549. Ten days after this, Fagius fell asleep in Christ, aged forty-five years: this event caused great sorrow to "all pious men that wished well to religion."

Fagius dies, Nov 15, 1549

Tremellius succeeds him.

Upon the death of Fagius, he was succeeded as Hebrew professor by Immanuel Tremellius, who probably would have had that portion of the work which had been appointed to his predecessor, if the scheme of this translation had gone forward.

Bucer's death, Feb 1551

This, however, was prevented by the death of Bucer, which took place in the end of February, 1551; his loss was much felt by the Reformed in England, to whom he had been of great service, as regarded the defence and confirmation of the Gospel of Christ.*

We do not know, very exactly, the particulars of the plan, according to which the proposed translation or revision was to have been executed; it is probable, however, that Bucer and Fagius would have had much aid from English scholars, as to the more accurate manner of expressing the originals according to the idiom of our language; otherwise, it is probable, that however learned their version might have been, it would be one but little fitted for the use of mere English readers.

Before concluding all mention of Bucer, it is to be observed, that England had, for several years before, been mediately benefited by his services. The Argentine English Psalter, published in 1530, was a translation from his Latin Version; it is not impossible that this fact may have suggested the idea of a revision of the whole of the English translation in which he was to be engaged.

Sir J. Cheek translates part of the New Testament

During some part of this reign, Sir John Cheek (the king's Greek preceptor) executed a version of a part, at least, of the New Testament. This, if completed, would probably have been published; but it is not unlikely that it may have been begun towards the end of the reign, and thus discontinued in consequence of the change of events relative to religion and the Reformation. The following verse is given by Lewis, as a specimen of Sir John Cheek's manuscript version:—"When Jesus was boorn in Bethlem a citi of Juri in King Herood's dais, lo then the Wisards cam fro thest parties." Lewis says, "He has many other such peculiarities, as *toller*, for *publicane*, &c." Perhaps this version was never intended for publication, but merely executed for private use.

Matt. ii 1

Having thus concluded an account of the events of this reign, relative either to the translation or the diffusion of the Scriptures in English, together with briefly noticing the instruments by whom these objects were principally effected; it will be well to give a general estimate of the probable number of copies of the Scriptures, which were in circulation at the close of this reign.†

Copies in circulation.

The New Testament was printed in the very first year, and very frequently in those which succeeded; some of these editions were of the translation of Tyndale, some according to the "Great Bible," some few Coverdale's version. The number of these editions amounts together to at least *twenty-five;* so that, perhaps, it would not be too high an estimate, if we regard them to have together comprised *seventy-five thousand copies.* The editions of the Bible varied as to the text, just in the same manner as did

Twenty-five editions of the New Test.

75,000 copies.

* The friends of the Reformation showed what honour was in their power to both Fagius and Bucer in their burial; a few years afterwards, however, they were disinterred, and their bodies burned, as being those of heretics It was but a weak and foolish triumph of the restorers of popery, in the days of Mary, thus to attack the bodies of the dead; yet it was a very honourable testimony to those whose remains were thus treated.

† In the estimate given, nothing has been mentioned except what has been and is commonly acknowledged to have been published: how far the editions have been understated as to number and variety, by Dr Cotton, &c it is not easy to say, but probably *many* editions have not been, notwithstanding the diligence and ability of Dr. Cotton in this pursuit, properly noticed.

those of the New Testament; the first of these was printed in the year 1549, in which year there were also several other editions. The total number of impressions in the reign of Edward was at least *thirteen*, containing probably together more than *thirty thousand* copies: besides these, there were various editions of separate books of Scripture; and likewise it is to be remembered that at least twelve thousand copies of the "Great Bible" were in existence, and probably in use. At the close of the reign of Edward (July 6th, 1553), there were in circulation and use in England, at least *one hundred and seventeen thousand copies* of the whole Bible or the New Testament in English; including those used in the parish churches.

Thirteen editions of the Bible. 30,000 copies

117,000 copies at the close of Edward's reign, July 6, 1553.

Little need be said here of the effects which resulted from this diffusion of truth; when the copies of the Scriptures were few and forbidden, results might be marked with comparative ease; not so when the word of God was so widely diffused, and the working of the Spirit of God was bringing it to so many hearts with quickening power. The occurrences of the reign of Mary give ample proof of the working of the truth of God during the time of quiet which had preceded.

XI.

THE REIGN OF MARY.—RESTORATION OF ROMANISM.—SUFFERINGS OF REFORMERS.—PARTICULARS RELATIVE TO ROGERS AND COVERDALE.

THE death of Edward VI., on the 6th of July, 1553, immediately changed the whole scene. The liberty of the circulation of the word of God, and that of the preaching of the Gospel, were no longer continued. It is probable that the attempts which were made by ambitious and designing men to hinder the accession of Queen Mary, had no inconsiderable sway in prejudicing her mind yet more than it had been before against those who held the Reformed doctrines. Mary very soon declared her dislike of all the changes, with regard to religion, which had taken place. One of the first overt acts against the spread of Reformed doctrine was the prohibition of any to preach unless they were particularly licensed by the queen so to do; at the same time the Scriptures were forbidden to be read in the churches.

Edward's death, July 6, 1553. Its consequences. Mary's accession and conduct

Prohibition to preach

A circumstance had occurred, just at this time, which led to the publication of this restriction. Gilbert Bourne, one of the canons of St. Paul's (afterwards bishop of Bath and Wells), who was strongly attached to the Popish doctrines, and to those who upheld them, was appointed (probably by those now in power) to preach at Paul's Cross. In his sermon, he largely justified Bonner, who was present; and he spoke of the harsh usage which he had really received in the preceding reign. The auditors, offended at the praise which they heard so bestowed upon Bonner, interrupted the preacher, telling him that the doctrine preached by Bonner was most abominable. The tumult increased, until at length some zealots sought to pull the preacher down from the pulpit: at this crisis, John Bradford, a prebendary of St. Paul's, and a faithful preacher of Christ, was requested by Bourne's brother to appease the people if possible. This he sought to do, by setting before them the duty of obedience to "the powers that be," as the ordinance of God: and this was effectual in causing the greater part of the multitude to disperse. Bourne, however, continued in fear (a dagger having been thrown at him in some part of the tumult); he therefore requested Bradford not to leave him until he should be in safety. Accordingly, Bradford and John Rogers (whose name has been already mentioned in this account as the editor of Matthew's Bible) guarded him until he was safely sheltered. The same afternoon Bradford preached in Bow Church, where he again reproved the people for the insubordination and sedition which they had just manifested.

Aug 13, 1553. Bourne's sermon at Paul's Cross. Fox, iii 14, 233.

A disturbance

Bradford interferes

The date assigned to these occurrences at Paul's Cross is the thirteenth of August, 1553; and, on the next day, the restrictions which have just been mentioned, were commanded to be published. The Lord Mayor and the Recorder of London were directed to state to the Common Council that the queen had informed them, on the twelfth of the month, of the substance of the restrictions, both with regard to preaching, and to the diffusion of the Scriptures. The calling of the Common Council, to which this statement was to be made, was avowedly in consequence of the tumult at Paul's Cross. The ante-dating of the restriction, so as to make it seem to have been issued previous to this affair, was either done to make it appear that the queen was not desirous of paying too much attention to what had passed, and that she was not acting upon that provocation;—or else, the date may have been the true one: only an opportunity had to be waited for, which might seem a fit occasion for making it public.

Publication of the restrictions in preaching Aug. 14, 1553

To prove that this proclamation against preaching and publicly reading the Scriptures was illegal, and so

This restriction wholly illegal

far invalid, would be sufficiently easy: however, it was acted upon, and thus it comes under notice here. Rogers and Bradford found but little favour with the queen: it may be, she was offended that their preaching should be so much more influential over the minds and conduct of the people, than was that of the preacher of whom she approved. On the sixteenth of August (only three days after the tumult) Bradford was committed to the Tower, and Rogers commanded to restrain himself to his own house, "without having any conference with any other than those of his own household."

Bradford committed to the Tower Rogers restrained to his own house, Aug 16.

Thus the queen was resolved that if no attention were given to her preachers, no others should be listened to. By far the greater part of the clergy obeyed this order, while those who had been much marked as friends of the Reformation, were either committed to prison, or else restrained to their own houses. Those who had been in any way concerned in the setting up of the Lady Jane as queen, were sufficiently obnoxious on that account; while those who were not involved in that affair, were troubled upon real or pretended grounds. Those who were Romishly affected (however they might have previously complied with the steps which had been taken for the carrying on of the Reformation) now shewed themselves ready even to anticipate the queen's will; they set up the altars which had been removed, and again officiated in the Latin service of the Mass.

The Mass, &c. restored.

Several Bishops imprisoned and deprived

Cranmer, Ridley, Hooper, and others of the bishops, were committed to prison: others were deprived of their bishoprics on various grounds, while their places were supplied by those who might, from their attachment to Romanism, be regarded as sure to comply with the queen's will. Gardiner was again placed in the see of Winchester, of which he had been deprived; and Bonner was a second time similarly put in possession of the bishopric of London. The common grounds on which the prelates who favoured the Reformation were ejected, were either—of their being married men, or else their being in possession of bishoprics of which some Romish prelates had been deprived during the previous reign. Many finding that there was no liberty in England for the profession of the Gospel, sought a refuge on the continent; while some few, at the peril of their lives (as the events proved), continued to preach to the people in various parts of England, as they might find opportunity. One of those who so remained in England was John Harley, who had been made bishop of Hereford but a little while before the death of King Edward; and having been deprived of his bishopric on the ground of his being married, he continued in England preaching when and where he could, being frequently concealed in woods and similar places, and died at length "like a banished man in his own country." This conclusion of his labours was not until the last year of the reign of Mary, when he had seen enough to shew him the resolute opposition of the Romanists to all who favoured the Reformation.

Romish bishops restored

Many leave England

Some preachers remain.

Bp Harley

Efforts to restore Romanism

The latter half of the year 1553, and the whole of the following year, were spent by those in power in doing what they could diligently to eradicate all that had been sown of the seed of the Reformation. The prisons were crowded with those who had been active in the setting forth of the Gospel, and who had thus opposed the whole system of Rome. It does not appear that any particular measures were taken to suppress the Scriptures; indeed, *that* might be deemed a hopeless task, the copies in circulation were now so numerous. The attempts which were made, were rather directed to the expulsion from England of all those doctrines concerning the Gospel which had been learned from the Scriptures.

No attempt apparently to destroy the Scriptures

Amongst the sufferers and exiles in this reign, we find two who had been peculiarly prominent in publishing and translating the Scriptures into English; namely, John Rogers and Myles Coverdale.

Some account of Rogers. His marriage, 1537

Rogers, about the time of the publication of Matthew's Bible, took a wife; which was, no doubt in a great measure, the reason of his quitting England when the Act of the Six Articles was passed. Upon this he went to Wittemberg, where he was appointed to the charge of a congregation; for this he was well qualified, as having not only the needful gifts from God to fit him spiritually for the work, but likewise being so well acquainted with the German language, that his being an Englishman was no impediment to his preaching. There he remained, until the death of King Henry VIII. emboldened the exiles to return; which they did with the more confidence, seeing how fully the duke of Somerset was bent upon providing, so far as in him lay, that the word of God and the Gospel should be unhindered. Hereupon Rogers returned to England, leaving behind him the competent maintenance which he had in Saxony, in order that he might preach the Gospel of Christ in his own country, without any certainty concerning temporal things. He thus laboured diligently for some years: at length Ridley, when he was bishop of London, gave him a prebend in St. Paul's, and the Dean and Chapter chose him to lecture on divinity in the cathedral. His parochial charge was at this time the vicarage of the parish of St. Sepulchre.

Quits England, 1539.

At Wittemberg till the death of Henry, 1547

His return to England

He preaches

Made prebend of St Paul's

Divinity lecturer

Vicar of St. Sepulchre's

There he continued until the accession of Queen Mary; when he, preaching at Paul's Cross, earnestly exhorted his auditors to continue in the profession of the faith of Christ's Gospel. This sermon gave offence to the court, and he was summoned on account of it before the privy council. For the time he was discharged, until a little while after, when the queen had prohibited preaching, and the tumult had arisen about Bourne's sermon, he was again summoned before the council (August 16th, 1553); and then (as has been related) he was required to remain as a prisoner in his own house. He had now the opportunity of escaping if he would, but the obligation under which he was placed, as having been commanded by the council, as well as other causes, restrained him. He remained thus as a prisoner in his own house for several months, and then was sent by Bishop Bonner to Newgate.

Preaches at Paul's Cross after Mary's accession.

Imprisoned in his own house, Aug 16, 1553

Sent to Newgate.

In order that the bishops and other prominent persons, who were friends to the Reformation, might be under the power of the council, they were, summoned soon after the acccession of Mary. Thus, on the 22nd of August, 1553, Coverdale and Hooper, bishop of Gloucester, were both of them ordered to repair to court without delay, where they were to attend the pleasure of the council. Accordingly, on the 26th Hooper appeared, and on the 31st Coverdale did the same. It is probable that the longer period between the summons and the appearance of Coverdale, than there was in the case of Hooper, was owing to his being absent in his diocese.

Bishops Coverdale and Hooper summoned before the council, Aug 22, 1553

On the 1st of September, Hooper and Coverdale again appeared before the council; the former was committed a prisoner to the Fleet, and the latter was commanded to attend the pleasure of the Lords of the council. It is probable that he gave security for his appearance when summoned, and that this was deemed sufficient. It is to be observed that the systematic persecution of this reign did not commence for a considerable time; indeed as yet there were no laws enacted, which would authorise such a mode of procedure. Any of the bishops who were possessed of sees from which others had been ejected, were now in their turn deprived. Coverdale had his bishopric taken away from him on this ground; for although his predecessor had resigned, yet it was said that he had done this from intimidation.

Hooper sent to the Fleet, Sept 1, 1553

Coverdale deprived of his bishopric

In October, the Parliament and the Convocation met. In the former of these, measures were taken for the restoration of every thing connected with the worship permitted by law, to much the same state in which it had been in the latter part of the reign of Henry VIII. In the Convocation, a proposition was made that the whole of the lower house should subscribe certain articles, of which one asserted the Romish doctrine of the "real presence" in the Lord's Supper. This doctrine had gradually been relinquished during the reign of Edward VI.; Ridley was convinced that it was not supported by the testimony of God in His word; and after he had suggested his doubts, Cranmer was induced to examine the subject, and he too, arrived at a negative conclusion. Latimer soon after accorded with them in judgment. The opposition to the Romish doctrine continued to spread just in proportion as the Gospel was known; so that at the accession of Mary the number was considerable of those who had on this subject renounced the Romish dogma.

Meeting of Parliament and the Convocation, Oct 1553.

The "real presence" discussed

Weston, the prolocutor of the Convocation, in proposing the recognition of the Romish doctrine on this subject, made a deliberate attack upon the Reformation. The whole of the lower house of Convocation were fully disposed (with the exception of six persons) to subscribe the article proposed. John Philpot, archdeacon of Winchester, one of the six who maintained on this point the reformed doctrine, requested the prolocutor that the matter might be considered and debated, instead of the whole house subscribing without consideration. He desired farther, that if a disputation were held on the subject, Bishop Ridley and John Rogers, together with a few others on the same side, might be allowed to take a part in it, as well as the six dissentients of that house.

The Reforma- attacked.

All but Six subscribers

Archdeacon Philpot opposes

The former part of this request, namely, that there might be a disputation, was acceded to, the other was not allowed. The disputation lasted, accordingly, several days, but as might be expected, no benefit really resulted from it; to overcome in argument is a very different thing from conviction being brought to the *conscience* by the power of the Holy Ghost. One thing, however, was fully proved, namely, how earnestly the doctrines of Rome were held and pressed by many who had pretended to conform to all the changes adopted in the days of King Edward. Philpot and his coadjutors, although the truth was on their side, argued in vain; their adversaries were resolved to crush them by some means or other. In consequence of what passed in the Convocation house, Philpot was committed to the King's Bench prison; there he remained (after having been once examined before Gardiner, his diocesan) for a considerable time after that of which I am speaking, until the second of October, 1555, when he was examined before the queen's commissioners, who sent him to Bonner's coal-house, where other prisoners were confined. He was repeatedly examined before Bonner and others; and in these examinations Christ fulfilled unto him His gracious promise, "I will give you a mouth and wisdom which none of your adversaries shall be able to

A disputation

Philpot sent to the King's Bench

Examined before the Commissioners, Oct 2, 1552.

Before Bonner

Luke xxi 15

gainsay nor resist." In consequence of his confession of Christ, he was condemned as a heretic: one of the grounds of accusation against him was very remarkable; a sentence of Bernard's was found written in his Bible, importing that *the Spirit is the vicar of Christ upon earth.* This was deemed an heretical statement, and thus Bernard (and constructively our Lord himself—see John xiv—xvi.) was condemned with Philpot. He was burned, December 18th, 1555.

" Quod Spiritus est Vicarius Christi in terrâ."

Philpot burned, Dec. 18, 1555.

The Lady Jane, Lord Guildford Dudley, and Cranmer tried, Nov. 1553.

In November, 1553, the Lady Jane and her husband were tried for high treason: as was also Archbishop Cranmer. This was not a little harsh; for although he had acknowledged Jane as queen, yet he was far less implicated in the matter than were many others who were freely pardoned by Mary: it is not to be doubted that reasons connected with religion led to his being selected for trial.

Disputation on the Lord's Supper at Oxford, April 14, 1554.

Cranmer, Ridley, and Latimer sent thither

In the spring of the following year it was determined, for the better establishing of the Romish doctrine of the Lord's Supper, that a solemn disputation should be held on the subject at Oxford; not, let it be observed, for the inquiring what the true doctrine in the matter is, but in order to triumph over those who were already in the power of their adversaries. Cranmer, although attainted of treason, was to be sent to Oxford to dispute, and with him Ridley and Latimer. A deputation was sent from Cambridge to take a part in the contest; so that the conclusion might appear to be the determination of both Universities.

The disputation commenced on the 14th of April, 1554, the points were three:—

Articles disputed, Fox, iii. 36.

"I Whether the natural body of Christ be present in the Sacrament, after the words spoken by the priest, or no?

"II. Whether in the Sacrament, after the words of consecration, any other substance do remain than the substance of the body and blood of Christ?

"III Whether the Mass be a sacrifice propitiatory for the sins of the quick and the dead?"

The two former of these articles were questions in which much of the important truth of God was concerned; but as to the third, the very substance and essence of the Gospel was at stake; the finished work of Christ to which the Holy Ghost bears witness was set at nought, and the sacrifice of Christ was made like unto the oft-repeated offerings of the Mosaic law.

Cranmer and Ridley dispute.

Latimer's written statement

Against the first and second of these especially, Cranmer and Ridley held much and long contention; Latimer, because of his age and infirmities, refused to dispute: he gave in a written statement in answer to the articles, in which he briefly and solidly refuted them from Scripture. He was, however, led into some discussion, in the course of which his adversaries actually tried to confound him by appealing from the Latin version to the Greek original (of which Latimer was ignorant), and in doing so *falsely* affirmed that passages were other than they really are. Truly this was handling the word of God deceitfully!*

All three condemned as heretics April 20, 1554

Of course the three advocates for the truth were condemned as heretics; this was on the 20th of April, 1554. The Romish party by dint of numbers and authority claimed a triumphant victory over the three prisoners (one of them being already under sentence of death), against whom they had contended in the disputation.

After Dr. Weston had, in St. Mary's church, solemnly condemned them, their fautors, and patrons, they each gave a brief reply:—

Their replies to the sentence.

Cranmer.—"From this your judgment and sentence, I appeal to the just judgment of God Almighty, trusting to be present with Him in heaven, for whose presence in the altar I am thus condemned."

* The sufficiency of the word of God, as applied by the Spirit, to meet the exigencies of Christians has been so often opposed that it will be fitting to give a small portion of Latimer's disputation; it shews how the opposers of the scripture seek to pervert it to their own ends. Latimer, when asked the meaning of ἀγάπη, replied, "I understand no Greek; yet I think it meaneth charity." Upon this his opponents seem to have thought that they might practise as they pleased upon Latimer's ignorance; Dr. Weston asked presently after,—"Will you have all things done that Christ did then [in the institution of the Lord's Supper]. . . And where find you, I pray you, that a woman should receive the sacrament?" To this Latimer replied—"Will you give me leave to turn my book? I find it in the 11th chap. to the Corinthians. I trow these be his words—*Probet autem seipsum homo,* &c. I pray you, good master, which gender is *homo?*" Weston thus pressed, replied truly enough—"Marry, the common gender." This seemed to be a concession of point at issue, but Cole interposed, saying—"It is in the Greek ὁ ἄνθρωπος." His object in saying this is not very apparent; it may be that he ignorantly thought the masculine article, which he quoted (which is not really in the Greek), proved the point against Latimer. Harpsfield now interposed, making a false allegation, which was much more to the purpose; he boldly uttered this deliberate untruth, "It is ἀνηρ, that is *vir*" To this impudent falsehood Latimer simply and sufficiently replied, "It is in my book of Erasmus's translation, *Probet seipsum* HOMO." They dared not allege that Erasmus had erred in his version, they only quibbled about the word *seipsum* being of the masculine gender

The self-same argument, that the Scripture does not speak of women receiving the Lord's Supper, has *often* been brought forward by ignorant cavillers in more recent times; but it is probable that it has rarely been supported in so unprincipled a manner.

Ridley.—" Although I be not of your company, yet doubt I not but my name is written in another place, whither this sentence will send us sooner, than we should, by the course of nature, have come."

Latimer.—" I thank God most heartily, that He hath prolonged my life to this end, that I may in this case glorify God by that kind of death."

The Protestants had regarded the Oxford disputation with great interest, judging that it might serve as an indication of the treatment which they might expect: they looked upon the three advocates for the truth as being the representatives of all the Gospellers; and when they heard of the unfairness with which the dispute was conducted, and the consequent condemnation of the prisoners, they read the history of their own treatment.

In the following month (May) it was reported that a similar discussion was to take place at Cambridge, in which John Bradford, John Rogers, Laurence Saunders, and others of the Protestant prisoners were to be opposed and condemned, as their brethren had been at Oxford. In consequence of this, a declaration was drawn up by Bradford and Saunders, and signed by them and several other prisoners. They state that they do not refuse to dispute, but they would only do it in writing; for this, their determination, they give various reasons. They speak of their readiness to maintain the truth by any death which might be adjudged to them; at the same time earnestly disclaiming every thing which might seem like rebellion against the Queen or her authority. Then they set forth a statement of the Christian doctrine which they had received and taught; they declare their belief in the paramount authority of Scripture; that none can be the true church which does not listen to Scripture; they acknowledge various creeds and confessions as containing sound doctrine; and, in the fourth place, they declare very fully what they believed respecting the vital point of justification:—

A similar discussion proposed at Cambridge

A statement signed by certain of the prisoners, May 8, 1554.

The doctrine they held

" We believe and confess, concerning justification, that as it comes only from God's mercy, through Christ, so it is perceived and had of none which be of years of discretion, otherwise than by faith only: which faith is not an opinion, but a certain persuasion wrought by the Holy Ghost in the mind and heart of man; wherethrough, as the mind is illuminated, so the heart is suppled to submit itself to the will of God unfeignedly, and so sheweth forth an inherent righteousness; which is to be discerned in the article of justification, from the righteousness with which God endueth us withal, justifying us, although inseparably they go together. And thus we do not for curiosity or contention sake, but for conscience' sake, that it might be quiet, which it never can be, if we confound without distinction *forgiveness of sins and Christ's justice* IMPUTED *to us*, with *regeneration and* INHERENT *righteousness*. By this we disallow Papistical doctrine of free-will, of works of supererogation, of merits, of the necessity of auricular confession, and satisfaction to Godwards."

Justification by faith only

It is evident that by "*inherent* righteousness" is here meant what might be now more simply understood by the term "*infused* righteousness;" the distinction between our being justified and our being regenerate (although they ever go together) is, as they state, most important as regards the purging of the *conscience*.

After this they speak of other points of doctrine, including the articles of the Oxford disputation; they conclude with praying for the Queen, and promising submission and obedience, to which they exhort all; and "where they cannot obey, but [i. e. unless] they must disobey God, there to submit themselves with all patience and humility, to suffer as the will and pleasure of the higher powers shall adjudge." This declaration was dated the 8th of May, 1554. It was signed by several of the most prominent upholders of the Reformation, namely:—" Robert Menaven, *alias* Robert Ferrar; Rowland Taylor; John Philpot; John Bradford; John Wigorn, & Glou. Episcopus, *alias* John Hooper; Edward Crome; John Rogers; Lawrence Saunders; Edmund Lawrence; F. P., T. M." Besides these, who were prisoners in the King's Bench, the Fleet, the Marshalsea, and Newgate, there was the following subscription:—" To these things abovesaid, do I, Myles Coverdale, late of Exon, consent and agree, with these mine afflicted brethren being prisoners, mine own hand." It does not appear that Coverdale had been actually put in prison; and it is very probable that he it was who conveyed this declaration from one to another amongst those by whom it was signed.

Obedience to "the powers that be."

Signatures

Coverdale's subscription

In the course of this year, the queen was married to Philip of Spain (July 25th). Cardinal Pole came as legate from the Pope into England, and the realm was "reconciled" to the see of Rome (Nov. 30); and thus the whole of the system of Romanism was formally re-established.

The queen's marriage, July 25, 1555

Pole "recconciles" the realm, Nov 30

Early in the ensuing year (1555), measures were taken for punishing some of those who were already in prison as heretics. This probably was intended to be done by way of example; and, therefore, a few of those whose opposition to the Romish rule and doctrine had been most marked were selected as victims.

It is unlikely that any of the persecutors thought that the constancy of the Gospellers would furnish so vast a number of sufferers.

John Rogers, the first martyr in Mary's reign.

The *first* of that band who sealed their testimony for the doctrine of Christ by their death, was John Rogers, of whom previous mention has often been made. He remained a prisoner, at first in his own house, and afterwards at Newgate, from the 16th of August, 1553, until the 22nd of January, 1555; when he was brought, together with other preachers, before Gardiner, bishop of Winchester, the lord chancellor, in the church of St. Mary Overy, Southwark. Here he was examined upon numerous points of doctrine, and many endeavours were made to induce him to submit himself to the authority of the papal church. One of the charges against him was his being married, which he had been for eighteen years. He was again and again called on to answer to the interrogatories of the bishop on the following days: one of the things principally insisted on was, of course, the "real presence" in the Lord's supper. On these same days, Bishop Hooper and others were likewise examined. On the 29th of January, Rogers and Hooper were condemned by Gardiner as obstinate heretics, and delivered over to the secular power to be punished, "to the extirpation, terror, and confusion of the heretics;" and yet (according to the form) the rigour was directed not to be too extreme—as if burning men alive was not proceeding to extremities.

Brought before Gardiner, Jan 22. Fox, iii 98. Examined

Condemned, Jan 29

After Rogers and Hooper were thus condemned, Gardiner declared them to be under the sentence of the greater curse, denouncing the same against all who should eat, drink, aid, or have any communication with them. To this Rogers replied:

His reply to his sentence.

"Well, my lord, here I stand before God and you, and all this honourable audience, and take Him to witness, that I never wittingly or willingly taught any false doctrine; and therefore have I a good Conscience before God and all good men I am sure that you and I shall come before a Judge that is righteous, before whom I shall be as good a man as you: as I nothing doubt but that I shall be found there a true member of the true Catholic Church of Christ, and everlastingly saved And as for your false Church, ye need not to excommunicate me forth of it. I have not been in it these twenty years, the Lord be thanked therefore.

"But now ye have done what ye can, my lord, I pray you yet grant me one thing.

"*Gardiner*—What is that?

His wife forbidden to come to him.

"*Rogers*—That my wife, being a stranger, may come and speak with me so long as I live For she hath ten children which are hers and mine, and somewhat I would counsel her, what were best for her to do

"*Gardiner*—No She is not thy wife

"*Rogers*—Yes, my lord, and hath been these eighteen years.

"*Gardiner*—Should I grant her to be thy wife?

"*Rogers*—Choose you, whether ye will or not; she shall be so nevertheless.

"*Gardiner*—She shall not come to thee.

"*Rogers*—Then I have tried out all your charity!"

After this, Rogers and Hooper were taken until night to the Clink, and then conveyed to Newgate. There they both remained until the martyrdom of Rogers, and then, on the following day, Hooper was sent to suffer at Gloucester.

While in prison, at this time, Rogers spake thus (amongst other things) to John Day, the printer, then in Newgate on account of religion:—"Thou shalt live to see the alteration of this religion, and the Gospel to be freely preached again. And therefore have me commended to my brethren, as well in exile as others, and bid them be circumspect in displacing the Papists, and putting good ministers into churches, or else their end will be worse than ours."

On the morning of Monday the 4th of February, Rogers was awaked very early by the wife of the keeper of Newgate, and was thus suddenly warned that he was then to be burned. He was sleeping so soundly that he could with difficulty be awaked. When he was aroused, and understood what they wanted, he said, "Then I need not tie my points."* He was then taken with Hooper to Bonner to be degraded in the chapel of Newgate; after which he petitioned him, as he had Gardiner, to be allowed to speak a few words to his wife: this was again refused him. He was then delivered to the sheriffs, Chester and Woodroofe, to be burned. On his way to Smithfield, his request, which the two bishops had refused, was granted by the gracious providence of God. "His wife and children, being eleven in number, and ten able to go, and one sucking on her breast, met him by the way as he went towards Smithfield: this sorrowful sight of his own flesh and blood could nothing move him, but that he constantly and cheerfully took his death with wonderful patience in the defence and quarrel of Christ's Gospel."

Degraded by Bonner

* Alluding to a part of the dress then worn; if his points had been tied, his undressing, in order to be burned, would have taken the longer.

Woodroofe, one of the sheriffs, asked him, whether he would not revoke what he called "his abominable doctrine, and his evil opinion of the sacrament of the altar," Rogers replied, "That which I have preached, I will seal with my blood." "Then," replied Woodroofe, "thou art an heretic." Rogers answered, "That shall be known at the day of judgment." "Well," replied Woodroofe, "I will never pray for thee." "But I," said Rogers, "will pray for you!" Thus did he act on the command of the apostle, "Overcome evil with good."

On his way towards Smithfield, he repeated the fifty-first Psalm; "all the people wonderfully rejoicing at his constancy, with great praises and thanks to God for the same." The distance from Newgate to Smithfield is very little; but in that little space, he had to pass his own parish church of St. Sepulchre's; the people, probably, were many of them his own parishioners, to whom, close to the very street through which he went (Giltspur Street), he had often preached the Gospel of Christ.* He goes to Smithfield.

After he reached Smithfield, his pardon was brought, to be given him in case he would have recanted; but this he utterly refused. Pardon offered him He refuses to revoke

"He shewed most constant patience, not using many words, for he could not be permitted, but only exhorting the people constantly to remain in that faith and true doctrine which he before had taught, and they had learned; and for the confirmation whereof he was not only content patiently to suffer and bear all such bitterness and cruelty as had been shewn him, but also most gladly to resign up his life, and to give his flesh to the consuming fire, for the testimony of the same"

Thus died the faithful servant and martyr of Christ, John Rogers, who was honoured by his Master, not only to be a preacher of His Gospel for twenty years, and a setter forth of His holy word, but likewise thus to yield his body to be burned, as the first of that blessed company of saints who were at this time called to suffer for their Lord. What, though their bodies endured bitter torture, and their ashes were scattered far and wide—they were the Lord's; and even as He ransomed them by His own precious blood, so did He care for and strengthen them in the hour of their need; and so will He, when He comes in glory, gather these His saints unto Him, making their once destroyed bodies glorious and incorruptible like unto His own. His death.

A few days after the burning of Rogers, that faithful servant of Christ, John Bradford, addressed a letter to Cranmer, Ridley, and Latimer, at Oxford. He thus adverted to the condemnation of certain of the prisoners in London:— Bradford's mention of Rogers, Feb 8

"I had thought that every one of your staves had stood next the door, but now it is otherwise perceived. *Our dear brother Rogers hath broken the ice valiantly:* as this day (I think) or to-morrow at the uttermost, hearty Hooper, sincere Saunders, and trusty Taylor, take their course and receive their crown. The next am I, which hourly look for the Porter to open me the gates after them, to enter into the desired rest God forgive me mine unthankfulness for this exceeding great mercy to choose me to be one in whom He will suffer."

This letter is dated the 8th of February.

Gardiner appears to have hoped that a few suffering as a terrible example would so intimidate all others, that the compliance with Romanism would be universal. However, he was disappointed; for, on the 8th of February, before all those who had been condemned were put to death, six others were examined on similar charges. But Gardiner would not meddle with their examination and condemnation, and left the whole matter in the hands of Bonner, who seemed to have found in this bloody persecution a work for which he was well suited; these six were all of them condemned the next day, although their death for the present was delayed; this was supposed to have been partly caused by a sermon which Alphonso, the confessor of King Philip, preached on the 10th of February against burning men for religion. But after a few weeks the flames were again kindled; and in less than four years, *two hundred and seventy seven* persons laid down their lives for the testimony of Christ. Ridley and Latimer suffered together on the 16th of October in this year; and on the following March 21st, Cranmer similarly suffered, after having been induced to recant, and then, by the merciful kindness of God, being enabled to see and condemn his weakness in having so acted. Gardiner leaves persecution to Bonner Alphonso preaches against burning. 277 persons burned in 4 years

It has been already noticed that many escaped to the continent in the early part of this reign, and were thus preserved from the bitter persecution which afterwards commenced. Some of the deprived bishops were among the number of these exiles: for instance, Poinet, bishop of Winchester; and also Barlow and Many escape to the continent.

* One who had been converted by the ministry of Rogers, was a youth named John Leaf, who, in the following July, was burned for the confession of the truth, together with John Bradford.—Fox, iii. 254

Scory: the two latter, however, had been taken before they could effect their escape, and only obtained their liberation by submitting to the doctrines of Rome. This submission was, it is true, only nominal: neither of them did really in their hearts renounce the doctrines which they had previously held; they did, however, by their submission, most effectually mar their testimony for Christ, and thus lost the honour which so many had, of being witnesses for Him in patient endurance.

Coverdale at length escapes.

Amongst others who at length found a refuge in a foreign country was Coverdale. Although he had not been in prison, yet the "security" under which he was to appear before the council when called upon, bound him in conscience not to leave England: so that he was as one kept waiting the will of the persecutors. The Lord, however, in whose hands his cause was, had other things in store for him. His connection with Dr. Johannes Macchabæus Alpinus (they having married two sisters) has been already noticed; in consequence of the circumstances of danger in which Coverdale was placed in England, Macchabæus had besought the king of Denmark to intercede for him with Queen Mary. The king had, accordingly, written to her on the 25th of April, 1554. He speaks of having heard that Coverdale was in prison, and in danger of his life, on account of some charge connected with the political changes which had taken place in England, notwithstanding he was assured that he was entirely innocent. He therefore besought Mary to pardon him freely; and if, on any account, he could not be allowed to remain in England, he requested that he might be sent in safety to Denmark. In return, King Christiern promised to do what he could to oblige her.

Christiern of Denmark intercedes for him. April 25, 1554. Fox, iii 149

It has been questioned how Christiern could suppose that Coverdale was in trouble on account of any thing which had taken place "in hâc recenti perturbatione ac motu regni Angliæ," when Wyatt and the duke of Suffolk's insurrection did not take place until some time after his summons before the council. It is probable, however, that Christiern looked at the setting up of the Lady Jane as queen, and the subsequent revolt, as belonging to one affair; and thus he may, very probably, have thought that Coverdale was called in question about something connected with the first attempt for making Jane queen.

The queen's reply.

Mary replied to the application of the king of Denmark, that Coverdale was not under restraint on the ground of religion, as he might have supposed, but for certain debts which were due from him.* She seemed, however, to intimate that Coverdale should feel the good effects of the king's interest for him. Nothing, however, was done towards his liberation; and, consequently, the king wrote again, on the 24th of September. In this letter, he expresses his satisfaction that there was nothing more serious laid to Coverdale's charge than a matter of debt; but as he understood that this must have arisen from something connected with his bishopric, of which he had been deprived, and from which he had received very little emolument; he hoped that even if his accounts should be involved, that the queen would shew him favour. He wrote as if not questioning at all that the queen would pardon Coverdale, and only apparently was glad that it was for nothing more serious than an alleged debt.

The king writes again, Sep. 24.

Some months passed, however, and no notice was taken of this letter. At length, however, even after the first selected band of witnesses had been condemned, and the fires of persecution were again kindled, the queen gave permission to Coverdale to leave England. She wrote to King Christiern, on February the 18th, 1555, stating that she complied with his request in consideration of the desire which he had expressed that Coverdale should be sent to him, although he was her subject, and had not paid certain sums of money which he owed to her treasury. What this complaint respecting debt might mean, is not very clear. It would harldly refer to any demand concerning his bishopric, for he had been excused his first-fruits in Edward's reign: it may, after all, have been nothing but the sum in which he was bound, together with his sureties, to appear when called upon. It may be questioned why Mary deferred so long to liberate Coverdale, and then complied just at this juncture. It is to be observed, that she had distinctly stated to King Christiern, that he was not in trouble for any matter of religion, but solely on a ground of debt; this might have been felt to be a pledge that he should not be molested on account of his non-compliance with the restoration of Romanism; and thus Mary would have been bound not to have allowed him to suffer with his brethren. It may be, indeed, that the wholesale slaughter of Protestants had not then been determined on. At a later period of this reign, so firm an adherent of the Gospel would not have been allowed to escape the flames.

Mary writes to king Christiern, Feb 18, 1555

Debt alleged as the ground of Coverdale's detention.

Coverdale had his passport granted him for himself and two servants, February 19th, 1555. It is probable that his wife had left England, and was with her sister in Denmark. Coverdale, on his arrival thither, was

Coverdale receives his passport, Feb. 19, 1555

* This had been also made the pretext for the imprisonment of Hooper:—"He was commanded to ward, it being declared unto him at his departure that the cause of his imprisonment was only for certain sums of money, for which he was indebted to the queen, and not for religion" (Fox, iii. 122).

received joyfully by Macchabæus and his other friends, who, from the recent occurrences in England, had little reason to expect to see him amongst them. It was like Peter coming to the house of Mary where the saints were met in prayer for his liberation. He reaches Denmark.

The English exiles scattered on the continent were mostly at Frankfort, Strasburgh, Wesel in Friesland, Bâle, Geneva, and a few of eminence at Zurich. After having remained for a little while in Denmark, Coverdale went away from that country, in order to be where he might have the opportunity of preaching the Lord Jesus Christ. The king of Denmark would gladly have retained this honoured confessor of Christ in his country, but he could not speak Danish, which hindered him from preaching there, and made some part of Germany a more eligible station for him; besides, in Denmark he had no opportunity of building up his own exiled countrymen in the doctrine of Christ. Places of the abode of English exiles.

After leaving Denmark he went to Wesel, and preached for some time to the English exiles there. It was at this place that Bishop Scory remained, and regularly ministered to the exiles. He appears to have bewailed bitterly his weakness and sinful compliance in his submission, before his escape from England. Coverdale had not been long at Wesel, before Wolfgang, duke of Deux Ponts, offered him the benefice of Bergzabern, which he formerly had during his second exile in the days of Henry. It must have been to him deeply interesting again to labour, in the service of the Lord, amongst those to whom he had ministered the truth of God eight years before. At this place he probably remained for several months. Coverdale goes to Wesel. He goes to Bergzabern

Now leaving for a while the exiles on the continent, let us take a brief glance at some of the occurrences in England. It is not to be supposed that the edicts of man could frustrate the power of the Spirit of God: there were not a few who, at the peril of their lives, continued to teach and preach the Lord Jesus Christ. This was now done, it is true, without courting publicity, but at the same time without shrinking from the confession of Christ. This continued during the whole of the reign of Mary, in such sort that it seemed like a revival of the days of the Lollards, when for one hundred years and more, there were not lacking such men as William Thorp and Thomas Mann, to testify and instruct, according to the gift which they had received of God. Occurrences in England

One of the most laborious of these evangelists, in the days of Mary, was George Eagles; who was commonly known, from his itinerant labours, by the name of *Trudge-over-the-world.* He would gather little companies together, and preach to them; and then secrete himself in the woods to avoid capture. At length the council offered a reward for his apprehension; and a diligent search was made, so that he was arrested. He was tried on a charge of high treason, which was endeavoured to be supported by the allegation that the small congregations to whom he preached, were traitorous assemblies: he was likewise charged with having prayed that the Lord would change the queen's heart, *or else take her away:* this latter clause being a mere false accusation. He was condemned, and suffered the penalties of treason at Chelmsford. This was in the middle of 1557. George Eagles a diligent labourer Fox, iii. 700 Arrested and tried for treason. Executed, 1557.

In London there was throughout this reign a congregation of Gospellers, who used to assemble, sometimes all together, sometimes in separate companies, to worship God, and to shew the death of Christ in the Lord's supper. Several of them were taken and put to death from time to time, but still they rather increased: several, at different times, were wont to minister among them. Two of the most prominent of these, were Cuthbert Symson, the deacon, and Augustine Bernher, a devoted Christian who had been Latimer's servant. Amongst the exiles at Wesel was one named John Rough, a Scotchman, who had laboured much in England, as a preacher, in the days of King Edward. During his exile he supported himself by knitting; to purchase yarn he came to London, on the 10th of November, 1557, and during his stay he associated with and ministered amongst the congregation of Gospellers. On the following 12th of December, they held a meeting (at which they were going to have received the Lord's supper), at the Saracen's Head, in Islington. At this meeting, through the treachery of a false brother, they were surprised, and many of them were taken; amongst others, John Rough and Cuthbert Symson. John Rough was burned in Smithfield, on the 22nd of December; and with him suffered Margaret Mearings, who belonged to the London congregation of Gospellers. She had been a little before excluded from their communion by an act of discipline, in which John Rough had taken a principal part: but so graciously did the Lord manifest the power of his restoring grace, that she sought repentantly to minister to the necessities of Rough while in prison, and thus being taken and condemned, they suffered martyrdom together. The London congregation of Gospellers Their sufferings. Labourers, Cuthbert Symson, Aug Bernher. John Rough comes to London, Nov. 10, 1557 A meeting in Islington, Dec 12, 1557 Many arrested, Rough, Symson, and others Rough burned, Dec 22. Margaret Mearings burned with him.

Cuthbert Symson was not put to death until the 28th of March, 1558. He was cruelly tortured, in order to force him to disclose the names and abodes of those who belonged to this congregation. Cuthbert Symson burned, Mar 28, 1558.

T. Bentham returns to England.

In 1558, Thomas Bentham, one of the exiles, returned into England for the express purpose of ministering amongst those who were "counted as sheep for the slaughter." He appears to have been greatly strengthened by the Lord, and to have been a great blessing to those to whom he had thus gone. He thus wrote to Lever in Switzerland:—

His letter to Lever. Strype, Mem. Ecc v 273.

"Whiles I was in Germany at liberty of body, havyng sufficient for it for the time, I was yet many tymes in great greyf of mynd, and terrible torments of hell; and now here beyng every moment of an hour in danger of takyng, and fear of bodily death, I am in mynd, the Lord be praysed, most quiet and joyful, seying the fervent zeal of so many, and such increase of our congregation in the myddest of thys cruel and violent persecution. What shold I say but, *A Domino, factum est?*"

A meeting at Islington, April, 1558. Seven burned in Smithfield, June 27. All forbidden to pray for them. Bentham's conduct

In April, 1558, about forty Gospellers met in a field at Islington; and several of them were taken and imprisoned: seven of these were examined before Bonner on the 14th of June, and on the 27th were burned in Smithfield. At the burning of these martyrs, there was a proclamation made in the name of the king and queen, that no man under pain of death should approach them, touch them, speak to them, comfort them, PRAY FOR THEM, or once say, "God help them!" Such a proclamation needs no comment. Thomas Bentham, however, as well as others of the congregation who were present, in spite of the threatening proclamation, comforted, exhorted, and strengthened the souls of the sufferers.

When the fire was set to them, he turned to the people who were assembled, and said to them:—"We know that they are the people of God, and, therefore, we cannot choose but wish well to them, and say, *God strengthen them!*" He then prayed, "Almighty God, for Christ's sake, strengthen them!" Upon this the whole assembled multitude responded, "Amen! Amen!" So many were there that joined in the cry, that the officers, amazed, knew neither whom to take or whom to accuse. After this Bonner, fearing lest such scenes might be repeated, sent six of the prisoners to Brentford, and had them burned there.

Six burned at Brentford

It was thus that the Lord wrought by His Holy Spirit in providing witnesses for Himself, and preserving them (almost as the three in the fiery furnace) throughout the bitter days of this persecution.

XII.

A TRANSLATION OF THE SCRIPTURES MADE BY THE EXILES AT GENEVA. THE NEW TESTAMENT PUBLISHED.

A translation of the Scriptures by the exiles at Geneva. NewTestament published, 1557

It has been already stated, that the accession of Mary had hindered the printing and circulation of the Scriptures in English; but notwithstanding the hindrances constantly thrown in their way, those who longed to see the word of God in the hands of their countrymen, continued their efforts to this end. Certain of the exiles from England, during this reign, made a new translation of the New Testament, and also advanced considerably in a version of the Old. It was at Geneva that this work was accomplished, and on that account the version is commonly called the Genevan translation. The New Testament was published in 1557, the printing being finished (according to a statement at the end of the volume) on the tenth of June. It is not known how long before this time the work was commenced: several of the parties concerned in it had taken up their abode at Geneva, in the spring of 1555; and they seem to have used the rest which was thus afforded them, in preparing this version. The greater part of those engaged in this work had taken a part in the grievous contentions which were carried on by the refugees about the service-book and the habits. It is not my place to discuss these questions which so divided at this time those who were one in Christ, I have only to speak of the results to which they led. Many of those who left Frankfort in consequence of their objections to these things, went to Geneva and formed an English congregation there; upon this, others who held similar sentiments joined them from Strasburgh and other places, some of whom undertook the work referred to.

English congregation formed at Geneva

They probably had motives which sufficiently influenced them in executing a new translation, instead of giving a mere reprint or revision of any which had preceded. The intention of such a work had been entertained in the reign of Edward VI.; and it is probable that in this projected revision, from the manner in which the name of Bucer was connected with it, there would have been embodied whatever might be learned from the Biblical knowledge possessed by reformers on the continent. The exiles at Geneva possessed ample opportunity of profiting by such aid; and this may have been a leading motive with them for making the work entirely new, or at least entirely remodelled. Another reason which the translators themselves assign for making a new version, was, that the knowledge of Greek and Hebrew had greatly increased since the earlier English translations were made, and thus it was possible to translate with far more accuracy than could have been done some years before.

Reasons for a new version

The last place at which it was noticed that Coverdale had arrived, was his old parish of Bergzabern, in the duchy of Deux Ponts; we next find him at Geneva, engaged in the execution of this translation. Whether he was invited to join the others who undertook the version, or whether he himself, hearing of what they had in hand, bent his steps to Geneva in order to aid them, does not appear. ' However, we find him as one of those who took the work in hand; and, therefore, we may regard the version, which was the result of much united labour, as containing Coverdale's last review of a version of the New Testament. It is very probable, however, that the principal part of the toil was borne by those who were his associates in this work. These are said to have been the following persons.

Coverdale goes to Geneva

Thomas Sampson, who had been educated at Oxford, and who afterwards studied at one of the inns of court, being convinced of the erroneousness of the doctrines of Popery, and desiring to preach the truth which his own soul had received, was ordained by Bishop Ridley, and almost immediately afterwards became known as a preacher. Archbishop Cranmer collated him, in 1551, to the rectory of Allhallows, Bread Street. On the accession of Mary, in 1553, when so many of the Gospellers were compelled to leave England, or else were doomed to suffer imprisonment, he went to the continent, and remained for some time at Strasburgh, at which place he became very intimate with Immanuel Tremellius, who had, in the reign of Edward, succeeded Paulus Fagius at Cambridge. At the time when the unhappy contentions troubled the English exiles, he was one of those who opposed the introduction of the service book and the habits; and, in consequence of this, it is probable that he retired to Geneva.

Thos Sampson one of the translators.

He returned to England after the accession of Queen Elizabeth, and, in 1561, received from her the deanery of Christ Church, Oxford. In 1564, he and Laurence Humphreys, president of Magdalen College, were cited before the ecclesiastical commissioners on a charge of not wearing the appointed habits; the result of which was that Sampson was deprived of his deanery. He appears to have been regarded, in the reign of Elizabeth, as one of the principal non-conformists.

Dean of Christ-Church, 1561

Deprived, 1564

William Whittingham was another of the translators; he was born in the city of Chester, and was educated at Oxford, at Brazen-nose College, having been admitted about the year 1540, where he became eminent as a scholar. He was elected, in 1545, fellow of All Souls; and, in 1547, was made one of the senior students of Christ Church. He was one of those who, during the exile of the Reformers, went to Frankfort, and took the part of those who opposed the introduction of the English Liturgy, &c.: on this account he went to Geneva.

Wm. Whittingham

Having returned to England, after the accession of Queen Elizabeth, he was made dean of Durham, July 19th, 1563. He was the translator of certain of the metrical Psalms in the version commonly called Sternhold and Hopkins's, to which the initials "W. W." are prefixed.

Dean of Durham, 1563

Another of these translators was Christopher Goodman; who was, like Whittingham, a native of Cheshire, and, like him too, educated at Brazen-nose College, Oxford. He also became one of the senior students of Christ Church in 1547, and was appointed Margaret Professor of Divinity.

Chr Goodman

On the accession of Mary, he fled to Strasburgh, where he joined with others in writing to the English at Frankfort, endeavouring to induce them to adhere to what had been instituted in England, respecting religious worship, in the days of King Edward. The ground on which they based this argument was, the scandal which variations from it might occasion amongst the Papists. After this, however, Goodman joined the refugees of Geneva: and he seems to have fully acquiesced in the Geneva model. During his exile, he wrote against Queen Mary and her government, in a manner which must be regarded as very reprehensible by those who have learned to reverence "the powers that be" (be their character or conduct what it may), as "the ordinance of God." Whittingham, and others of the exiles, approved both of his sentiments and their expression; they yielded to that provocation to which the flesh is prone, and which, at a later period, led to the lamentable resistance of the constituted powers by the Covenanters in Scotland.

A violent writer against Queen Mary.

Goodman, however, it is only right to say, retracted the statements which he had published. The warmth of his feelings sometimes carried him away; but Christian grace led him afterwards to acknowledge his error.

Anthony Gilby was another of these translators: he appears to have pretty nearly accorded in sentiment with Goodman.

Anthony Gilby.

Thomas Cole.

Another, was Thomas Cole. The place of his exile, after the accession of Mary, was Frankfort; from whence, in consequence of the dissension, he went to Geneva.

In the reign of Elizabeth, Edmund Grindall, who had been his fellow exile, and was now become bishop of London, collated him to the archdeaconry of Essex, January 3rd, 1559; he likewise was appointed rector of High Ongar.

Besides these, it has been said that the well known Scottish Reformer, John Knox, as well as John Bodleigh and John Pullain, took some part in the execution of this version. It does not seem very probable that the former took any active part in the translation; but there can, I think, be hardly any question that John Bodleigh was connected with this version: this may be inferred from the proprietorship of it seeming to be in his hands in the reign of Elizabeth. It does not, however, prove him to have been one of the *translators*.

Characteristics of this version

This translation differed from all that had preceded it, not only in its plan, but also in its execution. The other versions had been generally the work or the revision of an individual; or at most, a revision in which certain individuals executed certain particular parts: in this translation we find, on the contrary, many acting unitedly in the formation of a version, and thus, in the plan of operation, there was a principle of completeness which had not been acted on previously.

Italic supplements

The execution of the work also is very different from that of preceding translations. This will be evident to any one who compares a portion of it with the translation of Tyndale, or its revision in Cranmer's Bible; the Geneva translators, by the use of *italic supplements*, often aided the sense without seeming to insert what was not found in the original. Perhaps, in some cases, they may have carried this liberty too far; but on the whole, it enabled them to give more exactly the force of the original.

The N Test of this version

Division of verses

The New Testament rendered by these translators, was published (as has been already stated) in 1557, before the entire Bible. This was a small square volume printed in Roman letters, divided into verses, and with a good many notes in the margin. With regard to the division into verses, it is to be observed, that *this* was the first time the Scriptures had been printed thus broken into these sections. In Robert Stephens's fourth edition of the Greek Testament (1551), the notation of the verses had been for the first time appended: and in this edition, the numbers were put in the margin, while the text went on continuously. These numbers were found so convenient for purposes of reference, that they soon became universally adopted; the Geneva translators being the first to break the text into little paragraphs. It is probable, that they used Stephens's fourth edition when engaged in this work, while at the same time, in the manner of rendering not a few passages, they followed the judgment which Beza had expressed. In some places they paid a decided deference to his criticisms; with regard even to what he had considered (without adequate evidence) to be errors in the Greek text.

Deference paid to Beza

The following was the title of this New Testament:—

THE

NEVVE TESTA-

MENT OF OVR LORD IE-

fus Chrift.

Conferred diligently with the Greke, and best approued translations.

VVith the arguments, af wel before the chapters, as for euery Boke & Epistle, also diuersities of readings, and mofte proffitable annotations of all harde places: wherunto is added a copious Table

AT GENEVA

Printed By Conrad Badius.

M. D LVII

In an address headed, "To the Reader Mercie and Peace through Christ our Sauiour," some account is given of the plan pursued by the translators. This address runs in the singular number, as though some particular person had been the principal conductor of the work.* He says,

"To these therfore which are of the flocke of Christ which knowe their Fathers wil, and are affectioned to the trueth, I rendre a reason of my doing in fewe lines. First, as touching the perusing of the text, it was diligently reuised by the moste approued Greke examples, and conference of translations in other tonges, as the learned may easely iudge, both by the faithful rendering of the sentence, and also by the proprietie of the wordes, and perspicuitie of the phrase. Forthermore that the Reader might be by all meanes proffited, I haue deuided the text into verses and sections, according to the best editions in other langages, and also as to this day the ancient Greke copies mention it was wont to be used. And because the Hebrewe and Greke phrases, which are strange to rendre in other tongues, and also short, shulde not be to harde, I haue sometyme interpreted them without any whit

* This edition of the New Testament, with its copious marginal annotations, has been carefully reprinted, somewhat in its original form, page for page, and line for line, with facsimile initial wood cuts, &c. &c. The prefaces and the index at the end of the volume, are also exactly reprinted. 1 vol. fscp 8vo.; large paper copies 4to.

diminishing the grace of the sense, as our langage doth vse them, and sometyme haue put to that worde which lacking made the sentence obscure, but haue set it in such letters as may easely be discerned from the commun text."

The anonymous writer of this preface then goes on to speak of the annotations which constitute so prominent a part of the editions of this version. The Annotations noticed.

"As concerning the Annotations, wherunto these letters a. b c. &c leade vs, I haue endeuored so to proffit al therby, that both the learned & others might be holpen: for to my knollage I haue omitted nothing vnexpounded, wherby he that is any thing exercised in the Scriptures of God, might iustely complayn of hardenes: and also in respect of them that haue more proffited in the same, I haue explicat all suche places by the best learned interpreters as ether were falsely expounded of some or els absurdely applyed by others: so that by this meanes both they which haue not abilitie to by the Commentaries vpon the New testament, and they also which haue not opportunitie & leasure to reade them because of their prolixitie may vse this booke in stede therof"

In the conclusion of this address, the preservation of the New Testament by the nominal church throughout the long period of Romish apostasy is alluded to. He says:— Preservation of Scripture.

"So may we glorifie him [God] more and more rendring to him eternal thankes and praises for his heauenly and inestimable giftes bestowed vpon his churche, that all thogh Satan, Antichrist, and all his ennemies rage and burste, yet are they not able to suppresse them, nether wil he diminishe them: for seing he doth not only brydel his ennemies furie, but causeth them to defende and preserue his giftes for the vse of his Churche (as we se the Iewes Christs professed ennemies preserue the olde testament in moste integritie) what shulde we doute of his bontiful liberalitie towards vs? or why do we not rather with all humilitie and submission of mynde obey him, loue & feare him which is God blessed for euer?"

The margins of this New Testament (as well as those of the entire Bible when published) were plentifully filled with notes on the text. These were much in request amongst those who loved the word of God; so much so that several editions of King James's version were published with these notes appended to them. They appear, generally speaking, to be well written, and in them the doctrines of the Gospel are very prominently set forth. It is not unlikely that their character was partly influenced by the circumstances in which they were written; namely, by exiles, who were toiling for the benefit of their country, where Popery was again taking its stand.

XIII.

ACCESSION OF ELIZABETH.—RETURN OF THE EXILES. GENEVA BIBLE PUBLISHED.

THE time of severe trial and persecution to the professors of the Gospel, during the reign of Mary, closed at her death, November 17th, 1558. The accession of Queen Elizabeth was one of those circumstances which, through the merciful ordering of God, led to the restored circulation both of the Scriptures and of the testimony of the Gospel in England; the *former* of these having never since that time been withdrawn. The transfer of the crown from Mary to her sister was an event which occasioned much joy and thankfulness. The persecutions in the preceding reign had failed to commend the religion of Rome to the people at large; and it is most likely that very many besides the two hundred and seventy-seven, who gave their lives in the defence and quarrel of Christ and His Gospel, and the several hundreds who were exiles on the continent, knew and prized the Gospel of the grace of God. The previous circulation of the Scriptures had been as the sowing of the seed of truth; and the harvest was springing up, even though external circumstances caused its progress to be seen but dimly. Accession of Queen Eliz. Nov 17, 1558 End of the persecution. Rejoicings

It is evident that the number of Christians in England, who were not ashamed of the profession of Christ, was considerable. Of course, the word of the Lord was then true even as it is now, that, "Wide is the gate and broad is the way that leadeth unto destruction, and *many* there are go in thereat:" the word of Christ in this, as in all things else, must stand steadfast, even though heaven and earth pass away; and never can we (if Scripture be our guide) expect to find the *few* and the *many* belong to different classes until that coming of the Son of man, when every eye shall see Him, and all kindreds of the earth shall wail because of Him. Many in England not ashamed to confess Christ.

The preservation of the London congregation of Gospellers

Amongst those in England who were faithful to the profession of the Gospel, those Christians in London have, in the first place, to be mentioned, who continued to meet together throughout all this bitter time of trial. Their preservation was in itself a very gracious proof of the overruling care of God. It was just as the Lollards had been a continuous chain of witnesses, in the midst of almost uninterrupted persecution, connecting Wiclif and Tyndale; so these, set in the very fire, as it were, in the midst of persecution such as had never been equalled in England, were witnesses for the truth against those who slew the holy servants of the Lord. Some of the circumstances relative both to the sufferings of some of these saints in London, and to the preservation of others, have been already stated; in addition to which, it may be well here to notice, that they had collections in their meetings for the prisoners of the Lord, which sometimes, at a single meeting, amounted to ten pounds.

See above, p. 129

Additional notices respecting them

Their collections

Attempts to ensnare them.

Many were the devices used for ensnaring them,—sometimes through treachery, sometimes through force. On one occasion, a person who had gone amongst them in order to take an opportunity of betraying them, was arrested by the grace of God: so that, instead of opposing, he cast in his lot with this company, so seemingly devoted to destruction.

At Stoke in Suffolk, and other places.

In other places, likewise, there were many who were, humanly speaking, by the accession of Elizabeth snatched from impending destruction. There was a company of such at Stoke in Suffolk; while in the North of England, where, through the lenity of Archbishop Heath and Bishop Tonstall, the persecution was comparatively little felt, there was much of testimony for the Gospel of Christ.

The exiles on the continent.

None, however, hailed the change more than did the scattered exiles who had taken refuge on the continent. Most truly might it be said of them, that their hearts yearned for their native country, which they sorrowed to see ruled over by superstition and persecution. As to themselves, they were indeed mourners and pilgrims during their exile: their subsistence was very precarious, depending mostly upon the pecuniary aid which was furnished them either from England, or else from the reformed in the countries in which they had found an asylum. Their books likewise are supposed to have aided them by their sale, but I think it may well be doubted whether they did as much as pay their own expenses. The importation of the books which the exiles might publish (amongst others those of Coverdale by name), were prohibited by a proclamation dated June the 13th, 1555; at the same time search was made for those who either had any correspondence with the exiles, or transmitted any money to them.

Importation of their books prohibited June 13, 1555.

The minds of the exiles were much turned to the hope of again being permitted to dwell in their native land: and not only had they this as a matter of hope, but their speedy return was spoken of with confidence, even before the occurrence of that event which brought it to pass.

Fox's sermon at Basle. Strype, Mem. Ecc v. p. 304. Bp Elmer present

"Those at Basil had the news of their speedy return told them the day before the Queen's death It was strange, but true; for Elmer (bishop of London afterwards) was present when John Fox preached there, when, among other arguments which he used for the consolation of the poor English, he bad them to be of good comfort, for the time drew near that they should be restored to their own country; and said that this he told them *Dei monitu*, being *warned of God* so to do. He was reproved by the elder sort for thus preaching, but the issue of things excused him And by comparing the times, it appeared that he preached this sermon but the day before the Queen's death."

After the tidings of the accession of Elizabeth reached Strasburgh, messengers were sent to Zurich, through whom the English there learned the happy intelligence on the last day of November, 1558. On the following day, Peter Martyr, who had been professor of divinity at Oxford in the reign of Edward, and who at this time was professor at Zurich, wrote to Calvin; and thus the English at Geneva learned that they might return to their native land. The work of the translation of the Bible, in which Coverdale and some others of these were engaged, has been already noticed. The New Testament had now been printed nearly a year and a half, and thus it is probable that the version of the Old was by this time pretty far advanced: its actual publication did not take place until the year 1560, after many of the exiles had returned home. In this completed Bible it is to be observed, that the translation of the New Testament *differs* in several respects from that which had been separately printed in 1557. This Bible, which was stored with marginal notes, continued for many years to be the popular version in England, having been displaced only by King James's translation, which appeared fifty-one years afterwards. Even then the new version did but *gradually* supersede the Geneva translation, for from the year 1611 to 1621 inclusive, there were at least six editions printed of this latter version, besides the vast number of copies which were still in the hands of private possessors on every side. In some families it continued to be used for very many years after this,

The Geneva version of the whole Bible published 1560

Editions of it after the publication of King James's

and I have *occasionally* met with copies of it which have been from the days of Queen Elizabeth, and *are still* in common use.

Copies *still* in use.

The Geneva Bible of 1560 was the first edition printed in the reign of Elizabeth: hence it is probable that the copies of previous translations, which had been in use in the reign of Edward VI., were yet in existence; and were now doubtless once more freely circulated and openly used. Thus there was again the same liberty which had been enjoyed for a little season during the reign of Henry, and fully during that of Edward. The labours of the Geneva translators had been like those of Tyndale, in 1526—an endeavour to shed the light of God's word upon England from a foreign land: and if we do not find these labours as reiterated as those had been, it evidently was only because the change of events rendered such efforts needless.

Previous editions in circulation, 1560.

And now having brought down the narrative of the connection between the circulation of the Scriptures and the progress of the Reformation, as far as the point at which the *uninterrupted* use of the Bible in English commenced; it is needless farther to trace the history of editions, and of circumstances relative to them. There are, however, various separate matters, such as the conclusion of the life of that veteran translator, Myles Coverdale, as well as the history of the translations called the Bishop's Bible, the Rhemish and Douay version, and King James's, which remain to be briefly noticed.

No interruption to the circulation of the Scriptures, from the accession of Elizabeth to this day Laus Deo

---

XIV.

THE LATTER PART OF COVERDALE'S LIFE.

Myles Coverdale was at Geneva at the time of the accession of Queen Elizabeth; for he, with others at that place, wrote (December 15th, 1558) on the occasion a letter to the congregation at Frankfort, in which they congratulate them on the event, and desire that all their private dissension might cease, concerning ceremonies, &c. It is indeed pleasant to find that such gracious sentiments had a place in the hearts of the Geneva exiles towards their brethren: for it appears to be commonly supposed, that those who retired to Geneva had been by no means well treated by their brethren who remained at Frankfort. Indeed, it would have been well if both parties had ever been free from the charge of forcing things confessedly non-scriptural upon the consciences of their brethren.

Coverdale at Geneva at the accession of Elizabeth. Letter of the Geneva exiles to those at Frankfort, Dec 15, 1558. Hallam

The first intimation of Coverdale's having actually reached England is this:—That on the 12th of November, 1559, he took his turn as preacher at Paul's Cross. He may probably have been already some months in England. Coverdale now occupied a remarkable position: he was the only patriarch of the English Reformation that was left; the only one of those whose testimony had commenced forty years before, at Cambridge; and who, by preaching the Gospel, or diffusing the Scriptures in English, had introduced the bright shining of the lamp of God's truth. Coverdale had done this in both ways.

Coverdale returns to England

Preaches at Paul's Cross, 1559.

Coverdale was likewise the only one of the English bishops who had aided the Reformation in the days of Edward, and who still lived without having made any compromise of conscience. Barlow and Scory, who had been bishops, the one of Bath and Wells, the other of Chichester, still survived; but they had made compliances, in the reign of Mary, to preserve their liberty. Thus, in many respects, Coverdale stood alone in a place of pre-eminence, and thus we find him honoured by those who most valued the truth and word of God.

The only English bishop who had not conformed to popery.

On the 17th of December, 1559, Coverdale was one of those who took a part in the consecration of Matthew Parker, archbishop of Canterbury. On this occasion he shewed how deeply rooted was his objection to the use of the "habits," for he chose only to appear in a plain black gown. It is not unlikely that it was his non-conformity in this matter that hindered his being again appointed to a bishopric. Barlow and Scory were again so appointed, but not to the same sees which they had before held. However, at the time of Archbishop Parker's consecration, the see of Exeter had not become vacant, for Turberville, who had been appointed bishop of that diocese in the reign of Mary, was not deprived until the commencement of January, 1560; so that Coverdale could not, as yet, have had his former bishopric

Coverdale at the consecration of Abp Parker, Dec 17, 1559

His opposition to the "habits"

Bp Turberville deprived, Jan 1560.

Wm Alley made bishop of Exeter, June 9, 1560

offered to him. It seems probable that he was not offered any of the vacant sees, and that the cause of this was his non-conformity in the matter of the "habits," &c. William Alley was made bishop of Exeter on the 9th of June, 1560.

Bp. Grindall befriends Coverdale. Proposes him for the see of Llandaff.

Coverdale, although poor and destitute of any preferment, was befriended by Edmund Grindall, bishop of London, who, on the vacancy of the see of Llandaff, wrote to the secretary of Queen Elizabeth, strongly recommending Coverdale as the bishop of that diocese. This makes it highly improbable that Coverdale had previously refused a bishopric. Grindall, however, expressed his doubts whether the see of Llandaff, despoiled as it was of its revenue, would yield sufficient for Coverdale to live on. He speaks in high commendation of Coverdale, "who was in Christ before us all," lamenting that thus in his old age he should be without means of subsistence. It is not known whether any attention was paid to Grindall's recommendation: this only is certain, that Coverdale did not receive the bishopric of Llandaff. Grindall made various attempts to befriend Coverdale, and complained that he did not receive the attention which was his due. "I cannot," he said, "excuse us bishops," although, as to himself, he stated that he had offered him many things, of which he had not thought fit to accept.

Gives him the parish of St. Magnus London Bridge, 1563. His poverty at this time. He petitions to be excused his "first fruits."

Coverdale was, however, for a short period, appointed to the rectorship of a parish; his friend, bishop Grindall having, in the beginning of 1563, presented him with the living of St. Magnus, near London Bridge. Some delay occurred in consequence of his being too poor to pay the queen her "first fruits," which amounted to 66*l.* 16*s.* 10*d.*, and thus he had to wait until he could get Elizabeth to excuse him the payment. He wrote to Archbishop Parker, as well as to others, requesting them to represent to the queen how utterly unable he was to meet this demand. He besought the archbishop to join with Grindall in soliciting her to forgive him the "first fruits." He represented how his bishopric had been taken from him ten years before, and how he had since remained in poverty. He likewise represented, that at his age it was not likely that he could enjoy the benefice, "going (he said) upon my grave as they say, and not like to live a year." If the queen would grant him this favour, he said to the archbishop, "so am I fully persuaded, God willing, to shew myself again as thankful, and in my vocation, during my short time, as fruitful and as quiet as I can." This letter to Archbishop Parker was dated, "29 Jan., New Year," and signed, "Myles Coverdale, quondam Exon."

The Queen grants his request.

A few days after, he wrote to Cecil on the same subject; thanking him for former help which he had received, and telling him, that if it would please him to obtain this for him, he should think this enough "to be as good as a feast." This was on the 6th of February. A few weeks afterwards, Coverdale wrote again to Archbishop Parker, stating that he had received a message from Lord Robert Dudley, (better known as the earl of Leicester), to let him know that the queen had granted his request concerning the first fruits.

Coverdale collated to the rectory of St Magnus, March 3, 1563. Strict conformity not yet pressed.

Coverdale was collated to this rectory of St. Magnus the Martyr, March 3rd, 1563. He was allowed at the time to remain a nonconformist, as regards the "habits" and other matters which troubled his conscience, so that there was no compromise in his having accepted the rectory. The strict compulsion to conformity which subsequently took place, had not as yet begun; and thus, under the protection of Grindall, he enjoyed much liberty. The Act of Uniformity, which had been passed at the commencement of the reign of Elizabeth, was not, as yet, brought into any thing like full practical operation.

Coverdale taken with the plague Strype

In this year he was taken with the plague, and, old as he was (seventy-five), recovered again, "as though God had some more work for him to do in the church before his death." What his subsequent labours may have proved as to *result* is not known; but he continued to preach the Gospel of Christ. It is the day of account which must shew the fruit of his subsequent, as well as of his prior testimony.

Made D D by the university of Cambridge. Appointed to admit Bishop Grindall. Ap. 15, 1564.

In the same year, 1563, Coverdale received the degree of Doctor of Divinity from the University of Cambridge, *per gratiam;* he had received this degree from that of Tübingen several years before. Barkley, bishop of Bath and Wells, took this degree at the same time as Coverdale. In the following year, Bishop Grindall desired to take his degree of Doctor of Divinity; and accordingly he wrote to the vice-chancellor of the University of Cambridge, requesting that he would either admit him himself, or else authorize some other person to do so. Upon this, the vice-chancellor transmitted the authority for this purpose (bearing date, April 10, 1564) to Coverdale, who admitted Grindall to his degree at the bishop's palace in London, on the 15th of the same month. This, at least, shews that both by the vice-chancellor and the bishop, this poor and aged servant of Christ was held in high respect.

Conformity pressed, 1564 and the following years.

Coverdale continued to hold the rectory of St. Magnus until the year 1566; when he, and many others, were compelled either to conform or to resign whatever benefices they held. In 1564, the Act of Uniformity was pressed in several cases: and in the two following years, it was brought into full operation.

It has been questioned, but I think needlessly, whether it was on account of age and infirmity that Coverdale resigned, or whether it was on account of the uniformity required. That it was the latter is evident from the fact, that he was a nonconformist, and it was needful for him to conform, unless he preferred resigning; and he did not cease preaching until after this time.

Coverdale in consequence resigns his rectory, 1566

Other ministers in London (about forty-six in all), were deprived at the same time, on the same ground. Strype thus speaks of them : —

Forty-six ministers deprived, Mar. 26, 1566. Collier, vi 429.

"After the deprivation of the London ministers for seven or eight weeks, their hearers either came to the churches and heard the conformable preachers, or went no whither. Many of them ran after father Coverdale, who took that occasion to preach the more constantly; but yet with much fear, so that he would not be known where he preached, though many came to his house to ask where he would preach the next Lord's day. This it is likely he did, because he did not care for tumultuous meetings, lest he might give offence to the government"

He was now more than seventy-eight years old; and yet we find him still continuing to preach thus diligently: this, indeed, was what had peculiarly marked him forty years before amongst his cotemporaries, when the profession of the Gospel began at Cambridge.

Coverdale a zealous preacher.

His long and laborious life was now near its close: of its conclusion we know no particulars beyond what is learned from his having continued to preach until, at the farthest, a few months of his death. This took place in the beginning of the year 1569; and, on the 19th of February, he was buried in the chancel of St. Bartholomew's Church, behind the Royal Exchange. His funeral was attended by vast crowds of persons, by whom he had been admired and loved.

Coverdale's death, 1569 His funeral, Feb. 19

His tomb was marked by "a fair plated stone," with an inscription stating his age—*eighty-one years;* but this stone, together with much of the building, was destroyed by the fire of London. In the year 1840, this church was pulled down, to make way for certain improvements; on which occasion much care was taken in the removal of the remains of those who had been interred within its walls. A particular search was made for the bones of Coverdale; and the remains which were supposed to be his were carefully raised and removed to the church of St. Magnus, of which, till forced to resign, he had been rector. In this place the supposed remains of Coverdale were re-interred. The parishioners of St. Magnus had erected a monument to his memory in the year 1837; so that now his mouldering ashes are located in the place in which he has been more honoured in death than he was in life.

The disinterment of his remains, 1840 Re-interred at St Magnus, London Bridge

The long and weary life of service, exile, and suffering which Coverdale led, was but the result of the knowledge of grace received; proving blessedly that he who is freely forgiven, instead of being careless about the bringing forth of fruit, is the most diligent and devoted in so doing.

Coverdale seems in himself to connect together the two distinct periods of the history of the circulation of the English Scriptures—the time of restriction and that of liberty. He had been the associate of Tyndale, the martyr for the word of God; he was, in part, the means of the conversion of Rogers, another honoured instrument; and now, surviving his former fellow-workers, both his predecessors and successors in labour, he lived to see that liberty of circulation of the word of God restored in England which still exists, and has continued without interruption. There are but two names which occupy as high a place with regard to the diffusion of the word of God in English, and these are Wiclif and Tyndale; each of these three had his distinct work, and each was honoured by the blessing of God.

Long period of Coverdale's connection with the history of the English Scriptures

It is impossible to take leave of Coverdale without regarding him as one of the most devoted and honoured amongst the many instruments of the Reformation raised up by God in the sixteenth century. He appears as the successor of Tyndale,—toiling to the same end, aided by the same grace, and, after a longer pilgrimage, entering into the same rest, and waiting for the full fruition of glory when Christ comes again, and raises all his sleeping saints in bodies of glory like unto His own.

XV.

THE "BISHOPS' BIBLE" PREPARED AND PUBLISHED.

AFTER the Scriptures were again permitted, in the reign of Elizabeth, to be freely read and used, one of the first steps for bringing them publicly into notice was their being again set up in the parish churches, where they were publicly read every Lord's day. The version which was thus "authorized" was of course

The Bibles again placed in the parish churches.

the "Great Bible," which had been adopted for this purpose in the reigns of Henry and of Edward: indeed no other Bibles would be so placed, unless, perhaps, enough copies of the Bible which bears the name of Thomas Matthew could have been gathered together for the purpose. The new version, by the Geneva exiles, was not yet published. It would therefore have been a needless delay, to have waited till that were obtainable; and even if it had been already completed, it is not very likely that those who now held ecclesiastical authority in England would have regarded, without suspicion, the version which had been executed by those who had separated from the other English exiles, on account of their dislike to the English service-book, "habits," &c.

Complaints made of Cranmer's Bible.

In the early part of the reign of Elizabeth, Cranmer's Bible was thus restored to the place which it had previously occupied. It was not, however, long before many complaints were made against this translation; various statements were alleged as reasons for condemning the version altogether. It is probable that many now set to work to examine the English Bible more critically than had been done before, and thus many real or supposed corrections were suggested. The advocates of the Geneva version are mentioned as having depreciated Cranmer's. It is probable that the charges of *corruption* which they made might have had some reference to the insertion in it (in smaller type) of passages from the Latin Vulgate, which do not exist in the Hebrew or Greek originals. The Romanists of course objected to this version; but they had done the same with regard to every previous translation; and they have now done so with regard to all since, except indeed their own.

Bishop Sandys writes to Abp. Parker, Feb. 6, 1564-5. Strype's Par. i 415

One of the Protestant objectors was Edwin Sandys, at this time bishop of Worcester, and, subsequently, archbishop of York. In writing to Archbishop Parker, Feb. 6, 1564-5, he charged the setters forth of Cranmer's Bible with having "followed Munster too much, who doubtless was a very negligent man in his doings, and often swerved very much from the Hebrew." This was after the preparation for a new Bible had commenced, for with this letter he returned a certain portion of the Bible, which the archbishop had sent to him for revision. Now let us see, first, how far Cranmer's Bible followed the Latin interpretation of Munster; and, secondly, how far the character which Archbishop Sandys thus gave to Munster is correct.

The criticisms of Bp. Sandys considered How far does the "Great Bible" follow Munster?

First, then, the basis of the Old Testament, in Cranmer's Bible, is in part the translation of Tyndale, and in part that of Coverdale. Now Tyndale published his version of the Pentateuch four years before Munster put forth his Hebrew and Latin Bible, so that in that part Tyndale could not possibly have followed Munster. Again, the other portion of Tyndale's labour, namely, from Joshua to the Chronicles inclusive, was in all probability executed before his imprisonment, which took place in the year when the first volume of Munster's Bible appeared. Tyndale could have made no use of it: for his occupation, during several months previous to his imprisonment, was not the translation of the Old Testament, but the revision of his version of the New. The basis of the rest of the Old Testament was Coverdale's version; one of his "subsidia" was certainly Munster's Latin version; but it cannot be proved that he followed it servilely: nay, it is most easy to shew, that while he used it as an aid, he did not take it as his basis. It would be difficult to prove, that the revisors of the joint labour of Tyndale and Coverdale, made too great a use of Munster.

Was Munster a careful translator?

Secondly, it has to be inquired whether Munster really "executed his version negligently, often swerving from the Hebrew." I do not think that this charge can be proved: for it appears to me that Munster adheres very closely to the original, always preferring literal exactness to elegance of phraseology. It is not to be denied that he has committed oversights (Who has not?); but the character here given to him was one by no means deserved. If particular examples had been brought forward, the question could have been fairly examined; but as it now stands, the general charge made by Archbishop Sandys can only receive a general answer. It seems to me that the existing version, which was publicly read, was made an object of attack; and those who disliked it, without having any particular objection which they could define, stated reasons which they supposed were sound. All such charges ought, however, to be examined, if we would form a true judgment.

Laurence's objections to Cranmer's Bible

Another objector was a person named Laurence, who is described as being "a noted Grecian at this time." He stated to Archbishop Parker, that various passages in the New Testament of the existing versions were inadequately rendered. He gave a list of particular texts, in which he noticed something to be amended; referring apparently, in his criticisms, to any of the existing translations indiscriminately. Several of his remarks apply apparently to some particular edition of these various versions; so that they refer not merely to errors of translation, but to those of editing and printing likewise. Although Laurence may be classed amongst the objectors to the "Great Bible;" yet his suggestions, if acted on, would not have amounted to any thing more than a revision.

Another reason, which had probably a good deal of weight in causing a new translation to be undertaken, was the fact of the Geneva version having become the one in daily use, in private families: this at least was the case very soon; and it is probable that it had begun to be preferred, before the Bishop's Bible was undertaken. It is likely that a version was thus desired by Archbishop Parker, which should be free from the objections urged by Bishop Sandys, Laurence, and others; and which should not only be authorised and appointed for public use, but also be calculated to compete with the Geneva translation for private reading. This last mentioned version had been, like all that had originally preceded it, the undertaking of private individuals. What Archbishop Parker wished for was, a version executed by those whose position and station might give the translation a kind of weight. In this Parker acted very differently from Cranmer. Cranmer had taken the best version that he could find which was then in existence, and used it with comparatively little revision: Parker, on the contrary, would have the work to be thoroughly remodelled, and made, not the adoption of the previous labours of others, but a version of a different character; in this respect resembling more the Geneva translation, than any of those of an earlier date.

Spread of the Geneva translation

The "Bishops Bible" intended to supersede it

Bishop Sandys, in another letter, urged on the archbishop to complete and carry out his design of publishing a new version of the Bible. He says, "Those which we have be not only false printed, but also give great offence to many, by reason of the depravity in reading."

Bp. Sandys again writes to Abp. Parker

Strype's Par i. 416.

The Book of Psalms had been sent to Guest, bishop of Rochester, for revision. He sent it back "with his notes and advertisements." In writing to Parker, he said—

The Psalms revised by Bp Guest.

That he "had not altered the translation but where it gave occasion of an error. As at the first Psalm, at the beginning, I turn the preterperfect tense into the present tense; because the sense is too harsh in the preterperfect tense. Where in the New Testament one piece of a Psalm is reported, I translate it in the Psalms according to the translation thereof in the New Testament, for the avoiding of the offence that may rise to the people upon divers translations. Where two great letters be joined together or one great letter is twice put, it signifieth that both the sentences or the words be expounded together"

This latter sentence evidently refers to some of the marks of reference which Guest had made use of, in his manuscript.

Another portion was sent to Parkhurst, bishop of Norwich, who wrote in reply to Archbishop Parker, that he would labour in it to the best of his ability.

A portion revised by Bp Parkhurst

Davies, bishop of St. David's, had another part. He was at this time employed in aiding William Salesbury, in translating the New Testament into Welsh; he was thus taken away from his previous work, and the whole Bible in Welsh (which apparently they would have undertaken) was not executed for twenty years.

Another by Bp Davies.

In the year 1566, Bishop Cox, of Ely, wrote to Archbishop Parker (May 3), in which he thus refers to the progress of the translation:—

Bp. Cox writes to Abp. Parker, May 3, 1566

"I trust your grace is well forward with the Bible by this time. I perceive the greatest burden will lie upon your neck, touching care and travail I would wish that such usual words as we English people be acquainted with, might still remain in their form & sound, so far forth as the Hebrew will well bear; ink-horn terms to be avoided."

The version of the Bible which Archbishop Parker thus superintended was published in the year 1568, with simply the following title:—

The "Bishops' Bible" published 1568

The holie Bible.

This is in the upper compartment of an engraved plate, the centre of which is occupied with a portrait of the queen, having the arms of England and France quarterly in a shield over her head, with those of Ireland in a shield to the right of it, and those of Wales in a shield to the left. Beneath the portrait of the queen is the following text:—

Non me pudet Euangelii Christi
Virtus enim Dei est ad salutem
Omni credenti. Rom. i.

At the end of various portions of this Bible there are initial letters, which are supposed to intimate the respective individuals by whom they were executed. However, it is doubtful, in some instances, who were the persons intimated.

Initials at the ends of various portions

At the end of the Pentateuch are the letters, W. E., standing, as is supposed, for William Exoniensis; that is, William Alley, bishop of Exeter. This translator was born at Great Wycombe, in Buckinghamshire; he was educated at Eton, and afterwards, in 1528, was admitted at King's College, Cambridge; he

End of Pentateuch, W. E.

Wm. Alley, bishop of Exeter.

Notice of him

Bliss's Wood's Athenæ Oxon

took his degree of Bachelor of Arts and then removed to Oxford, where he continued for some time. He became a zealous reformer, and like many others married (this was, I suppose, in the reign of Edward VI.). He had a benefice, which he left on the accession of Queen Mary, being probably deprived on the ground of matrimony. He spent his time during the reign of Mary in wandering "from place to place in the north parts of England where he was not known; and by his sometimes practising of physic and teaching of youths he obtained a comfortable subsistence for himself and his wife." Several of the professors of the Gospel appear to have found at the same time a shelter in the northern counties of England, where they were comparatively safe in the dioceses of the non-persecuting prelates, Heath, Tonstall, and Oglethorp. Thus there were many thrown together who were the means of strengthening one another's hands.

On the accession of Elizabeth, Alley was appointed Divinity Lecturer at St. Paul's, the situation which had six years before been filled by John Rogers. Some of his lectures thus delivered on the first epistle of St. Peter, were published under the title of "The Poor Man's Library."

In 1560 he was appointed bishop of Exeter, and consecrated in July of that year. He died April 15, 1570.

It is probable that he was one of the best Hebraists at this time in England: he wrote a Hebrew grammar, which he appears to have left behind in manuscript. In his epitaph he is described as being, "acerrimus Evangelicæ veritatis propugnator," no mean commendation, when it is remembered that earnestly contending for the faith once delivered to the saints would, in a part of his days, have put a man in peril of his life.

End of 2 Sam R M

Rd. Davies, bishop of St. David's

A notice of him

Bliss's Wood's Athenæ Oxon

The next portion appears to conclude at the end of the second book of Samuel, where the initials R. M. are placed. These are regarded as standing for "Richard Menevensis." Richard Davies, bishop of St. David's, has been already mentioned as having been previously engaged about a version in his native language—the Welsh. He was born probably in Denbighshire, about the year 1509, and educated at New Inn, Oxford. He was one of the exiles in the reign of Mary; but, returning on the accession of Elizabeth, he was made bishop of St. Asaph, from which see he was in the following year translated to that of St. David's. He died in October, 1581. He published some small works in his native language, especially designed to set before them the Gospel which had been so long obscured and kept out of sight. In the Welsh New Testament, already referred to, he translated certain of the epistles.

End of 2 Chr E. W

Edwin Sandys, bishop of Worcester.

Some notice of him.

The third portion concludes at the end of the second book of Chronicles, where the letters E. W. appear, standing for "Edwin Wigornensis." This was Edwin Sandys, who has already been mentioned as one of the great promoters of this version. He was born near Hawkshead, in Lancashire, in the year 1519. He went to St. John's College, Cambridge, in the year 1532, or the following year. This college was, at that time, and for many years afterwards, the most remarkable place for the number of persons it contained who were professors of the Gospel; and it is probable that whilst there Sandys was converted. In 1547, Sandys was elected master of Catherine Hall. During the reign of Edward he received various benefices, but continued to reside at Cambridge. In 1552 he married a lady who appears from her surname to have been a relative of his own.

Master of Catherine Hall, 1547.

Vice-chancellor of Cambridge, 1553.

His troubles.

In the following year, when he was vice-chancellor of the University, Edward VI. died, and the Lady Jane having been proclaimed queen, he preached in support of her title. In consequence of this, he was, after the close of her brief reign, deprived of his vice-chancellorship, and committed to the Tower. Here he was deprived of everything, except a Bible, which his faithful servant, Quintin Swainton, brought to him. After having been kept in a vile prison for three weeks, he was removed to the same apartment with John Bradford, who was his companion for more than half a year. By the joint labour of Bradford and Sandys, their gaoler was converted, not only from Romanism, but to Christ: he used, from time to time, to bring them bread and wine, and thus these three united in happily receiving the Lord's supper.

His liberation and escape to the continent.

He was subsequently removed to the Marshalsea; whence, after nine weeks, he was liberated by the intercession of Sir Thomas Holcroft, knight-marshal. Upon this he escaped from England, although with great difficulty, the lord chancellor, bishop Gardiner, being very earnest to retake him. On the 6th May, 1554, he embarked for Flanders; two emissaries, sent to apprehend him, arriving at the shore while the vessel was yet in sight. His last act, before leaving England, had been preaching on the beach, to a congregation of sailors.

When he reached Antwerp, he found that even there orders had been already given for his apprehension. However, by the good hand of his God upon him, he escaped; and, at length, reached Strasburgh. His life at this place was saddened in very many ways; he was one who took some part in the grievous dissension, which divided the English exiles; but not, of course, to the same extent as was done by those at Frankfort.

At the time of the accession of queen Elizabeth, he was at Zurich, with Peter Martyr: but he forthwith set out for England; and after preaching at Strasburgh, he returned with Grindall, and reached England on the day of the coronation of Queen Elizabeth. He was very soon after this appointed bishop of Worcester, and was consecrated by Archbishop Parker, December 21st, 1559. In 1570, when Grindall, bishop of London, was translated to the arch-diocese of York, Sandys succeeded him; and six years afterwards, when Grindall was translated to Canterbury, Sandys succeeded him at York. He died July 10th, 1588. His life, after his return to England, was disquieted by the schemes and projects of various enemies; so that few have experienced more continued turmoil. His judgment respecting the earlier English translations, and respecting Sebastian Munster, are, I think, very erroneous; but, in spite of his errors in judgment, he is to be regarded as a man deeply attached to the principles of the Reformation, and willing, if called upon, to suffer for their defence.

His return to England. Bp. of Worcester, 1559. Of London, 1570 Abp. of York, 1576 Died, 1588.

The fourth portion of Archbishop Parker's Bible concludes with the book of Job, where the letters A. P. C. appear; these are supposed to indicate Andreas Peerson, Cantuarensis; Andrew Peerson, prebend of Canterbury, being at this time one of Archbishop Parker's chaplains. He had been fellow of Bene't College, Cambridge; he was the reader of the service at the consecration of Archbishop Parker. Throughout the archbishop's life, he appears to have been highly esteemed by him.

End of Job, A P C. Andrew Peerson, prebend of Canterbury.

The fifth portion consists of the book of Psalms; after which occur the letters T. B. It is very uncertain who was indicated by these letters: some have thought that they stand for Thomas Bentham; but as Bentham was at this time bishop of Lichfield and Coventry, it seems very unlikely that the initial of his surname would be used; especially, considering that the other bishops used the initial indicating their respective sees. It is, I think, much more probable, that Thomas Becon was the translator of this portion. It may be that he gave it a final revision, since it is certain that Edmund Guest, bishop of Rochester, had sent Archbishop Parker his "notes and advertisements" for this book.

End of Psalms, T B. Probably Thos Becon

Thomas Becon was distinguished amongst the Reformers by his writings. He was born in 1512, and was educated at Cambridge, where he took his bachelor's degree, in 1530; this was at the time when the Reformed doctrines had made considerable progress in that University. He was for some time one of Cranmer's chaplains; and, on May 24th, 1547, he was presented to the rectory of St. Stephen, Walbrook. In the reign of Mary, after having been twice imprisoned, he escaped to the continent, where he continued, by writing, to do what he could for the upholding of the doctrines of the Gospel amongst his countrymen. Becon died about the year 1570.

Notice of him

At the close of the Proverbs, the letters A. P. C. again occur; making this book a sixth portion. It has been supposed that the person indicated, was not the same as the previous A. P. C.; but for this I see no sufficient ground. The reason assigned for this opinion has been, that the C. stands at a greater distance from the A. P. in the latter case, than in the former. It is true that the space is a *minute particle* greater (not more than a *thin space*, in printing); but in each case the C. is purposely separated. I believe the indication to be simply that of the same individual, namely, Andrew Peerson.

End of Proverbs, A P C

The seventh portion consists only of Ecclesiastes and the Canticles. At the end is A.P. E, denoting, it is said, Andreas Pern Eliensis, Andrew Perne being at this time prebendary of Ely.

End of Canticles, A P. E Andrew Perne, Prebend of Ely

The eighth portion concludes with the Lamentations, at the end of which the letters R. W. occur, indicating, as is supposed, Robert Wintonensis. Robert Horne, bishop of Winchester, was a person of considerable eminence amongst the reformers. He had been an exile at Frankfort during the reign of Queen Mary, and afterwards at Zurich. On his return to England at the accession of Queen Elizabeth, he was employed in various steps which were taken for the re-establishment of the Protestant doctrines as the professed religion. When he was made bishop of Winchester, he was regarded as one of those who were very friendly to the nonconformists with respect to the "habits," &c.

R W. Robert Horne, Bp of Winchester.

At the end of the ninth allotment, which contains the two books, Ezekiel and Daniel, the initials are T. C. L. Strype asks, "Might it not be Thomas Cole of Lincolnshire?" Lewis assents to this without hesitation; but it would have been expected, if this had been the case, that the L would have been (as in the similar instances) at a distance from the other two letters, and in a different character, whereas the

End of Daniel T C L Probably Thos Bentham, Bp. of Lichfield and Coventry.

interval is between the T and the two other letters, all being in the same character. This shews, I think, that it must have been Thomas Bentham, bishop of Lichfield and Coventry (who in his signature used to place Coventry the first), who had this portion assigned him. Thomas Bentham was born about the year 1513, in Yorkshire. He was admitted a fellow of Magdalen College, November 16, 1546, and became one of the most eminently learned in Hebrew of any of his cotemporaries at Oxford. In the reign of Mary he was deprived of his fellowship, because of the zeal which he shewed for the reformed doctrines; and in consequence of the proceedings against the reformers, he fled to the continent. His return to preach to the London congregation of Gospellers, and his merciful preservation through the close of the reign of Mary, have been already narrated.

On the accession of Elizabeth, when the popish bishops were deprived, he was appointed to the see of Lichfield and Coventry, to which he was consecrated March 24, 1560. He was one of the most learned in the original languages of Scripture of all who were occupied in the preparation of the Bishops' Bible. He died February 21, 1579.

End of Malachi E. L, Edmund Grindall, Bp. of London

Notice of him

The minor prophets form the tenth of the allotted portions. At the end of them are the letters E. L., for Edmund Londinensis, as is supposed. Edmund Grindall, who was at this time bishop of London, was born in Cumberland in 1519. He was educated at Cambridge, belonging first to Magdalen College, then to Christ's, and afterwards to Pembroke Hall, of which in 1538 he was chosen fellow. In 1549 he became president (vice-master) of his college, and being now a bachelor of divinity, he was chosen Lady Margaret preacher.

In 1550, Bishop Ridley appointed him his chaplain, and in 1551 he was made precentor of St. Paul's, and also chaplain to the king. Not long after, when it was intended to divide the bishopric of Durham into two, Grindall was nominated to be one of the bishops. Ridley himself was to have been translated to the other portion.

At the accession of Mary, when so many fled for safety wherever they could find shelter, Grindall took up his abode at Strasburgh, where he studied German, in order to be able to preach in the churches in that city. He took some part, but not a prominent one, in the unhappy disputes by which the English exiles were divided. On the accession of Elizabeth he returned, arriving with Sandys on the day of her coronation. On the deprivation of Bonner, he was appointed to the bishopric of London, after having been chosen Master of Pembroke Hall, Cambridge. As bishop of London, he has been already noticed for the care and consideration with which he treated Myles Coverdale; indeed, he appears to have done what he could to hinder the deprivation of the non-conformist ministers. In several things he had to act with Archbishop Parker, to whom his unwillingness to molest those who scrupled about the "habits," &c., soon became very apparent. He was translated to the see of York in 1570; Parker is said to have procured this promotion, in order that there might be a bishop of London more decided in his promotion of uniformity.

Bp. of London on Bonner's deprivation

Abp. of York, 1570

Abp of Canterbury, 1576

On the death of Archbishop Parker, he was appointed his successor, in 1576; but in that very year he fell under the displeasure of the queen, because of the favour which he shewed to what were termed "prophesyings." These "prophesyings" were expositions or exhortations, mutually delivered by various ministers, others also being present as auditors. Grindall also encouraged the preaching of the Gospel; while, on the other hand, Elizabeth thought that it was good for the church that the preachers should be few, and that three or four in a county were amply sufficient. The queen, on these grounds, required Grindall to lessen the number of preachers, and to put down the "prophesyings." In consequence of his refusal to comply, the queen sequestrated him from his office, and for some time confined him to his own house. His sequestration continued almost up to the time of his death, which occurred July 6th, 1583. It may be interesting to mention that he aided Fox in the compilation of his "Acts and Monuments."

His sequestration.

His death, 1583

End of Apocrypha, J N

J. Parkhurst, bishop of Norwich

At the end of the Apocrypha, which forms the eleventh portion, are the letters *J. N.* indicating, as is supposed, Johannes Norwicensis. John Parkhurst, bishop of Norwich, had been educated at Oxford, at Merton College, of which he was elected a probationer-fellow in 1529. In the reign of Edward VI. he was appointed rector of Cleve, in Gloucestershire; but, on the accession of Mary, he became one of the Protestant exiles.

After his return, on the accession of Elizabeth, he was appointed bishop of Norwich. In this situation he was regarded as being more favourable to those who did not conform to the "habits" than any of the other prelates; this often brought him into collision with Archbishop Parker. He died in 1574.

End of Gospels and Acts. R. E. Richard Cox.

The Four Gospels and the Acts formed the twelfth portion: the letters at the end are R. E. for, as is supposed, Richardus Eliensis. This was Richard Cox, who forty years before had been brought into trouble when the Scriptures were first printed in English. He had been elected from Eton as a scholar to King's College, Cambridge, whence, in December, 1525, he was removed to the New College of St. Frideswide at Oxford, which Cardinal Wolsey had founded. Here he, together with Frith and others, as has been already narrated, were persecuted and imprisoned on account of charges of heresy connected with the diffusion of Tyndale's New Testament.

At a subsequent period, we find him (1540) made archdeacon of Ely, and afterwards dean, first of Osney, and afterwards of Christ Church. In 1547, he was made chancellor of the University of Oxford, where he carried on the work of Reformation in a manner which has been bitterly censured. The search for superstitious books, which he instituted, is said to have led to the destruction of most valuable documents.

During the reign of Mary, he, like others, left England, when he fixed his abode at Frankfort, where he took a very prominent part in the unhappy contentions by which the English there were divided. So forward was he in pressing the introduction of the English service-book, &c., that the party who urged these things were denominated, from him, "the Coxians."

After his return to England, on the accession of Elizabeth, he was appointed bishop of Ely. He died in 1581.

End of Romans, R. E Doubtful who is meant.

At the end of the Epistle to the Romans, the letters R. E. are again placed: this is supposed to be by mistake for E. R., Edmund Roffensis. Edmund Guest, bishop of Rochester, has been already mentioned as one who took a part in this translation, having in some measure revised the book of Psalms. This makes it not improbable that the Romans was really his portion as a final revision, and that the letters, which as they stand, seem to intimate Bishop Cox of Ely, are really transposed.

End of 1 Cor G. B. Gabriel Goodman

At the end of the First Epistle to the Corinthians are the letters G. G, which are supposed to be for Gabriel Goodman, Dean of Westminster. No initials are subjoined to the remainder of the New Testament.

To this Bible was prefixed, amongst other things, *the sum of Scripture*, setting forth the Scripture doctrines, tables of genealogy, &c., and a preface written by Archbishop Parker.

The providential care of God in preserving the Scriptures is noticed, and also the endeavours which had been made to decree the translating of Scripture to be so perilous a thing that it can scarcely be hoped that it may be well performed.

Character of the Bishops' Bible.

This Bible was known by the name of "The Bishop's Bible," either from the greater part of those who were engaged in its preparation being bishops, or else from its having been executed under their direction. The name of "Matthew Parker's Bible" has sometimes been given to it, from the archbishop who first set it on foot. It continued to be the version authorised to be read in the parish churches for forty-three years; but in private use it never displaced the Geneva version. As a whole, it was not nearly so good a translation as that of the Geneva exiles, and *now* one of the things which especially gives it importance, is the fact of its having been the basis in the reign of James I. of the translation which we still use. But although the avowed basis of our authorised version, this latter was executed upon wholly different principles, and is very different in its general character from that which is now under consideration.

XVI.

THE ANGLO-RHEMISH VERSION.

Circumstances leading to the making of the Rhemish version.

THE circumstances which led to the execution and publication of this version, are to be found in the history of the expulsion of Romanism during the reign of Elizabeth. The versions of the New Testament previously executed, from that of Tyndale to the Bishops' Bible inclusively (the English text of Coverdale's Duoglott New Testament excepted), had been made from the original Greek; but the Rhemish translators took for their basis the Vulgate Latin.

The authority of the Latin Vulgate was a point of dissension between Papists and Protestants: the latter were disposed to depreciate it very much, the former to extol it, as though it surpassed in authority even the original texts themselves. Its *authenticity* (whatever that may mean) had been declared by the Council of Trent, so that it could not be expected that zealous Romanists, in translating the Scriptures into English, would use any other basis than that version. One of the principal objects which the Rhemish translators had in view, was evidently to circulate their doctrinal and controversial notes, together with the Scripture translated by them. This had been done by the Geneva translators with regard to their version, and from this probably the idea was taken by the Rhemish translators.

Cardinal Allen, the chief director of the Rhemish version Some account of him

The chief agent in causing the Rhemish version to be made, was WILLIAM ALLEN (or Alleyn), more commonly known as Cardinal Allen. He was born about the year 1532, at Rossal, in Lancashire; and in 1547, entered at Oriel College, Oxford, where he became very distinguished for his learning and abilities: in 1550, he was chosen fellow of his college. He became principal of St. Mary's Hall in 1556, and in 1558 he was appointed canon of York.

He leaves England on the accession of Elizabeth

On the accession of Elizabeth, Allen quitted his country, and gave up his church preferment. About the year 1560, he went to Louvain, where many of the more zealous English Romanists had taken up their abode. After this he returned to England for his health.

He subsequently removed to Douay, where an academy had been set up about the year 1562; at this place he took the degree of Doctor of Divinity. Soon after he was made canon of Cambray; and about the year 1568, by his endeavours, the English seminary at Douay was established, to receive such of the English Romanists as fled from their country on account of their religion.

English seminary of Douay founded 1568.

English seminary at Rheims

Upon the appointment of Dr. Allen to be canon of Rheims, he exerted himself to establish an English seminary at this latter place; the state of the Netherlands having become so unsettled, that the English scholars were driven from Douay. Allen's efforts did not stop here; he procured the establishment of a similar institution at Rome, and two others in Spain, for the express object of furnishing England with missionaries for the dissemination of Romanism.

The Rhemish version an effort to oppose the Reformation

Allen was a strenuous opposer of Queen Elizabeth's interest in every way: he was one who fully carried out the principles enjoined by the excommunicating bull of Pope Pius against her. Amongst his other efforts against Protestantism, the execution of the Rhemish and Douay version must be regarded as one. It is to be questioned whether he was personally concerned in its execution; but at all events, his counsels and directions led to its being undertaken. In 1589, Pope Sixtus V. created him a cardinal, and two years afterwards he was made archbishop of Mechlin.

His principal coadjutors in this translation were Gregory Martin, Richard Bristow, and Thomas Worthington: of these, it is probable that the first was the one chiefly concerned in the translation.

The New Testament prepared by these translators was published under the following title:—

THE

NEVV TESTAMENT

OF IESVS CHRIST, TRANSLATED FAITHFVLLY INTO ENGLISH,

out of the authentical Latin, according to the best corrected copies of the same, diligently conferred vvith the Greeke and other editions in diuers languages: Vvith ARGVMENTS of bookes and chapters, ANNOTATIONS, and other necessarie helpes, for the better vnderstanding of the text, and specially for the discouerie of the CORRVPTIONS of diuers late translations, and for cleering the CONTROVERSIES in religion of these daies:

IN THE ENGLISH COLLEGE OF RHEMES

Psal 118.

Da mihi intellectum, & scrutabor legem tuam, & custodiam illam in toto corde meo.

That is,

Giue me vnderstanding, and I vvil searche thy lavv, and vvil keepe it vvith my vvhole hart.

S. Aug. tract. 2. in Epist Ioan.

Omuia quæ leguntur in scripturis sanctis, ad instructionem & salutem nostram intentè oportet audire: maximæ tamen memoriè commendanda sunt, quæ adversus Hæreticos valent plurimùm: quorum insidiæ, infirmiores quosque & negligentiores circumuenire non cessant

That is,

Al things that are readde in holy Scriptures, vve must heare vvith great attention, to our instruction and saluation: but those things specially must be commended to memorie, vvhich make most against Heretikes: whose deceites cease not to circumuent and beguile al the vveaker sort and the more negligent persons.

PRINTED AT RHEMES.
by Iohn Fogny.

1582.
CVM PRIVILEGIO.

Translator's preface

In a preface to the Reader of some length, they state their reasons for having translated out of the Latin instead of from the Greek; together with noticing various other matters connected with translations of the Scripture in general, and this version in particular.

Account of the version

They say that they had their translation of the whole Bible lying by them for some time; and that at length having means of publishing the New Testament, they have this printed first.

Reasons why it was made.

"which translation vve doe not for all that publish, vpon erroneous opinion of necessitie, that the holy Scriptures should alvvaies be in our mother tonge, or that they ought or vvere ordained by God, to be read indifferently of all, or could be easily vnderstood of euery one that readeth or heareth them in a knovven language: or that they vvere not often, through mans malice or infirmitie, pernicious and much hurtful to many: or that vve generally and absolutely deemed it more conuenient in itself, & more agreable to Gods word and honour, or edification of the faithful, to haue them turned into vulgar tonges, then to be kept & studied only in the Ecclesiastical learned languages Not for these nor any such like causes doe vve translate this sacred booke, but vpon special consideration of the present time, state, and condition of our countrie, vnto vvhich, diuers thinges are either necessarie, or profitable and medicinable novv, that othervvise in the peace of the Church vvere neither much requisite, nor perchance vvholy tolerable."

Thus cautiously do they guard against the supposition that the publication of this version was to be deemed an acknowledgment that the former opposition which had been made to the circulation of the English Scriptures, had been an error on the part of the Church of Rome.

Wisdom of the church in regulating translations commended.

They speak of the wisdom of the church in making regulations, both as to what translations of the Scriptures might be published, and also by whom they might be read. On the latter point they recite that it had been lately decreed by the Council of Trent, " that the holy Scriptures, though truely and Catholikely translated into vulgar tonges, yet may not be indifferently readde of all men, nor of any other then such as haue expresse licence therevnto of their lawful ordinaries, with good testimonie from their Curates or Confessors, that they be humble, discrete, and deuout persons, and like to take much good, and no harme thereby."

They enlarge on the subjection with which Scripture is to be read; not, however, subjection to what God has seen fit there to reveal, but subjection with regard to Scripture to the authorities in the church: as if any authority could be in any way so constituted of God as to make void the requirements of His holy word.

Protestant versions blamed.

The Rhemish Translators find great fault with all the Protestant versions which had been made; they speak of the liberties taken with the text as having been most unwarranted: the translations of words deemed " ecclesiastical," and the manner in which proper names were expressed, being part of the ground of this charge. In consideration of the alleged state of the English translations of the Bible, they say:—

" Vve therfore hauing compassion to see our beloued countrie men, vvith extreme danger of their soules, to vse onely such prophane translations, and erroneous mens mere phantasies, for the pure and blessed vvord of truth, much also moued thervnto by the desires of many deuout persons: haue set forth, for you (benigne readers) the nevv Testament to begin vvithal, trusting that it may giue occasion to you, after diligent perusing thereof, to lay avvay at lest such their impure versions as hitherto you haue ben forced to occupie "

The Rhemish version intended to supersede them

Alleged object of the annotations

They state that the annotations appended were for the purpose of proving that the Romish Church was conformable to the Scripture. If this had been the case, why should she have taken such pains to keep them back, until they could no longer be withheld. In fact, the real truth was most unconsciously acknowledged in the demands of the Popish insurgents in the West, in the reign of Edward VI., who required that the English Scriptures might be suppressed; because they said that " they had heard that until this were done their priests could not refute the 'heretics.' "

Reasons for translating from the Latin

The translators, in their preface, give ten reasons why they adopted the Latin Vulgate as their basis. They speak of its antiquity, gravity, sincerity, impartiality, and the like; but what were all these worth when assigned as reasons for preferring the Latin version to the Greek original? The fifth of their reasons for this preference was clearly that which decided the point in their minds, namely, that the Latin Vulgate had been declared, by the Council of Trent, to be authentic, and to be refused of none.

The Latin asserted to be better than the Greek.

The ninth reason which they assign is this, " It is not onely better then al other Latin translations, but then the Greeke text it selfe, in those places where they disagree." This is a bold assertion, and one which at the time when it was made no one was competent to advance. It is quite true that the Vulgate Latin is valuable as an aid for judging amongst discrepant readings of Greek manuscripts; but to praise the version more than the original was, to say the least, a mere gratuitous assertion.

They strengthen their arguments in favour of the Vulgate by alleging that various interpreters had, in some places, at least preferred its readings to those of the Greek copies then in use. This argument, however, amounts to very little worth for their purpose; the alleged passages in which the Greek was said to be deserted, and the Latin followed being in fact such as contained some supplied word or words to make the rendering clear.

Critical reasons advanced for deserting the Greek text.

The Rhemish translators likewise object to the authority of the Greek text, that in some places Erasmus and other critics had regarded it as preserving the genuine reading, when the Greek text, as then commonly read, had some variation; this argument has considerable weight when applied solely to the individual passages in question. In fact, the Rhemish translators incline to speak of the Latin Vulgate very much in the same strain as did the Complutensian editors: these latter actually compared the Latin text in the Old Testament of their Bible, standing between the Hebrew and the Septuagint, to Christ crucified between two thieves!

" Posuimus, tanquam duos hinc et inde latrones, medium autem Jesum "

The Latin Vulgate defended.

The Rhemish translators afterwards defend the Vulgate on critical grounds; and in this they speak with much more propriety. They defend it thus: first, that it commonly agrees with the Greek text; secondly, that when it differs from the common Greek text, it frequently accords with some of the various readings of Stephens's third edition; thirdly, they say that even Protestants do not unfrequently prefer the marginal reading to that in the text; fourthly, that in the passages in which the printed Greek authority does not agree with the Latin, there is sometimes to be found a manuscript Greek copy which does accord with the Latin; fifthly, they allege that where no Greek copy accords with the Latin text, not unfrequently the citation of some ancient Greek "father" supplies a confirmation; sixthly, they suppose in passages where some variation is found which cannot otherwise be accounted for, that the Latin interpreter followed some other Greek copy; seventhly, they bring forward the Latin "fathers" as witnesses of what the reading of the text was in their days; lastly, they account for variations in the citations made by the Latin "fathers" by the fact that the Latin versions were in the early days very numerous, and thus when their quotations vary from the Vulgate, they suppose that they may have cited some other of these versions. This last reason is merely apologetic; the rest contain, on the whole, a great deal of truth. One thing, however, they ought to have stated, namely, that the Vulgate contains not a few passages which are clearly the corruptions of copyists. Candour on the part of the Rhemish translators would have acknowledged this; but as that version had been declared "authentic" they were willing fully to carry out this Tridentine decree.

It is quite true that they do acknowledge some faults to have crept in, but merely such as would, in a printed book, be regarded as typographical errata; those to which I have just referred, are such as have a more serious character.

The Greek text asserted to favour Romanism more than the Latin

They strenuously deny that they prefer the Latin to the Greek text, because of its being more favourable to their views and opinions; alleging that the Greek text makes for them more than the Latin. This they endeavour to prove by examples which they bring forward; and I think that it must be admitted, by any one who dispassionately considers the subject, that very few of the variations of the Latin from the Greek text bear the mark of having been made to serve a purpose. They almost all must have crept in just like various readings in Greek copies, through the negligence or oversight of transcribers.

The Rhemish translators give the following account of their version:—

The Rhemists' account of their version.

"In this ovr translation, because we wish it to be most sincere, as becommeth a Catholike translation, and haue endeuoured so to make it: we are very precise & religious in folowing our copie, the old vulgar approued Latin: not onely in sense, which we hope we alwaies do, but sometime in the very wordes also and phrases, which may seeme to the vulgar Reader & to common English eares, not yet acquainted there with, rudenesse or ignorance: but to the discrete Reader that deepely weigheth and considereth the importance of sacred wordes and speaches, and how easily the voluntarie Translatour may misse the true sense of the Holy Ghost, we doubt not but our consideration and doing therein, shal seem reasonable and necessarie: yea and that al sortes of Catholike Readers wil in short time thinke that familiar which at the first may seeme strange, & wil esteeme it more when they shal otherwise be taught to vnderstand it, then if it were the common knowen English"

By "otherwise," they mean by a table of explanations given at the end of the book.

Examples of unusual words.

They give several examples of unusual words which they introduced. They do not, however, give any good reason for not translating them; and, what is more, the meaning given in their glossary would, generally speaking, be far better if introduced into the text, than the comparatively unused word which they have adopted. The following are a few of the strange words thus introduced: *Parasceue, Pasche, Azymes, Depositum*, and such like.

Some of the words which they thus use, and speak of as newly introduced, are, however good and intelligible, such, for instance, as *Evangelize*, which alone fittingly and fully expresses εὐαγγελίζω; and, in such cases, this novelty of the Rhemish translators is not to be reprehended.

"Our Lord" substituted for "The Lord."

One of their peculiarities is, the use of the expression, "Our Lord," in cases where the Scripture has simply "The Lord." For an explanation of this, they refer from their preface to their notes on the 6th of Timothy. In the note they give no better reason for thus altering the text than this;—that the heretics (i. e. the Reformed) used the simple phrase; a strange reason, truly.

They farther thus expound their manner of translating:—

Their manner of translating.

"Moreouer, we presume not in hard places to mollifie the speaches or phrases, but religiously keepe them vvord for vvord, and point for point, for feare of missing, or restraining the sense of the holy Ghost to our phantasie: as Eph 6 *Against the spirituals of vvickedness in the celestials. And vvhat to me and thee, woman.*"

They then give other instances, in some of which they not only add no new sense of their own, but absolutely exclude all meaning from the passages.

This account of portions of the preface will serve to give some idea of the plan pursued by these translators. They had their minds fully bent upon preserving, untouched, the whole of what they deemed "Catholic verity;" and their minds recoiled from whatever seemed to oppose this. In a previous part of their preface, they had spoken thus of their version:—

"Hovv vvell vve haue done it, vve must not be iudges, but referre all to Gods Church and our superiors in the same. to them vve submit our selues, and this, and all other our labours, to be in part or in the vvhole, reformed, corrected, altered, or quite abolished: most humbly desiring pardon, if through our ignorance, temeritie, or other humane infirmitie, vve haue any vvhere mistaken the sense of the holy Ghost further promising, that if hereafter vve espie any of our ovvne errors, or if any other, either frende of good vvil, or aduersarie for desire of reprehension, shal open vnto vs the same: vve vvil not (as Protestants doe) for defense of our estimation, or of pride and contention, by vvrangling vvordes vvilfully persist in them, but be most glad to heare of them, and in the next edition or othervvise to correct them: for it is truth that vve seek for, and Gods honour: which being had, either by good intention or by occasion, al is vvel. This vve professe onely, that vve haue done our endeuour vvith praier, much feare and trembling, lest vve should dangerously erre in so sacred, high, and diuine a vvorke: that vve haue done it vvith all faith, diligence, and sinceritie: that vve haue used no partialitie for the disaduantage of our aduersaries, nor no more licence then is sufferable in translating of holy Scriptures: continually keeping our selues as neere as is possible, to our text & to the very vvordes and phrases vvhich by long vse are made venerable, though to some prophane or delicate eares they may seeme more hard or barbarous, as the whole style of Scripture doth lightly to such at the beginning: acknowledging with S Hierom, that in other writings it is ynough to giue in translation, sense for sense, but that in Scriptures, lest vve misse the sense vve must keepe the very vvordes."

The professions of the translators

They thus invite criticism as to their labours, and the invitation has been very fully responded to. They attacked all previous versions, and in their turn were attacked, both as it regards their text and their notes.* It may, I believe, be said, as an impartial judgment on this version, that the translators were fully competent to execute the task before them, so far as learning and ability could go; but their minds were so imbued with the same feelings which had led but fifty years before, to persecution in England for the word of God, that they desired any thing rather than to give the rendering of the text simply and fairly. Very few passages, however, shew in their rendering a really dishonest perversion; but very many exhibit a desire of expressing the sense obscurely, or at least, in such a way that a common reader may find not a little difficulty in gathering from the words a definite meaning. If we take the whole version, we shall, however, find a very large portion well translated, and truly exhibiting the sense of the Latin Vulgate such as they had it. I say, such as they had it; for although the council of Trent had defined the Latin Vulgate to be the "authentic" version, it remained a considerable question what copy was to be regarded as such.

Criticism invited

Learning of the translators.

Intentional obscurity.

At the time when the Rhemish version was printed, there had been no decision as to what this "authentic" Latin Vulgate might be. In 1589, Pope Sixtus V. published an edition, which by his bull prefixed, was declared to be what the Tridentine Council sought to establish. This edition was presently suppressed. Romish writers say, that it was in consequence of Pope Sixtus perceiving that it contained errors. But be that as it may, Pope Clement VIII. published his edition of the Vulgate in 1592, which he declared by his prefixed bull to be the only authentic edition of the Latin Vulgate. This has fared better, for this continues to be the standard text adopted and used by the Church of Rome.

The "authentic" Latin Vulgate.

Edition of Pope Sixtus V 1589.

Edition of Pope Clement VIII 1592

The Rhemish translators, as may be supposed, do not exactly agree with either the Clementine or the Sixtine edition. Sometimes they have the reading adopted afterwards by the one, sometimes that which is found in the other. This may be said to be a matter of comparatively small importance, so long as they used the best readings which were within their reach: it is, however, thus far of importance, that they give as a conclusive reason for translating from the Latin rather than the Greek, that the Council of Trent had decreed the authenticity of the Latin Vulgate. Now of what avail was this decree, if it could not be definitely said what this authentic copy was?

In the same year (1582) in which this New Testament appeared, Gregory Martin, one of the translators, published an attack upon the hitherto printed English Bibles and Testaments. This was evidently done to make way for this version. Dr. William Fulke, master of Pembroke Hall, Cambridge, published in the following year an ample refutation of the most part of the objections made, shewing very conclusively that the true ground of objection in the mind of Martin was the opposition which the circulation of the Scriptures gave to Romish doctrine.

Gregory Martin's attack on the English versions. 1582

Answered by Fulke, 1583.

* A complete confutation of these arguments, glosses, and annotations, was published in 1617, by Fulke: and a second, in 1618, by Cartwright.

Rom Cath. version of Old Test published. 1609-10

The Roman Catholic translation of the Old Testament, which appears to have been executed on the same principles as that of the New, was not published till the years 1609 and 1610, when it was printed at Douay, in two volumes. The editors of this part of the version, speak of it as having been executed many years before, but that the poor estate of the English Romanists, in their banishment, hindered its publication. They say, that they have revised the version according to the Clementine edition of the Vulgate, that thus it might be fully in accordance with "the authentical Latin."

The Rhemish translation has a considerable value to a Protestant reader; for if he would see what can be done, in order to evade the force of those passages which set forth *the Gospel*, the great weapon against Rome, it may, of course, be expected here. While the general and substantial accordance of this version with Protestant translations, is a cause for great thankfulness to the overruling providence of God.

Modern editions of this version

In the modern editions of the Douay Bible and the Rhemish Testament but few changes have been introduced: these are, however, some of them, not improvements.

XVII.

KING JAMES'S TRANSLATION.

THERE were, at the commencement of the reign of James I., two translations of the Bible in common use —that of Geneva and the Bishops'; the latter being what might be termed the then "authorised" version, while the former was the one in daily use among the people. It is not, therefore, surprising that another version, or revision, should have been projected. The following were the actual circumstances which led to the undertaking of a new version,—which has succeeded in supplanting both the one and the other of those which were at that time in use.

Accession of James I Mar 24, 1603.

At the time of the accession of James I. to the throne, March 24, 1603, many of those whose conformity to the Church of England by law established was of an uneasy character, hoped that the accession of a monarch who had been educated like James in Presbyterianism, might lead either to a change in the system of the Anglican Establishment, or else to a permission of non-conformity. Accordingly, a petition running in the name of more than a thousand ministers was presented to the king, in which the "redress of divers abuses in the Church" was earnestly solicited. From the number of ministers in whose names it ran, it was called the "Millenary Petition," although the names actually subscribed are said to have been very far short of a thousand. Their complaints were ranged under four heads; 1st. Things connected with the Church service; 2nd. Church ministers; 3rd. Church living and maintenance; and 4th. Church discipline.

The "Millenary" petition

The Oxford answer

Hampton Court conference, Jan. 12, 1604 Collier

The University of Oxford drew up an answer to this petition, for which a letter of thanks was sent them by that of Cambridge. The king, however, chose to interfere in the matter, and bring it to a public conference. To this end certain delegates of each party received a summons to be at the palace of Hampton Court on the ensuing 12th of January. On the part of the Anglican establishment there were, the archbishop of Canterbury, Whitgift; the bishop of London, Bancroft, and several other prelates and dignitaries. The delegates on the part of the petitioners were, Dr. John Reynolds, and Dr. Thomas Sparke of Oxford, and Mr. Chadderton and Mr. Knewstubbs from Cambridge.

Dr Reynolds requests that a new version of the Bible should be made

Faults in previous versions

This conference led incidentally to the execution of the translation of the Scriptures which is still in use. Dr. Reynolds, who took the lead on the part of the petitioners, made a request to the king on the second day of the conference "for a New Translation of the Bible." The ground upon which this request was made was, that the versions which were extant, did not in all places come up to the force and meaning of the original text. In proof of this, Dr. Reynolds brought forward a few instances; first, that in Gal. iv. 25, the word συστοχεῖ is rendered in the Bishops' Bible by "bordreth," which is very wide of the mark; next in Psalm cv. 28, the translation says, "they were not obedient," whereas it ought to have been just the contrary; and thirdly, in Psalm cvi. 30, the translation said, "then stood up Phineas and prayed," whereas the last of these words should have been rendered "executed judgment."* It is probable that Dr. Reynolds, in specifying these three instances of mistranslation, did it in order to shew that a

* The last two of these objections applied to the version of the Psalms in Cranmer's Bible, which is still retained in the Liturgy

revision of the existing versions was desirable, if the full meaning of the original text were wished to be transfused into the English version.

Little notice appears to have been taken of these specific objections themselves: they had, it was said, been often brought before, and were already answered in print; what the *answering* of these objections may mean I do not know; for if they be mistranslations they ought to be acknowledged as such; if they had not been such, then they ought to have been preserved when a new version was made.

During the whole of this conference, Bancroft, the bishop of London, (who soon after succeeded Whitgift as archbishop of Canterbury,) had been foremost in the opposition to everything which was proposed by Dr. Reynolds and his fellow-delegates. On this ground he seems to have offered a kind of opposition to the proposal for a new version or recension of the Bible in English: he said, that there would be no end of translating if this were to be done to please every man's humour; the king, however, liked Dr. Reynolds's proposition, and said that he had never seen a good English version of the Bible as yet, though he thought that of all hitherto executed, the Geneva Bible was the worst. He wished the work of translation to be taken up, and that some special pains might be taken for there to be one uniform translation. The method proposed by the king was this;—that the version should be made by some of the most learned men in both the Universities, that it should then be reviewed by the bishops and other of the most learned ecclesiastics, that it should then be laid before the Privy Council, and last of all be ratified by Royal authority, so that in the whole Anglican establishment this translation so made should be used, and no other. Bancroft hinted the undesirableness of any marginal notes being allowed to be appended, to which the king assented, on the ground of his having found in those annexed to the Geneva Bible some that were very partial, untrue, seditious, and savouring too much of dangerous and traitorous conceits.

Bancroft opposes the making of a new version.

King James wishes a new version.

The plan proposed.

Marginal notes objected to.

This assent of the king to the proposal of Dr. Reynolds requires a little explanation: perhaps the judgment of the king, relative to the previously existing English versions, may be regarded by all as very unjust and severe: granted that they were all of them capable of a good deal of emendation in many places, but still to say that none of them was a good translation, was going a great deal too far. In this point, the judgment of the translators employed by the king, differed greatly from that which the king himself had expressed. They say, in their preface, that their object was to make a *good* version better;—that it was *good* before, but they sought to improve it, and the like, and in this they clearly spoke the truth. It is to be observed, that the translation of the Bible had become a kind of party question between the thorough conformists and the partial conformists; the latter were considered to prefer and uphold the Geneva version, which was by far the most read in private, while the former were considered to uphold the Bishops' Bible, as being the one authoritatively set forth as being appointed to be read in public service. Thus the proposition of Dr. Reynolds for a new version might be regarded as savouring strongly of his party, while the whole of the king's reply was so directed as to express a very severe though not a deserved censure on the Geneva Bible. The proposal of Dr. Reynolds would, if acceded to, have the effect of rendering the Bishops' Bible obsolete; the king, however, so turns the matter, as to make it appear as though it were the Geneva version of which the suppression was desired, a result which, it is probable, was but little desired by Dr. Reynolds.

The king's censures on previous versions.

The Geneva Bible depreciated for party reasons.

The exclusion of marginal notes was, doubtless, a good suggestion: but the remarks made by King James with respect to those annexed to the Geneva version, were very far from just. The notes to which the king is said to have referred were the following:—On Exodus i. 19, where the non-compliance of the Hebrew midwives with the orders of Pharaoh is spoken of, they say, "Their disobedience herein was lawfull, but their dissembling euill." Now, I do not see what objection can be made to this note, the very next verse speaks of the blessing of God being bestowed upon these women, on the very ground of their non-compliance with the king's murderous commands, and the object of the note seems to be to shew, that although they acted rightly, yet they excused themselves to the king in a manner in which they ought not to have done. But if the non-compliance of the midwives was wrong, what would follow? That a king is to be obeyed, even if he command *murder* to be committed: and further, that this is to be done even when it is the murder of an indefinite number of helpless infants; and yet further, that it is to be done even when it is nothing short of a deliberate attempt to frustrate the declared purpose and counsel of God. I think that even King James would have acknowledged that *some* non-compliance with the orders of a king were more admissible than all this train of necessary consequences.

The king's objections to the Geneva notes.

Ex. i. 19.

The other note to which the king objected, was that on 2 Chron. xv. 16, where the account is given of Asa deposing Maachah, his mother, or grandmother, from being queen, on account of her idolatry. They say, "Herein he shewed that he lacked zeale, for she ought to have died, both by the couenant, as verse

2 Chr. xv. 16.

13, & by the Law of God: but he gaue place to foolish pitie, and would also seeme after a sort to satisfie the Lawe." Would king James or any other objector say, that the law of Moses did not command the punishing of idolatry with *death;* death without pity, and without respect of persons? Or, can it be said that the covenant into which Asa and the people had just entered, did not pledge them to the self-same thing? I really believe, that such objections, however they arose, must have rested upon a basis of prejudice, and not of dispassionate judgment.

King James's judgment that the Geneva notes encourage insubordination.

It seems, however, that King James thought the Geneva notes to be opposed to that obedience which is due from subjects to their sovereigns: if they had been, they would have been highly reprehensible; but before judgment is given let the facts be proved. "The powers that be are ordained of *God*, he therefore that resisteth the power resisteth the ordinance of *God;* and they that resist shall receive to themselves damnation," is the recorded sentence of the Holy Ghost against all who, under what lying pretext soever it be, dare to act in insubordination: but if we would see where the limit of obedience is to be found, we have only to look at the history of the three servants of God whom He preserved in the midst of the fiery furnace (Dan. iii.).

The king's plan for a version excellent.

Thus it is very plain, that King James acquiesced in the proposal of Dr. Reynolds upon grounds wholly different from those upon which it was originally suggested; but whatever were the circumstances which led to the execution of the translation which was in consequence made, it cannot be controverted that the plan which was suggested by the king (and with some modifications at length adopted) was admirably devised for the procuring of a version well considered in all its parts. There was, as might have been expected, some little delay before the preliminary arrangements could be brought to bear. Some time probably was needed for the consideration of the fittest scholars to be employed upon the work, and also in the arrangement of the different companies of translators who should work together, and in the allotment of their respective portions of the Bible.

The king writes to Bancroft, July 22, 1604 Fifty-four translators appointed.

Lewis

Some progress had been made in the outline of the proceedings before the lapse of many months; for on the 22d of July, 1604, the king wrote to the archbishop of Canterbury (Bancroft*) concerning some provision to be made for those who were to be employed in the proposed work. He states that he had appointed certain learned men, to the number of *fifty-four*, for the translation of the Bible into English. Of those who were so appointed, some had very little church preferment, some none, and for this cause he directs the archbishop to write to the archbishop of York, and also to the other bishops, commanding them in the king's name, that when any benefice valued in the king's books at twenty pounds or upwards should become void, that instead of presenting any one to supply the vacancy, the king should be informed, in order that some of the learned persons whom he had appointed might be presented. This was to be done by the bishop whether the benefice were in his own gift or in any other patronage. The latter part of the letter chiefly relates to the obtaining of aid from other learned men, besides those who had been named as the four and fifty appointed by the king.

Inquiry to be made for learned men.

He says :—"Furthermore, we require you to move all our bishops to inform themselves of such learned men within their several dioceses, as having especial skill in the Hebrew and Greek tongues, have taken pains in their private studies of the Scriptures, for the clearing of any obscurities, either in the Hebrew or in the Greek, or touching any difficulties or mistakings in the former English translation, which we have now commanded to be thoroughly viewed and amended; and thereupon to write unto them, earnestly charging them, and signifying our pleasure therein, that they send such their observations, either to Mr. Livelie, our Hebrew reader in Cambridge, or to Dr Harding, our Hebrew reader in Oxford, or to Dr. Andrewes, dean of Westminster, to be imparted to the rest of their several companies, that so our said intended translation may have the help and furtherance of all our principal learned men within this our kingdom."

Translators nominated by the Universities

It is not known what arrangements were made relative to the selection and appointment of the translators; but it would seem that some part of them were chosen by the University of Cambridge, and approved by the king: it is probable also, that the University of Oxford made a similar nomination. This selection at Cambridge must have taken place previous to the day on which the king wrote the letter already referred to, and in part quoted, namely, July 22, 1604, for on the same day the chancellor of the University of Cambridge, Robert Cecil, earl of Salisbury, wrote to the vice chancellor and heads, mentioning that such an appointment had been made by the king. The order for the translation was stated to be placed in the hands of Livelie, the Hebrew lecturer. The king's commandment was, that if they could remember any

* In some of the proceedings at this time, Bancroft is spoken of as archbishop of Canterbury, in some as bishop of London The proceedings relative to his translation to the archiepiscopal see were not complete, although he was Archbishop elect.

fit men to join with those already appointed, they should, in the king's name, add such to those who had been previously selected for the work. The king likewise required that the University should give to those employed all the aid that could be afforded:—

"That such as are to be called out of the countrie may be intertayned in such colleges as they shall make choice of, without any charge unto them either for their entrance, their chamber, or their commons, except it happen that any doe make choice to remayne in any of the poorer colleges, that are not well able to beare that charge; and then such order will be taken by the Lord Bishop of London, as that the same shall be defrayed." Cecil's letter to the Vice-Chancellor of Cambridge

On the last day of the same month (July, 1604), Bancroft sent a copy of the king's letter in favour of the translators, to all of those at Cambridge, whose names appear in the list. From this it would appear, that that University had not made any addition to the number originally appointed. The bishop, in his letter, told them, that the king (as Mr. Livelie could inform them), very much approved of the choice. And because the king was very desirous that the work should proceed with as little delay as possible, his pleasure was, that they should, with all possible speed, meet together in the University, and begin the same. They were directed to write to the bishop so soon as they were actually assembled, and had prepared themselves for the work. Bancroft's letter. July 31, 1604 The work urged on

On the same day, the bishop wrote to the vice-chancellor and the heads of the University of Cambridge, earnestly urging them to expedite the work which had been assigned to the translators. They were particularly desired to write to any who might be absent from Cambridge, in order that they might, without any delay, repair thither, and commence their work.

It is probable, that similar letters were sent also to the University of Oxford at the same time; and that, just as the copy of the rules to be observed in the translation, were sent to Cambridge, to Livelie, the king's Hebrew reader, so were they, probably, to Dr. Harding, who held the similar station at Oxford. Similar letters probably sent to Oxford

The list of persons actually employed in the work (which will be given after the preliminary proceedings have been detailed), contains only *forty-seven* names, whereas, the king's letter to the archbishop mentions *fifty-four* as having been appointed. Some have supposed, that the deficiency was occasioned by the decease of certain who had been named for the work: but this is improbable; because, the number of those who actually met at Cambridge, was exactly the same, and the individuals were the same, as those who were at first proposed; whereas, if there had been any deficiencies through the decease of those appointed, it is very unlikely that the Oxford and Cambridge numbers would have been precisely the same. Others have supposed, that some who were appointed at first, were afterwards withdrawn; and that thus the numbers were reduced to forty-seven. But this, likewise, is improbable; for the learned Hugh Broughton, who has been *supposed* to have been thus excluded from having a part in the execution of this version, was clearly *not* one of the persons named; for on the 30th of August, 1604, the bishop of London sent to Cambridge, for the perusal of Livelie, and the rest of the translators there, "a certain learned epistle of Mr. Broughton's:" this, it can hardly be supposed, he would have done, had Broughton himself been proposed as a translator. Lewis suggests another way of accounting for the discrepancy, which, however, is equally open to objection. A kind of supplementary rule directed, that three or four of the most learned and grave divines of each University, should be assigned as having an oversight of the version; especially to see that the rules prescribed were attended to. He supposes, that these three or four may make up the deficiency; but, however, it is to be observed, that this rule was not communicated until August 30, 1604; whereas, the number of translators is spoken of by the king, as having been completed on the 22nd of July: and, farther, the fifty-four persons are distinctly said to be appointed for the purpose of executing the translation; whereas, the three or four of each University are distinctly excluded from that work. *Forty-seven* names in the list of those actually engaged; *Fifty-four* mentioned in the king's letter Hugh Broughton not named

Who then were the seven whose names do not appear in the list? It is to be remembered, that at the Hampton Court conference the method of translating proposed by the king was, that the version should be made by the most learned of the Universities, and then pass the examination of certain of the *Bishops*. Now, in the list of persons appointed, although several of them were made bishops before the work was completed, yet none of them were so at the time of their appointment; and thus the plan would have been incomplete (according to the king's original draught), had not certain prelates been named as having the work in some manner under their control. I do not doubt but that the number needed to make up the deficiency is to be found in the fact of certain bishops having been especially named to this work; *who* these were, it may be more difficult to say: but Dr. Bancroft, the archbishop of Canterbury, has been said to have made some alterations in the version. This (if true) he would hardly have done, had he not been in some manner appointed to an oversight of it; and (if incorrect) it would hardly have been said, if he Who were the seven not in the list? Certain bishops appointed to superintend the work Abp Bancroft connected with the version.

had not been connected with the work. It is evident, from the letters which were written by him (as bishop of London), that he had some important share in the conducting of the preliminary arrangements for the commencement of the work; so that I think it is not too much to conclude that he was one of the prelates so appointed. Bilson, bishop of Winchester, was one of those who gave the work its final revision; so that it may be deemed probable that *he* too was one appointed to the work.

Bp. Bilson a reviser

The translators were, as has been said, some of them appointed by the University of Cambridge, some, in all probability, by that of Oxford, in a similar manner; while, besides these, there were several who were to meet at Westminster: these may have been appointed directly by the king. The translators meeting at each of these three places, were severally divided into two companies, so that there were in all six companies of translators. The instructions for their proceedings were conveyed for their information to the several places at which they were to meet, about the month of July, 1604. I give the instructions themselves, together with any elucidatory remarks which may appear needful.

Some of the translators at Westminster.

Six companies in all

Instructions.

Bishops' Bible to be the basis

"(1.) The Bible ordinarily read in the church, commonly called the 'Bishops' Bible,' to receive as few alterations as may be. And to pass throughout, unless the originals plainly call for an amendment." It was a good plan to take a previously existing version, and make it, as much as might be, the material of the new recension. The Bishops' Bible was apparently specified as the one which was to be used for this purpose, because else, some of the translators might have been disposed to have taken the more popular Geneva translation as their basis.

Proper names to be unchanged

"(2.) The names of the prophets and the holy writers, with the other names in the text, to be kept as near as may be, according as they are vulgarly used." There was good sense in this rule; for it makes extremely little difference what the precise form may be in which any Hebrew or Greek *name* is transfused into English; and, indeed, we have good authority for acting on such a rule as this, from the manner in which Old Testament names are found written in the New. We read those names which were known and familiar in their accustomed forms, while those which were altogether still unnaturalized, are taken in the forms in which they had been written in Greek letters by the Septuagint translators. We do not find the inspired writers busying themselves about writing Hebrew proper names in precisely equivalent Greek characters. Thus, in English, *Hezekiah* serves for all practical purposes, as well as "*Yekhizkiyahû*," and so on of the rest. However, it would have been well if the translators had been admonished to give the same person the same name, whether found in Hebrew or in Greek; for instance, to have used the name *Hosea* in the New Testament, instead of *Osee;* and likewise to translate the same proper name uniformly in the same manner; for instance, not to call the same person sometimes Luke, and sometimes Lucas.

Ecclesiastical words to be retained

"(3) The old ecclesiastical words to be kept, as the word *Church* not to be rendered *Congregation*." It would have been desirable if some more explicit statement had been made as to *what* words are to be regarded as "ecclesiastical." For instance, ἐπίσκοπος is rendered in Acts xx. by "overseer" (though the vulgate Latin takes it literally), and in other places by "bishops." Probably the want of sufficient definitiveness prevented the full observance of this rule.

Doubtful words according to the "Fathers"

"(4) When any word hath divers significations, that to be kept which hath been most commonly used by the most eminent Fathers, being agreeable to the propriety of the place, and the analogy of faith." This may perhaps be regarded, as well as the preceding, as a check against the introduction of what might be deemed *Puritanism:* but, however intended, I suppose that no right-minded Chrristian (whether called Episcopalian or Puritan), could object to words being used in the same sense in which they are taken by the writers called "*Fathers*," *with the defined limitation above expressed.*

Division of chapters.

"(5) The division of the chapters to be altered either not at all, or as little as may be, if necessity so require."

No marginal notes

"(6) No marginal notes at all to be affixed, but only for the explanation of the Hebrew or Greek words, which cannot, without some circumlocution, so briefly and fitly be expressed in the text." This regulation is one of great importance; because its tendency was to cause the translators to do what they could to give, in the text, the precise meaning of the original. A loose translation may be aided by an expository note; but if the original is to be transfused into another tongue, without any such appendage, it can only be achieved by a version as close as may be made. One great evil of notes, in a commonly circulated version of the Scriptures, is this, that they lead the thoughts of a reader away from the text which the Spirit of God has given forth, to the thoughts and judgments of men (often perhaps very true, but still not authoritative) about that very text.

Marginal references.

"(7) Such quotations of places to be marginally set down, as shall serve for the fit reference of one Scripture to another."

The preceding seven rules are the general directions for proceeding in the work; the rest contain the precise directions for its execution.

"(8) Every particular man of each company to take the same chapter or chapters; and having translated or amended them severally by himself, where he thinks good, all to meet together, to confer what they have done, and agree for their part what shall stand." Thus in each company there would be as many separate revisions made, as there were individuals in the company (that is, from seven to ten); these various revisions would then be compared together, and from the whole they would digest one revised or re-translated copy of the particular portion.

Manner of proceeding with the execution of the translation

"(9) As any one company hath dispatched any one book in this manner, they shall send it to the rest, to be considered of seriously and judiciously; for his Majesty is very careful in this point.

"(10) If any company, upon the review of the book so sent, shall doubt or differ upon any places, to send them word thereof, to note the places, and therewithal to send their reasons; to which, if they consent not, the difference to be compounded at the general meeting, which is to be of the chief persons of each company, at the end of the work."

These rules would have to be carried into execution thus:—Each company, when they had made their version of a book, would have to send a transcript of it to each of the other five companies, for their judgments and criticism; so that every portion of the Bible would pass through the hands of the whole body of translators. Every part of the Bible would thus have been considered: first, by each of the translators in the company to which it was assigned, *separately;* secondly, by the whole of that company unitedly; thirdly, by the other five companies separately; and fourthly, by the committee of revision, who are hinted at in the close of the tenth rule. As the number of companies was six, and the numbers in each company varied from seven to ten, it follows that every several part would be examined at the least *fourteen* times distinctly; many parts *fifteen* times, and some *seventeen.* These rules were framed, in this part, with remarkable judgment and sagacity.

All the companies to revise each part

Every part examined fourteen times at least

"(11) When any place of special obscurity is doubted of, letters to be directed by authority, to send to any learned in the land for his judgment in such a place.

"(12) Letters to be sent from every bishop to the rest of his clergy, admonishing them of this translation in hand, and to move and charge as many as being skilful in the tongues have taken pains in that kind, to send their particular observations to the company, either at Westminster, Cambridge, or Oxford, according as it was directed before in the king's letter to the archbishop." This regulation explains why Bancroft communicated the king's letter to all of those who had been appointed at Cambridge as translators, the letter itself containing some things which related to the ordering of the version itself.

Inquiry to be made for learned men

"(13.) The directors in each company to be the deans of Westminster and Chester for the Westminster company, and the king's professors in Hebrew and Greek in the two Universities.

The directors in the companies

"(14.) These translations to be used, when they agree better with the text than the Bishops' Bible, viz. Tyndale's, Coverdale's, Matthew's, Whitchurch's, Geneva." In this list "Matthew's Bible" might quite as well have been omitted, as containing simply, in part the translation of Tyndale, in part that of Coverdale. "Whitchurch's Bible" evidently means the Bible commonly known as Cranmer's, or the Great Bible, of which Whitchurch was, in conjunction with Grafton, the printer. This regulation was a good one for making the newly revised translation as little as possible with the character of novelty stamped upon it. It is likely that in many cases, when they deserted the version of the Bishops' Bible, they might find some one or other of the four above-named versions expressing the sense which they wanted to give.

Early English versions to be used.

These fourteen were the whole of the original rules as sent to Livelie, at Cambridge; similar ones being, of course, also transmitted to Oxford and Westminster. Questions, however, seem to have arisen at Cambridge on two points connected with the third and fourth of the above regulations. *What* words are to be deemed old "ecclesiastical," and as such to be retained? How should it be determined in what sense words were used by the most eminent fathers, and when should such a sense be regarded as agreeable to the propriety of the place and the analogy of faith? It is evident that queries of this kind did actually arise, for Bancroft wrote a letter on the 30th of August, 1604, to Dr. Cowell, vice-chancellor of the University of Cambridge, in which he answers the difficulty. He states that it was the king's pleasure, that besides the learned persons employed for the Hebrew and Greek, there should be three or four of the most eminent and grave divines of the University assigned by the vice-chancellor upon conference with the rest of the heads, to be overseers of the translations, as well Hebrew as Greek, for the better observing of the rules appointed by the king; and especially concerning the *third* and *fourth* rule. The bishop further directed the vice-chancellor to inform him who the persons appointed for this part of the work were, when they

Questions with regard to the third and fourth rules

Bancroft's letter to the Vice-Chancellor of Cambridge, Aug. 30, 1604

Overseers of the translation to be appointed.

should have been agreed on. It does not appear whether any such appointments were actually made, or how the difficulties which the third and fourth rules might occasion were actually met.

A copy of H. Broughton's letter sent to Cambridge.

The bishop mentioned a letter of Hugh Broughton's, which was, he says, brought to him at that very time: he sends a copy of it to Cambridge, in order that Livelie and the rest of the translators there might have the perusal of it, if they had not seen it before. This letter was doubtless one of those which this learned but untoward man had written relative to the manner in which a translation of the Bible should be undertaken and executed.

Bancroft writes to the bishops, July 31, 1604.

On the 31st of July, Bancroft had written to the other bishops, in pursuance of the king's command, with regard to a provision being made for those of the translators who possessed but little, or else no church preferment; he explains the king's meaning to be, that in each diocese two livings should be reserved, one in the presentation of the bishop himself, and another belonging to a lay-patron.

Money to be raised for the expenses of the work.

It was, however, necessary to raise money for the current expenses of the work. The king spoke in his letter about another point to be by the bishops imparted to the deans: this Bancroft also communicated to the bishops. On the same day as his letter just mentioned, he wrote to them a distinct letter on this point, which was, he said, reserved for his relation: it was simply this, that in order to meet the expenses, the king requested that the bishops and the deans and chapters would raise a contribution. Bancroft suggested that a thousand marks would be a sufficient sum to meet the whole charges, and thus he left it to the several bishops and deans to judge what their respective proportions ought to be. Bancroft's letters contained the following clause:—"I must requier yow, in his Majesty's name, accordinge to his good pleasure in that behalfe, that, as soon as possibly yow can, yow send me word what shall be expected from yow and your said Deane and Chapter. For I am to acquainte his Majestie with every man's liberality towards this most godly worke."

1000 marks supposed to be sufficient.

A considerable delay

And now, after all things were so far arranged, a considerable delay took place before the work was actually commenced. No sufficient or satisfactory reason for this detention has, I think, been assigned.

Livelie's death, 1605.

The death of Livelie, which took place in the year subsequent to the above proceedings, has been supposed to have been one reason; this may be quite true as it regards Cambridge, but how need this have affected the other companies of translators? Besides, if this had been the cause of detention, how was it that they had not begun their labour during the several months which elapsed after the appointment was made before Livelie's death took place? To me, it seems not improbable, that the delay was in some measure connected with the difficulty which the king found in raising the sum needed for the purpose, and thus, until something else could be devised, the matter was obliged to rest.

The translators not easily brought together.

Commencement of the work, 1607

It might also be a difficult thing to get together the various translators, whose abodes were in such different parts; and this would be especially difficult, if the needful aid were not provided, in order to defray their expenses. At length, however, the work commenced in the early part of the year 1607. The companies who met at Oxford and Cambridge being provided for in several of the colleges, but receiving no farther compensation for their labours. Those who met at Westminster, probably provided for themselves, which the most part of them were well able to do.

List of the translators

In giving the list of the translators (as preserved by Fuller), together with the respective portions of the Bible which were appropriated to the several companies, it will be well briefly to state who and what they respectively were. It is a matter of peculiar interest to trace out by what means the Lord was pleased to work, in first causing the printed Scriptures to be published in English, and just so it ought to be of no small interest to know to whose labours we are indebted for the translation which has now continued as that daily used for two hundred and thirty years wherever the English language is spoken.

The First Company ten, at Westminster.

The First Company of Translators met at WESTMINSTER: they were ten in number; and the portion which was assigned them was the *Pentateuch*, and *the historical books to the Kings*, inclusive.

Genesis to Kings inclusive.

They consisted of the following persons:—

Bp Andrews

1st DR LAUNCELOT ANDREWS, who presided in this company, and who was, at the time of his having been appointed to the work of translation, dean of Westminster

He was born in the year 1565, in London; he went to Pembroke Hall, Cambridge, having received one of the then newly founded Greek fellowships at that house After the erection of Jesus College, he became one of the first fellows upon that foundation; subsequently he became one of the fellows of Pembroke Hall, of which, on the death of Dr Fulke, he was afterwards master. Previously to this, however, his lectures at his college had attracted considerable attention. He became subsequently particularly known as a preacher After having received preferment in various ways, he became a prebendary of Westminster, when Bancroft was made bishop of London He afterwards succeeded

Dean of Westminster

Dr Gabriel Goodman (one of the translators of the "Bishops' Bible") as dean of Westminster. This was his position when appointed president of the first company of translators. Before, however, the work itself commenced, he was made bishop of Chichester (consecrated Nov. 3, 1605). From this see he was translated to that of Ely, Sep. 22, 1609; this was before the translation was completed. He was made bishop of Winchester, February 18, 1618. He died, September 25, 1626, in the seventy-first year of his age, leaving behind a high reputation for learning, no less than for godliness. His labour as presiding over the translation of so large a portion of the Old Testament, must have been considerable.

Bp. of Chichester
Of Ely
Of Winchester.

2nd. Dr John Overall. He was born in 1559; became a fellow of Trinity College, Cambridge; and in 1596 he was appointed Regius professor of Divinity in that university, In 1601, he succeeded Dr Alexander Nowell, as dean of St Paul's. This was the station which he held when appointed one of the translators In April, 1614, he was made bishop of Lichfield and Coventry; and in 1618, he was translated to the see of Norwich. He died May 12, 1619.

Bp. Overall dean of St. Paul's, Bp. of Lichfield, Coventry, and of Norwich.

3rd Dr. Adrian de Saravia. This translator was a learned foreigner, of Spanish extraction, but born at Artois, in the year 1531. In 1582, he was invited to become professor of divinity at Leyden; where he was also preacher in the French church. He continued there about five years, and then removed to Jersey; where he kept a school, and preached in French. He subsequently removed to Southampton, where he also became a schoolmaster He was treated with much favour by Archbishop Whitgift; and was successively appointed a prebendary of Gloucester, Canterbury, and Westminster He was reinvited to Leyden after he had settled in England, with which request he did not incline to comply He died, aged eighty-two, in 1613; two years after the publication of King James's translation of the Bible. It is probable that he was appointed to this work, rather on account of his great abilities as a linguist, than as being peculiarly qualified to translate critically *into* the English language.

Dr Saravia
Prebendary of Gloucester,&c.

4th. Dr. Richard Clarke, vicar of Mynstre and Monkton, in Thanet, and one of the six preachers, Canterbury. Dr. Clarke.

5th Dr. John Laifield, rector of St Clement Danes, fellow of Trinity College, Cambridge. "Being skilled in architecture, his judgment was much relied on for the fabric of the tabernacle and temple." Dr. Laifield

6th. Dr Leigh, archdeacon of Middlesex, parson of Allhallows, Barking. Dr. Leigh.

7th. Master Burgley. [Lewis adds "Stretford."] Burgley.

8th. Mr King [Lewis adds "Sussex."] King

9th. Mr. Thomson. [Lewis adds "Clare."] Thomson.

10th Wilhelm Bedwell, of St. John's College, Cambridge. He was appointed vicar of Tottenham 1607, where he died, May 5, 1632. He appears to have been an eminent oriental scholar. Bedwell.

The Second Company of Translators assembled at Cambridge, having for their portion of the translation, from the commencement of the *Chronicles* to the end of the *Canticles*, inclusive.

Those who belonged to this company were the following persons:—

Second company of eight at Cambridge. Chron to Cant. inclusive.

1st Edward Livelie; who has been already mentioned as the Regius professor of Hebrew, as such, he was *nominated* the president of this company; but he died before the work was actually commenced. This is supposed to have occasioned a considerable delay. Livelie.

2nd. Dr. John Richardson, fellow of Emanuel College, then master of Peterhouse, and, lastly, master of Trinity College. Dr. Richardson.

3rd. Dr Laurence Chaderton. He was one of the Cambridge delegates at the conference at Hampton Court; and, as such, has been already mentioned, together with Dr. Reynolds. In his early life, he suffered much from the unkind treatment of his parents, in consequence of his embracing the reformed doctrines. He studied at Cambridge; where he became a fellow of Christ's College, in 1567 When Emanuel College was refounded, in 1584, he was appointed the first master. In the latter part of his life, when Arminianism was spreading in England, he so much feared, lest he might have a successor who did not hold the doctrines of grace, that he resigned in favour of one who held the same doctrine as himself. However, he not only survived this successor, but lived to see two other masters of the college. He died in November, 1640, aged ninety-four. Dr Chaderton

4th. Francis Dillingham, "fellow of Christ-College, beneficed at ——, in Bedfordshire, where he died." Dillingham

5th. Mr. Andrews, afterwards D D., brother to the bishop of Winchester, and master of Jesus-College. Dr. Andrews

6th. Thomas Harrison, vice-master of Trinity College. Harrison

7th. Robert Spalding, fellow of St. John's. He succeeded Livelie, as Regius professor of Hebrew. Spalding

8th Andrew Bing, fellow of Peterhouse. He succeeded Spalding in his professorship. Bing.

The Third Company of Translators met at Oxford, their portion being the remainder of the Old Testament, namely, from *Isaiah* to *Malachi*, inclusive. This company consisted of the following individuals:—

The Third Company of Seven at Oxford. Isaiah to Malachi inclusive

1st. Dr. John Harding, president of Magdalen College, the Regius professor of Hebrew. He presided in this company. Dr. Harding.

Dr. Reynolds.

2nd. Dr. John Reynolds, who has been already mentioned as one of the delegates at the Hampton Court Conference; at whose suggestion, indeed, this translation itself (as has been already said) was undertaken. This eminent scholar was born at Pinhoe, near Exeter, about the year 1549, he studied at Corpus Christi College, Oxford, of which, in 1598, he became president. In the reign of Queen Elizabeth, he refused to be promoted to a bishopric; probably objecting then to many of those things which were afterwards discussed in the conference at Hampton Court. He did not live long after the work of translation was commenced, dying on the 21st of May, 1607. Had he lived to continue the work, it is probable, that from his extraordinary learning, his aid would have been peculiarly valuable to his coadjutors.

Dr. Holland.

3rd. Dr. Thomas Holland, who was for many years rector of Exeter College, and stood high as a scholar. He is particularly mentioned for the part which he took in the labour of this translation, for which he was qualified, not merely by his extensive learning, but also by his knowledge of Scripture. He died, March 17th, 1612, a few months after the completion and publication of the version itself.

Dr. Kilbye.

4th. Dr. Richard Kilbye, rector of Lincoln College; he was eminent as a Hebrew Scholar, and became Regius professor in the University of Oxford. He died in 1620, aged about sixty years.

Bp. Smith. Bp. of Glo'ster.

5th. Dr. Miles Smith. He was, on the whole, regarded as the person who had the chief hand in the execution of this version, he was very learned, both as a classical and as an oriental scholar. He was made, in 1612 (Sept. 20th), bishop of Gloucester. This see was conferred upon him for the indefatigable pains which he had taken in the execution and final revision of the translation, to which he wrote the preface. He died in November, 1624. In doctrine he strenuously opposed Laud, during the time when the latter was dean of Gloucester.

Dr. Brett.

6th. Richard Brett, B.D. This translator was for some time fellow of Lincoln College. He became rector of Quainton, near Aylesbury, in or about the year 1595. He died, April 15th, 1637, aged seventy.

Faireclowe.

7th. "Mr. Faireclowe." This must, I think, have have been Daniel Fairclough (otherwise called Featley), who was afterwards rector of Northill, in Cornwall. He died in 1645, aged sixty-three. He was the author of many works.

Fourth Company of Eight at Oxford. Gospels, Acts, Rev.

A Fourth Company who met at Oxford, had assigned to them, for their portion, *the four Gospels, the Acts of the Apostles*, and *the Revelations.*

This company consisted of eight persons:—

Bp. Ravis. Of Gloucester. Of London.

1st. Dr. Thomas Ravis, the president of this company. He was, at the time of his appointment as a translator, dean of Christ Church. On March 19th, 1605, he was made bishop of Gloucester; from whence he was translated to London, June 2nd, 1607, but a little while after the labour of this translation of the Bible had commenced. He died, December 14th, 1609, before the work was completed.

Abp. Abbott. Bp. of Lichfield. Of London. Abp. of Canterbury.

2nd. Dr. George Abbot. He was, at the time of his appointment, dean of Winchester, and master of University College. He was made bishop of Lichfield and Coventry in 1609 (December 3). In February, 1610, he was translated to the see of London, vacant by the death of Dr. Ravis, and, in the following year (April 9), he was made archbishop of Canterbury. He died in 1633, aged 71. In doctrine, he was a striking contrast to his successor, Archbishop Laud.

Dr. Eedes.

3rd. Dr. Richard Eedes. He was at this time dean of Worcester; but although appointed to this part of the translation he did not live until it was actually commenced. He died, November 19, 1604.

Bp. Tomson. Of Gloucester.

4th. Dr. Giles Tomson, dean of Windsor, bishop of Gloucester, June 9, 1611, died June 14, 1612, aged fifty-nine.

Savile.

5th. "Mr. Savile;" this may perhaps be Sir Henry Savile, knighted in the latter part of 1604. If not, I do not know who it can have been.

Dr. Peryn.

6th. "Dr. Peryn." This was, I conceive, Dr. John Perin, Regius Greek Professor: he was of St. John's College. He died May 9, 1615.

Dr. Ravens.

7th. "Dr. Ravens." This must have been Ralph Ravens, D.D., Jan. 20, 1596, afterwards rector of Eystan Magna. He died in 1616.

Dr. Harmer.

8th. Dr. John Harmer, he was some time Regius Greek professor, chief master of Winchester School for nine years, and warden of the college there for seventeen years. He died October 11, 1613.

Fifth Company of Seven at Westminster. The Epistles.

A Fifth Company of Translators met at Westminster, whose portion of the work was the whole of *the Epistles of the New Testament.*

This company consisted of the following persons:—

Bp. Barlowe, of Rochester, of Lincoln.

1st. Dr. William Barlowe, then dean of Chester: before the translation was commenced, he was made bishop of Rochester, 1605, he subsequently became bishop of Lincoln.

2nd. "Dr. Hutchinson." 4th. "Mr. Fenton." 6th. "Mr. Sanderson."

3rd. "Dr. Spencer." 5th. "Mr. Rabbet." 7th. "Mr. Dakins."

The Sixth Company of Translators met at CAMBRIDGE. They had the *Apocrypha* for their portion; the whole of the Canonical Scripture having been distributed to the other companies. This body of translators, however, had as much to do as any of the others, in revising those portions which when completed by any one company, were sent to the rest for revision.

Sixth company of seven at Cambridge

The Apocrypha

In this company of translators there were the following individuals:—

1st. DR. JOHN DUPORT, master of Jesus College, and prebendary of Ely. Dr Duport.

2nd. DR. BRAINTHWAITE, fellow of Emanuel, then master of Gonvil and Caius College." Dr Brainthwaite

3rd. DR JEREMIAH RATCLIFFE, one of the senior fellows of Trinity College. Dr Ratcliffe.

4th DR. SAMUEL WARD, then of Emanuel College He afterwards became master of Sidney College, and Lady Margaret professor of divinity In 1618, he was one of the English delegates to the Synod of Dort. Dr. Ward

5th. ANDREW DOWNES, fellow of St John's College, and Regius Greek professor. Downes

6th. JOHN BOYS, fellow of St John's Collage, prebendary of Ely, rector of Boxworth, near Cambridge. This was one of the most learned and laborious of all the body of translators It is difficult to say whether he was more distinguished for his knowledge of Greek or of Hebrew. After the portion which was assigned to him was completed, he acceded to the earnest request that was made to him to undertake another; this must have been the portion from the Chronicles to Canticles inclusive, which had been assigned to the other company who met at Cambridge It is probable that the loss of Livelie's assistance was much felt; and they were glad to call in the aid of so distinguished a scholar as Boys. He appears to have been regarded as the principal Hebraist in that company whom he thus joined; although the then Hebrew professor, as well as his successor, belonged to it This may be inferred from the fact, that he and Andrew Downes, the Regius professor of Greek, were the two who were delegated from Cambridge to the kind of committee of revision, which met in London Boys

7th. DR. WARD, of King's College, prebendary of Chichester, rector of Bishop-Waltham, in Hampshire. Dr. Ward.

These are the forty-seven men to whose hands the task was assigned of preparing a new translation of the Bible. It will be seen that this list contains the names of many, who were eminent no less as scholars than as Christians; while it is also probable that those of whom but little is known, were men of very competent learning. Two persons are omitted in this list, who, although of singular eminence as Hebrew scholars, were not appointed to this service, Hugh Broughton, and William Bedell. The former was probably omitted on account of his overbearing spirit and temper: the latter was scarcely known in England till about the year 1613, although in other countries he was famed as an Oriental scholar: he subsequently became bishop of Kilmore.

Broughton and Bedell not employed

The manner in which the translators proceeded has been already described: according to this system of management, each company formed a copy of the whole Bible, with the version revised. For convenience' sake, as it would seem, the translators at each of the three places met respectively together, and digested their corrections: this reduced the number of copies to *three*, and then it remained for *one* corrected Bible to be framed out of them. It must have been about the beginning of the year 1610, that they had proceeded thus far in their labour.

Three revised copies of the Bible

For the completion of the work, two persons were dispatched from each place. The delegates from Cambridge, were John Boys and Andrew Downes, who went to London; where they were joined by the two delegates from Westminster, and the two from Oxford. These met daily at Stationers' Hall, for about three quarters of a year; during this part of their work they received, each of them, from the Stationers' Company, thirty pounds a week, although before they had received nothing.

Six delegates form a Committee of Revision.

Selden says that the translators, in one part of their work, met together and read what had been done; each one of them having a Bible in some language in his hand: if any thing struck any of them as requiring alteration, he spoke, otherwise they read on. It is probable that this was when one company received some book of the Scripture from another, that this was done: it seems to have been a very good method of observing variations in rendering. This *may* perhaps have belonged to some other stage of the proceedings; I therefore mention it in this place.

Selden's account of the revision

At the Synod of Dort in 1618, when a new Dutch translation of the Scriptures was proposed (November 20) the English delegates who were present gave an account of the manner in which the authorized English version had been made. Their account states that, out of the whole number to whom the work was committed, *twelve* select men met together to review the version which had been prepared. This is not to be questioned; for, to say nothing of the notoriety of events which had occurred but seven years before, one of the English delegates, namely, Dr. Samuel Ward, was one of those who had been engaged

Account of the version given at the Synod of Dort

Six revisers besides the delegates.

in the work. Thus, in the committee of revision, there were six persons besides the six delegates; *who* those were cannot be positively stated; but it appears probable that they were six bishops to whom the task was assigned by the King. This accords with what has been before said relative to the number of the translators.

Bp Bilson one of them. He and Bp. Smith finally revise the version

One of these six bishops was, I suppose, Dr. Bilson, of Winchester, who, with one of the Oxford translators, Dr. Miles Smith (soon afterwards bishop of Gloucester), gave the version a final revision. In doing this they prefixed the summaries of contents to the several chapters, and then Dr. Smith wrote the preface which was appended to this Bible when first printed, and which is in some editions still retained.

The Bible published 1611.

This Bible was published in London in 1611, in a large black letter folio, with the following title:—

THE
HOLY
BIBLE
Conteyning the Old Testament, and the New:
¶ Newly translated out of the Originall Tongues: and with the former Translations diligently compared and reuised by his Maiesties speciall Commandement
¶ *Appointed to be read in Churches*

¶ IMPRINTED at London by *Robert Barker*, Printer to the Kings most excellent Maiestie.
ANNO DOM. 1611

The dedication to King James

The dedication of the translators to King James the First is still prefixed to almost all the editions of this version, so that any reference to it would be almost superfluous. It is couched in a strain sufficiently adulatory for a court like that of King James; while, at the same time, the recognition of the hand of God, and the blessings coming from Him, are equally unlike what is found in modern times. Mere foolish adulation may be well dispensed with; but how rarely in later times have those who have addressed monarchs, rejoiced in the "preaching of God's sacred word," as being "that inestimable treasure which excelleth all the riches of the earth!"

The translator's preface

The Scripture to be circulated in vernacular tongues

The preface of the translators to the reader, which is of some length, is not often now printed with the Bible. In it Dr. Miles Smith, in the name of his colleagues, brings before the reader a great variety of topics connected with the translations of the Scripture which had been made in former times, demonstrating that it is not a new fancy of any that the Scriptures ought to be diffused in the vernacular tongues. One argument used on this point is good and simple; amongst the Jews, when God gave a revelation of his will, He gave it in Hebrew, the language of the people; had the Scripture been intended by Him *not* to be circulated amongst men at large, surely He would at first have veiled it in a language not commonly known by the nation to whom it was given.

A new version desirable.

They speak of various versions which had been made both in early and in then recent times; after which they defend what had been by some opposed, namely, that a new version or revision was a desirable work. These objectors appear to have been chiefly Romanists, who were only too glad to find something against which to cavil with regard to the translation of the Scriptures. The objections are stated thus:—"Was their translation good before? Why do they now mend it? Was it not good? Why then was it obtruded upon the people?" The reply made to such objections is this:—"We do not deny; nay, we affirm and avow, that the very meanest translation of the Bible in English, set forth by men of our profession . . . . containeth the word of God, nay, is the word of God." They then speak of the substantial correctness of any version not being any reason for abstaining from seeking to make it exact in every respect.

Objectors answered

Other objections answered.

Another class of objectors to whom they reply, consisted of "certain brethren" who were, it seems, scandalized by a new version having been long in hand, asking why such a thing should be necessary? and whether the church had been deceived through all the time of the Reformation as to what the Scripture is? To these they reply, by speaking in terms of high commendation of all who had preceded them in their work, in the reign of Henry VIII. or since; while they speak of their own work as having consisted in the perusal of translations already made. In this reply, they refer to the objections of the Puritans and the Hampton Court conference, in consequence of which this version had been made.

The labours of the translators.

After discoursing at some length upon these topics, they at last speak of their own labours:—

"We never thought from the beginning, that we should need to make a new Translation, nor yet to make of a bad one a good one, . . . but to make a good one better, or out of many good ones, one principal good one, not justly to be excepted against; that hath been our endeavour, that our mark To that purpose there were many chosen, that were greater in other men's eyes than in their own, and that sought the truth rather than their own praise. . And in what sort did these assemble? In the trust of their own knowledge, or of their sharpness of wit, or deepness of judgment, as it were in an arm of flesh? At no hand. They trusted in him that hath the key of David, opening and no man shutting; they prayed to the Lord the Father of our Lord, to the effect that S. Augustine did; O let thy Scriptures be my pure delight, let me not be deceived in them, neither let me deceive by them In this confidence, and with this devotion did they assemble together; not too many, lest one should trouble another; and yet many, lest many things haply might escape them. If you ask what they had before them, truly it was the Hebrew text of the Old Testament, the Greek of the New. . . . . These tongues therefore the Scriptures we say in those tongues, we set before us to translate, being the tongues wherein God was pleased to speak to his Church by his Prophets and Apostles. Neither did we run over the work with that posting haste that the Septuagint did, if that be true which is reported of them, that they finished it in seventy-two days; neither were we barred or hindered from going over it again, having once done it, . . . neither, to be short, were we the first that fell in hand with translating the Scripture into English, and consequently destitute of former helps. . . . . None of these things: the work hath not been huddled up in seventy-two days, but hath cost the workmen, as light as it seemeth, the pains of twice seven times seventy-two days and more: . . . . Neither did we think much to consult the Translators or Commentators, Chaldee, Hebrew, Syrian, Greek, or Latin; no, nor the Spanish, French, Italian, or Dutch; neither did we disdain to revise that which we had done, and to bring back to the anvil that which we had hammered: but having and using as great helps as were needful, and fearing no reproach for slowness, nor coveting praise for expedition, we have at the length, through the good hand of the Lord upon us, brought the work to that pass that you see."

The length of time which is thus intimated as having been occupied in this version, is about *three years;* it refers, probably, to all that was done previous to the three copies of the Bible being put into the hands of the committee for revision at Stationer's Hall. This revision lasted three quarters of a year more.

The work three years in hand.

After this, they speak of the reasons which induced them to put sometimes another version in the margin than that which they let stand in the text. They assign as the reason, that they thought it not well to dogmatize with regard to passages of which the rendering, whether from the words occurring but rarely, or from the construction being peculiar, were in some measure doubtful.

The marginal renderings explained

They next speak of the variety of phraseology which they have used in translating, not having tied themselves down to rendering any one Greek or Hebrew word constantly by the same English term, even when the sense is identical. They seem, in fact, to have been fond of using synonyms: indeed they could hardly avoid it; for how could the three different companies to whom the Old Testament was assigned, without some previous concert, know what particular word to take to represent the same in Hebrew? Some of the variations are evidently to be accounted for in this manner, while others seem simply to have arisen from a love of synonyms. This was, I think, a mistake in judgment: it was one, however, which Coverdale had made before them; but a mistake it was, for how could an unlearned person be supposed to apprehend that one and the same thing is meant when the word varies? Would not such a one rather suppose, that if the word is varied there is at least some shade of variation in the meaning also? It is not with unkindly feelings that I mention this as being a flaw in our version. It was not occasioned by the incompetency of the translators, nor by their negligence, but simply from the judgment which they formed with regard to minor points in translating, and from the separation of the companies.

Variations in phraseology

Synonyms to be avoided

Before concluding the preface, they state how they have sought to steer clear between Puritanism and Popery. The former would have sought to change what were then termed *ecclesiastical* words, such (they say) as *Baptism* into *Washing, Church* into *Congregation;* the latter sought (they say) by an affected obscurity to hinder the true meaning of the Scripture from appearing. Perhaps the former of these would have seemed too much like innovation for the mere sake of it; but still it is to be observed, that the early English printed versions used *Congregation* as the representative of ἐκκλησία, and thus the introduction of the word *Church* into printed Bibles and New Testament, had been an innovation. The great thing, after all is, that all such words should be so rendered as to give the most intelligible meaning in the language of the version.

Popery and Puritanism avoided.

In concluding, they thus address the "gentle reader":—

"It remaineth, that we commend thee to God, and to the Spirit of his grace, which is able to build further than we can ask or think. He removeth the scales from our eyes, the vail from our hearts, opening our wits that we may understand his word, enlarging our hearts, yea correcting our affections, that we may love it above gold and silver, yea that we may love it to the end......It is a fearful thing to fall into the hands of the living God; but a blessed thing it is, and will bring us to everlasting blessedness in the end, when God speaketh unto us, to hearken; when he setteth His word before us, to read it; when he stretcheth out his hand and calleth, to answer, Here am I; here we are to do thy will, O God, The Lord work a care and conscience in us to know him and serve him, that we may be acknowledged of him at the appearing of our Lord Jesus Christ, to whom with the holy Ghost, be all praise and thanksgiving Amen"

Concluding address to the reader

As to the execution of this translation, it combined the advantages both of the Geneva version and the

Advantages of

The Geneva and Bishops' Bible combined.

Bishops' Bible. In the latter of these, different portions were distributed to various persons; so here a similar distribution was made to companies of translators. In the former, many acted in concert with regard to the version; so here, the translations made separately by each individual in a company were compared together, and the compared translations were, as has been already said, repeatedly revised.

How was this version received? The Bishops' Bible had been the translation read in churches previously, and this became wholly superseded by the new version: the Geneva Bible, which was the *household* version, maintained its ground for some time, but *gradually* gave way; so that this translation soon became the only one in general use. Perhaps it has too entirely superseded all those which were formerly in use: at least, the advantage which was enjoyed during the reign of Elizabeth has been let go, namely, that of comparing the various renderings of the same passage as a help to the true understanding of what the Scripture teaches.

The ground maintained by this version.

If a testimony were needed to the general excellence of this version, an appeal need only be made to the fact, that it has maintained its ground for two hundred and thirty years. It has been as highly esteemed by the learned as by the unlearned; and although many minor particulars might (as has often been shewn,) be corrected to advantage, yet the version taken as a whole is admirable. It is impossible to form any estimate of the blessing in result which has flowed from this version: the translators acted in their labour as being the servants of Christ; they knew that it was vain to trust in themselves, and thus, like Tyndale and Coverdale before them, they laid their work before the Lord in prayer, and found, in so doing, that He to whom they trusted was indeed faithful.